STATE
AND
LOCAL
GOVERNMENT

W9-ABS-055

Sixth Edition

Annual Editions
A Library of Information from the Public Press

Editor

Bruce Stinebrickner
DePauw University

Bruce Stinebrickner received his Ph.D. from Yale University
in 1974. He has taught at Lehman College of the City
University of New York and at the University of Queensland
in Brisbane, Australia. He currently teaches in the
Department of Political Science at DePauw University in
Greencastle, Indiana. Dr. Stinebrickner teaches and writes
about American politics and brings to *Annual Editions*
valuable perspectives on the American political system
gained from working and living abroad.

TECHNICAL COLLEGE OF THE LOWCOUNTRY
LEARNING RESOURCES CENTER
POST OFFICE BOX 1288
BEAUFORT, SOUTH CAROLINA 29901-1288

Cover illustration by Mike Eagle

The Dushkin Publishing Group, Inc.
Sluice Dock, Guilford, Connecticut 06437

The Annual Editions Series

Annual Editions is a series of over 55 volumes designed to provide the reader with convenient, low-cost access to a wide range of current, carefully selected articles from some of the most important magazines, newspapers, and journals published today. Annual Editions are updated on an annual basis through a continuous monitoring of over 300 periodical sources. All Annual Editions have a number of features designed to make them particularly useful, including topic guides, annotated tables of contents, unit overviews, and indexes. For the teacher using Annual Editions in the classroom, an Instructor's Resource Guide with test questions is available for each volume.

VOLUMES AVAILABLE

Africa
Aging
American Government
American History, Pre-Civil War
American History, Post-Civil War
Anthropology
Biology
Business Ethics
Canadian Politics
China
Commonwealth of Independent States
Comparative Politics
Computers in Education
Computers in Business
Computers in Society
Criminal Justice
Drugs, Society, and Behavior
Dying, Death, and Bereavement
Early Childhood Education
Economics
Educating Exceptional Children
Education
Educational Psychology
Environment
Geography
Global Issues
Health
Human Development
Human Resources
Human Sexuality
India and South Asia

International Business
Japan and the Pacific Rim
Latin America
Life Management
Macroeconomics
Management
Marketing
Marriage and Family
Microeconomics
Middle East and the Islamic World
Money and Banking
Nutrition
Personal Growth and Behavior
Physical Anthropology
Psychology
Public Administration
Race and Ethnic Relations
Social Problems
Sociology
State and Local Government
Third World
Urban Society
Violence and Terrorism
Western Civilization, Pre-Reformation
Western Civilization, Post-Reformation
Western Europe
World History, Pre-Modern
World History, Modern
World Politics

Library of Congress Cataloging in Publication Data
Main entry under title: Annual Editions: State and local government. 6/E.
        1. Local government—United States—Periodicals. 2. State governments—United States—Periodicals. I. Title: State and local government.
352'.000973'05   ISBN 1-56134-215-7

Sixth Edition

Printed in the United States of America

To the Reader

In publishing ANNUAL EDITIONS we recognize the enormous role played by the magazines, newspapers, and journals of the *public press* in providing current, first-rate educational information in a broad spectrum of interest areas. Within the articles, the best scientists, practitioners, researchers, and commentators draw issues into new perspective as accepted theories and viewpoints are called into account by new events, recent discoveries change old facts, and fresh debate breaks out over important controversies.

Many of the articles resulting from this enormous editorial effort are appropriate for students, researchers, and professionals seeking accurate, current material to help bridge the gap between principles and theories and the real world. These articles, however, become more useful for study when those of lasting value are carefully *collected, organized, indexed,* and *reproduced* in a *low-cost format*, which provides easy and permanent access when the material is needed. That is the role played by *Annual Editions*. Under the direction of each volume's *Editor*, who is an expert in the subject area, and with the guidance of an *Advisory Board*, we seek each year to provide in each *ANNUAL EDITION* a current, well-balanced, carefully selected collection of the best of the public press for your study and enjoyment. We think you'll find this volume useful, and we hope you'll take a moment to let us know what you think.

This collection of readings is the sixth edition in a series on state and local government. The book is designed for use in courses on state and local government and in state and local government segments of courses on American government. The educational goal is to provide a collection of up-to-date articles that are informative and interesting to students studying the area.

The 50 state governments and approximately 83,000 local governments in the United States have a great deal in common. They also exhibit remarkable diversity. The contents of the book as a whole inevitably reflect this theme of commonality *and* diversity. Some of the selections treat individual states or localities in considerable detail. Other articles focus on particular aspects of more than one state or local government. Still other articles explicitly compare and contrast regions, states, or localities. Taken together, the selections provide an overview of similarities and differences among state and local governments in the United States.

Keeping the idea of similarities and dissimilarities in mind can help students who are beginning their study of state and local governments. In many state and local government courses, a home state or region is given special attention. In such courses, the theme of commonality and diversity can serve to highlight what is and is not typical about the home state or region.

One objective of Reagan administration policies in the 1980s was to reduce the national government's direct spending on domestic programs and to cut national government aid to state and local governments. In response, many state and local governments sought to fill gaps in services available to the public, and the fiscal situation of many state and local governments worsened substantially during the Reagan years. With national government budgetary woes continuing during the Bush presidency and the nation going into a recession at the halfway mark in President Bush's term in office, the fiscal situation of many state and local governments remained precarious. As this book goes to press, it is too early to tell whether the Clinton administration will bring policies that lessen the fiscal woes of state and local governments.

The book is divided into eight units. Unit 1 is devoted to several eighteenth- and nineteenth-century commentaries on American federalism and state and local governments. Unit 2 treats relations among national, state, and local governments. Unit 3 covers elections, parties, referenda, and related matters, and pays considerable attention to unusual features of state and local "linkages." Unit 4 turns to government institutions and officeholders. Unit 5 focuses explicitly on diversity among regions and states. Cities and suburbs provide the material for unit 6, while unit 7 is devoted to finances and development. Unit 8 concludes the book with an examination of service delivery options available (including privatization) and of selected policy issues confronting state and local governments.

The book generally groups articles treating particular aspects of the governing process, be it state *or* local government, in the same units or sections. For example, unit 4 covers governmental institutions at both state and local levels, with sections 4A, 4B, and 4C treating state *and* local legislatures, executives, and courts, respectively. Unit 6, which treats metropolitan areas, is an exception to this rule in that it focuses primarily on issues involving *local* governments.

Deciding what articles to use in this revised edition was not an easy task. I tried to assess articles according to significance and relevance of subject matter, readability for students, and utility in stimulating students' interest in state and local government. Potential selections were evaluated not only as they stood alone, but also as complements to other likely selections. I want to thank the Advisory Board members who provided detailed critiques of the fifth edition as well as suggestions for improvements.

The next edition of this book will bring another opportunity to make changes. State and local government is a particularly diverse field of study, and numerous newspapers and regional magazines across the country carry articles that might be suitable for use. I earnestly solicit reactions to this book as well as suggestions of articles for use in the next edition. In other words, readers are cordially invited to become advisors and collaborators in future editions by completing and mailing the article rating form on the last page of this book.

Bruce Stinebrickner

Bruce Stinebrickner
Editor

Contents

Unit 1

Early Commentaries

Three selections provide historic perspectives on federalism and on state and local governments in the United States.

Unit 2

Intergovernmental Relations

Four selections discuss relations between national, state, and local governments in the United States' three-tier system of government.

The concepts in bold italics are developed in the article. For further expansion please refer to the Topic Guide and the Index.

Unit 3

Linkages Between Citizens and Governments

Nine articles explore various mechanisms that are supposed to help make state and local governments responsive to citizens: elections, parties, referenda, initiatives, and so forth.

The concepts in bold italics are developed in the article. For further expansion please refer to the Topic Guide and the Index.

Unit 4

Government Institutions and Officeholders

Thirteen selections treat the functioning of legislatures, executives, courts, and other institutions in state and local governments.

The concepts in bold italics are developed in the article. For further expansion please refer to the Topic Guide and the Index.

Unit 5

Regionalism and Variations Among Regions and States

Five articles cover differences between states and regions as well as regional efforts among neighboring states to combat common problems.

Unit 6

Cities and Suburbs

Nine selections comment on issues, problems, and opportunities facing governments of metropolitan areas.

Unit 7

Finances and Development

Nine articles examine revenue-raising methods that state and local governments use, as well as challenges and problems of development that state and local governments face.

The concepts in bold italics are developed in the article. For further expansion please refer to the Topic Guide and the Index.

Unit
8

Service Delivery and Policy Issues

Eleven selections treat, the means that state and local
governments use in delivering services to the public
and policy issues in such areas as education, zoning,
abortion, and so forth.

The concepts in bold italics are developed in the article. For further expansion please refer to the Topic Guide and the Index.

Topic Guide

This topic guide indicates how the selections in this book relate to topics likely to be treated in state and local government textbooks and courses. It is useful for locating articles that relate to each other for reading and research. The guide is arranged alphabetically according to topic. Articles may, of course, treat topics that do not appear in the topic guide. In turn, entries in the topic guide do not necessarily constitute a comprehensive listing of all the contents of each selection.

TOPIC	TREATED IN:	TOPIC	TREATED IN:
Administration and Bureaucracy	20. Practicing Political Science 21. Gubernatorial Styles 23. "City Managers Don't Make Policy" 29. Bringing Government Back to Life 31. Resurgence of Multistate Regionalism 36. Snow White and 17 Dwarfs 53. Privatization Is a Means 54. Privatization Presents Problems 57. Schoolhouse Equality	**Elections and Electoral Systems**	8. Maps That Will Stand Up in Court 9. Dickering Over the Districts 10. Mirage of Campaign Reform 11. Throwing Out the Rascals 12. Local Redistricting 13. Should Judges Be Elected? 20. Practicing Political Science
Charters	28. Charter Reform	**Federalism**	All selections in Unit 2 1. *The Federalist* No. 17 2. *The Federalist* No. 45 3. Nature of American State
Cities	All selections in Unit 6 12. Local Redistricting 23. "City Managers Don't Make Policy" 25. View From the Bench 28. Charter Reform	**Governors**	21. Gubernatorial Styles 22. Wisconsin's 'Quirky' Veto Power
City Managers	23. "City Managers Don't Make Policy"	**Interest Groups**	10. Mirage of Campaign Reform 20. Practicing Political Science 61. Of LULUs, NIMBYs, and NIMTOOs 63. Other People's Garbage
Courts	All selections in Unit 4C 13. Should Judges Be Elected? 57. Schoolhouse Equality	**Item Veto**	22. Wisconsin's 'Quirky' Veto Power
Criminal Justice System	25. View From the Bench 40. How to Hold a Riot 60. Do We Need More Prisons?	**Lotteries**	45. Not Quite the Pot of Gold
		Mayors	23. "City Managers Don't Make Policy"
Diversity	All selections in Unit 5	**News Media**	14. News Judgments
Economic Development	33. State Stats 35. Business Flees to the Urban Fringe 39. Cities Get Into the Game 50. Taxes and the Wealth of States 56. State Agenda for the Coming Years	**Parties**	8. Maps That Will Stand Up in Court 10. Mirage of Campaign Reform
		Privatization	53. Privatization Is a Means 54. Privatization Presents Problems
		Race and Racial Issues	32. Delta Looks Up 38. Health Problems of Inner City Poor 41. After the Los Angeles Riots

TOPIC	TREATED IN:	TOPIC	TREATED IN:
Referenda and Initiatives	All selections in Unit 3B	**State Legislatures/State Legislators**	8. Maps That Will Stand Up in Court 9. Dickering Over the Districts 10. Mirage of Campaign Reform 17. Legislature 2010 18. Embattled Institution
Regions and Regionalism	All selections in Unit 5		
Revenue Raising	All selections in Unit 7A 4. American Federalism: Past, Present, and Future	**Suburbs**	36. Snow White and 17 Dwarfs 57. Schoolhouse Equality
		Term Limits	11. Throwing Out the Rascals
Riots, Urban	40. How to Hold a Riot 41. After the Los Angeles Riots	**Town Meetings**	19. Running a Town the 17th-Century Way
Schooling/School Boards/School Districts	20. Practicing Political Science 34. School Days' Primer 36. Snow White and 17 Dwarfs 56. State Agenda for the Coming Years 57. Schoolhouse Equality 58. Reform School Confidential 62. Dismantling the Ivory Tower	**Towns and Townships**	19. Running a Town the 17th-Century Way

Early Commentaries

The American political system includes three levels of government—national, state, and local. Although not unique among nations today, this arrangement was unusual in the late eighteenth century when the United States became independent. Early commentaries on the American political system paid considerable attention to each of the levels of government as well as to relations among the three levels. These writings suggest the important role that state and local governments have always played in the United States.

Debate about the desirability of the proposed new Constitution of 1787—the constitution that remains in force to this day—often focused on the relationship between the national government and the states. Some people thought that the states were going to be too strong in the proposed new union, and others argued that the national government would be. Three prominent supporters of the new Constitution—Alexander Hamilton, James Madison, and John Jay—wrote a series of articles in 1787–1788 explaining and defending it. Many of these articles, which came to be known as *The Federalist Papers*, treated the federal relationship between the national government and the states. So did many of the writings of other early observers. This shows the importance that was attached to the new federal relationship right from the start.

Local government was also the subject of considerable attention in early commentaries on the American political system. Alexis de Tocqueville, a French nobleman visiting the United States early in the nineteenth century, recorded his observations in a book entitled *Democracy in America* (1835). Tocqueville remarked on the extraordinary vitality of American local government institutions, comparing what he saw in the United States with European institutions at the time. Today American local government still plays a prominent role in the overall governing process, probably more so than in any other nation in the world.

Later in the nineteenth century, a second foreign observer, James Bryce, published another historic commentary on the United States, *The American Commonwealth* (1888). Bryce, an Englishman, discussed American federalism and American state and local governments. He described the similarities and differences among local government structures in different regions of the country, the nature of the states, and the lamentable performance of city governments. Like Tocqueville, Bryce was able to identify and analyze distinctive elements of the American system of government and make a lasting contribution to the study of the American political system.

Selections in this first section of the book come from *The Federalist Papers* and Bryce's *American Commonwealth*. These historic observations on American federalism and state and local governments provide a baseline against which to assess the picture of contemporary state and local government that emerges in the rest of the book.

Looking Ahead: Challenge Questions

How does the picture of local governments provided by Bryce compare with American local governments today?

Do you think that the observations of Hamilton, Madison, and Bryce are out of date by now? Why or why not?

Students of politics frequently refer to the "historic" writings of Plato, Aristotle, Machiavelli, Hobbes, Locke, Rousseau, and others. Selections in this section are examples of early or historic writings on American politics. Why do you think that those who study politics so often look to the classics, even centuries after they were first written?

Do you find the arguments and logic of *Federalist* No. 17 and No. 45 persuasive? Can you detect any flaws or mistakes?

Which author do you find most interesting and helpful—Hamilton, Madison, or Bryce? Why?

THE FEDERALIST NO. 17
(HAMILTON)

To the People of the State of New York:

AN OBJECTION, of a nature different from that which has been stated and answered, in my last address, may perhaps be likewise urged against the principle of legislation for the individual citizens of America. It may be said that it would tend to render the government of the Union too powerful, and to enable it to absorb those residuary authorities, which it might be judged proper to leave with the States for local purposes. Allowing the utmost latitude to the love of power which any reasonable man can require, I confess I am at a loss to discover what temptation the persons intrusted with the administration of the general government could ever feel to divest the States of the authorities of that description. The regulation of the mere domestic police of a State appears to me to hold out slender allurements to ambition. Commerce, finance, negotiation, and war seem to comprehend all the objects which have charms for minds governed by that passion; and all the powers necessary to those objects ought, in the first instance, to be lodged in the national depository. The administration of private justice between the citizens of the same State, the supervision of agriculture and of other concerns of a similar nature, all those things, in short, which are proper to be provided for by local legislation, can never be desirable cares of a general jurisdiction. It is therefore improbable that there should exist a disposition in the federal councils to usurp the powers with which they are connected; because the attempt to exercise those powers would be as troublesome as it would be nugatory; and the possession of them, for that reason, would contribute nothing to the dignity, to the importance, or to the splendor of the national government.

But let it be admitted, for argument's sake, that mere wantonness and lust of domination would be sufficient to beget that disposition; still it may be safely affirmed, that the sense of the constituent body of the national representatives, or, in other words, the people of the several States, would control the indulgence of so extravagant an appetite. It will always be far more easy for the State governments to encroach upon the national authorities, than for the national government to encroach upon the State authorities. The proof of this proposition turns upon the greater degree of influence which the State governments, if they administer their affairs with uprightness and prudence, will generally possess over the people; a circumstance which at the same time teaches us that there is an inherent and intrinsic weakness in all federal constitutions; and that too much pains cannot be taken in their organization, to give them all the force which is compatible with the principles of liberty.

The superiority of influence in favor of the particular governments would result partly from the diffusive construction of the national government, but chiefly from the nature of the objects to which the attention of the State administrations would be directed.

It is a known fact in human nature, that its affections are commonly weak in proportion to the distance or diffusiveness of the object. Upon the same principle that a man is more attached to his family than to his neighborhood, to his neighborhood than to the community at large, the people of each State would be apt to feel a stronger bias towards their local governments than towards the government of the Union; unless the force of that principle should be destroyed by a much better administration of the latter.

This strong propensity of the human heart would find powerful auxiliaries in the objects of State regulation.

The variety of more minute interests, which will necessarily fall under the superintendence of the local administrations, and which will form so many rivulets of influence, running through every part of the society, cannot be particularized, without involving a detail too tedious and uninteresting to compensate for the instruction it might afford.

There is one transcendent advantage belonging to the province of the State governments, which alone suffices to place the matter in a clear and satisfactory light,—I mean

The Federalist, No. 17, Alexander Hamilton, 1787.

the ordinary administration of criminal and civil justice. This, of all others, is the most powerful, most universal, and most attractive source of popular obedience and attachment. It is that which, being the immediate and visible guardian of life and property, having its benefits and its terrors in constant activity before the public eye, regulating all those personal interests and familiar concerns to which the sensibility of individuals is more immediately awake, contributes, more than any other circumstance, to impressing upon the minds of the people, affection, esteem, and reverence towards the government. This great cement of society, which will diffuse itself almost wholly through the channels of the particular governments, independent of all other causes of influence, would insure them so decided an empire over their respective citizens as to render them at all times a complete counterpoise, and, not unfrequently, dangerous rivals to the power of the Union.

The operations of the national government, on the other hand, falling less immediately under the observation of the mass of the citizens, the benefits derived from it will chiefly be perceived and attended to by speculative men. Relating to more general interests, they will be less apt to come home to the feelings of the people; and, in proportion, less likely to inspire an habitual sense of obligation, and an active sentiment of attachment.

The reasoning on this head has been abundantly exemplified by the experience of all federal constitutions with which we are acquainted, and of all others which have borne the least analogy to them.

Though the ancient feudal systems were not, strictly speaking, confederacies, yet they partook of the nature of that species of association. There was a common head, chieftain, or sovereign, whose authority extended over the whole nation; and a number of subordinate vassals, or feudatories, who had large portions of land allotted to them, and numerous trains of *inferior* vassals or retainers, who occupied and cultivated that land upon the tenure of fealty or obedience to the persons of whom they held it. Each principal vassal was a kind of sovereign within his particular demesnes. The consequences of this situation were a continual opposition to authority of the sovereign, and frequent wars between the great barons or chief feudatories themselves. The power of the head of the nation was commonly too weak, either to preserve the public peace, or to protect the people against the oppressions of their immediate lords. This period of European affairs is emphatically styled by historians, the times of feudal anarchy.

When the sovereign happened to be a man of vigorous and warlike temper and of superior abilities, he would acquire a personal weight and influence, which answered, for the time, the purposes of a more regular authority. But in general, the power of the barons triumphed over that of the prince; and in many instances his dominion was entirely thrown off, and the great fiefs were erected into independent principalities or States. In those instances in which the monarch finally prevailed over his vassals, his success was chiefly owing to the tyranny of those vassals over their dependents. The barons, or nobles, equally the enemies of the sovereign and the oppressors of the common people, were dreaded and detested by both; till mutual danger and mutual interest effected a union between them fatal to the power of the aristocracy. Had the nobles, by a conduct of clemency and justice, preserved the fidelity and devotion of their retainers and followers, the contests between them and the prince must almost always have ended in their favor, and in the abridgment or subversion of the royal authority.

This is not an assertion founded merely in speculation or conjecture. Among other illustrations of its truth which might be cited, Scotland will furnish a cogent example. The spirit of clanship which was, at an early day, introduced into that kingdom, uniting the nobles and their dependents by ties equivalent to those of kindred, rendered the aristocracy a constant overmatch for the power of the monarch, till the incorporation with England subdued its fierce and ungovernable spirit, and reduced it within those rules of subordination which a more rational and more energetic system of civil polity had previously established in the latter kingdom.

The separate governments in a confederacy may aptly be compared with the feudal baronies; with this advantage in their favor, that from the reasons already explained, they will generally possess the confidence and good-will of the people, and with so important a support, will be able effectually to oppose all encroachments of the national government. It will be well if they are not able to counteract its legitimate and necessary authority. The points of similitude consist in the rivalship of power, applicable to both, and in the CONCENTRATION of large portions of the strength of the community into particular DEPOSITS, in one case at the disposal of individuals, in the other case at the disposal of political bodies.

A concise review of the events that have attended confederate governments will further illustrate this important doctrine; an inattention to which has been the great source of our political mistakes, and has given our jealousy a direction to the wrong side. This review shall form the subject of some ensuing papers. PUBLIUS

THE FEDERALIST NO. 45
(MADISON)

To the People of the State of New York:

HAVING shown that no one of the powers transferred to the federal government is unnecessary or improper, the next question to be considered is, whether the whole mass of them will be dangerous to the portion of authority left in the several States.

The adversaries to the plan of the convention, instead of considering in the first place what degree of power was absolutely necessary for the purposes of the federal government, have exhausted themselves in a secondary inquiry into the possible consequences of the proposed degree of power to the governments of the particular States. But if the Union, as has been shown, be essential to the security of the people of America against foreign danger; if it be essential to their security against contentions and wars among the different States; if it be essential to guard them against those violent and oppressive factions which embitter the blessings of liberty, and against those military establishments which must gradually poison its very fountain; if, in a word, the Union be essential to the happiness of the people of America, is it not preposterous, to urge as an objection to a government, without which the objects of the Union cannot be attained, that such a government may derogate from the importance of the governments of the individual States? Was, then, the American Revolution effected, was the American Confederacy formed, was the precious blood of thousands spilt, and the hard-earned substance of millions lavished, not that the people of America should enjoy peace, liberty, and safety, but that the government of the individual States, that particular municipal establishments, might enjoy a certain extent of power, and be arrayed with certain dignities and attributes of sovereignty? We have heard of the impious doctrine in the Old World, that the people were made for kings, not kings for the people. Is the same doctrine to be revived in the New, in another shape —that the solid happiness of the people is to be sacrificed to the views of political institutions of a different form? It is too early for politicians to presume on our forgetting that the public good, the real welfare of the great body of the people, is the supreme object to be pursued; and that no form of government whatever has any other value than as it may be fitted for the attainment of this object. Were the plan of the convention adverse to the public happiness, my voice would be, Reject the plan. Were the Union itself inconsistent with the public happiness, it would be, Abolish the Union. In like manner, as far as the sovereignty of the States cannot be reconciled to the happiness of the people, the voice of every good citizen must be, Let the former be sacrificed to the latter. How far the sacrifice is necessary, has been shown. How far the unsacrificed residue will be endangered, is the question before us.

Several important considerations have been touched in the course of these papers, which discountenance the supposition that the operation of the federal government will by degrees prove fatal to the State governments. The more I revolve the subject, the more fully I am persuaded that the balance is much more likely to be disturbed by the preponderancy of the last than of the first scale.

We have seen, in all the examples of ancient and modern confederacies, the strongest tendency continually betraying itself in the members, to despoil the general government of its authorities, with a very ineffectual capacity in the latter to defend itself against the encroachments. Although, in most of these examples, the system has been so dissimilar from that under consideration as greatly to weaken any inference concerning the latter from the fate of the former, yet, as the States will retain, under the proposed Constitution, a very extensive portion of active sovereignty, the inference ought not to be wholly disregarded. In the Achæan league it is probable that the federal head had a degree and species of power, which gave it a considerable likeness to the government framed by the convention. The Lycian Confederacy, as far as its principles and form are transmitted, must have borne a still greater analogy to it. Yet history does not inform us that either of them ever degenerated, or tended to degenerate, into one consolidated government. On the contrary, we know that the ruin of one of them proceeded from the incapacity of the federal authority to prevent the dissensions, and finally the disunion, of the subordinate authorities. These cases are the more worthy of our attention, as the external causes by which the component parts were pressed together were much more numerous and powerful than in our case; and consequently less powerful ligaments within would be sufficient to bind the members to the head, and to each other.

In the feudal system, we have seen a similar propensity exemplified. Notwithstanding the want of proper sympathy in every instance between the local sovereigns and the people, and the sympathy in some instances between the general sovereign and the latter, it usually happened that the local sovereigns prevailed in the rivalship for encroachments. Had no external dangers enforced internal harmony and subordination, and particularly, had the local sovereigns possessed the affections of the people, the great kingdoms in Europe would at this time consist of as many independent princes as there were formerly feudatory barons.

The State governments will have the advantage of the Federal government, whether we compare them in respect to the immediate dependence of the one on the other; to the weight of personal influence which each side will possess; to the powers respectively vested in them; to the predilection and probable support of the people; to the disposition and faculty of resisting and frustrating the measures of each other.

The State governments may be regarded as constituent and essential parts of the federal government; whilst the latter is nowise essential to the operation or organization of the former. Without the intervention of the State legislatures, the President of the United States cannot be elected at all. They must in all cases have a great share in his appointment, and will, perhaps, in most cases, of themselves determine it. The Senate will be elected absolutely and exclusively by the State legislatures. Even the House of Representatives, though drawn immediately from the people, will be chosen very much under the influence of that class of men, whose influence over the people obtains for themselves an election into the State legislatures. Thus, each of the principal branches of the federal government will owe its existence more or less to the favor of the State governments, and must consequently feel a dependence, which is much more likely to beget a disposition too obsequious than too overbearing towards them. On the other side, the component parts of the State governments will in no instance be indebted for their appointment to the direct agency of the federal government, and very little, if at all, to the local influence of its members.

The number of individuals employed under the Constitution of the United States will be much smaller than the number employed under the particular States. There will consequently be less of personal influence on the side of the former than of the latter. The members of the legislative, executive, and judiciary departments of thirteen and more States, the justices of peace, officers of militia, ministerial officers of justice, with all the county, corporation, and town officers, for three millions and more of people, intermixed, and having particular acquaintance with every class and circle of people, must exceed, beyond all proportion, both in number and influence, those of every description who will be employed in the administration of the federal system. Compare the members of the three great departments of the thirteen States, excluding from the judiciary department the justices of peace, with the members of the corresponding departments of the single government of the Union; compare the militia officers of three millions of people with the military and marine officers of any establishment which is within the compass of probability, or, I may add, of possibility, and in this view alone, we may pronounce the advantage of the States to be decisive. If the federal government is to have collectors of revenue, the State governments will have theirs also. And as those of the former will be principally on the sea-coast, and not very numerous, whilst those of the latter will be spread over the face of the country, and will be very numerous, the advantage in this view also lies on the same side. It is true, that the Confederacy is to possess, and may exercise, the power of collecting internal as well as external taxes throughout the States; but it is probable that this power will not be resorted to, except for supplemental purposes of revenue; that an option will then be given to the States to supply their quotas by previous collections of their own; and that the eventual collection, under the immediate authority of the Union, will generally be made by the officers, and according to the rules, appointed by the several States. Indeed it is extremely probable, that in other instances, particularly in the organization of the judicial power, the officers of the States will be clothed with the correspondent authority of the Union. Should it happen, however, that separate collectors of internal revenue should be appointed under the federal government, the influence of the whole number would not bear a comparison with that of the multitude of State officers in the opposite scale. Within every district to which a federal collector would be allotted, there would not be less than thirty or forty, or even more, officers of different descriptions, and many of them persons of character and weight, whose influence would lie on the side of the State.

The powers delegated by the proposed Constitution to the federal government are few and defined. Those which are to remain in the State governments are numerous and indefinite. The former will be exercised principally on external objects, as war, peace, negotiation, and foreign commerce; with which last the power of taxation will, for the most part, be connected. The powers reserved to the several States will extend to all the objects which, in the ordinary course of affairs; concern the lives, liberties, and properties of the people, and the internal order, improvement, and prosperity of the State.

The operations of the federal government will be most extensive and important in times of war and danger; those of the State governments in times of peace and security. As the former periods will probably bear a small proportion to the latter, the State governments will here enjoy another advantage over the federal government. The more adequate, indeed, the federal powers may be rendered to the national defence, the less frequent will be those scenes of danger which might favor their ascendancy over the governments of the particular States.

If the new Constitution be examined with accuracy and candor, it will be found that the change which it proposes consists much less in the addition of NEW POWERS to the Union, than in the invigoration of its ORIGINAL POWERS. The regulation of commerce, it is true, is a new power; but that seems to be an addition which few oppose, and from which no apprehensions are entertained. The powers relating to war and peace, armies and fleets, treaties and finance, with the other more considerable powers, are all vested in the existing Congress by the articles of Confederation. The proposed change does not enlarge these powers; it only substitutes a more effectual mode of administering them. The change relating to taxation may be regarded as the most important; and yet the present Congress have as complete authority to RE-QUIRE of the States indefinite supplies of money for the common defence and general welfare, as the future Congress will have to require them of individual citizens; and the latter will be no more bound than the States themselves have been, to pay the quotas respectively taxed on them. Had the States complied punctually with the articles of Confederation, or could their compliance have been enforced by as peaceable means as may be used with success towards single persons, our past experience is very far from countenancing an opinion, that the State governments would have lost their constitutional powers, and have gradually undergone an entire consolidation. To maintain that such an event would have ensued, would be to say at once, that the existence of the State governments is incompatible with any system whatever that accomplishes the essential purposes of the Union.

PUBLIUS

Nature of the American State

James Bryce

. . . As the dissimilarity of population and of external conditions seems to make for a diversity of constitutional and political arrangements between the States, so also does the large measure of legal independence which each of them enjoys under the Federal Constitution. No State can, as a commonwealth, politically deal with or act upon any other State. No diplomatic relations can exist nor treaties be made between States, no coercion can be exercised by one upon another. And although the government of the Union can act on a State, it rarely does act, and then only in certain strictly limited directions, which do not touch the inner political life of the commonwealth.

Let us pass on to consider the circumstances which work for uniformity among the States, and work more powerfully as time goes on.

He who looks at a map of the Union will be struck by the fact that so many of the boundary lines of the States are straight lines. Those lines tell the same tale as the geometrical plans of cities like St. Petersburg or Washington, where every street runs at the same angle to every other. The States are not natural growths. Their boundaries are for the most part not natural boundaries fixed by mountain ranges, nor even historical boundaries due to a series of events, but purely artificial boundaries, determined by an authority which carved the national territory into strips of convenient size, as a building company lays out its suburban lots. Of the States subsequent to the original thirteen, California is the only one with a genuine natural boundary, finding it in the chain of the Sierra Nevada on the east and the Pacific ocean on the west. No one of these later States can be regarded as a naturally developed political organism. They are trees planted by the forester, not self-sown with the help of the seed-scattering wind. This absence of physical lines of demarcation has tended and must tend to prevent the growth of local distinctions. Nature herself seems to have designed the Mississippi basin, as she has designed the unbroken levels of Russia, to be the dwelling-place of one people.

Each State makes its own Constitution; that is, the people agree on their form of government for themselves, with no interference from the other States or from the Union. This form is subject to one condition only: it must be republican.[1] But in each State the people who make the constitution have lately come from other States, where they have lived under and worked constitutions which are to their eyes the natural and almost necessary model for their new State to follow; and in the absence of an inventive spirit among the citizens, it was the obvious course for the newer States to copy the organizations of the older States, especially as these agreed with certain familiar features of the Federal Constitution. Hence the outlines, and even the phrases of the elder constitutions reappear in those of the more recently formed States. The precedents set by Virginia, for instance, had much influence on Tennessee, Alabama, Mississippi, and Florida, when they were engaged in making or amending their constitutions during the early part of this century.

Nowhere is population in such constant movement as in America. In some of the newer States only one-fourth or one-fifth of the inhabitants are natives of the United States. Many of the townsfolk, not a few even of the farmers, have been till lately citizens of some other State, and will, perhaps, soon move on farther west. These Western States are like a chain of lakes through which there flows a stream which mingles the waters of the higher with those of the lower. In such a constant flux of population local peculiarities are not readily developed, or if they have grown up when the district was still isolated, they disappear as the country becomes filled. Each State takes from its neighbours and gives to its neighbours, so that the process of assimilation is always going on over the whole wide area.

Still more important is the influence of railway communication, of newspapers, of the telegraph. A Greek city like Samos or Mitylene, holding her own island, preserved a distinctive character in spite of commercial intercourse and the sway of Athens. A Swiss canton like Uri or Appenzell, entrenched behind its mountain ramparts, remains, even now under the strengthened central government of the Swiss nation, unlike its neighbours of the lower country. But an American State traversed by great trunk lines of railway, and depending on the markets of the Atlantic cities and of Europe for the sale of its grain, cattle, bacon, and minerals, is attached by a hundred always tightening ties to other States, and touched by their weal or woe as nearly as by what befalls within its own limits. The leading newspapers are read over a vast area. The inhabitants of each State know every morning the events of yesterday over the whole Union.

Finally the political parties are the same in all the States. The tenets (if any) of each party are the same everywhere, their methods the same, their leaders the same, although of course a prominent man enjoys especial influence in his own State. Hence, State politics are largely swayed by forces and motives external to the particular State, and common to the whole country, or to great sections of it; and the growth of local parties, the emergence of local issues and development of local political schemes, are correspondingly restrained.

These considerations explain why the States, notwithstanding the original diversities between some of them, and the wide scope for political divergence which they all enjoy under the Federal Constitution, are so much less dissimilar and less peculiar than might have been expected. European statesmen have of late years been accustomed to think of federalism and local autonomy as convenient methods either for recognizing and giving free scope to the sentiment of nationality which may exist in any part of an empire, or for meeting the need for local institutions and distinct legislation which may arise from differences between such a part and the rest of the empire. It is one or other or both of these reasons that have moved statesmen in such cases as those of Finland in her relations to Russia, Hungary

in her relations to German Austria, Iceland in her relations to Denmark, Bulgaria in her relations to the Turkish Sultan, Ireland in her relations to the United Kingdom. But the final causes, so to speak, of the recognition of the States of the American Union as autonomous commonwealths, have been different. Their self-government is not the consequence of differences which can be made harmless to the whole body politic only by being allowed free course. It has been due primarily to the historical fact that they existed as commonwealths before the Union came into being; secondarily, to the belief that localized government is the best guarantee for civic freedom, and to a sense of the difficulty of administering a vast territory and population from one centre and by one government.

I return to indicate the points in which the legal independence and right of self-government of the several States appears. Each of the forty-two has its own—

Constitution (whereof more anon).

Executive, consisting of a governor, and various other officials.

Legislature of two Houses.

System of local government in counties, cities, townships, and school districts.

System of State and local taxation.

Debts, which it may (and sometimes does) repudiate at its own pleasure.

Body of private law, including the whole law of real and personal property, of contracts, of torts, and of family relations.

Courts, from which no appeal lies (except in cases touching Federal legislation or the Federal constitution) to any Federal court.

System of procedure, civil and criminal.

Citizenship, which may admit persons (e.g. recent immigrants) to be citizens at times, or on conditions, wholly different from those prescribed by other States.

Three points deserve to be noted as illustrating what these attributes include.

I. A man gains active citizenship of the United States (i.e. a share in the government of the Union) only by becoming a citizen of some particular State. Being such citizen, he is forthwith entitled to the national franchise. That is to say, voting power in the State carries voting power in Federal elections, and however lax a State may be in its grant of such power, e.g. to foreigners just landed or to persons convicted of crime, these State voters will have the right of voting in congressional and presidential elections.[2] The only restriction on the States in this matter is that of the fourteenth and fifteenth Constitutional amendments, . . . They were intended to secure equal treatment to the negroes, and incidentally they declare the protection given to all citizens of the United States.[3] Whether they really enlarge it, that is to say, whether it did not exist by implication before, is a legal question, which I need not discuss.

II. The power of a State over all communities within its limits is absolute. It may grant or refuse local government as it pleases. The population of the city of Providence is more than one-third of that of the State of Rhode Island, the population of New York city more than one-fifth that of the State of New York. But the State might in either case extinguish the municipality, and govern the city by a single State commissioner appointed for the purpose, or leave it without any government whatever. The city would have no right of complaint to the Federal President or Congress against such a measure. Massachusetts has lately remodelled the city government of Boston just as the British Parliament might remodel that of Birmingham. Let an Englishman imagine a county council for Warwickshire suppressing the muncipality of Birmingham, or a Frenchman imagine the department of the Rhone extinguishing the municipality of Lyons, with no possibility of intervention by the central authority, and he will measure the difference between the American States and the local governments of Western Europe.

III. A State commands the allegiance of its citizens, and may punish them for treason against it. The power has rarely been exercised, but its undoubted legal existence had much to do with inducing the citizens of the Southern States to follow their governments into secession in 1861. They conceived themselves to owe allegiance to the State as well as to the Union, and when it became impossible to preserve both, because the State had declared its secession from the Union, they might hold the earlier and nearer authority to be paramount. Allegiance to the State must now, since the war, be taken to be subordinate to the Union. But allegiance to the State still exists; treason against the State is still possible. One cannot think of treason against Warwickshire or the department of the Rhone.

These are illustrations of the doctrine which Europeans often fail to grasp, that the American States were originally in a certain sense, and still for certain purposes remain, sovereign States. Each of the original thirteen became sovereign when it revolted from the mother country in 1776. By entering the Confederation of 1781-88 it parted with one or two of the attributes of sovereignty, by accepting the Federal Constitution in 1788 it subjected itself for certain specified purposes to a central government, but claimed to retain its sovereignty for all other purposes. That is to say, the authority of a State is an inherent, not a delegated, authority. It has all the powers which any independent government can have, except such as it can be affirmatively shown to have stripped itself of, while the Federal Government has only such powers as it can be affirmatively shown to have received. To use the legal expression, the presumption is always for a State, and the burden of proof lies upon any one who denies its authority in a particular matter.[4]

What State sovereignty means and includes is a question which incessantly engaged the most active legal and political minds of the nation, from 1789 down to 1870. Some thought it paramount to the rights of the Union. Some considered it as held in suspense by the Constitution, but capable of reviving as soon as a State should desire to separate from the Union. Some maintained that each State had in accepting the Constitution finally renounced its sovereignty, which thereafter existed only in the sense of such an undefined domestic legislative and administrative authority as had not been conferred upon Congress. The conflict of these views, which became acute in 1830 when South Carolina claimed the right of nullification, produced Secession and the war of 1861-65. Since the defeat of the Secessionists, the last of these views may be deemed to have been established, and the term "State sovereignty" is now but seldom heard. Even "States rights" have a different meaning from that which they had thirty years ago.[5] . . .

The Constitution, which had rendered many services to the American people, did them an inevitable disservice when it fixed their minds on the legal aspects of the question. Law was meant to be the servant of politics, and must not be suffered to become the master. A case had arisen which its formulae were unfit to deal with, a case which had to be settled on large moral and historical grounds. It was not merely the superior physical force of the North that prevailed; it was the moral forces which rule the world, forces which had long worked against slavery, and were ordained to save North America from the curse of hostile nations established side by side.

The word "sovereignty," which has in many ways clouded the domain of public law and jurisprudence, confused men's minds by making them assume that there must in every country exist, and be discoverable by legal inquiry, either one body invested legally with supreme power over all minor bodies, or several bodies which, though they had consented to form part of a larger body, were each in the last resort independent of it, and responsible to none but themselves.[6] They forgot that a Constitution may not have determined where legal supremacy shall dwell. Where the Constitution of the United States placed it was at any rate doubtful, so doubtful that it would have been better to drop technicalities, and recognize the broad fact that the legal claims of the States had become incompatible with the historical as well as legal claims of the nation. In the uncertainty as to where legal right resided, it would have been prudent to consider where physical force resided. The South however thought herself able to resist any physical force which the rest of the nation might bring against her. Thus encouraged, she took her stand on the doctrine of States Rights: and then followed a pouring out of blood and treasure such as was never spent on determining a point of law before, not even when Edward III and his successors waged war for a hundred years to establish the claim of females to inherit the crown of France.

What, then, do the rights of a State now include? Every right or power of a Government except:—

> The right of secession (not abrogated in terms, but admitted since the war to be no longer claimable. It is expressly negatived in the recent Constitutions of several Southern States).
> Powers which the Constitution withholds from the States (including that of intercourse with foreign governments).
> Powers which the Constitution expressly confers on the Federal Government.

As respects some powers of the last class, however, the States may act concurrently with, or in default of action by, the Federal Government. It is only from contravention of its action that they must abstain. And where contravention is alleged to exist, whether legislative or executive, it is by a court of law, and, in case the decision is in the first instance favourable to the pretensions of the State, ultimately by a Federal court, that the question falls to be decided.[7]

A reference to the preceding list of what each State may create in the way of distinct institutions will show that these rights practically cover nearly all the ordinary relations of citizens to one another and to their Government.[8] An American may, through a long life, never be reminded of the Federal Government, except when he votes at presidential and congressional elections, lodges a complaint against the post-office, and opens his trunks for a custom-house officer on the pier at New York when he returns from a tour in Europe. His direct taxes are paid to officials acting under State laws. The State, or a local authority constituted by State statutes, registers his birth, appoints his guardian, pays for his schooling, gives him a share in the estate of his father deceased, licenses him when he enters a trade (if it be one needing a licence), marries him, divorces him, entertains civil actions against him, declares him a bankrupt, hangs him for murder. The police that guard his house, the local boards which look after the poor, control highways, impose water rates, manage schools— all these derive their legal powers from his State alone. Looking at this immense compass of State functions, Jefferson would seem to have been not far wrong when he said that the Federal government was nothing more than the American department of foreign affairs. But although the National government touches the direct interests of the citizen less than does the State government, it touches his sentiment more. Hence the strength of his attachment to the former and his interest in it must not be measured by the frequency of his dealings with it. In the partitionment of governmental functions between nation and State, the State gets the most but the nation the highest, so the balance between the two is preserved.

Thus every American citizen lives in a duality of which Europeans, always excepting the Swiss, and to some extent the Germans, have no experience. He lives under two governments and two sets of laws; he is animated by two patriotisms and owes two allegiances. That these should both be strong and rarely be in conflict is most fortunate. It is the result of skilful adjustment and long habit, of the fact that those whose votes control the two sets of governments are the same persons, but above all of that harmony of each set of institutions with the other set, a harmony due to the identity of the principles whereon both are founded, which makes each appear necessary to the stability of the other, the States to the nation as its basis, the National Government to the States as their protector.

Notes

1. The case of Kansas immediately before the War of Secession, and the cases of the rebel States, which were not readmitted after the war till they had accepted the constitutional amendments forbidding slavery and protecting the freedmen, are quite exceptional cases.

2. Congress has power to pass a uniform rule of naturalization (Const. Art. i. § 8).

Under the present naturalization laws a foreigner must have resided in the United States for five years, and for one year in the State or Territory where he seeks admission to United States citizenship, and must declare two years before he is admitted that he renounces allegiance to any foreign prince or state. Naturalization makes him a citizen not only of the United States, but of the State or Territory where he is admitted, but does not necessarily confer the electoral franchise, for that depends on State laws.

In more than a third of the States the electoral franchise is now enjoyed by persons not naturalized as United States citizens.

3. "The line of distinction between the privileges and immunities of citizens of the United States, and those of citizens of the several States, must be traced along the boundary of their respective spheres of action, and the two classes must be as different in their nature as are the functions of their respective governments. A citizen of the United States as such has a right to participate in foreign and inter-state commerce, to have the benefit of the postal laws, to make use in common with others of the navigable waters of the United States, and to pass from State to State, and into foreign countries, because over all these subjects the jurisdiction of the United States extends, and they are covered by its laws. The privileges suggest the immunities. Wherever it is the duty of the United States to give protection to a citizen against any harm, inconvenience, or deprivation, the citizen is entitled to an immunity which pertains to Federal citizenship. One very plain immunity is exemption from any tax, burden, or imposition under State laws as a condition to the enjoyment of any right or privilege under the laws of the United States. . . . Whatever one may claim as of right under the Constitution and laws of the United States by virtue of his citizenship, is a privilege of a citizen of the United States. Whatever the Constitution and laws of the United States entitle him to exemption from, he may claim an exemption in respect to. And such a right or privilege is abridged whenever the State law interferes with any legitimate operation of Federal authority which concerns his interest, whether it be an authority actively exerted, or resting only in the express or implied command or assurance of the Federal Constitution or law. But the United States can neither grant nor secure to its citizens rights or privileges which are not expressly or by reasonable implication placed under its jurisdiction, and all not so placed are left to the exclusive protection of the States."—Cooley, *Principles,* pp. 245-247.

4. It may of course be said that as the colonies associated themselves into a league, at the very time at which they revolted from the British Crown, and as their foreign relations were always managed

by the authority and organs of this league, no one of them ever was for international purposes a free and independent sovereign State. This is true, and Abraham Lincoln was in this sense justified in saying that the Union was older than the States. But what are we to say of North Carolina and Rhode Island, after the acceptance of the Constitution of 1787-89 by the other eleven States? They were out of the old Confederation, for it had expired. They were not in the new Union, for they refused during many months to enter it. What else can they have been during these months except sovereign commonwealths?

5. States rights was a watchword in the South for many years. In 1851 there was a student at Harvard College from South Carolina who bore the name of States Rights Gist, baptized, so to speak, into Calhounism. He rose to be a brigadier-general in the Confederate army, and fell in the Civil War.

6. A further confusion arises from the fact that men are apt in talking of sovereignty to mix up legal supremacy with practical predominance. They ought to go together, and law seeks to make them go together. But it may happen that the person or body in whom law vests supreme authority is unable to enforce that authority: so the legal sovereign and the actual sovereign—that is to say, the force which will prevail in physical conflict—are different. There is always a strongest force; but the force recognized by law may not be really the strongest; and of several forces it may be impossible to tell, till they have come into actual physical conflict, which is the strongest.

7. See Chapter XXII. *ante.*

8. A recent American writer well observes that nearly all the great questions which have agitated England during the last sixty years would, had they arisen in America, have fallen within the sphere of State legislation.—Jameson, "Introduction to the Constitutional and Political History of the States," in *Johns Hopkins University Studies.*

Intergovernmental Relations

Three levels of government—national, state, and local—coexist in the American political system. They not only survive alongside one another, but they also cooperate and conflict with each other in carrying out functions.

Legal bases for relationships among governments in the American political system include the United States Constitution, 50 state constitutions, court decisions by both state and federal courts, and state and national legislation. But legal guidelines do not prevent complications from arising in a system of government with three tiers. Problems requiring attention often overlap more than one state or local jurisdiction. Governments closest to the scene seem best able to handle certain kinds of problems, but at the same time higher, more "distant" levels of government often have access to better sources of revenue with which to finance such government activities. Citizens give different degrees of loyalty and support to different levels of government, and competing ambitions of politicians at different levels of government obstruct needed cooperation.

The formal relationship between the national government and the states is quite different from that between the states and their local governments. The national-state relationship is formally "federal" in character, which means that in theory the states and the national government each have autonomous spheres of responsibility. In contrast, the state-local relationship is not a federal one. Local governments are mere "creatures" of the states and are not on equal footing with their creators and masters. In practical terms, however, the national government has gained the upper hand in its dealings with the states, and often localities are more nearly on equal footing with state governments than their inferior legal position suggests.

The three tiers of American government have often been likened to a layer cake: three layers in one overarching system of government. Still using the cake analogy, political scientist Morton Grodzins argued that a marble cake better represents the interactions of local, state, and national governments. According to Grodzins, these interactions are far less tidy than the model of a layer cake suggests.

It is easy to think, for example, that public schooling is a local government function. This impression is supported by the prominent role of special-purpose local governments called "school districts" in governing public education. But, as Grodzins pointed out, such a view overlooks the powerful role that state governments play by providing financial aid, certifying teachers, prescribing curriculum requirements, regulating school safety and pupil health, and generally overseeing what school districts do. The national government is also involved in public schooling. In the last 40 years, the United States Supreme Court and lower federal courts have made numerous decisions aimed at ending racial segregation in public schools. In addition, national government grants finance various activities such as school breakfasts and lunches and special education programs. Even this brief review of local, state, and national involvement in one area, schooling, can show why Grodzins believed that a marble cake better reflects the reality of the American three-level system of government than a layer cake does.

Intergovernmental transfers of money are an important form of interaction among local, state, and national governments. "Strings" are almost always attached to money that one level of government transfers to another level. For example, when the national government provides grants to states and localities, requirements concerning use of the money accompany the funds, although the extensiveness and specificity of requirements vary greatly in different grant programs. Similarly, state governments aid local governments, and state money also brings strings of one kind or another.

Presidents often set forth proposals about how to structure relations and divide responsibilities among national, state, and local governments. President Reagan's "new federalism" was aimed at shifting greater responsibility back to the states and localities, thereby reversing a long-term trend toward greater national government involvement in providing an increasing number of services. Moreover, the amount of revenue that the national government transferred to states and localities was significantly reduced during the Reagan years. The change in direction begun under Reagan continued under President Bush, and state and local governments had to operate in the context of what has been called "fend-for-yourself federalism." Whether the Clinton administration will bring about a reversal of Reagan-Bush policies in this area remains to be seen.

Selections in this unit treat various aspects of relationships among national, state, and local governments.

Looking Ahead: Challenge Questions

Do you think that the current state of intergovernmental relations in the United States is satisfactory or unsatisfactory?

Which level of government do you think is contributing the most to the welfare of Americans? Why?

Under what circumstances do you think the national government should try to impose national standards on state and local governments? Under what circumstances do you think state governments should impose state standards on local governments?

Should states and localities have responsibility for performing more tasks and for raising money to pay for them? Why or why not?

American Federalism:
Past, Present and Future

Where stands American federalism at the close of the Reagan years and what is its future? Understanding how the formal features of our government have shaped and been shaped by socio-cultural, economic, technological and international challenges of the last two centuries is a basic prerequisite for grappling with federal-state-local issues.

David B. Walker

David B. Walker is director, Institute of Public and Urban Affairs at the University of Connecticut. He was assistant director of the U.S. Advisory Commission on Intergovernmental Relations from 1966 to 1984.

The study of federal systems in other countries and a close probe of our own version of this form of government reveal that three factors have undermined the fundamental bases of a genuine federalist regime. These factors or "conditioners" are: (1) the representational and indirectly the political; (2) the functional or operational, and (3) the judicial and jurisdictional. All three are incorporated in constitutions purporting to establish a federal system of free government. They also influence in part the social, economic and technological development of nations possessing federalist governmental arrangements.

The Shaping of Our Federalist Tradition: 1789-1963

During the first 175 years of American federalism, these three conditioners served to reinforce each other and thus to sustain a territorial division of power and influence.

Although the representational and political facets of American federalism experienced major shifts during the period that stretched from Presidents Washington through Kennedy, they continued to support the federal principle. Popular representation at the national and state-local levels steadily broadened during this time. Examples are the Voting Rights Act of 1965 and the 26th Amendment, giving 18-year-olds the vote in 1971.

Direct election of U.S. senators in 1913 possessed the potential of reducing direct state involvement in national policy-making. Yet, a special concern for states' rights lingered on in the Senate for 50 years following enactment of the 17th Amendment, thanks to the strength of state-local party systems and the political ascendancy of the "conservative coalition" in Congress from 1939 to 1964.

These formal actions to democratize the representational system were significant, but the political developments during this 175-year period more than matched them. The advent of the Constitution initially nurtured a party system that was strong at the national level. With the emergence of decentralized, state-based parties in the late 1820s, relations changed between state officials and political parties. The major parties of the day — the Jacksonian Democrats and Whigs — were loose alliances of state and local parties, generally undisciplined, lacking in doctrine and in clear programs, and composed of diverse socioeconomic and regional interests (Ladd 1970, 8-34).

These pluralistic characteristics also applied to their latter-day national successors. State and local parties, though in some cases more cohesive and disciplined, reflected most of these traits. Yet, collectively they were stronger than their national counterparts and this helped make the states the prime arenas in which policy choices were made. These political organizations not only dominated the nominating process at their own levels, but also dominated nomination and election of candidates for federal public offices.

Clearly, the formal representational features of all levels helped nurture these political developments. Moreover, while centralizing periods can be identified — 1861-1876, 1901-1917, and 1933-1938, — the general tendency was that the major national parties with their confederative structures, strong state-local foundations, loose and heterogeneous socio-economic composition, and concomitant lack of discipline at the national level preserved the federal principle both operationally and jurisdictionally (ACIR 1986, 17-46).

In broad terms, the workings of the American federal system until the early 1930s adhered quite closely to the dual or compartmentalized model that the Framers sought to establish, where the power of states and the federal government were fixed so that the national government could not overstep powers reserved to the states. Moreover, even with the marked growth of national regulatory, grant-in-aid and subsidizing roles during the New Deal and the immediate post-war years, dual federalism in most servicing and financing areas was still part of the system as late as the early 1960s (Walker 1981, 76-95). New federal-state relationships emerged as a consequence of the Great Depression and World War II. In addition, during the Truman and Eisenhower years the federal regulatory, promotional and assistance roles increased. Increased federal-state collaboration in domestic programs gave rise to the concept of "Cooperative Federalism." Yet, by 1963 the degree of national activism was moderate, and most responsibilities were still left wholly to state and local discretion and control. The continued strength of the old non-centralized party system maintained its constraining impact on national decision-making.

The umpiring role of the federal judiciary was another vital force shaping American federalism. Under Chief Justice John Marshall, the Supreme Court protected its institutional independence under the separation of powers arrangement, asserted its authority to render judgment on unconstitutional actions of the national political branches and the states, and selectively protected Congress' powers under the Constitution. In the court of Marshall's successor, Roger Taney, a full-fledged doctrine of dual federalism emerged which expanded the states' police powers and capacity to regulate commerce in the absence of federal action. Yet, the Supreme Court still vigorously asserted its right to control state judiciaries in matters of constitutional interpretation.

During the 75 years following the Civil War, the Supreme Court played a highly activist role. From 1874 to 1937, 62 acts of Congress and 525 state laws were found unconstitutional. The latter development indirectly highlights the emergence during this period of the states as laboratories of novel social and economic policies. By the

end of the judicial era (1937), the Supreme Court had chalked up an impressive record of aggressively acting as the ultimate interpreter of the constitutionality of state laws enacted pursuant to their police powers and of national statutes passed in furtherance of Congress' commerce, conditional spending and taxing powers.

With the advent of the "New Deal" Court in 1938, a generally deferential position was adopted regarding Congress' interpretation of commerce, pre-emption and conditional spending powers. The question of national constraint was left largely to the central government's political processes. Yet, these processes were relatively restrained until the early 1960s, thanks to the continuing ascendancy of the "Conservative Coalition" and its general propensity to resist most federal domestic initiatives. On the other hand, civil rights, the 14th Amendment and efforts to include some of the Bill of Rights within the provisions of the 14th Amendment provided the basis for a renewed activism on the part of the Supreme Court.

Dual federalism as previously applied judicially was a dead doctrine after 1937. The states' police powers, however, expanded during the 1940s and 1950s, thanks in part to the Supreme Court's elimination of the "twilight zone" wherein neither the national nor state governments could regulate authoritatively various social and economic areas. By 1963, however, it was apparent that the judicial enlargement of the national sphere was at the expense of the states and the private sector. The Court's constitutional interpretation made the national government the more authoritative federal partner. Some scholars trace the beginning of the demise of the states' preferential legal status to this development.

Recent Trends: From Cooperative to Co-optive Federalism (1964-1980)

American federalism and the web of federal-state-local relationships it engenders experienced their greatest challenges and transformations during the current intergovernmental era. By 1980, there were no vestiges of "dual federalism." The triumph of "Cooperative Federalism," however, was brief and transitional — leading to a "Co-optive Federalism" in the 1970s that receded somewhat during the Reagan years of ideological, then fiscal constraint. Contemporary federalism still is highly centralized. Its chief feature is "Permissive Federalism" as described by Michael Reagan: "There is a sharing of power and authority between the national and state governments, but . . . the state's share rests upon the permissiveness of the national government" (Reagan and Sanzone 1981, 75). The chief reasons for this troubling transformation were the collapse of the old, non-centralized party system, the continued activism and centralizing tendencies of the federal judiciary and a parallel explosive expansion of the nation's domestic agenda until reined in by Carter in the late 1970s and Reagan in the 1980s.

The dimensions of the governmental transformation from 1964 to 1980 are so numerous that it would require a volume to catalog them. In the area of functional federalism, the federal government experienced major shifts from Presidents Johnson through Carter. In quantitative and qualitative terms, the national government's domestic role expanded exuberantly. Its breadth and depth far surpassed New Deal actions and, as analysis of the Reagan years indicate, the federal "heavy duty" domestic agenda was not drastically reduced as a result of major devolutions of the national roles and functions between 1964 and 1980.

A frequently overlooked but historic development of these years was the assumption by localities and especially the states of greater — even indispensable — fiscal, administrative and operational responsibilities in functional federalism. State governments became the paramount field managers, planners and partial funders of the majority and largest of the federal intergovernmental assistance and regulatory programs. States also experienced a dramatic revitalization of their historic role as a source of significant innovative policy initiatives. They carved out a more positive pattern of state-local relationships and again served as the dominant source of local fiscal assistance.

These developments resulted, in part, from the unwillingness of the national government to assume the responsibility for administering and fully funding most of its domestic programs, and, in part, from the transformation of the states during this 16-year period. At the same time, new regulatory thrusts and other national policy and centripetal federal judicial actions were reducing state and local governments in constitutional and jurisdiction terms to only a notch above the level of a pressure group. Thus, our federal system appeared by the late 1970s to be increasingly dysfunctional, given the centralization of major domestic policy decisions and the federal reliance on state and local governments and others to implement these policies. The efficiencies of a territorial division of servicing responsibilities, that a federal system helps assure, were being lost.

In addition to functional changes in federalism, from Johnson to Carter a transformation occurred in the representational and political areas. As to the representational, the Supreme Court's reapportionment decisions from 1962 to 1965 and Congress' enactment of the 1965 Voting Rights Act produced a dramatic democratization of state and local representational arrangements. The electorates expanded in states that had systematically barred racial and ethnic minorities. State legislatures were recast to reflect the Court's one man-one vote dictum, largely ending rural he-gemony. State and local politics have not been the same since that time. State policy-making processes are more accessible, responsive and representative than ever.

The deference that had been accorded states and localities eroded by the late 1970s so that Congress and administrative agencies treated them as just another interest group.

At the national level, however, far less favorable developments took place from the late 1960s through the 1970s. The deference that had been accorded states and localities eroded by the late 1970s so that Congress and administrative agencies treated them as just another interest group. Four reasons explain this. First, lobbying by states and localities for new aid programs and more funds, as pressure groups were doing, harmed their image. Second, the collapse, beginning in the mid-1960s, of the "Conservative Coalition's" domination of Congress and the concomitant increased control of congressional committees by northern and western Democrats combined to produce a major centripetal force. The third factor was that state and local elected officials could no longer exert the controlling voice in the nominating processes for elective national offices, as well as their own, as they had for 140 years. And fourth, the rise of more powerful pressure groups in Washington with centralizing agendas was another significant reason for the undercutting of state and local influence.

These developments produced the paradox: that as the governors moved their National Governors' Association headquarters to Washington, as the state legislatures merged three national associations and set up a major office there, and as the county and municipal associations beefed up their Washington staffs — all with a view toward presenting the views of their respective groups — the clout of state and local governments in the nation's capital was eroding.

Many factors contributed to the demise of the "old party system." One was the decline in state and local party control over the nominating processes in their own jurisdictions, thanks to the increased use of primaries, the impact of heavy state governmental regulation, national party requirements that pre-empted certain state and local party decisions, expansion of merit coverage of state and local employees, and a new generation of voters who were more independent, issue-oriented, and less dependent on state and local political organizations for services.

Another fundamental cause of party decline was the emergence of tough competitors who took on assignments that political parties formerly monopolized or dominated. Voter contact now is largely achieved through the independent mass media rather than by party stalwarts and mechanisms. Hired consultants provide much of the expert assistance in campaigning and a range of non-party providers are the main sources of campaign funds. The historically weak party role in Congress was further undermined by reforms adopted in the early 1970s and by the explosion in the number and types of Washington-based interest groups (ACIR 1986, 223-236).

Despite and partly because of these developments, state and national party organizations have endeavored to adapt to the new milieu. At the national level, party organizations — the Republicans more than the Democrats — are stronger than ever. Their financial aid to state parties, direct fund-raising assistance, polling and data processing capacities, voter registration efforts, and candidate recruitment and training reflect activities and roles vis-a-vis state parties that would have amazed their predecessors of a generation ago (ACIR 1986, 85-86).

One might question whether these intra-party federalist changes can correct the overall imbalance in the system. The answer is "No." The electorate is no more strongly committed to a party than it was two decades ago. A majority of those expressing an opinion in a 1983 survey indicated they preferred to work through interest groups to advance their political concerns (ACIR 1986, 52). Moreover, the potent role of the media, PACs, consultants and pressure groups seems unlikely to fade.

The federal judiciary's record throughout the 1964-1980 period was to aggressively expand trends initiated in the 1950s. In the 1960s, the federal court system upheld controversial congressional enactments and assumed the role of "a leader in the process of social change quite at odds with its traditional position as a defender of legalistic tradition and social continuity" (Kelly and Harbison 1976, 856). Generally, judicial decisions enlarged national power by placing severe limits on the states. The few instances where federal courts reflected some sensitivity to a powerful state role included reapportionment and educational finance cases that strengthened the states.

Some observers predicted a reversal or reduction of the Warren Court's libertarian and egalitarian tendencies with the appointment of Chief Justice Warren E. Burger. However, analysis of key 1970s' civil rights and liberties cases indicates the Court maintained its sensitivity to libertarian and racial justice values. In cases involving the criminal defendant rights, sex discrimination, local zoning ordinances and state legislative appropriation of federal grant funds, however, the Court exhibited concern for state autonomy and awareness of intergovernmental "comity" and "forbearance."

Yet, in constitutional areas of crucial significance to federalism — the conditional spending power, regulation of interstate commerce, the supremacy of congressional enactments and taxation — the Court generally played a nationalizing role (Walker 1981, 135-157). Only in *National League of Cities* vs. *Usery* (1976) did the Court by a 5-4 vote enunciate an extraordinary exception to this "trend." But later cases eroded *Usery's* significance, until the decision was specifically overturned in the *Garcia* (1985) case.

Reagan's Record: 1981-1988

Reagan federalism as revealed in his 1980 campaign speeches and early term proposals reacted to and rejected intergovernmental developments of the previous 16 years: the massive expansion of the national agenda; the highly centralized policy-making process; the regulation of state and local governments and the private sector; the resulting administrative ineffectiveness, economic inefficiencies and lack of accountability; the increasingly co-optive approach of federal legislators, administrators and regulators; the dangers of interest group ascendancy; and the lack of clear national domestic purposes.

President Reagan ignored, as did most politicians, the positive results of earlier programs (Schwarz 1988). For example, from 1960 to 1980, the number of Americans living in poverty was halved and the gap between the economically stronger and weaker did not widen despite the massive influx of "baby boom" generation job applicants. An additional 30 million Americans joined the work force, in part because of federal actions. Life expectancy lengthened and child mortality rates declined. A revolution was achieved in civil rights and liberties.

These salutary aspects of the Johnson-Nixon-Ford-Carter years were overlooked, while the negative ones were highlighted. Hence, Reagan's federalist creed stressed: a severe reduction in the federal intergovernmental role, a major devolution of program responsibilities, deregulation, a reduction in government activism and a return to a federal-state partnership in intergovernmental relations.

The administration's drive to reduce the federal intergovernmental role achieved an absolute reduction of $8 billion (from the Carter figure) in grant programs for fiscal year 1982. However, the projected slashing of federal aid over the following three years never materialized. What is more, during Reagan's second administration, federal aid increased to nearly $115 billion for fiscal 1987 (ACIR I 1987, 15; U.S. Census Bureau 1987, 2). This glacial increase in federal aid, however, produced a 25 percent aid reduction in constant dollars between 1978 and 1988 and a 22 percent decline as a proportion of state-local revenues between 1981 and 1987.

Another dimension of this drive to reduce the federal role was the reduction in grant programs from 539 in 1980 to 405 by January 1984. Most reductions were initiated in 1981 and new programs gradually increased after 1982. The increase in grant programs to 435 by 1987 suggests that the dynamics of program proliferation that characterized the 1970s have not been totally eclipsed by retrenchment concerns.

In related moves to devolve programs and responsibilities to state and local levels, the administration scored its greatest successes in 1981. Some 60 aid programs were scrapped by the Omnibus Budget Reconciliation Act (OBRA) and 77 were merged into nine new block grants. By the end of 1986, the total reached 12 as Congress enacted three more in three years and continued the older entitlement Community Development Block Grant. Only one of the 1981 clusters proved inoperative. The renewal of general revenue sharing for local general governments in 1983, with White House support, marked another phase of this devolutionary drive. Revenue sharing's demise in 1986 with the administration's approval was the kind of federal unilateral devolution that subnational governments resent. The Environmental Protection Agency's assignment of greater program authority to states under its regulatory programs was another devolutionary action.

To fully gauge the significance of these centrifugal achievements, they should be placed in a broader context. The major Reagan effort to effect a massive devolution of program responsibilities reached a total impasse by the fall of 1982. Not to be overlooked is that in 1987 federal outlays of block and general purpose grants accounted for only about 14.4 percent of the total budget, compared to 20 percent for the last year of the Carter administration. Moreover, most major domestic programs of the 1960s and 1970s are still on the national agenda (regional economic development and housing were the chief victims of budget cuts). Many enactments of the 100th Congress (catastrophic illness, welfare reform, clean water amendments, housing, trade, etc.) suggest a rise in national activism softened by ingeniously inexpensive draw-downs on the federal fisc.

Intergovernmental deregulation as such was not the basic focus of the Reagan administration; instead, the curbing and softening of the regulatory process was sought. The softening strategy involved appointing Reagan loyalists to key regulatory posts; cutting agency personnel; relaxing, if not forgetting, agency procedures; and establishing a centralized review of proposed new or changed regulations. All these administrative actions slowed dramatically the rate of issuances in the early Reagan years and considerably eased the burden for the private sector, but only marginally for state and local governments (Conlan 1988, 217-218).

No major deregulatory legislative initiative — other than the block grant proposals — accompanied these efforts, however. Moreover, Congress' propensity to pre-empt and regulate did not slacken. Moreover, the administration supported trailer truck and teen-age drinking regulations and mandated procedures for responding to reports of hospital neglect of handicapped infants. The administration also led the fight for tougher conditions on social welfare programs.

The administration's philosophical goal of reducing governmental activism met with little success. From 1980-87, federal spending rose from $602.1 billion to $1,067 billion, and state outlays from $108.1 billion to an estimated $209 billion (ACIR II 1988, 22). Combined outlays rose from 33 percent of GNP in 1981 to 35 percent six years later (ACIR II 1988, 22).

Another facet of national activism is the government's credit programs. Following a slight decline in new direct federal loans between 1980 and 1988, new guaranteed loans soared to an outstanding balance of $507 billion by the end of 1987. Federal government-sponsored enterprises surpassed the $580 billion level in loans outstanding by 1987. By 1987, the federal government directly or indirectly had influenced the allocation of $1.3 trillion in outstanding credit to homeowners, farmers, foreign governments, exporters, utilities, shipbuilders, and state and local governments. This contrasts markedly with the grant-in-aid story. Governmental activism, as reflected in expenditures and credit programs, has not been tamed, despite the curbing of the federal grant portion of domestic program outlays.

With Reagan's unstated goal of returning to the pre-1964 pattern of intergovernmental relations, the score board indicates major successes. The states have been the prime recipients of all the new block grants. Four governors were the prime spokespersons for state and local governments during the "great debate" over the president's 1982 "Big Swap" proposal. The states were assigned the chief responsibility for administering the regional "clearinghouse" process under Executive Order 12372. During 1981-1987, the state share of total federal aid rose from 75 percent to 83 percent. With the scrapping of the Urban Direct Action Grant program in 1988 and probably the last remaining major federal-local block grant (the entitlement Community Development program) in 1989, the state share will approximate what it was in the final Eisenhower years. The union of public interest groups with strong state leadership in advancing federal welfare reform helped bring about the first overhaul of the program since its inception in 1935.

On a more negative note, the states have borne the brunt of implementing stiff conditions added to welfare programs during the Reagan years. They have had to finance a larger share of some programs based on changes in matching ratios. States also have been affected by the expansion in federal regulations since 1981, including uniform federal standards on truck size, a national minimum drinking age and tougher environmental protection provisions (Conlan 1988, 211-217). Above all, states and localities have been significantly affected by "de facto federalism," as the federal fiscal role in intergovernmental programs has gradually shrunk or disappeared. For the localities, all but a few direct federal-local grants have expired in the past four years. This shrinking federal role has increased state funding, program and regulatory responsibilities as states attempt to make up federal cuts. From the state vantage point, Washington-initiated actions since 1981 have undercut the basis for real partnership. Such a relationship must be founded on mutual trust and shared decision-making on prime concerns.

An assessment of the Reagan record would be remiss if it did not examine the administration's effect in changing attitudes. State and local officials no longer look to Washington to solve problems as many did in the late 1960s and 1970s.

This shrinking federal role has increased state funding, program and regulatory responsibilities as states attempt to make up federal cuts.

This is not to say the national government is being ignored. Far from it. Too many legal, regulatory, pre-emptive and fiscal actions are taken there to permit that luxury. But the images of Uncle Sam as the sage problem solver and bountiful banker have faded in the minds of state and local governmental officials, the electorate and most leaders of Washington pressure groups.

A positive result from this change in attitudes has been the revival of the states' historic role of launching unusual policy initiatives. In primary and secondary education, work-related welfare reform, consumer protection and economic development, states initiated innovative, wide-spread and, in some instances, expensive actions. This state (and to a lesser degree local) renaissance following the severe recession of 1982 prompted some to proclaim the advent of the more balanced federal system sought by reformers in the 1970s (Conlan 1988, 228-229).

Federalism's Current Condition

With the Reagan years at a close, one way to gauge the health of American federalism is to examine the differences and similarities between its conditioners and condition in 1980 and those of today.

Regarding the differences, at least six developments highlight the sharp contrasts between American federalism in the last year of Presidents Carter and Reagan.

1) Most of today's national agenda is markedly different from nine years ago. Witness the over-riding challenge of eight years of three-figure (billions) national deficits and the near tripling of

the national debt, continuing trade deficits and the advent of the United States as the world's largest debtor nation, efforts to sustain the prolonged economic growth without inflation, the pent-up popular and political demands for renewed governmental activism, the struggle to maintain political consensus on the usefulness of most domestic (grant) programs and the uncertain disciplining effect of the two deficits.

2) The current operational role of the federal government in the federal system is quite unlike that of 1980; in the sustaining, funding and supervision of intergovernmental programs, the national government's role is still significant. Yet, it is not as extensive, expensive and entangling as it was in 1980. The shortening of Washington's state and local agenda, the proportionate decline in its funding of programs, the slash in the number of grant recipients (especially localities) and the easing of certain conditions in intergovernmental programs are signs of this moderately reduced federal role. In addition, state and local governments have assumed a larger role as a result of greater fiscal efforts and expanded policy initiatives. These developments suggest a slight tilt in power to the states, but not to the extent of undercutting the national government's policy ascendancy in key programs and regulatory areas.

3) The recognition given now to the states' pivotal role in the system stands in contrast to the earlier failure to recognize that during the 1970s states had become the prime planners, administrators and partial funders of most major federal domestic programs. The reductionist posture of the national government, the surge of state activism, and the greater local governmental dependence on states help explain this greater awareness of the states' indispensable functional roles in the system (Osborne 1988).

4) As a result of these changed federal, state and local relationships, the federal government is no longer so broadly indicted as it was in 1980. Less than a decade ago, the federal system was described as dysfunctional, out-of-control and pressure group propelled. Put differently, the grim gridlock politics of the national deficits have refocused perceptions of the problems and perils of our federal system. Now, it is a matter of the minimum acceptable level of federal participation and what can be expected of state and local governments to compensate for federal defaults on domestic responsibilities.

5) State and local efforts to be represented at the national level are more diverse, difficult and depressingly frustrating than they were in the 1970s. Their lobbying then chiefly focused on grant programs — their conditions, funding, allocation and management. In the 1980s, these concerns have not disappeared, though the growth of most grants is at a glacial pace. In addition, state and local spokesmen must focus on three other major fronts: regulatory, taxation and

judicial. Each has presented major problems to state and local governments over the past eight years.

6) Turning to the four criteria for evaluating governmental systems — economic efficiency, administrative effectiveness, accountability and equity — different assessments are made regarding each of these compared to those of the late Carter years. Better program targeting (i.e., the "safety net" cluster), the pruning of marginal and ineffective grants, the federal tax reform act of 1986, and the remarkable resourcefulness of current state and local revenue systems (e.g., state and local general revenues experienced a 42 percent surge from 1981 to 1987) are all signs of greater economic efficiency. The fewer partners, conditions, regulations and dollars for federal grants along with the re-emergence of state and local government have tended to enhance administrative effectiveness at all levels. To the extent that these developments have produced a disentangling of interlevel program responsibilities and helped clear the lines of intergovernmental communication in the remaining 430 plus grants, accountability has been enhanced. Regarding equity, concerns have been raised about the fairness of tax actions taken from 1981 to 1986. In addition, spending levels fell for programs aiding the working poor while the poverty figure rose to 13 percent. The comparatively low public expenditures on poor children compared to extraordinarily high ones for the middle-class elderly suggest fundamental faults in our understanding of the minimal standards for social decency.

Continuing Trends

Trends present in 1980 that continued unabated during the Reagan era included:

1) The Supreme Court continued to favor centralized government. The Court includes seven appointees by Republican presidents (four of them Reagan's) and the conservative Justice White (a Kennedy selection). Yet this ostensibly conservative court continues to favor the central government in about four out of five instances. *Garcia* vs. *San Antonio Metropolitan Transit Authority* (1985), *South Carolina* vs. *Baker* (1988) and *J.A. Croson Co.* vs. *City of Richmond* (1989) are the tip of the judicial centripetal iceberg.

2) Congress' inclination — frequently buttressed by administration support — to regulate and pre-empt has continued during the Reagan years. If anything, this trend of the 1970s has been strengthened, since in a retrenchment period regulations can be just as significant politically as grant programs, and they usually involve few federal dollars.

3) The power and influence of the major political parties are as weak today as in 1980. Despite efforts to strengthen the role of elected officials in Democratic national conventions, the national party units are as authoritative now as then and the state and local organizations remain weak (Kayden, 1981, 276). Moreover, the parties continue to relinquish many of their functions to the media, PACs, private consultants, pollsters and pressure groups. State and local officials still are not accorded deference by congressional committees, national administrative bodies and the Supreme Court (ACIR 1986, 242,243).

4) Yet another dimension of adhering rigidly to the status quo is the federal fixation with relying on non-federal employees to implement domestic (and sometimes foreign) policies. Much has been made of the Reagan emphasis on privatization, but ever since FDR and especially since LBJ the national government has relied on "third parties" to administer most domestic initiatives (Salomon 1980, 2-4). The Reagan years are no different in this respect, except that the practice has been extended to defense and foreign policy efforts that would have been deemed unthinkable a few years back.

5) The political and popular appetites for a welfare state are as strong now as they were in 1980. The activist surge was reined in slightly by President Carter's last two budgets. Today, pent-up domestic pressures are being gradually released. Witness the remarkable legacy of the 100th Congress: welfare reform, housing the homeless, catastrophic-illness insurance, clean water amendments, stronger civil rights, drug control and transportation (*Economist* 15-21, Oct. 1988, 29-30). Note also President Bush's domestic agenda — environmental: wetlands preservation, outdoor recreation, clean air renewal, ocean dumping, and superfund viability; education: head start, magnet schools and excellence in teaching; and health: child care, and Medicaid "buy in" for 37 million uninsured Americans. The Democratic Congress has on its domestic agenda such "carry overs" as the clean air act renewal, banking reform, savings and loan bailout, child care, parental leave, and the required statutory renewals of child nutrition, school lunch, food stamps, library services, vocational education, education of the handicapped, Indian education, energy policy and conservation programs. Congress and the president will continue to joust over domestic programs and, despite budget constraints, they will adopt new and re-enact old measures just as in 1980. However, some will have ingenious to nonexistent funding mechanisms.

6) The Washington scene also resembles the 1970s in the policy-making model now in ascendancy. That model is the neo-Madisonian, pluralistic, multiple-actor scenario that dominated President Carter's term, the Reagan administration from 1983 to 1988 and probably will characterize Bush's term. What this means is that the president is an actor on the Washington stage; that Congress is as important in domestic matters as the executive branch; that interest groups remain powerful, plentiful and persuasive,

though not as much as in the 1970s; that state and local governments must exert extraordinary efforts to compete successfully with potent conflicting forces; and that the budget dominates this policy-making approach and the attention of these diverse players just as it began to at the end of the Carter years. This non-hierarchical, pluralistic mode of decision-making can produce the expensive and harmful effects of gridlock budgetary politics as happened from 1982 to 1987. It also can skillfully resolve seemingly irresolvable issues such as, Social Security bailout, 1986, tax overhaul and welfare reform. Let us hope the latter cooperative approach is the version of this traditional American approach to policy-making that prevails.

As this analysis shows, many of the changes since 1980 are welcome ones: the somewhat smaller federal domestic agenda, the growing bipartisan consensus on domestic priorities, the less panoramic partnership principle and the remarkable resilience and responsiveness of the localities and states. These, in turn, suggest far less systemic overload, more balance and a degree of vitality in our federalism that has astonished many observers.

Yet, the continuities with the past are just as significant and some are not promising. Above all is the verdict that Reagan and Sanzone's "permis-

---

Localities and states continue to be incapable of asserting by any means an authoritative role in national governmental actions affecting their jurisdictional and operational integrity. This does not bode well for the future of American federalism.

---

sive federalism" description is still valid. Most state and local actions could have been initiated, modified or pre-empted by the central government, budgetary constraints permitting. Localities and states continue to be incapable of asserting by any means an authoritative role in national governmental actions affecting their jurisdictional and operational integrity. This does not bode well for the future of American federalism.

The Future of Federalism?

If the condition of American federalism is functionally good, but systemically disturbing, what does this mean for the future?

One school of federalist thought is optimistic (Conlan 1988, 228-231). The positivist activism of state and local governments will continue, so its members argue, and there will be no return to the days of "overwhelming Federal dominance" (Herbers 1987, 28, 34). The fiscal dilemmas confronting the national government, the public's de-

mand for welfare programs and the better fiscal position of state and local governments support this interpretation. A more historically based version holds that federalism is a cyclical affair and that "the states . . . are taking on new life and moving in response to the demands of modern society" (Keller 1988, 57). The "tensions and discontents of modern life have increased the need — social, even psychological — for units of government" that have the "geographic capabilities" to govern effectively, while not being beyond the "reach and comprehension of the average citizen" (Keller 1988, 57).

A second more pessimistic assessment of federalism's prospects rejects this functional theory as unmindful of the long-term centripetal dynamics of our system. This view, which is largely my own, holds that "the systemic position of state and local governments, while operationally powerful, is weak constitutionally and politically. . . . Reagan federalism . . . has done little to . . . place the American states on a par with their counterparts in . . . other federal systems" (Bender and Steven 1988, 344). The combination of centralizing national judicial decisions and political developments have placed the localities and states in a second-class position, compared to that of a generation ago. The change in relations between the levels is probably permanent. The states' inability to convert their functional clout into political power and balanced treatment before the federal judiciary leaves them in a perennially precarious position — legally, jurisdictionally, politically and operationally. This nightmarish condition confronts none of their counterparts in Australia, Canada, Switzerland or West Germany.

A third forecast focuses on correcting legal deficiencies. This view holds that only constitutional and judicial changes will restore the states to a healthy position. The judicial portion of this interpretation emphasizes that because nearly half of all federal judges are Reagan appointees along with four of the Supreme Court justices and at least two future Supreme Court appointments will be made by Bush, there will be a solidly conservative federal judiciary in the near future, including the Supreme Court. With this would come reversals of recent centripetalist court decisions, starting with *Garcia* as then-Justice Rehnquist promised in his dissent.

The constitutional facet of this formulation for the future is provided by former New Hampshire Gov. John Sununu's (and the National Governors' Association's) proposed amendment to the U.S. Constitution. Were it adopted, should two-thirds of the states memorialize Congress for a specific constitutional change, Congress would be required to vote on the proposed amendment. A two-thirds vote in both houses would be needed to stop the measure from going back to the states for ratification (Sununu Fall 1988, 8). Given

Sununu's pivotal chief of staff position in the Bush administration, it would be a mistake to dismiss this proposal out of hand.

The judicial part of this third scenario for federalism's future is on firmer ground. Yet, judicial observers might caution against expecting a massive reversal of centralizing decisions. The record of three of the five Nixon-Ford Supreme Court appointees is instructive, because they ultimately favored the position of the central government as much as that of the states and localities in federalist cases. So there is uncertainty surrounding this scenario as well.

What then seems certain? First, the nation's need to confront the deficit will have a constraining effect on Washington's domestic activist propensities. That will increase pressures on states and localities to help fill the gap left by the federal government's preoccupation with its floundering treasury. Some shifts in the Court's composition are inevitable, but not a mass conversion to any dual federalist position. Also unlikely are significant decentralizing or devolutionary actions by political parties and pressure groups.

All this prompts the guesstimate that elements of all three of these scenarios may play out, but with the author of the second and more pessimistic script writing the final version of this next act of American federalism's 200-year-old drama.

Sources

Bender, Lewis G. and James A. Stever, eds. 1986. *Administering the New Federalism*. Boulder, Colo.: Westview.

Conlan, Timothy. 1988. *New Federalism*. Washington, D.C.: The Brookings Institution.

The Economist. 15-21 October, 1988.

Kayden, Xandra. 1981. "The Nationalizing of the Party System." *Parties, Interest Groups, and Campaign Finance Laws*. Michael J. Malbin, ed. Washington, D.C.: American Enterprise Institute, 276 ff.

Keller, Morton. Oct. 1988. "State Power Needn't Be Ressurrected Because It Never Died," *Governing the States and Localities*. Washington, D.C.: Congressional Quarterly, Inc.

Kelly, Alfred H. and Winifred A. Harbison. 1976. *The American Constitution, Its Origins and Develoment*. New York: W. W. Norton and Co.

Ladd, Everett Carll Jr. 1970. *American Political Parties*. New York: W.W. Norton and Co.

Osborne, David Osborne. 1988. *Laboratories of Democracy*. Boston: Harvard Business School Press.

Reagan, Michael and John G. Sanzone. 1981. *The New Federalism*. New York: Oxford University Press.

Salomon, Lester. 1980. *Rethinking Public Management*, Washington, D.C.: The Urban Institute.

Schwarz, John E. 1988. *America's Hidden Success*. New York: W.W. Norton and Co.

Sununu, John. Fall 1988. "The Spirit of Federalism: Restoring the Balance." *Intergovernmental Perspective*, Washington, D.C.: Advisory Commission on Intergovernmental Relations.

U.S. Advisory Comission on Intergovernmental Relations. August 1986. *The Transformation of American Politics*. Washington, D.C.: ACIR.

____. December 1987. *Significant Features of Fiscal Federalism, 1988 Edition*, Vol. 1. Washington, D.C.: ACIR.

U.S. Census Bureau. *Governmental Finances*. Washington, D.C.: Government Printing Office.

Walker, David B. 1981. *Toward a Functioning Federalism*. Cambridge, MA: Winthrop Publications, Inc.

Rethinking Federalism

ROCHELLE L. STANFIELD

Should the federal government take charge of health care, thus freeing state and local governments to run and finance most other domestic programs? It's the centerpiece of a radical—but, to many, an increasingly attractive—plan to reorder federalism.

A lice M. Rivlin says that when she began working on *Reviving the American Dream*, she intended to write a prescription for the nation's current economic ills.

Whether or not she succeeded on that count, the former director of the Congressional Budget Office (CBO) ended up with a book that's rekindled a long-moribund debate over federalism—the distribution of power between the states and the federal government.

"The only way I see to get out of this [economic] bind is to think about whether the job [of raising revenues and performing government services] shouldn't be shared differently," Rivlin said in a recent interview in her office at the Brookings Institution, which published *Reviving the American Dream* earlier this year.

Although the economic logic of Rivlin's plan has been attracting a growing list of adherents, the political barriers between idea and action are steep. Many analysts, in fact, say that only a major national crisis could move Rivlin's proposal to the political front burner.

While President Bush and Gov. Bill Clinton of Arkansas, the Democratic presidential nominee, have been sparring over how to fix the economy, neither has talked about refashioning federalism as part of the solution. In his economic pamphlet "Agenda for American Renewal," Bush talks about "right-sizing government." In *Putting People First,* which has grown from pamphlet to paperback book in the past few months, Clinton advocates "revolutionizing government."

Strong on such superficials as reducing the size of the federal bureaucracy, both plans avoid specifics about fundamental changes in how government does business. But that apparently doesn't bother Rivlin. In the modern era, she said, presidential contenders "have not gotten much beyond generalities until they actually got elected."

But beginning on Nov. 4, Rivlin is hoping for some serious discussion about sorting out the federal system. Many economists, political analysts and a surprisingly large number of state and local government officials are coming to many of the same conclusions that Rivlin has, although they are quick to point out that they don't agree with all of her recommendations.

"To me, sorting out—not just of responsibilities but of financial resources—makes some sense," said Larry E. Naake, the executive director of the National Association of Counties.

Gov. Roy Romer, D-Colo., the new chairman of the National Governors' Association (NGA), carries around a well-thumbed copy of Rivlin's book and has said that he intends to make a restructuring of government one of his top priorities.

Part of the reason may be that federal aid to state and local governments has lost some of the luster that it had in the 1970s. "I don't think the salvation of American cities right now is in federal funding," Milwaukee Mayor John O. Norquist said in an interview. "It's often a onetime phenomenon that builds up your operating costs and then causes budget crises when it is withdrawn. I call it the gift that always stops giving."

Whether such discussions will trickle up to the White House next January is another question, of course.

"I don't see anything in what Bush has said or done that leads me to believe he'll act differently in a second term," said Charles Royer, a former mayor of Seattle who now directs Harvard University's Institute of Politics.

Clinton's advisers, on the other hand, are planning to press for a rethinking of federalism. David E. Osborne, the co-author of *Reinventing Government* (Addison-Wesley, 1992), whose catchphrases ("entrepreneurial government," for example) show up with remarkable regularity in Clinton's speeches, said in an interview that such a sorting out will be part of the blueprint for a Clinton Administration that he and others are drafting for the Washington-based Progressive Policy Institute.

"It will take a crisis, which we have—a severe political, economic and fiscal crisis, which will probably produce a new President who generally believes in a new federalism and in reinventing the federal government," Osborne said. "And it will take a new Congress with a new attitude. I think we're going to get that. So the conditions are right."

SORTING IT ALL OUT

Rivlin arrived at her one-fell-swoop proposal against the backdrop of a federal government that's neck deep in debt and unable to deal effectively with the wide array of domestic responsibilities it has accumulated over the past three decades.

To Rivlin, the bold swap she suggested would, at once, reduce the federal deficit, underwrite critical public investments and enable sweeping reforms. The only way to control health care costs is for the national government to take over the whole system, she figured. For their part, state and local governments would be better able to manage most domestic programs and to collect the additional taxes needed to pay for them.

States and localities may be better positioned for such decision making because of what intergovernmental phrasemaker John Shannon calls "the Alamo factor." Like those who defended the Alamo, state and local officials who must meet balanced-budget requirements do not have the same escape hatch as the federal government (the ability to engage in deficit spending), explained Shannon, the former executive director of the Advisory Commission on Intergovernmental Relations (ACIR) and now a senior fellow at the Urban Institute.

"All of our data show state and local governments can raise taxes, whereas taxes is a dirty word in Washington," Shannon said. "More and more of the run-of-the-mill domestic functions will be taken over by the state and local governments because their officials are forced to make tough decisions."

Accordingly, over the past 20 years, most states have adopted income taxes, comprehensive sales taxes and other mechanisms for raising big bucks from citizens. In 1964, Shannon figures, state and local governments collected about 60 per cent as much general revenue as the federal government. Now they are on a par. In 1990, the federal government raised about $1.1 trillion and the states and localities about $1 trillion, according to the Census Bureau.

"We used to think of the states as the fallen arches of the federal system," Shannon said. "But in the last 12 years, if anything, Washington has demonstrated that it has the Achilles' heel, because it can't pay its bills."

Why are state and local officials beginning to talk about a formal reshuffling of responsibilities? For more than a decade, they say, they've been the victims of a partial—and unpleasant—sorting out.

During the 1960s and 1970s, Congress poured federal aid into state and local governments. Grants soared from 14.5 per cent of state and local outlays in 1960 to a peak of 26.5 per cent in 1978 and dropped back to a low of about 18 per cent in 1988, according to the ACIR.

Along with the money came a lot of rules and regulations—"mandates." During the 1980s, federal policy makers "found it relatively easy to cut the money flow to local governments," county commissioner Randall Franke of Marion County, Ore., said. "But they haven't even slowed down in the unfunded mandates and the red tape they put on us."

The ACIR, for example, counted 36 major federal mandates enacted through 1980 and another 27 enacted from 1981-90. The CBO estimated that the 1986 amendments to the 1974 Safe Drinking Water Act, for example, cost local water systems up to $3 billion a year to implement.

The National Conference of State Legislatures publishes a newsletter that's devoted to federal mandates imposed on state and local governments. The *Mandate Watch List* tracks about 200 new mandates proposed by the 102nd Congress.

"If Congress passes a mandate," Bush said in his 1992 State of the Union message, "it should be forced to pay for it." Mandates, however, come not only from Congress, but also from the executive branch and the courts.

Nearly every state and local official seems to have a stock of mandate horror stories. Cook County (Ill.) Commissioner John H. Stroger Jr., for example, complained about a federal court decision that required improvements in the county jails. "Then it was mandated on us to immediately go forward and build" better facilities, he said, reflecting the biblical quality of mandates that many local officials feel. "There is something wrong with that type of decision."

States have also jumped into the mandating game by ordering county and city governments to meet standards or perform services for which they are not paid.

And sometimes state and federal mandates are at cross-purposes. Franke tells how Marion County ended up transferring its home health service from the county health department to a local hospital because of conflicting federal and state mandates. "Here we had different levels of government telling us what to do and how to do it, and that restricted our ability to respond to the citizens' needs," he said.

Milwaukee Mayor Norquist, on the other hand, expressed an ambivalence about mandates that could foreshadow the difficulty of achieving the unity needed to change the status quo in any major way. "Some of the mandates are more trouble than any funding you could get," he said. "But most of the mandates, if you really seriously check them out, are really commonsense things that you would do anyway."

MIXING IT UP

Advocates of a Rivlin-style New Federalism III say that the right conditions are now in place for reform: The federal government no longer can handle all the jobs it has taken on, and once the recession is over, state and local governments will be in a position to do so.

That wasn't the case the previous two times. President Nixon's first round of New Federalism didn't even contemplate a true sorting out—state and local governments were in no shape to handle that—but merely greater state and local flexibility in managing federal aid programs through general revenue sharing (which he got) and a series of block grants (which he didn't).

Rivlin's plan has some striking parallels to President Reagan's proposal. Among other things, Reagan would have swapped a federal takeover of medicaid for a state takeover of aid to families with dependent children. As they track state spending on medicaid (which rose from 9 per cent of state budgets in 1980 to 14 per cent in 1990 and is still climbing), many analysts wonder whether the states might have been better off had they accepted Reagan's offer.

If ever the New Federalism was to be pulled off, they say in retrospect, it was under Reagan, when the full weight of the White House was pushing for change.

"There was some political leadership behind it, and therefore people came to the table," recalled Royer, who was one of the mayors involved in negotiations at the time. "I don't see that going on now, even though the need is far greater."

Others involved in the negotiations say that the plan had a lot of drawbacks and, more important, that neither the governors nor the mayors trusted the Reagan

White House. Whether a New Federalism III could be negotiated in an atmosphere of trust is probably the most fundamental question. Other practical and political considerations, however, also come into play.

The first problem is getting all the actors together. Even on the hated mandate issue, "rarely have states and cities presented a united front," said Timothy J. Conlan, a professor of government at George Mason University who's written extensively about mandates.

"Southern governors went hat in hand to the Senate Finance Committee and asked for medicaid mandates, for example," recalled Paul Posner, a longtime government analyst who wrote a doctoral dissertation on mandates in the 99th Congress. "Governors are the strongest supporters of mandates."

In many cases, governors supported federal mandates because they wanted to maintain control but feared competition from other states. Most state and local officials agree that other mandates—such as environmental regulations—are the only practical way to achieve national goals. And the increasing globalization of the economy has resulted in more—not less—uniformity in banking, insurance, trucking and other forms of interstate commerce.

If they can't get together on mandates, can governors, mayors and county officials agree on other aspects of reform? The recent round of recession-induced state budget cuts, which substantially reduced state aid to localities, isn't contributing to a cooperative atmosphere.

"Our municipal league directors and big-city managers are telling me this year that they feel the relationship between state and local governments has deteriorated to maybe the lowest level anyone can remember, and some of them have been around for a very long time," said Frank Shafroth, the director of policy and federal relations for the National League of Cities. "One California guy said to me, 'Basically, we're at war with the state.'"

If the impetus doesn't come from the squabbling state and local officials, will it come from the White House?

Just about everyone seems to agree that if Bush wins, the debate over federalism will be less than robust. Although his economic plan talks about flattening out the federal government, Bush has never been particularly interested in state and local government. The governors say that the high point of their relationship with Bush came in his first year in the White House, when he met with representatives of the NGA on nine occasions.

This was at the urging of then-White House chief of staff John H. Sununu, the former governor of New Hampshire and a former chairman of the NGA. When he was governor, Sununu talked a lot about federalism and the need for reform. But at the White House, Sununu's interest in the issue waned.

Clinton is also a former chairman of the NGA and one of its most active members. But, close observers explain, his drive was never for matters of federalism or government structure but for particular issues such as education and child welfare and job training.

That, of course, doesn't preclude a new and improved federalism campaign should he be elected, advocates of reform say. Clinton is clearly interested in restructuring and decentralizing government, which would be the heart of any sorting-out initiative.[1]

"As a leading state innovator, he understands the importance of making sure the central government encourages innovation rather than getting in the way," Michael Waldman, the deputy communications director of the Clinton campaign, said. "He may not have written a law review article on federalism, but he has lived it."

[1]This article was written prior to the election of Bill Clinton in the 1992 presidential election. Ed.

Federal Government Mandates

WHY THE STATES ARE COMPLAINING

Martha Derthick

Martha Derthick, formerly director of the Brookings Governmental Studies program, is the Julia Allen Cooper Professor of Government and Foreign Affairs at the University of Virginia. She thanks John Dinan for research assistance.

Hard pressed by recession, state governments have been complaining that Congress keeps passing laws ordering them to undertake expensive new programs—but without providing the money to do so. Complaints about federal mandates are not new. In 1980 New York City Mayor Edward I. Koch wrote bitterly of the "mandate millstone" in an article in *The Public Interest,* giving currency to the term.

The main concern of state officials is political: who will pay the costs of government? But their complaints raise constitutional issues as well. In various ways the Constitution protects the states' existence as governments, having their own elected officials and the power to raise taxes and to enact, enforce, and interpret laws. How far can federal mandates be pushed without infringing on the states' governmental character?

The federal government influences state governments in four main ways—through court decrees, legislative regulations, preemptions, and conditional grants-in-aid. As a quick review will show, all four have grown significantly more coercive in the past half century.

Judicial Decrees

Until the mid-1950s federal courts interpreting the Constitution had habitually told the states what they might *not* do. They had struck down literally hundreds of state laws. But they had refrained from telling states what they *must* do. This changed with school desegregation. In 1955, with *Brown v. Board of Education II,* the Supreme Court gave federal district courts responsibility for entering the orders and decrees to desegregate public schools. The Court's ruling initiated a judicial effort to achieve racial integration with affirmative commands, telling school districts how to construct their attendance zones, where to build schools, where to bus their pupils, and how to assign their teachers.

Once courts and litigants discovered what could be done (or attempted) in the schools, other state institutions, especially prisons and institutions for the mentally ill and retarded, became targets. Nearly all state prison systems now operate under judicial decrees that address overcrowding and other conditions of prison life, and federal judges routinely mandate construction programs and modes of prison administration.

Needless to say, federal judicial mandates come without money, because courts have no way of raising money.

Legislative Regulations

Congress is also a source of affirmative commands to the states. When it imposes taxes and regulations—such as social security payroll taxes, wages-and-hours regulation, and emissions limits—on private parties, it must decide whether to cover state governments as well, for they and their local subdivisions are employers and, in some respects, producers.

For much of the nation's history, Congress did not tax and regulate state governments because it conceived of them as separate, sovereign, and equal. In a leading statement of this constitutional doctrine, the Supreme Court ruled in 1871 (*Collector v. Day*) that a federal income tax could not be levied against a county judge in Massachusetts. An earlier decision of the Court (*Dobbins v. The Commissioners of Erie,* 1842) had settled that the states could not tax the salary of an officer of the United States. Under 19th-century conceptions of federalism, it followed that the federal government could not tax the salaries of officers of the states.

When the Social Security Act of 1935 was passed, states as employers were routinely exempted from paying the payroll tax. Similarly, when the Fair Labor Standards Act of 1938 set maximum hours and minimum wages for industrial employers, no one would have imagined extending such regulation to state and local governments.

Yet as these New Deal measures were being enacted, the doctrine of sovereign immunity that had protected the states was collapsing. The Supreme Court overruled *Collector v. Day* in 1939. Eventually, under the nationalizing impact of the New Deal, Congress began regulating state governments just as if they were private parties. For example, Congress extended wages-and-hours regulation to some state and local employees in 1966, to the rest in 1974. The Supreme Court at first upheld the move, but then, in response to the law of 1974, changed its mind. In 1976 the Court forbade Congress from exercising its commerce power so as to "force directly upon the States its choices as to how essential decisions regarding the conduct of integral governmental functions are to be made" (*National League of Cities v. Usery*). But the standard proved impractical and was abandoned in 1985 (*Garcia v. San Antonio Metropolitan Transit Authority*). Speaking for the Court, Justice Blackmun wrote that the "political process ensures that laws that unduly burden the States will not be promulgated." The Court seemed to wash its hands of the subject, leaving the states to the mercy of what Justice O'Connor in dissent called Congress's "underdeveloped capacity for self-restraint."

Preemptions

Preemptions are commands to the states to *stop* doing something and let the federal government do it. They are sanctioned by the supremacy clause of the Constitution, which requires that state laws yield to federal ones in case of conflict. Historically, preemptions have been not so much a calculated technique of intergovernmental relations as something that "just happened" as a byproduct of congressional action. It was left to the courts to rule, in response to litigation, whether preemption had taken place.

Recently preemptions have become both more frequent and more explicit. Congress passed more than 90 new preemptive laws in the 1970s and again in the 1980s, more than double the number for any previous decade. Partly because of pressure from the courts to be explicit, Congress now often does declare an intention to preempt. And the states naturally experience such declarations as coercion, even if they are being prevented from doing things rather than commanded to do them.

There is also a modern variant on the use of preemption, called by students of federalism "partial preemption." In the 1970s, as it enacted a new wave of regulation, Congress hit on a way of making use of the states for administration. It would preempt a field—say, occupational health and safety or surface mining or air pollution control—but permit the states to continue to function providing that they adopted standards at least as exacting as those it stipulated. The Supreme Court upheld this technique (*Hodel v. Virginia Surface Mining and Reclamation Association*, 1981).

Technically, the states can refuse the federal government's invitation to serve as administrators of its regulations. But in practice they have responded. "Each State shall . . . adopt . . . a plan which provides for implementation, maintenance, and enforcement" of federal air quality standards, the Clean Air Act says—and each state does. Better to be subordinate governments than empty ones.

Grant-in-Aid Conditions

Federal grant-in-aid conditions addressed to the states have been around at least since the Morrill Act of 1862, which gave the states land—30,000 acres for each member of Congress—to endow colleges in the agricultural and mechanic arts.

In theory, states have always been able to refuse federal grants. In practice, they have generally found them irresistible. And as time passed, states' dependence increased: aid was habit-forming. In 1965 federal highway grants passed $4 billion a year. In 1970

grants for public assistance, including Medicaid, passed $7 billion a year. Altogether federal grants in 1970 amounted to nearly 30 percent of states' own-source revenues. It is absurd to hold, as constitutional doctrine formally does, that such grants can be rejected, and the burden of the accompanying conditions thereby avoided.

Over time, the conditions of grant programs expanded in scope and detail. Successful political movements left their mark on grant programs through conditions that apply to all or most grant programs. The rights revolution of the 1960s and 1970s, for example, left a legacy of anti-discrimination requirements, and the environmental movement a requirement that environmental impact statements be prepared for federally aided projects.

Similarly, conditions have multiplied program by program. Section 402 of Title IV of the Social Security Act of 1935 took 2 brief paragraphs to describe what should be contained in state plans for aid to dependent children. By 1976 section 402 had grown to 9 pages; by 1988, to 27.

Also, Congress in the 1970s began threatening to withhold grants, particularly those for Medicaid and highways, to achieve objectives connected only loosely or not at all to the underlying purpose of the grant. When Congress set a national speed limit of 55 miles per hour in 1974 and a minimum drinking age of 21 in 1984, it did so by threatening to withhold highway grants from states that failed to comply.

Finally, the language of grant-in-aid statutes has become more coercive. Federal law makes some Medicaid services "mandatory" and Congress keeps adding to the list.

From time to time presidents, especially Republicans, have tried to reduce and simplify grant conditions. The revisions that Nixon, Ford, and Reagan achieved, in the form of revenue sharing and block grants, have been modest and, in the case of general revenue sharing, short-lived. Conditioned grants for specific purposes have persisted and always predominated.

Historically, grant-in-aid conditions could be enforced only by administrative action, primarily the threat to withhold the grant. Because withholding was self-defeating, it was not often used. Federal administrators got what compliance they could through negotiation. However, with the rights revolution and the rise of judicial activism, many grant-in-aid conditions became judicially enforceable, particularly in programs of AFDC and education of handicapped children. A whole new set of commands emanated from an awe-inspiring source, the courts.

As grant conditions became more coercive, grants did not keep pace. Grants as a share of states' own-source revenues reached a peak at 32 percent in 1976 and then began to fall.

Do Mandates Matter?

The rise of the affirmative command, occurring subtly and on several different fronts, constitutes a sea-change in federal-state relations. The states have been converted from separate governments into subordinate

Congress is not much inclined to contemplate the deeper issues of federalism and to ask, self-critically, whether or where it should exercise restraint in its use of mandates.

ones, arguably mere "agents" in some programs. In constitutional significance, the change is comparable to the transformation by which the federal government ceased over the course of many years to be a government of limited, specified powers and became free to engage in any domestic activity not prohibited by the Bill of Rights.

That mandates developed only in the past 40 years does not necessarily mean that they are contrary to the Framers' intentions. That depends on which Framers one consults. Today's federalism is what the losing side of 1787 feared, but arguably what the winning side hoped for. Madison, after all, went into the Constitutional Convention saying that the states should be retained because they would be "subordinately useful." That is precisely what they have become. And there is at least a hint in *The Federalist* that affirmative commands would be acceptable. Number 27, written by by the ardently nationalistic Hamilton, anticipated that the federal government would employ the states to administer its laws. It is hard to see how that could have happened in the absence of mandates.

Yet most fundamentally, *The Federalist* saw federalism as a way to safeguard the public against abuses of governmental power and to sustain republicanism, the great central principle of the American regime. As Hamilton argued in number 28, "Power being almost always the rival of power, the general government will at all times stand ready to check the usurpations of the state governments, and these will have the same disposition towards the general government. The people, by throwing themselves into either scale, will infallibly make it preponderate. If their rights are invaded by either, they can make use of the other as the instrument of redress."

Indeed, the institutions of federalism can be used by the people to play different levels of government—and through them different policy choices—off against each other. One sees this happening most vividly in the prolonged contest over abortion policy, in which the federal courts "corrected" the restrictive excesses of state laws in the early 1970s and state legislatures responded by "correcting" the libertarian excesses of *Roe v. Wade*, and so on—in a heated intergovernmental exchange that threatens to be endless because the rival political movements are incapable of compromise.

Today mandates come in so many different forms and with so many different purposes that it is difficult to speak of them as a class. Limited, for the sake of discussion, to those that compel expenditure, they clearly raise important questions about republicanism. Judicial mandates come from a body that is not elected at all; congressional mandates, from a body that is not responsible to the various state electorates. When the federal judiciary commands the states to spend more on prisons and Congress commands them to spend more on Medicaid, they are making decisions that state electorates have no way to review. State officials lose their ability to weigh competing claims on state budgets. Of course, no such weighing is done at the federal level, where mandates are produced in isolation

from one another. Neither the courts nor Congress, framing commands to the states, asks the question, "how much, compared to what?" that is crucial to rational, responsible policymaking. At some point, federal commands to the states may come to implicate the guarantee clause of the Constitution: "The United States shall guarantee to every state in this Union a Republican Form of Government."

Can Mandates Be Curbed?

How strongly state officials oppose mandates may be questioned. Accepting subordination as a fact of life, they have produced scattered complaints but not concerted or doctrinaire opposition. Although the loss of budgetary discretion is a serious problem for governors, it is hard for all 50 of them to get together on anything, much less take a public stand *for* overcrowded prisons or *against* medical care for pregnant women.

Largely devoid of interest in constitutional issues except for its own battles with the president, today's Congress is not much inclined to contemplate the deeper issues of federalism and to ask, self-critically, whether or where it should exercise restraint in its use of mandates. If it can expand the benefits of government while imposing much of the cost on other governments in the system, why not do it?

By contrast, the Supreme Court, habituated to thinking in constitutional terms, and made conservative by a series of Republican appointments, is engaged in a wide-ranging retreat from the use of mandates. In school desegregation, prison administration, and enforcement of grant-in-aid conditions, not to mention voting rights, abortion, and *habeas corpus*, the Court has signaled that it will show more deference to the states. But it is one thing for the Court to practice self-restraint and quite another for it to attempt to restrain Congress. The Court does not lightly challenge a co-equal branch of government, nor has it had much success in the past in devising practical and enduring standards to protect the state governments.

There remains, nonetheless, a strong case for federalism, as Alice Rivlin, for one, has urged in the 1991 Webb Lecture before the National Academy of Public Administration and in *Reviving the American Dream*. As Madison foresaw, the task of governing so vast a country is too formidable for one government alone. It is significant that someone as thoughtful and experienced as Rivlin, whose whole career has been based in Washington and devoted to shaping national policy, should conclude that national uniformity is a liability in some areas of government. She names education and skills training, child care, housing, infrastructure, and economic development as activities that are "likely to succeed only if they are well adapted to local conditions, have strong local support and community participation and are managed by accountable officials who can be voted out if things go badly."

Rivlin's vision of revitalized state government calls, appropriately, for interstate equalization of revenues, to be achieved—and here her proposal becomes radical—by the states' adopting "one or more common

By contrast, the Supreme Court, habituated to thinking in constitutional terms, is engaged in a wide-ranging retreat from the use of mandates.

taxes (same base, same rate) and sharing the proceeds." She suggests a single state corporate income tax or a uniform value-added tax, shared on a per capita basis and substituted for state retail sales taxes. To achieve this, the states would need the "blessing and perhaps the assistance of the federal government."

Indeed. There is no plausible mechanism, formal or informal, by which the 50 states could voluntarily agree on a common tax. It would have to be imposed by Congress in a fresh stroke of centralization—a mandate, if you will—entailing preemption of a particular tax source and dedication of the proceeds to the states, with no conditions attached. The absence of conditions proved not to be politically durable when general revenue sharing was tried in the 1970s. State political leaders might be forgiven if they doubt whether Congress would be willing to take the heat for imposing a new tax while turning the proceeds over to them.

Perhaps no other of our governing institutions has been subject to so much change and yet so resistant to planned, deliberate reform as federalism. Its history is one of centralization, steady and seemingly irreversible. Yet the case for lodging a large measure of domestic responsibility and discretion with the states and their local subdivisions remains strong. So is the case for the states having governments—republican governments chosen by state electorates and accountable to them, and capable of raising their own revenues and deciding how those revenues should be spent. It is one of the ironies of federalism that deliberate acts of decentralization, such as Rivlin proposes, depend on centralization as a precondition.

Cities Have a Simple Message for States This Year:

SET US FREE

Jonathan Walters

LEGISLATURES 1992

City officials are taking one simple message to state legislators in 1992: If states can't do much to solve city problems—either because they are unwilling or because they are broke—then they ought to get out of the way and give local governments the tools to do the job themselves.

More than at any time in recent memory, cities are not pleading for additional money. They are pleading for authority. It's not that local officials wouldn't be as happy as ever with a big infusion of cash. They simply know there is not going to be one. So they want the authority to come up with new revenue sources on their own. They want to be able to consolidate services with other jurisdictions. And they want legislatures to be more disciplined about mandating local programs without providing the money to pay for them.

Authority is something states have been notably reluctant to grant their localities in the past. They may find themselves granting more of it this year than they ever imagined they would.

There are, of course, quite a few states where money will still be a very serious issue between states and cities. More than a dozen states cut direct local aid during the 1991 legislative session. In Massachusetts, state aid to localities has plummeted from more than $2.5 billion in 1989 to $1.8 billion

this fiscal year. Boston alone has lost $85 million in state aid over the last three years. New Mexico cities are having to swallow a new state tax that sends a portion of their own municipal revenues to Santa Fe. For cities in those straits, the overwhelming priority is getting the money back.

In a majority of states, though, the relationship has changed. The most intense arguments of 1992 won't necessarily be over the level of funding. They will be about how much freedom local officials are going to have when it comes to raising money and spending it in the way they want to.

City lobbyists feel they can bring to that argument a powerful point of political leverage: Voters seem increasingly inclined to trust the government that sits closest to the people, the one that provides the services that voters use and touch and see. In a recent survey by the Advisory Commission on Intergovernmental Relations, 35 percent of those polled chose localities as the level of government that spends tax money most wisely. Only 14 percent chose states.

Convinced he's reading the mood of voters correctly, Michael Sittig, lobbyist for the Florida League of Municipalities, says, "You have a $30 billion state budget, but if you're not in prison, if you don't have a kid in school and you're not receiving indigent aid, you have no idea where the hell your money goes." At the local level, Sittig insists, people know what the money goes for—roads, utilities and trash removal, police and fire protection. He believes voters will accept tax increases where they see the immediate need

and reap the immediate benefit. And so Sittig, along with his counterparts from cities all over the country, will be asking legislatures to turn communities loose to raise local money any way they feel like raising it.

It might seem odd that, at a time of widespread anti-tax resentment, localities would be working so hard to gain the power to make voters unhappy. But there is no real mystery about it. Localities are desperate to free themselves from the strictures of the most unpopular tax of all—the property tax, which currently accounts for around 50 percent of all local revenue.

Most local officials consider it a political advantage to be able to raise money from almost any new tax source—income, sales, gasoline, hotel occupancy—if it will allow them not to hit up homeowners for more property tax money. The problem is that localities are, in the old textbook phrase, "creatures of the state." Most legislatures allow them very little authority to tax anything without specific permission. Moreover, states put all sorts of conditions on where local-option tax money can be spent. The states may demand flexibility from the federal government, local lobbyists like to point out, but they have been unbending when it comes to their own localities.

Nevertheless, they started to bend in lots of places in 1991. Nearly 20 states gave localities some sort of new taxing authority. Some initiatives were sweeping. California turned $2.1 billion worth of revenue-raising authority over to counties last year in the form of new sales tax and vehicle registration fees. Other authority was more modest. In Pennsylvania, the legislature gave the city it loves to hate—Philadelphia— permission to tack 1 percent onto the state's 6 percent sales tax and skim off the new revenue. The legislature balked at extending the privilege to all Pennsylvania cities, but there will be a battle over the issue this year, and the result may be different.

Some of the new authority may turn out to be a mixed blessing. In California, counties won their new taxing powers only because they are taking back responsibility for several big-ticket health care programs. Those are not likely to get any cheaper to fund. Still, local officials consider the shift a coup.

The most radical of this year's tax autonomy plans comes from Florida. The Florida Municipal League may ask the state to give cities what amounts to carte blanche in setting up their own tax structures, from what gets taxed to the rate of the levy and the programs it can be used to finance.

Localities in Maine are pushing a more modest proposal, but an innovative one. It would establish a regional option tax. Regions would be defined by county boundaries, depending on the scope of economic activity in each cluster of counties. Some commercially strong counties will be economic regions unto themselves. Money from the tax would be distributed three ways: a percentage would go to the locality where the sale was made, a percentage would go to the region, and a percentage would go to all other regions that had adopted the tax. The beauty of the plan, says Christopher G. Lockwood, director of the Maine Municipal League, is that it accounts for Maine's wildly disparate economies, ranging from sparse and depressed agricultural areas to dense coastal tourist regions. Everybody gets a cut.

Beauty is, of course, in the eye of the beholder. The bill was narrowly defeated by the legislature last year. By statute it cannot be reintroduced until 1993. It will, however, be reintroduced then, Lockwood says. By next year, there may well be some conspicuous victories in other states for him to point to. Legislatures that have never shown a great deal of interest in local au-

tonomy before seem gradually to be recognizing that, in an era of state budget austerity, the time is finally coming. "It's appropriate," says Dean Conley, chairman of the Ohio House Ways and Means Committee, "as long as you're not destroying someone else's tax base."

There are skeptics, of course, who question whether localities will have the courage to use their new tax freedom, no matter how hard they may have lobbied to get it. Former Seattle Mayor Charles Royer, now teaching at Harvard, is one of those. "You can grant things like taxing flexibility," Royer says, "but you can't grant guts."

The mayor of Allentown, Pennsylvania, Joseph S. Daddona, responds that no such grant is necessary. "Give us the flexibility," he is telling his state legislators. "We'll take the heat." Daddona is simply asking them to grant Allentown the authority Philadelphia was given in the last session. With it, he says, his city could have reduced property taxes 24 percent this year. Instead, those taxes are heading up another 8 percent in 1992.

The other autonomy battle cities are fighting is the battle over mandates. Several states have passed some form of mandate relief in recent years, but it is the sort of relief only a state legislator could love. Illinois' law is typical. It requires the legislature to appropriate money whenever it imposes a mandate on a locality. But it has no provision for penalty if the legislature passes the mandate without including any money. The locality still has to comply. The history of these laws is that the legislatures seldom, if ever, ante up.

Two states, however, have now passed mandate-reform bills with teeth in them: Florida, and just last October, Louisiana.

Fed up with the legislature's intransigence on mandates, the Florida Municipal League took the issue to the voters in 1990. A petition was circulated to place a constitutional amendment on the ballot. The amendment was simple: No state mandate shall be enacted without including the funding needed to comply. Period. In just three months, the drive turned up 80,000 signatures—about a fourth of what would be required for putting the

STATE AID TO LOCAL GOVERNMENTS
PER CAPITA, 1990

(Excluding Education and Welfare Expenditures)

1.	Alaska	$497.65
2.	Wyoming	474.89
3.	Wisconsin	424.04
4.	Massachusetts	395.76
5.	Minnesota	350.65
6.	Nevada	329.70
7.	Michigan	298.18
8.	New Mexico	293.93
9.	Arizona	275.22
10.	Nebraska	258.62
11.	California	234.09
12.	Maryland	217.75
13.	Iowa	209.98
14.	New York	207.78
15.	Oregon	205.23
16.	Ohio	195.07
17.	New Jersey	193.01
18.	Mississippi	190.91
19.	Indiana	186.47
20.	North Dakota	185.92
	U.S. Average	**177.64**
21.	Illinois	172.13
22.	Pennsylvania	154.16
23.	Idaho	149.70
24.	North Carolina	146.98
25.	Florida	142.36
26.	Tennessee	137.00
27.	Connecticut	133.29
28.	Alabama	131.99
29.	Washington	127.61
30.	Virginia	125.17
31.	Oklahoma	115.51
32.	South Carolina	112.14
33.	Arkansas	110.97
34.	Kansas	107.71
35.	Colorado	97.99
36.	Kentucky	93.30
37.	Louisiana	88.49
38.	Maine	85.77
39.	Vermont	84.90
40.	Montana	83.85
41.	Hawaii	82.25
42.	South Dakota	82.18
43.	Delaware	81.32
44.	Georgia	77.71
45.	Utah	74.06
46.	Rhode Island	71.60
47.	Missouri	71.39
48.	New Hampshire	59.96
49.	Texas	44.24
50.	West Virginia	33.02

Source: U.S. Census Bureau

amendment on the ballot—and the drive was going strong.

Suddenly, after years of ignoring cities' pleas for relief, the legislature was intensely interested in compromise. An agreement was worked out: no mandates without money unless two-thirds of both houses vote otherwise. That modified constitutional amendment was placed on the ballot in November 1990, and it passed with 65 percent of the vote.

The Florida Municipal League believes several potentially expensive mandates were quashed by the legislative leadership last year on account of the new law. A proposal by public employee unions to mandate an increase in workers' compensation benefits never made it into committee, much less out. The same was true of an effort to strip municipalities of the right to collect impact fees from developers—which cities consider a form of mandate in reverse. Defeating public employee unions and business interests in the corridors of the legislature is a rare experience for municipal lobbyists. They enjoyed it.

The legislators, on the other hand, didn't. They spent part of the last session fashioning and passing an "implementation statute" to go with the new constitutional amendment. The bill was meant to spell out more clearly what a mandate is and at what point it becomes burdensome. The bill also set in place an elaborate procedure for localities trying to opt out of mandates. The legislative leadership claims the bill was an honest effort to help guide them in the fashioning of legislation; city officials think the legislature was trying to eviscerate the original amendment. City officials persuaded Governor Lawton Chiles to veto the bill, but it will be a point of battle again this session.

In Louisiana, it was old-fashioned political pressure that finally pushed a mandate-relief initiative over the top. The cities got fighting mad about having aid cut and mandates boosted while local taxing authority stayed capped. "We finally got elected local officials into a frenzy," says Charles J. Pasqua of the Louisiana Municipal Association. The message they delivered, Pasqua says, was this: "The state is in bad shape, so you cut our revenues, so goddamn it, no more mandates, or at least give us the money to comply, or if

you don't give us the money, then give us the authority to raise it ourselves."

The message made the intended dent. The legislature voted to put a constitutional amendment on last October's ballot allowing localities to ignore state mandates unless the state either includes the funding to comply or authorizes the localities to raise the funds themselves.

The latter requirement was not an easy one for legislators to swallow: They knew it would permit local officials to blame any future mandate-inspired tax increase on the legislature. But they placed it on the ballot, and of eight issues that appeared there, the mandates measure won by the widest margin, with nearly 60 percent of the vote. In Louisiana, as in Florida, the legislature can now impose an unfunded mandate only by mustering a two-thirds majority in each house.

This year, at least a dozen state municipal leagues are pushing for some type of general mandate reform. "It costs the state no money, but it could generate big relief for us," says Edward C. Farrell, executive director of the New York Conference of Mayors.

The third kind of autonomy localities are seeking this year is one that is only indirectly a matter of money. In addition to the freedom to tax and spend and freedom from mandates, they want the authority to consolidate. Localities in many states currently have to apply to their states for permission to consolidate services. Several municipal leagues will be asking this year for broader authority to combine efforts— police forces, fire departments, and especially public utilities—without having to ask permission on a case-by-case basis. More municipalities than ever seem to recognize that having contiguous towns or cities all with their own services, all clipped at the borders, does not make fiscal or practical sense. In some states, such as Kansas, where municipalities can do all the consolidation they want, the league wants some state money to help municipalities coordinate consolidation efforts.

There are states, however, where arguing over the future of consolidation or mandates seems to be something of a luxury right now. Local officials in those states are more likely to characterize what they are doing as fighting for their fiscal lives. Sheila Cheimets, executive director of the Massachusetts Municipal

Association, states her group's priorities succinctly: "We will spend this year trying to regularize state and local fiscal relations. They have fallen apart."

Remarkably, in spite of cutbacks in so many places, state aid to localities actually increased in 1991, as it did through virtually all of the 1980s. The reason, says Steve Gold, director of the Center for the Study of the States, "is because there is a lot of earmarking and built-in growth." Lots of the cutbacks were cutbacks in expansion. Still, Gold does not dispute the overall perception that "a lot of local governments took a serious hit."

This year, the hits will get harder. Many of the states that cut aid to localities in 1991 face another round of huge budget deficits again in 1992. Municipalities remain a large, tempting target. And states that didn't cut municipalities last year may cut them now. Nobody sees state budgets getting better very soon.

There is a certain bitterness in the local attitude toward states these days, a bitterness brought on by cutbacks, mandates and taxing restrictions, all in combination. "It's all part of what started in Washington," says New York's Edward Farrell. "It's just filtering down. There is less interest in the problems of local governments. The state governments and Washington have stopped looking at us as the providers of basic public services, and have started viewing local governments as another interest group."

It is worse than that, complains E.A. Mosher, who just retired after 31 years as executive director of the League of Kansas Municipalities: State legislatures have simply become large, bloated self-important bureaucracies in their own right. "Then they go to those National Conference of State Legislatures meetings and start believing what they hear about state government becoming increasingly important."

But beating up on state legislatures isn't going to help localities, warns Bill Pound, executive director of the National Conference of State Legislatures. "I know localities are frustrated by the cuts, but states are cutting themselves.... Last year the states raised taxes more than any year in history, but as we get into '92, the deficits are looking just as bad as in '91."

The fact is, some cities do seem to forget the previous largess of their legislatures. "A lot depends on the overall fiscal situation in the state," says Scott Mackey, who staffs NSCL's State-Local Relations Committee. "Take Connecticut. In the 1980s, the state was rolling in money, and it gave a lot of it to municipalities." State and local officials were great friends. "Then when trouble hits, the legislature is blamed for not doing enough on mandates or for not easing the local burden from tax-exempt property. That leaves legislators scratching their heads, wondering what localities did with all that money the state gave them in the 1980s."

Connecticut legislators see a city like Bridgeport crying bankruptcy after the state has poured in millions of dollars over the past 10 years. There is an inevitable feeling of suspicion. "I don't think more money is necessarily the answer," says Representative Linda N. Emmons. "I think there's going to have to be a change of direction in attitudes."

How many attitudes are going to change this year is impossible to tell. But it seems clear that the new drive for autonomy by local governments is more than a one-year lobbying campaign. It is an attempt to refashion the entire fiscal relationship between cities and states. Its leaders think they have a good chance to succeed. Don Benninghoven, executive director of the League of California Cities, is calling for a convention of a dozen or so of the largest municipal leagues later this year to hammer out a formal manifesto.

"The state-local budget argument can no longer be, 'Who is in the most fiscal trouble?'" Benninghoven says, "because we'll lose on that one. It's going to have to be, 'What are people willing to pay for?'" He thinks he knows the answer to that question, and he thinks it is an answer that will eventually force a more equal partnership between the legislatures and the "creatures of the state."

Linkages Between Citizens and Governments

- Elections, Parties, Computers, and News Media (Articles 8–14)
- Referenda, Initiatives, and Recalls (Articles 15 and 16)

The American political system is usually classified as a representative democracy. Top officials are elected by the people and, as a result, government is supposed to be responsive and accountable to citizens. Both the theory and practice of representative democracy are of interest to students of American politics. Political scientists study various processes that seem essential to the functioning of representative democracy: parties, interest groups, election laws, campaigning techniques, and so forth. Attention is not limited to the national government; state and local governments are also examined to assess responsiveness and accountability.

State and local governments operate under somewhat different circumstances and institutional arrangements than the national government. In many states and localities, voters can participate directly in the policy process through mechanisms known as *initiative* and *referendum*. In addition, some state and local voters can participate in removing elected officials from office by a procedure called *recall*. In many localities in the New England states, an open meeting of all local citizens, called a town meeting, functions as the local government legislature. These mechanisms provide additional avenues for citizens trying to influence state and local governments.

Generally speaking, party organization is strongest at the local level and weakest at the national level. Party "machines" are a well-known feature of the local political landscape in the United States, and colorful and powerful "bosses" have left their mark on local political history. While the heyday of "bosses" and "machines" is past, noteworthy examples of contemporary political machines still exist.

National elections, especially for the presidency, are usually contested vigorously by the two major parties and, over the long haul, the two parties tend to be reasonably competitive. This is less true in states and localities, because voters in some states and many localities are decidedly oriented toward one party or the other. Thus, in some states and localities, closer and more significant competition can occur within the nominating process of the dominant party than between the two parties in general elections.

Party labels do not appear on the ballot in many localities, and this may or may not affect the way elections are conducted. In "nonpartisan" elections, candidates of different parties may in fact openly oppose one another just as they do when party labels appear on the ballot. Another possibility is that parties field opposing candidates in a less than open fashion. As yet another alternative, elective offices may actually be contested without parties or the political party affiliations of candidates playing any part. One cannot assume that formally nonpartisan elections are accompanied by genuine nonpartisanship; nor can one assume that they are not.

One last feature of state and local political processes deserves mention here. While members of the Senate and House of Representatives in Washington, D.C., hold well-paid, prestigious positions, their state and local counterparts often do not. Many state legislators are only part-time politicians and earn the bulk of their livelihoods from other sources. This is also true of most general-purpose local government officials. In addition, most local school board members are unpaid, even though many devote long hours to their duties. That so many elected state and local officeholders do not get their primary incomes from their positions in government may well affect the way they respond to constituents. After all, while they and their families typically live in the community that they are representing, their livelihoods do not depend on being reelected.

Selections in the first section of this unit focus on elections, parties, and related matters. The second section treats referenda, initiatives, and recalls—three procedures that give voters in many states and localities a direct role in determining policies and overseeing the performances of elected officials during their terms in office.

Looking Ahead: Challenge Questions

If you were the head of an interest group, would you use different techniques in trying to influence a state government than in trying to influence a local government? What would the differences be?

Do you think there is much difference between running for office in a small town, running for a seat in a state legislature, and running to be a member of Congress?

Do you think people are more or less knowledgeable when they vote in state and local elections than in national elections? Why?

Which level of government seems most responsive to citizens—national, state, or local? Why?

Do you think citizens should be allowed to participate in policymaking through the initiative and referenda processes? Why or why not? What do you think about allowing citizens to recall officials during their term in office?

Maps That Will Stand Up in Court

Better do those redistricting plans with meticulous care and an eye on the courts, or risk having them undone.

Peter S. Wattson

Peter S. Wattson is counsel for the Minnesota Senate. He also is staff chair of NCSL's Reapportionment Task Force.

Legislators undertake the painful process of redistricting every 10 years, driven not only by a sense of duty, but also by a desire to control their own destiny. For they have learned that if they do not draw new boundaries for their legislative districts following each decennial census, the federal courts will do it for them.

It was a 1962 U.S. Supreme Court case involving the Tennessee General Assembly, *Baker vs. Carr*, that opened the floodgates of redistricting litigation by holding that legislative districts with unequal populations are subject to challenge in federal court.

The basic rule that all votes in a state election must have equal weight was laid down in the 1963 case of *Gray vs. Sanders*, where Justice Douglas made the now familiar assertion: "The conception of political equality from the Declaration of Independence, to Lincoln's Gettysburg Address, to the 15th, 17th and 19th Amendments can mean only one thing: one person, one vote."

In order to give each vote an equal weight, how equal do the district populations have to be? The federal courts use two different standards for judging the population equality of redistricting plans—one for congressional plans and a different one for legislative plans.*

The standard for congressional plans is strict indeed. In the 1964 case of *Wesberry vs. Sanders*, the U.S. Supreme Court articulated that standard as "as

[*"Legislative plans" refers here to *state* legislative plans. Throughout the article, the author tends to use "legislature" and "legislative" to refer to *state* legislatures. Ed.]

nearly equal in population as practicable."

Notice the choice of words. The Court did not say "as nearly equal as practical." The *American Heritage Dictionary* defines "practicable" as "capable of being done." It notes that something "practical" is not only capable of being done, but "also sensible and worthwhile." It illustrates the difference between the two by pointing out that "It might be *practicable* to transport children to school by balloon, but it would not be *practical*."

In 1983, in *Karcher vs. Daggett*, the U.S. Supreme Court struck down a congressional redistricting plan drawn by the New Jersey Legislature that had an overall range—the difference between the largest and the smallest district—of less than 1 percent. To be precise, 0.6984 percent, or 3,674 people, where the ideal population of a district was about 526,000. The plaintiffs showed that at least one other plan before the Legislature had an overall range less than the plan enacted by the Legislature, thus proving that the population differences could have been reduced or eliminated by a good-faith effort to draw districts of equal population.

If you can't draw congressional districts that are mathematically equal in population, don't assume that others can't. Assume that you risk having your plan challenged in court and replaced by another with a lower overall range.

Even if a challenger is able to draw a congressional plan with a lower overall range than yours, you may still be able to save your plan if you can show that each significant deviation from the ideal was necessary to achieve "some legitimate state objective." Writing for the 5-4 majority in *Karcher vs. Daggett*, Justice Brennan said: "Any number of consistently applied legislative policies might justify some variance, including, for

instance, making districts compact, respecting municipal boundaries, preserving the cores of prior districts and avoiding contests between incumbent representatives. . . . The state must, however, show with some specificity that a particular objective required the specific deviations in its plan, rather than simply relying on general assertions. . . . By necessity, whether deviations are justified requires case-by-case attention to these factors."

So, if you intend to rely on these "legitimate state objectives" to justify *any* degree of population inequality in a congressional plan, you would be well-advised to articulate those objectives in advance, follow them consistently and be prepared to show that you could not have achieved those objectives *in each district* with districts that had a smaller deviation from the ideal.

Fortunately for those who will be drawing redistricting plans after the 1990 census, the Supreme Court has adopted a less exacting standard for legislative plans. As Chief Justice Earl Warren observed in the 1964 case of *Reynolds vs. Sims*, "mathematical nicety is not a constitutional requisite" when drawing legislative plans. All that is necessary is that they achieve "substantial equality of population among the various districts."

"Substantial equality of population" has come to mean that a legislative plan will not be thrown out for inequality of population if its overall range is less than 10 percent.

The Supreme Court in *Reynolds vs. Sims* anticipated that some deviations from population equality in legislative plans might be justified if they were "based on legitimate considerations incident to the effectuation of a rational state policy." So far, the only "rational state policy" that has served to justify an overall range of more than 10 percent in a legislative plan has been respect for the boundaries of political subdivisions. And that has happened in only two cases: *Mahan vs. Howell* (1973) and *Brown vs.*

 From *State Legislatures*, September 1990, pp. 15, 17, 19. Copyright © 1989, National Conference of State Legislatures.

The Court Speaks on Redistricting

Eleven major Supreme Court cases have dealt with redistricting.

• *Baker vs. Carr*, 1962.

The Supreme Court holds that legislative districts with unequal populations may be challenged in federal court.

• *Gray vs. Sanders*, 1963.

Justice Douglas says that the basic rule for voting in state elections is "one person, one vote."

• *Wesberry vs. Sanders*, 1964.

The Supreme Court says that congressional districts must be "as nearly equal in population as practicable."

• *Reynolds vs. Sims*, 1964.

The Supreme Court holds that seats in both houses of a legislature must be apportioned on the basis of population, but "mathematical nicety is not a constitutional requisite" in drawing a legislative plan. It is necessary only to achieve "substantial equality of population among the various districts."

• *Mahan vs. Howell*, 1973.

The Supreme Court holds that respecting the boundaries of political subdivisions is a "rational state policy" that permits a legislature to deviate from population equality.

• *Gaffney vs. Cummings*, 1973.

Justice Brennan in dissent accuses the majority of establishing an overall range of 10 percent as the standard for legislative plans, with states not required to justify an overall range less than that.

• *City of Mobile vs. Bolden*, 1980.

The Supreme Court holds that Section 2 of the Voting Rights Act of 1965 applies only to election laws intended to discriminate against racial or language minorities, regardless of their effect.

• *Karcher vs. Daggett*, 1983.

The Supreme Court strikes down a congressional redistricting plan with an overall range of less than 1 percent, since plaintiffs showed that at least one other plan before the legislature had an overall range of less than that.

• *Brown vs. Thomson*, 1983.

The Supreme Court upholds a legislative reapportionment plan with an overall range of 89 percent.

• *Thornburg vs. Gingles*, 1986.

The Supreme Court upholds the 1982 amendments to the Voting Rights Act of 1965, designed to reverse *City of Mobile vs. Bolden*, and holds that a legislative redistricting plan must provide representation for racial and language minorities if they have previously been discriminated against and districts could be drawn where the minority has a fair chance to win.

• *Davis vs. Bandemer*, 1986.

The Supreme Court holds that legislative districts that result from partisan gerrymandering may be challenged in federal court.

Thomson (1983).

There may not be any other "rational state policies" that will justify a legislature's exceeding the 10-percent standard. But with the multitude of plans that are likely to be submitted for your consideration, you may wish to adopt other policies to govern plans that are within the 10-percent overall range.

Three-judge courts, called upon to draw redistricting plans when legislatures do not, often have adopted criteria for the parties to follow in submitting proposed plans to the court. These criteria are not constitutionally required, and have not been used to justify exceeding the 10-percent standard, but they have helped the three-judge courts to show the Supreme Court that they were fair in adopting their plans. These criteria often have included requirements that districts must be composed of contiguous territory, that they must be compact and that they should preserve "communities of interest."

In a democracy, "power to the people" means the power to vote. Section 2 of the Voting Rights Act of 1965 attempts to secure this political power for racial and language minorities by prohibiting states and political subdivisions from imposing qualifications for voting, prerequisites to voting or standards, practices or procedures to deny or abridge the right to vote on account of race or color or because a person is a member of a language minority group. Section 2 has been used to attack reapportionment and redistricting plans on the ground that they discriminated against blacks or Hispanics and abridged the right to vote by diluting the voting strength of those particular populations in the state.

In the 1986 case of *Thornburg vs. Gingles*, the Supreme Court held that a minority group challenging a redistricting plan must prove at least three things:

• That the minority is sufficiently large and geographically compact to constitute a majority in a single-member district;

• That it is politically cohesive;

• That, in the absence of special circumstances, bloc voting by the white majority usually defeats the minority's preferred candidate.

If you have a minority population that could elect a representative if given an ideal district, but bloc voting by whites has prevented members of the minority from being elected in the past, you will have to create a district that the minority has a fair chance to win. To do that, the minority will need an effective voting majority in the district.

How much of a majority is that? Under Section 2, that depends on "the totality of the circumstances." In other words, there is no fixed rule that applies to all cases.

The Court of Appeals for the Seventh Circuit, in the case of *Ketchum vs. Byrne* (1984), endorsed the use of a 65 percent black population majority to achieve an effective voting majority in the absence of empirical evidence that some other figure was more appropriate. The Court noted, "Judicial experience can provide a reliable guide to action where empirical data is ambiguous or not determinative and . . . a guideline of 65 percent of total population (or its equivalent) has achieved general acceptance in redistricting jurisprudence. . . . This figure is derived by augmenting a simple majority with an additional 5 percent for young population, 5 percent for low voter registration and 5 percent for low voter turn-out. . . ."

But the Court of Appeals in *Ketchum* also noted, "The 65 percent figure . . . should be reconsidered regularly to reflect new information and new statistical data," and "provision of majorities exceeding 65 percent to 70 percent may result in packing."

So, if you face a charge of a Section 2 violation, you had better be prepared with empirical data to show what is "reasonable and fair" under "the totality of the circumstances," because your plan may be invalidated for putting either too few or too many members of a minority group into a given district.

While Section 2 of the Voting Rights Act applies throughout the United States, Section 5 applies only to certain covered jurisdictions. If you're covered, you know it, because all of your election law changes since 1965—and not just your redistricting plans—have had to be cleared before they take effect by either the U.S. Department of Justice or the U.S. District Court for the District of Columbia.

Section 5 preclearance of a redistricting plan will be denied if it makes the members of a racial or language minority worse off than they were before. One measure of that is whether they are likely to be able to elect fewer minority representatives than before. To defend against a charge that your plan will make members of a racial or language minority group worse off than they were before, you will want to have at least a 10-year history of the success of the minority at electing representatives.

The Voting Rights Act does not apply to conduct that has the effect of diluting the voting strength of *partisan* minorities, such as Republicans in the South and Democrats in the West. Partisan minorities must look for protection to the Equal Protection Clause of the 14th Amendment.

While the federal courts have not yet developed criteria for judging whether a redistricting plan is so unfair as to deny a partisan minority the equal protection of the laws, the Supreme Court has held in *Davis vs. Bandemer* (1986) that partisan gerrymandering is now a justiciable issue. This means that you must be prepared to defend an action in federal court challenging your redistricting plans on the ground that they unconstitutionally discriminate against the partisan

minority.

Davis vs. Bandemer involved a legislative redistricting plan adopted by the Indiana General Assembly in 1981. Republicans controlled both houses. Before the 1982 election, several Indiana Democrats attacked the plan in federal court for denying them, as Democrats, equal protection of the laws.

The House plan included nine double-member districts and seven triple-member districts. The lower court found the multimember districts were "suspect in terms of compactness." Many of the districts were "unwieldy shapes." County and city lines were not consistently followed. Various House districts combined urban and suburban or rural voters with dissimilar interests. Democrats were packed into districts that already had large Democratic majorities, and fractured into districts where Republicans had a safe but not excessive majority. The speaker of the House candidly testified that the purpose of the multimember districts was "to save as many incumbent Republicans as possible."

The Supreme Court, in an opinion by Justice White, held that the issue of fair representation for Indiana Democrats was justiciable, but that the Democrats had failed to prove that the plan denied them fair representation. The Court denied that the Constitution "requires proportional representation or that legislatures in reapportioning must draw district lines to come as near as possible to allocating seats to the contending parties in proportion to what their anticipated statewide vote will be," since, if the vote in all districts were proportional to the vote statewide, the minority would win no seats at all. Further, if districts were drawn to give each party its proportional share of safe seats, the minority in each district would go unrepresented. Justice White concluded that a "group's electoral power is not unconstitutionally diminished by the simple fact of an apportionment scheme that makes winning elections more difficult, and a failure of proportional representation alone does not constitute impermissible discrimination under the Equal Protection Clause. Rather, unconstitutional discrimination occurs only when *the electoral system is arranged in a manner that will consistently degrade a voter's or a group of voters' influence on the political process as a whole.*" (Emphasis added.)

But merely showing that the minority

is likely to lose elections held under the plan is not enough. The Court pointed out: "The power to influence the political process is not limited to winning elections. . . . We cannot presume . . . , without actual proof to the contrary, that the candidate elected will entirely ignore the interests of those voters [who did not vote for him]."

How do the members of a major political party prove that they do not have "a fair chance to influence the political process?"

When California Republicans attacked the partisan gerrymander enacted by the Democratic Legislature to govern congressional redistricting, the Supreme Court in *Badham vs. March Fong Eu* (1989) summarily affirmed the decision of a three-judge court dismissing the suit on the ground that the Republicans had failed to show that they had been denied a fair chance to influence the political process. The lower court said: "Specifically, there are no factual allegations regarding California Republicans' role in 'the political process as a whole.' There are no allegations that California Republicans have been 'shut out' of the political process, nor are there allegations that anyone has ever interfered with Republican registration, organizing, voting, fundraising or campaigning. Republicans remain free to speak out on issues of public concern; plaintiffs do not allege that there are, or have ever been, any impediments to their full participation in the 'uninhibited, robust and wide-open' public debate on which our political system relies."

But just because unconstitutional partisan discrimination may be difficult to prove doesn't mean that major political parties won't challenge redistricting plans that appear to put them at a disadvantage. Rather, it more likely means that there will be a multitude of challenges before the standards of proof are clearly established.

Thus, state legislatures are now in about the same position with regard to partisan gerrymandering as they were in 1962 with regard to equal population requirements. The federal courts have clear authority to hear claims that redistricting plans violate the rights of a partisan minority, but it may take another decade or two of challenges to virtually every redistricting plan drawn by a legislature for the courts to settle the arguments over what that means.

Dickering Over the Districts

You can take redistricting out of the legislature but the politics remain.

Tim Storey

Tim Storey is NCSL's expert on redistricting.

Most states now have new state legislative district maps in place for the upcoming fall elections, but at least 23 of them are being challenged in court.

Every 10 years the U.S. Census Bureau counts Americans, and then states begin the arduous and often agonizing task of redrawing political boundaries for state legislative and congressional seats. In most states, it's the lawmakers who do the map drawing, and routinely they do it in a politically charged, contentious atmosphere. Inevitably, passing a redistricting plan comes down to the closing days of the session and is adopted in a cloud of partisanship. Not long after, disgruntled members, editorialists and public interest groups call for reform. "There must be a better way," they declare.

But is there?

Donald Stokes, dean of Princeton's Woodrow Wilson School, points out that the United States is the only nation with representative districts that leaves remapping to the normal legislative process. As a two-time member of New Jersey's redistricting commission, he argues that the public interest—not political interests—is served best when lawmakers are removed from redistricting. And indeed, nine states rely on commissions to redraw district lines, contending that lawmakers' priorities are to maximize partisan control and entrench incumbents rather than develop fair plans that can stand up in court.

But others argue that politics will never be absent from a process inherently political. For after all, commission members are appointed by politicians and bring their own agendas to the table. Some in Pennsylvania have called for an overhaul of their commission system and suggested that redistricting be brought back into the legislative process because they believe that the commission system invests too much power in the hands of too few people. Pennsylvania has a five-person commission for legislative redistricting.

Nevertheless, the appeal of removing redistricting from the legislative environment can be particularly tantalizing at least once every 10 years.

Following a contentious redistricting battle in Virginia in 1991, Delegate Steven Agee announced that he would introduce a bill during Virginia's next regular session calling for the creation of a redistricting commission. In Louisiana, several prominent public figures such as former governor Buddy Roemer and Senator Dennis Bagneris, who chairs the committee that handled redistricting, have been joined by various newspaper editorial writers in calling for the creation of some sort of entity to draw Bayou State districts that will take the process out of the hands of the Legislature.

Currently, redistricting of legislative seats is the responsibility of the legislature in 39 states. (In Alaska the governor is charged with redistricting, and Maryland's governor submits legislative maps to the legislature.) Reformers contend that redistricting done within the normal legislative process creates a clear conflict of interest since the outcome will have so many political ramifications.

Nine states have lifted the task of redistricting out of the legislature and given an independent commission the

Redistricting Via Commission

State	Members	Selection Requirements
Ark.	3	Governor, secretary of state and the attorney general serve.
Colo.	11	Legislature selects 4, governor 3, judiciary 4. Maximum of 4 from legislature; 6 from the same party. Each congressional district must have at least 1 but no more than 4 representatives; at least 1 member must live west of the Continental Divide.
Hawaii	9	Senate president selects 2, speaker 2, minority Senate 2, minority House 2. These 8 select 9th member to chair. No member may run for legislature in the two elections following redistricting.
Mo.	House—18 Senate—10	There are two committees. Governor picks 1 person from 2 lists submitted by the main political parties in each Congressional district to form the House committee. Governor picks 5 from lists of 10 submitted by the two parties to form the Senate committee. No member may hold legislative office for next 4 years.
Mont.	5	Majority and minority leaders of both houses each select a member. Those 4 select a 5th chair. If the 4 cannot select a 5th within 20 days, then a majority of the Supreme Court selects the chair. Public officials may not serve. Members may not run for office for 2 years.
N.J.	10	The chairs of the two major parties select 5 members each. If they cannot develop a plan in the allotted time, the chief justice of the Supreme Court appoints an 11th member.
Ohio	5	Board is the governor, auditor, secretary of state and 2 members selected by the legislative leaders of each major party.
Pa.	5	Majority and minority leaders of both houses each select 1 member. These 4 select a 5th to chair. If they fail to do so within 45 days, a majority of the Supreme Court will select the 5th. Chair may not be a public official.
Wash.	4	Majority and minority leaders of both houses each select 1. These 4 select a non-voting chair. If they fail to do so by a specific date, the Supreme Court selects the 5th. No commission member may be a public official.

Todd Rosenkranz, NCSL

initial responsibility for redrawing the lines. The states are Arkansas, Colorado, Hawaii, Missouri, Montana, New Jersey, Ohio, Pennsylvania and Washington. The makeup of these commissions varies. Arkansas has a three-member commission composed of the governor, secretary of state and attorney general. In Washington, the redistricting commission comprises four members, one each appointed by the minority and majority leaders in each house of the Legislature. None of the commissioners may hold public office while serving on the commission. The four appointed members select a fifth non-voting chairman. Several states have specific restrictions barring commission members from running for the legislature in subsequent elections.

Of the states that completed redistricting in 1991, several used the commission system successfully. New Jersey held legislative elections in November under districts drawn by an 11-member commission earlier in the year. The New Jersey commission adopted plans that have not been challenged in court, and no challenge is expected. Each of the two state party chairmen appoints five members to the commission, and the 10 commissioners have 30 days to produce new district maps. If they are unable to do so, an 11th commissioner is appointed by the chief justice of the state Supreme Court to break the tie and ensure the adoption of a fair plan with the public's interest as its top priority.

In 1991, as in 1981, Princeton's Donald Stokes was tapped by the chief justice as New Jersey's 11th member. Stokes lauds the New Jersey system as a model because it infuses the process with the wisdom of politics yet eliminates the conflict of interest that he believes is inherent when the legislature redistricts itself. Stokes says that the conflict of interest is so clear that "legislatures have been catching hell for the mischief that results (since) the early 19th century period in which Elbridge Gerry gave us the term *gerrymander*."

In 1981, Stokes was joined by the commission's five Democrats to pass a plan, and in 1991, the five Republicans voted with Stokes.

Iowa's method of redistricting is the most radical of the states. The Iowa approach seeks to eliminate political con-

cerns as the main force behind the line drawing. During the '60s and '70s, the courts repeatedly threw out redistricting proposals from the Iowa legislature; and in 1972, the Iowa Supreme Court imposed its own plan. With the frustrations of the past clear in their minds, Iowa lawmakers enacted the current redistricting statute in 1979.

Under Iowa law, the non-partisan Legislative Service Bureau submits a set of proposed redistricting maps to the legislature, which must approve or deny the plans without amending them. If the legislature rejects the first set of plans, the bureau supplies a second set also to be voted up or down without amendments. If the legislature rejects the second set, it gets a third set that it may amend. Only by stretching out the process to the third round can the legislature retake control of the line drawing.

Iowa's redistricting statute prohibits the Legislative Service Bureau from using any political data such as voter registration or past election results when drawing up the plans. Neither may the bureau take into consideration the residences of incumbent legislators. The bureau may use only population figures provided by the Census Bureau and apply criteria such as creating compact districts and preserving communities of interest.

Using this unusual system, Iowa became the first state in 1991 to adopt both state legislative and congressional districts, and no court challenges have been filed. Wyoming was actually the first state to complete redistricting using a process of apportioning seats out to counties, but their plans were thrown out by a federal court for violating the one person, one vote rule.

The Iowa experience was not without its anxious moments. One local television station declared the plans dead on arrival once the political results of the plans were revealed. The Iowa plans paired 20 of 50 incumbent senators and 40 of 100 incumbent representatives in the same districts; the Senate majority and minority leaders and the House speaker and majority leader were not spared. Nevertheless, the Iowa General Assembly accepted the first plans.

Iowa's ability to remove politics from redistricting is unusual. Even states with a commission or board admit that

politics still play a key role. Mark McKillop, who was the supervisor of the Senate Democratic reapportionment project in Pennsylvania, responds to those wanting to strip the process of politics by saying, "They're kidding themselves if they think they can take politics out of it." He does endorse a commission system like the one used in Pennsylvania on the grounds of efficiency. "If this were done in the legislature, we would still be doing it," McKillop said.

Anne Lee, the reapportionment chair for the League of Women Voters in Hawaii, agreed that politics were still very evident in the commission process used in her state. She did point out that the commission lifted the contentious process from the Legislature, thus allowing them to focus on substantive issues rather than being consumed by redistricting. She also noted that each political party had an equal voice on the Hawaii commission instead of one party dominating the process, which might occur if it were done within the Legislature.

Many states successfully adopt each decade redistricting plans that stand up in court and are produced within the crucible of the normal legislative process. Virginia Delegate Ford Quillen pointed out that his state "produced a good product using the typical legislative committee system." He also said that it would be very difficult "to design a pure commission system where the commission members don't have their own agendas." One of the principal criticisms of commissions is that the members invariably have political motives, and it merely concentrates substantial power in the hands of a smaller group than the legislature.

Using a commission system does not guarantee that new district plans will not be challenged. The Hawaii commission had its plans thrown out in 1982 and replaced by temporary court-drawn plans. Missouri, Ohio and Pennsylvania are currently in court defending plans drawn by commissions.

It is certain that redistricting will continue to be a divisive and time-consuming chore for legislatures every 10 years. Redistricting plans, whether drawn by the legislature or an independent commission, will always have dramatic political results. Whether you are a winner or loser in the redistricting sweepstakes may determine which system you advocate.

The Mirage of Campaign Reform

ROB GURWITT

We've spent the past 20 years talking about how to keep money from corrupting the political process. The more we talk, the worse the problem seems to get.

Let's start with a short test. Imagine a state somewhere in the Midwest. The public's disgust with politics has boiled over. A small band of reformers, arguing that campaign money has been corrupting the legislature, seizes the moment and puts a measure on the ballot to stifle the influence of private interests in the campaign process.

They propose setting aside enough public money every two years to give every candidate with a serious campaign as much as it takes to conduct it. Private funding would be legal, but everything possible would be done to discourage it; if your opponent took private funds, you would get public funds to match.

The campaign gets raucous. Some opponents of the measure argue that public funds have no place in campaigns. Others bombard radio talk shows with complaints that taxpayers' money shouldn't go to support politicians. The reformers counter that only when there's enough public funding to run a full-scale campaign will candidates stop bellying up to the special-interest bar. Even better, they say, candidates won't have any incentive to turn to fat cats in a close race because all it would do is generate more public money spent against them.

Throughout the fall, polls show a cynical electorate going back and forth on the question. Half the streets in the state are festooned with bright blue signs reading, "We Deserve Better. Yes on Public Financing," and red signs countering, "Your Money? For Politicians??? Vote No!" A to-do erupts when newspapers reveal that the opposition is being funded by the state's major corporations, but it quiets down after a report that the other side has been tapping the liberal Democratic network in Hollywood. Finally, Election Day rolls around. Early returns show the measure going down narrowly, but it pulls ahead when the numbers start flowing in from the cities, and finally passes.

Here's the question. It's now 2002, a decade later. Which of the following has happened?:

(A) The reform law has served mainly to create a multimillion-dollar industry of consultants, pollsters and campaign professionals, all of them skilled at running "independent expenditure" campaigns for the corporations, unions, trade associations and ideological groups that just want to "participate" on behalf of their favored candidates. The Supreme Court says it is unconstitutional to prohibit these expenditures. Because of them, special interests are as powerful in the state as ever.

(B) Legislators, faced with tight budgets, seem chronically unable to find enough money to fund the provision guaranteeing extra public funding for candidates whose opponents use private contributions. So the public money turns out to be nothing more than a floor. When a campaign is really close and hard-fought, private funding is what makes the difference.

(C) Campaign costs, which were supposed to go down after the reform law passed, keep going up. Candidates with rich friends believe their chances of winning go up if they spend every dollar of private money they can raise, even if their opponents are given public money to match them. The reform law not only hasn't controlled costs—there is talk that it is going to bankrupt the state.

(D) Nobody really knows what the reforms would have accomplished, because the Supreme Court has thrown them out. The court said that the provision matching public money against excess private funding violates the free speech rights of the person who wants to spend the extra private money.

(E) The reformers were right: The system survives all its court challenges, it wrings private money out of campaigns and holds costs down, it allows candidates to spend their time campaigning rather than raising funds, and it gives legislators the freedom to cast their votes without worrying about their campaign budgets. All in all, it is a tonic for democracy.

And now that you've made your choice, here's the real question: Why did you just snicker when you got to E?

It has been almost 20 years since the campaign reform movement built up its first real head of steam in the aftermath of Watergate. At the time, there was a widespread feeling of optimism, a belief that effective reform was just a matter of legislating the appropriate limits and disclosure laws. Congress passed them, states passed them, and now it is hard to find anyone who believes it's that simple anymore. A problem that seems as though it ought to be solvable—how to keep campaign money from influencing the decisions of government—is proving an enormously frustrating puzzle.

True, the country has made some progress since Watergate. There was a time when it was next to impossible to find out where candidates got their money. Now, every state requires disclosure of the amounts and sources of campaign contributions, although some—Ohio, for example—make gathering the information an unpardonable

SEARCHING FOR THE CHEAP SEATS

If you're hoping to break into politics with a run for the state legislature, you might want to think about heading for someplace as sparsely populated as Montana or Idaho. House seats in both states are flat-out bargains—winning one consumed less than $5,000 on average four years ago, and hasn't gone up much since.

There are plenty of other states where campaign costs haven't risen beyond the reach of ordinary folk, but identifying them can be difficult. Because the states treat campaign disclosure forms differently, it's almost impossible to compare legislative campaign costs for all 50 of them. The accompanying chart shows average and median costs for state House seats in 11 states—those covered in a joint project led by political scientists Anthony Gierzynski of Northern Illinois University and Gary Moncrief of Boise State.

In all cases, the average cost is higher than the median, or the mid-point of all campaigns, because a few high-spending contests have pulled the figure up.

Different costs among states can be traced to anything from varying district sizes to the expense of media markets to the degree of campaign professionalization that has taken place. It would be unthinkable, for example, to run for the California Assembly without paid staff, consultants and pollsters;

THE COST OF RUNNING
State House Campaign Expenditures, 1988

State	Average	Median
California	$370,722	$302,128
Idaho	4,425	2,244
Minnesota	13,244	13,144
Missouri	9,618	6,921
Montana	2,692	2,265
New Jersey	48,033	33,670
North Carolina	12,085	10,025
Oregon	35,982	30,333
Pennsylvania	18,462	13,944
Washington	25,811	20,145
Wisconsin	14,868	11,812

Sources: Created by Anthony Gierzynski from data collected in a joint project with David Breaux, William Cassey, Keith Hamm, Malcolm Jewell, Gary Moncrief and Joel Thompson.

in Montana, where legislative careerism has yet to take hold, you'd probably be laughed out of the state for using them.

There are other forces at play as well. Minnesota and Washington are close to each other in number of people and professionalization, but it costs a fair bit less to run in Minnesota. The reason probably is Minnesota's public financing law, which generally keeps spending down.

The escalation of campaign expense varies within states as well. Moncrief has found, for instance, that the cost of winning a House seat in Washington State grew by about 25 percent between 1980 and 1990, controlling for inflation. But the cost of a Senate seat rose by an inflation-adjusted 300 percent. The reason: The House remained under firm Democratic control during the decade, while the Senate became the crucial battleground between the parties. —R.G.

endurance test for the public.

In addition, some 20 states prohibit candidates from accepting direct corporate donations, and more than half the states have tried to curb the undue influence of any one contributor by limiting individual donations; a smaller number limit giving by political action committees. Twelve states provide direct public financing to individual candidates, although several of those systems have proved irrelevant in practice.

Still, it is hard to find people who think the system is significantly better; many insist it is worse. Private money is ubiquitous in all its forms—direct contributions, independent expenditures, "soft money," "bundled" donations—and the routes it travels to candidates only multiply with each new effort to restrict them. Campaigns continue to become more expensive. Legislators complain that the pressure of raising money is giving them less and less time for legislating or engaging voters. Donors complain that they are under increasing pressure to give to legislators who preside over their interests.

Perhaps most important, the voters themselves are increasingly cynical about the role of money in elections. They are convinced that monied interests can buy whatever they need in the legislative process, and they believe that the elections system perpetuates the status quo. "Most people perceive that politicians become careerists because the campaign finance system gives them the advantage as incumbents," says Gary Moncrief, a Boise State University political scientist.

In short, it's hard to escape the feeling that much of the campaign reform effort has been a waste of time. "The terms of the debate have not changed much since the early 1970s, when I first got into it," says Daniel Lowenstein, a law professor at UCLA and the first chairman of California's Fair Political Practices Commission. "And to the extent they have, they've changed for the worse: More prominence is being given to even more simple-minded ideas."

That may stem from simple frustration. If anything, the past two decades of campaign finance reform have given the country a lesson in the difficulties of legislating change. They have demonstrated that good intentions have little to do with actual results, that it's hard to keep reform efforts from falling prey to political maneuvering, that Republicans and Democrats diverge fundamentally in the way they view the issue, and that beyond a certain point no one seems able to agree even on what they want to accomplish.

Above all, they have made it clear that trying to force the system to conform to some preconceived set of ideals is doomed to fail. "We live in a democratic and pluralistic society, and you just cannot structure a regulatory system that will cover everything," says Herb Alexander, a campaign finance specialist and director of the Citizens' Research Foundation in Los Angeles.

The elections process is like a minor ecosystem; changing one small part of it can yield entirely unforeseen results elsewhere. Wisconsin, for instance, is one of three states that provide public financing for state House and Senate campaigns (the others are Minnesota and Hawaii). The idea was to level the playing field for incumbents and challengers, and to cut reliance on PAC contributions. But the system has gone off-kilter. Not only have legislative candidates been ignoring it routinely in close contests, opting to forego public money in exchange for freedom from spending limits, but the parties have been using it mainly to subsidize nuisance challenges to incumbents on the opposing side.

"If you want to keep an incumbent busy in some seat," says Democratic state Senator John Medinger, "you get a sacrificial lamb. He or she gets $8,000 or so of public money and keeps the incumbent home, and then the parties target the eight or nine seats where they're willing to blow the limits." Those eight or nine crucial elections, of course, are fought out with private funding.

"Public financing is a nice ethical thing to do," says Medinger, who is retiring this year, "and it's certainly good government. It just may not be good politics in every case." What has happened in Wisconsin is certainly not what the state's reformers had in mind.

One reason reforms can be counted on to produce unanticipated consequences is that campaign money is remarkably protean, not unlike the liquid-metal robot in *Terminator 2*. Just when you think you've dealt with it, it rises from the floor behind your back.

Take Arizona. The state has the strictest contribution limits in the country, $240 per candidate for individuals and most PACs this year. (The amount is indexed for inflation.) With contribution ceilings so low, you'd think that no legislator would feel a debt to any individual donor, and that interests trying to influence the legislature would look for some means other than campaign giving. You would, of course, be wrong.

For one thing, political committees don't sit still once they've given all they can to candidates. Instead, some mount independent expenditure campaigns—that is, campaigns on behalf of or against a particular candidate that are separate from the candidate's own campaign. In the 1990 elections, for example, the political action committee run by US West Corp. gave maximum contributions to the candidates it was supporting, and still had half of the money it had raised left over. But there were about a dozen key races that would decide the majority in each house, so the PAC mounted independent campaigns in several of them, trying to help the GOP win control. "I refused to sit back and not have the opportunity for US West to participate in the political process," says Barry Aarons, the PAC's director.

At the same time, Arizona's strict contribution limits have hardly wrung individual influence brokers out of the system. Since putting a viable campaign together in $240 increments is hard work, anyone who can convince others to contribute to candidate X is bound to become a pretty valuable friend of X's. In fact, some candidates are bypassing PACs altogether and searching out people—somehow, many of them turn out to be lobbyists—who can persuade donors who might have contributed to a PAC to contribute directly to the candidate instead. As one Arizona lobbyist points out, "Some candidates make a great to-do about the fact that they don't accept PAC contributions, but then they solicit individual PAC members for direct contributions."

The problem is by no means unique to Arizona: Donors and candidates all across the country have shown endless inventiveness in getting around contribution limits. A few years ago, the *Charlotte Observer* in North Carolina told the story of a party activist who reported being handed an envelope containing $15,000 in checks from optometrists to a statewide candidate. Each check was for less than $100, the level at which it would have had to be reported; the total amount, however, was well in excess of the $4,000 to which an optometrists' PAC would have been limited. The head of the state optometric association saw nothing wrong with that sort of "bundling." "The Optometric Society has not functioned politically as a group," he said. "If we were, we would be organized legally as a PAC."

In essence, says Alexander, "some of these laws just exchange the big giver for the big solicitor." Or as Paul Gillie, research director for Washington State's Public Disclosure Commission, puts it, "Money is like water: It will find its way no matter what obstacles it encounters."

This would be a sobering thought even under the most statesmanlike of circumstances, with incumbents committed to improving the system regardless of the impact on their own careers and parties willing to ignore partisan advantage in the interest of doing the right thing. But of course, we don't have those circumstances. We have incumbents who don't want to do anything to help challengers, and Democrats and Republicans whose main goal in legislative life is to achieve—or to keep—majority status.

That shouldn't be very surprising. "If you're in political office and like it and want to get reelected, why should you help your opponent?" asks Alan Rosenthal, director of the Eagleton Institute at Rutgers University. "There aren't many areas in which we believe that people should encourage their competition—we don't believe that Johnson & Johnson should go out and help Merck."

That applies to parties at least as much as it does to individuals. Democrats control most state legislative bodies in this country. They want the leaders of those bodies to continue to be able to shift money from their own campaign funds—stocked with PAC donations—to the campaigns of Democratic allies. Republicans have no trouble raising money from individual private donors. They do not like the idea of limiting the amount of money in private contributions that a candidate will be allowed to accept. "Campaign finance is a cutthroat business, and each party will try to devise a system that helps it best," says Ran Coble, who directs the North Carolina Center for Public Policy Research.

That dynamic is on display this year in Washington State, where two separate campaign reform initiatives have been proposed for the November ballot. One of them, backed by the GOP, qualified after a petition campaign in which people were paid to gather signatures—a new practice in Washington. The other, supported by a coalition that includes the League of Women Voters, Common Cause and a variety of prominent Democrats, collected barely enough signatures to qualify.

The Republicans' measure places limits on the size of contributions, prohibits transfers between candidates, and requires unions to get the written permission of members before using their payroll deductions to fund a PAC. It in no way tries to restrict spending, or

the overall amount a candidate can raise.

The rival measure, on the other hand, would involve spending limits. Candidates would not have to abide by them, but if they did, they would be given the reward of being allowed to take larger contributions. In addition, no candidate could get more than a third of his or her money from PACs and party caucuses.

No one knows whether variable contribution limits could pass constitutional muster—the Supreme Court essentially equates political spending with free speech—but Mark Brown of the Washington Federation of State Employees insists that spending limits are vital. "Campaign finance reform without expenditure limits will clearly favor Republicans," he says. That is because, he argues, the groups that support Democrats are currently being priced out of the market. "The labor movement in recent years has come to realize that we simply cannot remain competitive in the political arena with the cost of campaigns skyrocketing as they have," Brown says.

There are some problems with spending limits quite apart from the constitutional questions. There is evidence, for instance, that spending limits tend to hurt challengers. "Over the years," says Daniel Lowenstein, "we have found out that spending a substantial amount of money is more crucial to challengers than it is to incumbents. So spending limits are more of a problem than they may once have seemed." Moreover, as Herb Alexander once pointed out, "It is altogether impossible to prevent a savvy election lawyer from finding a hole in expenditure ceilings wide enough to drive a campaign message through."

The debate over spending limits, though, does serve to highlight a basic conflict between equally respectable political values: Trying to keep the barriers to entering politics as low as possible, versus giving challengers the freedom to spend whatever they need in order to win.

But there is another conflict that goes even further to explain the frustrations of campaign finance reform, and that is the discord between its fundamental aim—removing the influence of special interests from the legislative process—and the notion that everyone ought to be able to participate in elections by

giving money to his or her candidate of choice. "The problem in campaign finance," says Larry Sabato, a political scientist at the University of Virginia, "is that people will not accept the fact that we can't have it all. We want completely clean elections with no tainted money, and we want full and unfettered rights of free speech and association. You cannot have both. If you're not going to tinker with the First Amendment, you have to accept the fact that you can't dam the flow of political money."

Does that mean that effective campaign finance reform is a dead end? Given the conflicts between basic political values, the fluid dynamics of political money and the difficulties inherent in asking legislators and political parties to tackle the matter, it's understandable that many people think so. But despite all the disappointments and unpleasant consequences of the campaign reform movement over the past two decades, the fact remains that there is still useful work to be done.

At the very least, it is time to recognize that in this field, as in many others, there are limits to what government regulation can accomplish—that "good enough" is the best we can hope for. That is not to say that reform efforts are pointless. There are regulations, such as contribution limits and even public financing, that have helped temper some of the grossest excesses of the past, and proposals for free television time and cut-rate mailing costs may also help. But it's naive to expect new legislation to produce a perfect system, especially since campaigns have evolved to the point where every new limit seems to hurt as much as it helps. Boosting individual contributions at the expense of "special interest" donors, for example, has obvious public appeal, but it may also harm groups, such as teachers or anti-abortionists or women's rights advocates, whose ability to have an impact on a campaign rests in pooling many small donations. In the long run, legislation that works to keep the various sources of funding in balance, rather than trying to eliminate one or another, may prove the most stable reform.

It may also go the farthest toward

protecting the one element of reform that seems most in need of safeguarding: the system's openness. With strong disclosure laws, the system at least has a chance to correct itself. As Larry Sabato once wrote, disclosure "is the greatest single check on the excesses of campaign finance, for it encourages corrective action, whether by the politicians themselves, by the judiciary through prosecution in the courts, or by the voters at the polls."

"You've got to let the voters see what's going on, and then let them make their own decision," says Kent Cooper, a longtime official of the Federal Elections Commission. "If they want to re-elect a guy who's representing a cash constituency more than them, fine: If they make an informed choice, the system's not corrupt." Perhaps the most basic reform mechanism, in other words, is to make it as easy as possible for the public to find out who's getting money from whom, and to avoid reforms that force money underground.

That seems like an obvious idea, but you couldn't tell by looking at its reception in many legislatures. Most states require all candidates for statewide and legislative office to file campaign disclosure reports in a central state office,

Maybe we can't cut out special interest campaign money. But we can do a better job of tracking it.

although a few—Ohio, North Carolina, Vermont and Nevada—do not. But only 20 states require listing the occupation and principal place of employment of contributors, and only five—Florida, Louisiana, Maryland, Ohio and Wyoming—require all contributions to be itemized, regardless of the amount. There are even some states—Ohio and Wisconsin, for instance—that allow so-called "conduits," which are set up by special interest groups to funnel contributions by their members to candidates; the group can take credit for the money, but all that gets reported is the individual's contribution.

Even more important, in those states that have watchdog disclosure agencies, they are treated like poor stepchil-

dren. They rarely have the staff or resources to analyze what is happening to the campaign finance system as a whole, to perform specific audits of candidates' returns or even to make the data available in a form that allows people to figure out, say, how much the dairy industry has contributed to a particular candidate. Even the most highly regarded campaign disclosure agencies—New Jersey's Election Law Enforcement Commission and California's Fair Political Practices Commission, for example—have had to withstand severe budget cuts over the past few years. "We were like a thin man entering a famine as we went into this recession," says Fred Herrmann, director of New Jersey's ELEC. Until states get serious about disclosure, nothing else they do will amount to much.

That is especially true because, short of outlawing all private money—which the Supreme Court would not allow—money will always be a factor in elections. Reform legislation can force it further underground, or it can pull it into the open, but, as Cooper says, "the schemes will be there and the people operating in the gray area will be there." Disclosure is no ideal answer; it may simply be the best one we have.

Throwing Out the Rascals (And Those who Aren't)

Nobody's sure what is sparking term-limit proposals across the country. Maybe it's generalized rage; maybe it's a partisan plot. Whatever it is, it's spreading.

Nancy Rhyme

Nancy Rhyme is NCSL's specialist on term-limit proposals.

James Madison worried when he wrote in Federalist No. 53 that "a few members as happens in all such assemblies will by frequent re-election become members in long standing and will be masters of public business, and perhaps not unwilling to avail themselves of those advantages." Today's citizens are worried that there are far too many "members of long standing" in state legislatures and the Congress and they've reacted with term limit initiatives certified for the ballot in 15 states.

A movement to "throw the rascals out," that started two years ago in California, Colorado and Oklahoma, is raising a rumpus across the country. Some say it's an independent, grass-roots movement of state activists who believe that government under the status quo no longer works. Others believe it's an effort by the national Republican party to regain control of Congress. Whatever the motive, voters will have their say on the tenure of legislators on Nov. 3 in 15

of the 23 states with the initiative process, and it took hundreds of thousands of certified signatures to put the issue on those ballots. Whatever the outcome, the landscape of American politics has already been changed. In 29 states this year Democrats and Republicans alike introduced more than 100 bills to limit legislative terms, none of which survived.*

Turnover statistics evidently haven't been convincing. State senates turned over an average of 72 percent between 1979 and 1989. This means that roughly three out of every four senators elected in 1978 were not there when legislatures convened in 1989. In state assemblies and houses the average was 75 percent. The number of new state lawmakers

---

*On November 3, 1992, voters in twelve states approved term limits on their U.S. Senators, U.S. Representatives, *and* state legislators. In the two states (California and North Dakota) where only congressional term limits were on the ballot, a majority of voters also voted "yes." In eleven of the fourteen states, 60% or more of voters approved term limits. The closest vote was in Washington State, where 52% approved. In a fifteenth state, Nevada, the proposed state constitutional amendment on term limits has to be approved at two successive elections before going into effect.

coming into office after the November 1990 election was 18 percent. Of the 7,461 state legislators 1,374 were new members. Leadership figures show a similar turnover. A 10-year look indicates 88 percent of the senate presidents in 1989 were not senate presidents in 1979. The same for speakers. Ninety-four percent of those serving in 1989 were new since 1979.

No one can deny that public opinion of government and elected officials is at an all-time low. Citizens are frustrated by Congress' inability to reach consensus on budget matters, appalled by the U.S. Senate Judiciary Committee's performance in the confirmation hearings of Supreme Court Justice Clarence Thomas, and disgusted by the check bouncing fiasco in the House bank and the savings and loan scandal. They are equally frustrated by state and local governments' continual stalemate on a variety of issues. The Michigan Legislature and Governor John Engler locked horns over the elimination of general welfare assistance for 80,000 recipients. California Governor Pete Wilson and Speaker Willie Brown squared off for 64 days before the 1993 budget was adopted. Last year, 11 states missed their statutory

---

 From *State Legislatures*, November 1992, pp. 26-27. Copyright © 1992 by the National Conference of State Legislatures.

deadlines for enacting 1992 budgets, including Maine, where state government ground to a halt for 16 days.

Even though Washington state voters, fearful of losing the congressional clout of U.S. House Speaker Thomas Foley, turned down a term limit proposal there last November, all the 1992 initiatives (including another one in Washington) seek also to limit the terms of federal officeholders. In Missouri and Washington, limits would not be placed on the congressional delegation until other states pass similar measures. The initiatives in Arkansas, Michigan, Missouri and Oregon would place an absolute limit on the length of service allowed, similar to those passed in California and Oklahoma that place a lifetime ban on the years an individual can serve in public office.

Questions remain as to whether the states can limit congressional terms. A court challenge is planned in Colorado, currently the only state with federal limits, by the state chapter of the American Civil Liberties Union, which has petitioned the state Supreme Court.

Proponents of the Arizona, Arkansas, California, Florida, Nebraska, North Dakota and Washington measures hope their wording to deny ballot access to incumbents who have served a certain number of years—meaning their names could not be placed on the ballot—will keep their measures out of court. The U.S. Constitution, by giving states the right to control suffrage in elections (people under 18 can't vote, for example), allows states to regulate ballot access, but the Congress, by law, can alter those regulations. Court challenges are more likely with the proposals that change the state constitution by limiting terms. California, North Dakota, Washington and Wyoming are amending their statutes to implement term limits. Although California and North Dakota can change their constitution through the initiative process, Washington and Wyoming cannot.

Court challenges against the ballot proposals in Florida and Missouri were unsuccessful and a challenge is still pending on the Nevada initiative. More challenges may come with passage of proposals. However, California's 1990 law was challenged and upheld by the state Supreme Court and the U.S. Supreme Court declined to hear the case.

Term Limit Initiatives

Here's what the 1992 term limit initiatives look like. All of them would start counting years of service after voter approval.

Arizona: Limits U.S. senators to two consecutive terms and congressmen to three consecutive terms. Limits state lawmakers to four consecutive 2-year terms and members of the executive branch to two consecutive 4-year terms.

Arkansas: Limits statewide elected officials to two 4-year terms, state representatives to three 2-year terms and state senators to two 4-year terms. Holds U.S. representatives to three terms; U.S. senators to two terms.

California: Limits members of Congress: representatives can serve only six years in an 11-year period; senators can serve only 12 years during a 17-year period.

Florida: No one can run for re-election to the Legislature, executive branch or U.S. Congress if by the end of his current term he has served for eight consecutive years.

Michigan: State representatives may serve only three terms, state senators and the executive branch only two terms. Limits U.S. congressmen to three terms in any 12-year period and U.S. senators to two terms during 24 years.

Missouri: Restricts state lawmakers to eight years in the same house and total years of legislative service to 16. A separate initiative limits U.S. representatives to four terms and U.S. senators to two terms. Limits on congressional terms will not go into effect until enacted by half the states.

Montana: Limits state senators to eight years in a 16-year period, representatives to six years out of 12 years, and the executive branch to eight years of service in 16 years. Holds congressmen to six years out of 12 and U.S. senators to 12 years in a 24-year period.

Nebraska: Limits statewide officials and legislators to two consecutive terms. Prohibits U.S. representatives from placing their name on the ballot after four consecutive terms and U.S. senators after two consecutive terms.

Nevada: Limits federal officers effec-

tive Jan. 1, 1995. Restricts U.S. senators to 12 years in a 24-year period. Constitutional amendments must pass at two successive elections.

North Dakota: Restricts access to the ballot to members of the U.S. Sentate or House of Representatives after they have served 12 years in office in any combination. Can run again after a 2-year break.

Ohio: (#2) Limits U.S. senators to two consecutive terms and members of the U.S. House of Representatives to four consecutive terms.

Ohio: (#3) Limits state senators to two consecutive terms and state representatives to four consecutive terms.

Ohio: (#4) Limits members of the executive branch to two consecutive terms. Terms are consecutive in all three proposals unless there is a break of four years.

Oregon: Holds state lawmakers to six years in the House and eight years in the Senate and no more than 12 years of legislative service. Statewide officeholders limited to eight years and members of Congress to six years in the House and 12 years in the Senate.

South Dakota: Limits state lawmakers to four 2-year consecutive terms and statewide officers to two consecutive terms. Limits members of Congress to six consecutive terms in the House and two consecutive terms in the Senate.

Washington: Limits state senators to eight out of 14 years, representatives to six out of 12 years and the governor and lieutenant governor to eight out of 14 years. U.S. senators are held to 12 out of 18 years and U. S. representatives to six out of 12 years. Terms served before November 1992 will not count toward limits and the measure will not go into effect for federal officers until nine other states limit ballot access or terms.

Wyoming: Limits state senators to three terms in any 24-year period, representatives to three terms in any 12-year period, and constitutional officers to two terms in any 16-year period. U. S. senators are limited to serving two terms in any 24-year period and congressmen to three terms in 12 years.

LOCAL REDISTRICTING: THE DEMOGRAPHIC CONTEXT OF BOUNDARY DRAWING

The goal of minority representation has been pursued at the expense of policy-making bodies of wieldy size and electoral districts patterned after the principles of compactness, contiguity, and uniform population size. Can local redistricting plans in cosmopolitan communities respect the interests of diverse populations without succumbing to Byzantine complexity?

PETER A. MORRISON
WILLIAM A.V. CLARK

Peter A. Morrison is a demographer with RAND Corporation's Population Research Center and teaches at the RAND Graduate School. William A. V. Clark is a professor of Geography at the University of California, Los Angeles.

Counties, cities and other local jurisdictions rely on demographic analysis and expertise to draw local political boundaries and ensure their conformity with the law. Redistricting done in the 1990s will undergo more strident legal scrutiny than in the 1980s, and legislative bodies elected from single-member districts must be closely attentive to how minority electoral opportunities are created or obstructed by the positioning of district boundaries.

In this article we review the basic rules that govern the local boundary-drawing process and the current demographic context to which they apply. We illustrate how those rules may apply in demographically complex settings — juridictions with a multi-minority com-

position and significant concentrations of non-citizens. Our discussion highlights several recurrent issues in drawing political boundaries that are likely to intensify in the 1990s. Finally, we distinguish various technical roles that demographers can play at different stages in the redistricting process.

> **BOUNDARIES CAN SCATTER OR CONCENTRATE LIKE-MINDED PERSONS IN WAYS THAT MAY EITHER DISADVANTAGE THEM AS VOTERS OR EMPOWER THEM.**

The context of the 1990s

In many localities, the population has grown more diverse since 1980. The melting pot image has evolved into a more complex racial and ethnic mosaic, made up not just of blacks and Hispanics, but of a multitude of nationalities and ethnic sub-groups as well. The mosaic differs from place to place, with non-citizens adding additional complexity to the pattern in some areas.

As this human mosaic becomes more complex, it transforms the politics of local boundary drawing and the composition of local voting electorates. For example, diversity fosters ethnic coalitions, which form and reform alliances, thereby opening up new ways to make a majority (see Table 1). Separate ethnic and national identities also encourage the designation of protected minority groups in ever more specific terms. Such statistical umbrella terms as the "Hispanic vote" or the "Asian vote" may diminish in relevance as they are supplanted by terms like "Mexican-American," "Cuban," "Caribbean-American,"

Reprinted with permission from *National Civic Review*, 81:1, Winter/Spring 1992, pp. 59-63. Copyright © 1992 by National Civic League, Inc.

"Korean," and "Filipino," when used to characterize local electorates. Furthermore, certain jurisdictions have a sizable presence of non-citizens who (like all residents) are entitled to equal representation. The fact that non-citizens tend to be concentrated in particular places within jurisdictions, however, can complicate efforts to meet other legal requirements.

Purposes and Rules Governing Redistricting

Redistricting and the associated boundary drawing has both a political and a social purpose. It is helpful to grasp those purposes as we consider how courts have sought to implement laws on redistricting.

Boundaries can scatter or concentrate like-minded persons in ways that may either disadvantage them as voters or empower them. Laws that safeguard the right to vote are intended to prevent a disadvantage to minority voters or to empower them where they have been disadvantaged.

Three fundamental legal requirements pertain to political boundary drawing. First, the Constitutional "equal protection" clause embodies the principle of *electoral* equality. That is, each *citizen's* vote is supposed to carry equal weight ("one person, one vote"). In practice, this means that the jurisdiction's entire population should be distributed among the districts being formed such that the vote cast by a citizen in one district carries the same weight as that of a citizen in every other district. Second, principles of representative government accord *representational* equality. That is, each legislator should represent an equal number of *persons* as every other legislator. Third, Section 2 of the Federal Voting Rights Act prohibits abridging the right to vote by diluting the voting strength of a protected group. Section 2 sets forth certain requirements keyed specifically to demographic measurement.[1] Failure to meet those requirements, either directly (i.e., deliberately) or through technically flawed measurement, paves the way for legal challenge. One key legal standard discussed below pertains to the numerical size and residential compactness of a minority group.

Context and Boundary Drawing

We now consider three points at which the local demographic context and boundary drawing may interact: 1) measuring electoral and representational equality; 2) defining the "protected" group; and 3) evaluating the Section 2 "compactness" test.

City	Population (000 omitted)	White[*] (%)	Hispanic (%)	Asian[*] (%)	Black[*] (%)
Los Angeles	3,485	37.3	39.9	9.8	14.0
San Jose	782	49.6	26.6	19.5	4.7
San Francisco	724	46.6	13.9	29.1	10.9
Oakland	372	28.3	13.9	14.8	43.9
Stockton	211	43.6	25.0	22.8	9.6
Vallejo	109	46.2	10.8	23.0	21.2
Daly City	92	27.4	22.4	43.8	7.7
Carson	84	22.1	27.9	25.0	26.1
Alhambra	82	24.3	36.1	38.1	2.0
National City	54	26.0	49.6	17.7	8.5

Table 1
Illustrative California Cities without a Single Ethnic-Racial Majority by 1990

[*]non-Hispanic only
Source: United States Census of Population and Housing, 1990

Electoral equality and representational equality. Los Angeles County illustrates how demographic complexity can complicate redistricting, hampering the effort to achieve three goals simultaneously[2]: first, electoral equality among the people who vote (citizens 18 years and older); second, representational equality among the people being governed (all persons); and third, forming a district where Hispanics would be a majority of elegible voters, to encourage the election of a Hispanic-favored candidate.

The court imposed a new plan, drawn by plaintiffs, with five county supervisor districts. One of these (the "Garza district"), was designed to achieve a Hispanic majority among the district's eligible voters. An election was held in early 1991 (just before the demographics of the district became known from the 1990 Census). The voters in the Garza district elected a Hispanic (Gloria Molina). Shortly thereafter, however, the new census data revealed that the plan itself violated standards of representational equality and electoral equality. The Garza district, as it turned out, contains only 17.5 percent of the county's total population (short of representational equality) and 16.3 percent of the voting-age population (short of electoral equality). The Garza district, in effect, accorded one-fifth of the political voice to only 16 percent of the county's eligible voters — equivalent to "one person, 1.22 votes" — thereby devaluing the votes of individuals living in the other four districts.

Defining the "protected group." Applicable law designates protected minorities by name (e.g., blacks, Hispanics). Membership within a legally defined "protected group" ultimately translates into some precise quantification of that membership based on census-defined categories of people.

Where the local population is highly diverse, that membership may be ambiguous (or at least controversial). The New York City Districting Commission had to form 51 new city council districts reflective of New York's racial, ethnic and cultural diversity. In doing so, the Commission was obliged to enhance the opportunity for all voters to elect candidates of their choice while also maintaining the integrity of borough lines, neighborhoods and communities; minimizing the length of potential boundaries; and honoring the principle of "one person, one vote," while complying with Federal Voting Rights Act requirements for fair and effective representation of racial and language minority groups. With 51 districts to be formed, terms like "Asian" or "Hispanic" necessarily give way to more specific ancestral and ethnic affiliations whose voters seek candidates of their choice — voters identifying themselves as Korean, Chinese or Vietnamese; Haitian, Jamaican or Caribbean-American; Puerto Rican or Cuban; and so forth.

Meeting the "compactness test." Where people form a politically cohesive group, boundaries may disadvantage them by including either too few or too many of the group's eligible voters in a given district. Where boundaries spread the group too evenly across voting districts, they dilute its voting strength, as illustrated in Figure 1. Here, a hypothetical city has five election districts and an electorate that is 40 percent Hispanic. In no district, however, are Hispanics the majority among voters; their voting strength has been dissipated through "cracking." Alternatively, boundaries may excessively concentrate a politically cohesive group, thereby "wasting" its voting strength (illustrated in Figure 2). If Hispanics make up 80 percent of the votes in one city election district but only 30 percent in each of the other four, then Hispanics may have been disadvantaged through "packing." (An underlying assumption in both instances is that people vote exclusively along racial lines.)

Plaintiffs initiating a redistricting claim under Section 2 of the Voting Rights Act must demonstrate that they can form a system of districts that would enable the protected minority group to be the majority of the potential voters (i.e., citizens aged 18 years and older) in at least one district. This is known as the "compactness test." Under ordinary circumstances, the compactness test is a straightforward data-accumulation exercise, involving the rank-ordering of heavily minority census tracts (block groups, blocks, enumeration districts) and the combination of adjoining tracts until the district encompasses the requisite number of inhabitants.

The City of National City (within metropolitan San Diego) illustrates the potential pitfalls that may arise where significant non-citizen enclaves exist. In a Section 2 claim against National City, the "geographic compactness" issue before the court concerned whether Hispanics could constitute a majority in any conceivable single-member district in a four-district plan. The then-current

REDISTRICTING CAN BE AN OPEN PROCESS IN WHICH THE PUBLIC ARE INVOLVED AND INFORMED THROUGH HEARINGS AND ...LOCAL PARTICIPATION.

(1980) census data showed that 38.4 percent of National City's 48,772 inhabitants were Hispanic. We can estimate the hypothetical upper limit of Hispanic compactness by combining the city's most heavily Hispanic contiguous census block groups into an area containing one-fourth of National City's total population. This "packing" exercise shows that Hispanics could constitute up to 59 percent of the total population in such a hypothetical district of 12,193, and a majority of the voting-age population. However, only 48.5 percent of the voting-age *citizens* would be Hispanic.

Contrary to appearances, it often turns out that *non-Hispanics* are the majority of eligible voters in seemingly majority-Hispanic population districts. Inexact measurement of minority compactness can create the false impression that Hispanics are the majority among potential voters when, in fact, they are not.

Technical Issues for Municipalities

The boundary-drawing process

is subject to exacting legal standards which, if not met, may invite legal challenge under Section 2 of the Voting Rights Act. Increasingly, legal scrutiny and challenge focus on measurement and other technical demographic issues.

Demographic analysis necessarily enters in at several points prior to and after redistricting. Following the decennial census, jurisdictions need technical advice and assistance to draw boundaries in accordance with legal requirements. Initially, then, the demographer may refine measurement and adjust boundaries or redesign districts.

The actual crafting of redistricting plans exploits demographers' analytic and spatial skills and their technical familiarity with census data to ensure that redistricting meets the legal requirements, untainted by technical measurement problems. The presence of special populations (e.g., military residents registered to vote elsewhere, or felons ineligible to vote) may call for special adjustments.

A jurisdiction that anticipates a challenge to its election system may retain a demographer as a confidential advisor to explore the outer limits of what a hypothetical plaintiff might be able to demonstrate with respect to Section 2 preconditions. A jurisdiction, for example, may wish to ascertain whether it is even mathematically possible for a potential plaintiff to construct an election district where "minority group X" would comprise 50 percent of all voting-age citizens, or whether ther is a discernible pattern of racially polarized voting. If the answers here are "definitely not," then the jurisdiction may opt to defend

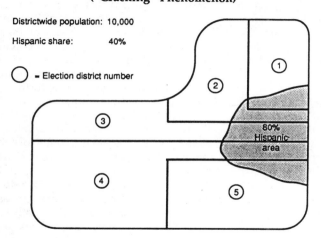

Figure 1
No Majority-Hispanic District
("Cracking" Phenomenon)

Districtwide population: 10,000

Hispanic share: 40%

◯ = Election district number

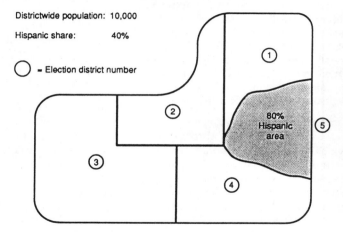

Figure 2
Single Extremely Hispanic District
("Packing" Phenomenon)

Districtwide population: 10,000

Hispanic share: 40%

◯ = Election district number

against any challenge rather than settle out of court. If one or both answers are "probably yes," however, the demographic facts may persuade the elected officials that it is better to alter district boundaries or even change the election system to avoid a challenge.

Conclusion

Redistricting can be an open process, one in which the public are involved and informed through hearings and other kinds of local participation. A jurisdiction may seek to formalize this process in a way that expresses its commitment to openness and its intent to recognize each protected group. Doing so from the outset may insulate the jurisdiction against subsequent charges that office holders created districts solely to protect their incumbency, at the expense of minority voting power.

Notes

[1]William A.V. Clark and Peter A. Morrison, "Demographic Paradoxes in the Los Angeles Voting Rights Case," *Evaluation Review*, Vol. 15, No. 6, December 1991, pp. 712-728.

[2]Peter A. Morrison, "Quantifying Legal Standards in Voting Rights Cases" (presented at the 1989 Population Association of America meetings).

Should judges be elected?

Point ►►►►►►►►►►►

Richard Lee Price

Richard Lee Price is an acting justice of the New York State Supreme Court in the Bronx and is president of the American Judges Association.

Although accused of politicizing what should be the branch of government above politics, most states still maintain that the best way to select judges is at the voting booth. I agree.

Those opposed to judicial elections say elected judges are politicians, beholden to their backers and special interest groups. They fail to acknowledge that judicial appointees suffer from the same fate.

One does not become appointed to a judicial position without cultivating supporters among the politicians with the power of appointment.

Gubernatorial appointments, the most common method of merit selection, do not routinely go to unknowns who, though bright and industrious, have no ties to the governor's office. Similarly, the members of judicial screening committees, who sometimes pick the pool from which the governor or other appointing official may select, are themselves either politicians or chosen by politicians.

Once one admits that both elected and appointed judges are politicians, it becomes clear that the public is better off with an elected judge. Such judges are accountable to the public and may be removed from office if their constituency is dissatisfied with the performance.

Take the case of the 1987 defeat of California Chief Justice Rose Bird, who was appointed to her post by Gov. Jerry Brown. During her tenure, she voted to reverse all 61 death sentences she reviewed.

When she ran in a retention election, she was ousted from judicial office. The lesson to be learned is that although the governor agreed with her death penalty reversals, the public was dissatisfied with her apparent refusal to enforce a law that the people supported.

Opponents of judicial elections insist that the judiciary must be capable of making decisions that may not, in some cases, adhere to the majority's ideas. Elected candidates, they proclaim, may be forced to compromise justice for the sake of pleasing their constituency.

While this concern may have some validity, judges should be re-elected not on the basis of a few decisions but on the basis of the body of work performed during their term. Moreover, public debate about controversial

◄◄◄◄◄◄◄ Counterpoint

Evan A. Davis

Evan A. Davis is a partner in the law firm of Cleary, Gottlieb, Steen and Hamilton. From 1985 through 1990, he served as counsel to New York Gov. Mario M. Cuomo.

Judges should apply the law, not make it. They should apply it objectively — without regard to the status or popularity of the parties before them. Litigants should not need an ideologically "correct" position to get justice, nor should they feel they lost because the other side had political connections.

The way we choose judges has a lot to do with how well we live up to these goals of objectivity, of fairness in fact and appearance and of wise judicial decisions.

New York chooses its judges in two ways — some by election, some by appointment. The election of judges is riddled with politics. Indeed, the process is controlled by the leaders of the two political parties in each county.

This approach is one of the last vestiges of patronage for the party leaders, who are accountable only to the party committee. Their job is to keep the party strong, ensure enough workers to get the party candidates elected, and raise money for the party.

Although there is technically an election, it is really these party leaders who choose the judges. First, they control the process for getting on the ballot. They are naturally inclined to choose people who have been active and helpful in the party.

Second, with other party leaders in the state, they control the party organization, an important resource for getting elected. For example, in New York state judicial candidates generally have to run in large, multi-county, multimember districts.

It is hard for many of them to raise money and remain within the bounds of the Code of Judicial Conduct. But political parties can raise money, and they have access to volunteers who will ring doorbells, hand out fliers and get out the vote. So in upstate New York, which the Republicans control, the Republican candidate wins. The Democrats have the same good fortune in New York City.

The rare contested election for a judgeship, is not a pretty sight. The soundness of the law a judge is required to apply becomes grist for the political millstone. Aid to parochial education can become a hot topic, as well as labor vs. management issues and criminal justice matters. One campaign commercial featured the sound of jail doors clanging shut.

Counterpoint

or unpopular decisions is healthy and should not be discouraged simply because the office to be filled is that of judge.

Judges perform a constitutional, as opposed to a majoritarian, function, and it is constitutional for the public to vote out a judge who does not enforce the laws passed by the majority.

Another benefit is that judicial elections can be scrutinized for discrimination, thereby encouraging minority candidates. This especially has become the case since the U.S. Supreme Court determined in 1991 that Section 2 of the Voting Rights Act, which prohibits the dilution of minority voting strength, applies to judicial elections. Gubernatorial and other judicial appointments do not have to comply with the provisions of the Voting Rights Act.

The right to contest a judicial election that appears to discriminate against minorities is a legitimate method of redressing discrimination in the judicial selection process.

Elections force candidates to go public with their qualifications, allowing voters to select a candidate with the qualifications and attributes they believe necessary.

Running for judicial office has drawbacks, most notably the expense. But judges invest more than money in their candidacy; they spend years in many beneficial, professional and community activities earning a reputation that entitles them to run for a judicial position.

Once elected, judges base decisions on their best understanding of the law. Because all judges are influenced by their own values and opinions and have varying degrees of ability, each performs differently.

However, when a term expires and re-election is sought, once again the public has the right to consider the candidate's qualifications.

The third branch of government, not unlike the other two, represents the people and upholds the laws. Excluding the public from the process of judicial selection is anti-democratic. The importance of a judgeship mandates application of a critical constitutional right — the right to vote.

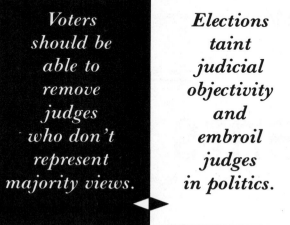

Voters should be able to remove judges who don't represent majority views.

Elections taint judicial objectivity and embroil judges in politics.

In light of such a history, the appointment process begun in 1979 for judges on New York's highest court, the Court of Appeals, was a breath of fresh air. A nominating commission composed of diverse members forwards to an accountable elected official a list of names. The official then chooses an appointee from the list with the advice and consent of the state Senate.

The advantages of this process are numerous:
• **Scrutiny.** Interested applicants must pass scrutiny at three levels: the commission, the appointing authority and the confirming authority. The bar association and the public have an opportunity for input at each level.

• **Accountability.** The list of names forwarded to the appointing authority and the makeup of the nominating commission are matters of public record. The elected official responsible for choosing an appointee is accountable to the voters for his or her choices. And the Senate is accountable for its decision about whether to confirm the appointee.

• **Diversity.** The bench needs a mix of race and gender to maintain public confidence and to be true to our constitutional principles of pluralism and inclusiveness. If the nominating commission is diverse and under a mandate to consider the need for improved diversity — which should be the legal requirement — that goal is likely to be achieved.

On the other hand, with racially polarized voting all too prevalent, many parts of the state are unlikely to elect a minority judge.

• **Judicial independence.** Merit selection greatly improves judges' independence. Judges can apply the law without acting as if they are politicians writing it. They are chosen for their competence and not because of their opinions of certain laws.

They can pledge faithful and impartial performance of their duties as judges, without worrying whether the party leader will approve and accordingly support them in the future.

• **Opportunity.** A lawyer or lower court judge without political connections can aspire to become a judge or gain a higher judicial office.

This does not mean that those with political connections will not become judges. But it does mean more competition, and from this better choices emerge.

To set out these two approaches is enough. Now, you be the judge.

Press row view:
News Judgments

Charles Wolfe

Charles Wolfe is a statehouse reporter for the Associated Press in Frankfort, Ky.

A television reporter I know has developed, through his years of statehouse coverage, a personal acid test for judging the newsworthiness of events.

He usually applies the test during the grand announcement of a task force's creation, a blue-ribbon commission's empanelment, an omnibus bill's introduction and the like. Turning his mind's eye toward one of the more socially circumscribed of his state's numerous rural nooks, he asks: "Will it mean a damned thing in Owsley County, Kentucky?"

The Owsley County test is one that reporters often don't take seriously enough. It's one that forces the media to acknowledge a basic fact: Most readers — or listeners or viewers — do not follow with rapt attention the daily occurrences at the seat of government.

The longer one pounds the state government beat, the easier it be-

comes to assume that everyone has been following the action in the statehouse and knows precisely what's going on.

News that House Bill 99 has cleared a Senate committee and is headed for a potentially final vote on the floor might be meaningful to the lobbyist who has faithfully tracked it. But it doesn't mean a thing to the rest of the public, including the good citizens of Owsley County — who don't give a fig about the bill's number, but only want to know how it will affect them.

A tendency to attach unwarranted importance to bill numbers and other institutional terms or titles is but one of many teeth in the trap for the capital press corps. Others include jargon, preoccupation with personalities and inattention to the less glamorous, albeit important, inner workings of government.

It is doubtful that any part of the governmental process gets more coverage than the state budget — from its formulation through its enactment — and the periodic tabu-

lations of income and outgo as the administration tries to make the books balance at the end of the fiscal year. The media often do a poor job, however, of reporting budget news. Their stories can be superficial, nothing more than a collection of numbers unconnected in any meaningful way to the circumstances of the public that coughs up the money on which the numbers are based.

Figures of millions and billions of dollars get tossed casually about in government and the danger of equally casual reporting always exists.

The late U.S. Sen. Everett Dirksen from Illinois was right in saying, "A million here and a million there and pretty soon you're talking about real money." We *are* talking about a lot of money; we're just numb to it.

It is a challenge for a reporter to follow the legislative odyssey of a budget bill, to cover its mark-ups, amendments, perhaps even its veto and to total up the relative winners and losers. But there is another challenge — to make that budget and its billions of dollars mean something to the average wage earner in Owsley County. Reporters need to find out what lies beneath the surface numbers. If a tax increase or rollback is at issue, they need to ask what the tab is per capita, not just the total dollar amount.

A part of state government that gets generally short shrift from the press corps is the process by which administrative regulations are written to implement new laws. It is tedious business to say the least, but many believe it is where the real lawmaking takes place.

Critics of the process contend a legislative mandate can be turned on its ear with a regulation or a lengthy delay in promulgating that regulation after the legislature has left town. Yet, so arcane is the process that the public rarely hears about it.

It became such a sore point with the Kentucky General Assembly, however, that legislation was passed to require that the state's mountains of administrative regulations be codified in statute, ostensibly giving the legislative branch greater control of its handiwork.

Reporting the story required an explanation of the Kentucky Administrative Regulations, the Kentucky Revised Statutes, the differences between them and why it was important. It was a story that was difficult to explain in paper and on the air and therefore it didn't get the coverage that many state officials thought it deserved.

Another common complaint about the media is that they tend to interview the same state officials over and over again. Reporters quickly learn which legislators, lobbyists and state officials are knowledgeable, influential and can be counted on for reliable, unbiased informa-

The amount of news to be generated at a governor's news conference is inversely proportional to the number of people standing behind the governor.

tion or reaction. But there is a natural tendency of reporters to gravitate to those known to be the most articulate, or provocative, or to hold the seats of greatest power.

There is a corresponding desire on the other side to have all events portrayed in the most favorable light. Attempts to manage the news are ongoing in state government. Such attempts, however, often backfire.

Some techniques will cause reporters reflexively to question the legitimacy of a news event. One is the standing room only news conference, in which the official making the announcement is accompanied by a crowd of associates. The idea seems to be that sheer force of numbers will compel press coverage. But it at times has had the opposite effect on capital press corps, which have developed their own irreverent rule of thumb: The amount of news to be generated at a governor's news conference is inversely proportional to the number of people standing behind the governor.

The press is frequently accused of overplaying the frictions and conflicts of government — a governor fighting with the legislature; legislators fighting with each other — but the process does not take place in a vacuum. If the executive and legislative branches are at a stale-

mate, that's serious news for the public.

It probably means crippling inaction on several fronts — education, tax reform, infrastructure, to name a few. The public needs to know the ramifications as well as the personalities.

The same thing holds in legislative leadership races. If there is factionalism, reporters need to know what is behind it and how is it likely to be translated into legislation.

Finally, woe to the reporter who slips into the habit of writing in the contrived style of the bureaucratic language.

Government officials are unlikely ever to talk about raising taxes to get more money to meet rising program costs. Instead, they will "dialogue about impacting a shortfall with revenue enhancements." Technocrats are wont to "prioritize." They are mindful of "opportunity windows." They might even "interface." They talk about people or things being "impacted" — an adjective, commonly describing a painful condition of the wisdom teeth, which has somehow been tortured into a verb.

If the capital press corps does its job, it will cut through the verbal clutter, all the way to Owsley County.

Civic Strategies
for Community Empowerment

JOSEPH F. ZIMMERMAN

*Joseph F. Zimmerman is a professor of political science at the State
University of New York at Albany, and editor of the* NATIONAL CIVIC
REVIEW *Metro Trends department.*

The past two decades have seen a serious erosion of "dynamic"
democracy in many parts of the United States as eligible citizens
vote less frequently and withdraw from other key aspects of local political life. Instead, we increasingly find a disturbing brand of "reluctant" democracy in which formal rights to participate are widely ignored
in practice.

Among the explanations given for this phenomenon is a spreading
sense of political impotency which discourages involvement. In many
communities today, one routinely hears that "you can't fight city hall."
While this theme is not new, when juxtaposed with a growing number
of "private" preoccupations (e.g., multiple jobs to support the family
or the explosion of recreational opportunities) and residential mobility, it provides good reason to keep out of the public arena.

However many communities (including larger jurisdictions) have effectively used certain structural mechanisms to combat feelings of political powerlessness and thus stem the potentially dangerous slide toward
"reluctant" democracy. In this article we examine the record of such
devices in three critical areas: the election system; ethics and openness
in public affairs; and the degree of local discretionary authority. These
areas offer future avenues for greater citizen participation.

Election Systems That Invite Participation

To encourage involvement, the formula used for electing officials must
be generally perceived as fair. The criteria for measuring systems include effectiveness of ballots cast, responsiveness of elected officials,
maximization of access to decision makers, equity in representation,
and legitimization of the legislative body! These canons can be used
to evaluate six electoral structures: at-large; combined ward and at-large;
limited voting; cumulative voting; and proportional representation.[2]

If an electoral system produces accurate community representation,
government may satisfy voter needs. Unfortunately, no means for selecting officials accurately represents the views of all citizens on all issues
at all times. The law making process can foster the illusion that each
measure is scrutinized carefully and fully prior to its approval, amendment, or rejection. However, elected representatives—whether ethical
or unscrupulous—are to a greater or lesser extent "trustees" who take
many of their cues from non-constituent sources, thus producing results
that never fully reflect voter consensus (if, indeed, there is one).

Three Mitigating Devices

Three devices can mitigate the problem: initiative, the referendum,
and recall. Ideally, these mechanisms should be available on a stand-
by basis as circuit breakers to be triggered only by gross misrepresen-
tation of the electorate.

The Binding Initiative. This approach allows the electorate to place
proposed laws on the referendum ballot. It can be traced to a 1715 Massachusetts law and to an 1898 constitutional amendment with respect
to other areas of the United States.[3] Today 23 state constitutions authorize its use. Seventeen provide for constitutional and 21 for statutory
initiatives. Placing a measure on the ballot requires petitions signed
by a certain number of registered voters (from 3 to 15% of votes cast
for Governor in the last election). Measures approved by the voters are
not subject to gubernatorial veto. State statutes and municipal charters often authorize local initiative.

*... elected representatives—whether ethical or
unscrupulous—are to a greater or lesser extent "trustees" who
take many of their cues from non-constituent sources, thus
producing results that never fully reflect voter consensus ...*

This direct method for circumventing the legislative process attracts
criticism. Opponents argue, for example, that elected representatives
produce better laws or that popular measures are often poorly drafted, confusing to voters, and not coordinated properly with other
statutes.[4]

An alternative, the indirect initiative, available in eight States including
Massachusetts, empowers voters (with requisite signatures) to refer measures to the legislature for its consideration (akin to submitting a bill).
If that body fails to approve the proposition within the stated time limit,
in five states it is automatically placed on the ballot. In three states,
sponsors of the proposal must collect additional signatures to force
a popular vote. Five states authorize their legislatures to place a competing proposition on the ballot.

Advisory Initiatives. Non-binding questions may be placed on the
referendum ballot to place pressure on law-making bodies to enact certain measures. The theory supporting this type of initiative suggests
that elected representatives will act in accordance with the clearly expressed desires of the voters. In the late 1970s, the environmental and
nuclear freeze movements often used such means to influence public
opinion and law makers.

The Referendum. Plebiscitarian techniques in the United States are
traceable to the Massachusetts Bay Colony where the General Court
(legislative body) in 1640 authorized the use of the referendum.[5]
However, this democratizing tool did not become established in most
parts of the country until the early 1800s when state legislatures and
constitutional conventions began to submit proposed constitutions for

Reprinted with permission from the May/June 1988 issue of *National Civic Review*, pp. 202-212. National Civic Review, 1601
Grant Street, Suite 250, Denver, CO 80203.

voter appoval. The first New York State Constitution of 1777, for example, was adopted in convention without popular vote.

In the late 19th century, several state legislatures, including New York's, so abused their powers that the public demanded (and won) the right to approve constitutional changes and a class of "conditional" laws which do not become effective unless approved by the voters. These restrictions are contained today in many state constitutions, including New York's, and typically involve taxation and the borrowing of funds.

A more dramatic development occurred in South Dakota in 1898 when voters amended the state constitution to authorize the electorate to employ the petition or protest referendum and the initiative.[6] This device allows voters to veto most laws enacted by a legislature. Exempted are laws designed to preserve "the public peace, health or safety, [and] support of the State Government and its existing institutions."[7]

The petition referendum, when signed by two to 15 percent of those voting in the last general election, suspends a law until a mandatory referendum on it can be held.

In 24 states, the protest referendum is authorized by the state constitution. In eight cases, it may be employed only to repeal an entire law while in the others it can be used like a line-item veto.

Specified topics (e.g., appropriation of funds, the judiciary, statutes applying to a single local government, and religion) usually are not subject to the petition referendum. The Commonwealth of Massachusetts excludes the largest number of items.[8]

Twenty states require a majority vote for repeal; the balance require from 30 to 50 percent of the vote in the last general election. Six constitutions forbid the state legislature to amend or repeal the voters' decision.

Local government charters and state statutes often allow for petition referenda to overrule municipal laws. The procedures are typically identical with those at the state level.

The Recall

This tool for popular involvement is a natural extension of the others. The recall or "imperative mandate" concept appeared in the Articles of Confederation and Perpetual Union, the national platforms of the Socialist Labor Party in 1892 and 1896, and the platform of the Populist Party in several states during the same period.[9] It was first authorized in the 1903 Los Angeles charter.[10] Currently, 14 state constitutions allow recall of state and certain local officers.[11] Also, 17 states authorize the recall of local officials by general law, special law, or a locally drafted and adopted charter. Although the California Constitution directed the State Legislature to provide for the recall of local officers, this provision does not affect cities and counties with "home rule" charters.

In Massachusetts, 52 locally drafted city and town charters allow recall. The Billerica town charter, for example, stipulates "any person who holds an elected town office, but not including an elected town meeting member, with more than six months remaining of the term of office, may be recalled from office by the voters"[12] The Oxford town charter simply states that "any elective officer of the town may be recalled and removed from public office by the voters of the town as herein provided."[13]

Charters of professionally managed cities typically include similar provisions to counterbalance the authority of that non-elected official. Although managers are theoretically accountable to the council, it is widely felt that intra-governmental politics can insulate them from popular opinion, thus requiring such protection.

In a few states, the recall ballot is also used to elect a replacement. If there is no prohibition, the target incumbent may simultaneously seek reelection (which, ironically, can occur if the other candidates split the opposing vote).

Like the initiative and the protest referendum, the recall process is launched by petition (usually requiring signatures equal to 25% of votes cast in the last election for governor or the position in question) and concluded by a special election.[14]

Several states require that recall petitions for statewide elected officials contain a geographical spread of signatures. California, for example, stipulates 1% of the last vote cast for the office in each of five counties.[15]

Typically a short justification for recall and defense appear on the ballot. San Francisco publishes a voter information pamphlet containing a sample ballot, the proponents' statement of reasons for the proposed recall, the officer's reply to the reasons, and paid advertisements. The 1983 pamphlet relative to the special recall election of the Mayor contained 49 paid advertisements (37 favoring the Mayor and 12 supporting recall).

In nine states, the electorate simply votes on the question of recalling an officer. In most jurisdictions, a majority affirmative vote *ipso facto* vacates the office which is then filled according to law, and may involve a second special election to select a successor.

In a few states, the recall ballot (e.g., Arizona) is also used to elect a replacement. If there is no prohibition, the target incumbent may simultaneously seek reelection (which, ironically, can occur if the other candidates split the opposing vote).

Arguments for and against the recall resemble those aimed at the initiative and petition referendum.[16] Not surprisingly, many elected officials oppose all three corrective devices. Yet it appears that their availability often promote dynamic democracy by enhancing governmental legitimacy and reducing feelings of political impotence.

Open and Ethical Government

These conditions are essential for effective, participatory democracy because citizens possess substantially fewer political resources than elected and appointed officials. As Aristotle insisted:

> If the citizens are to judge officers according to merit, then they must know each other's characters; where they do not possess this knowledge, both the election to office and the decision of lawsuits will go wrong.[17]

Information and resulting citizen inputs alone, however, generally do not provide a sufficient antidote to unethical official behavior. Other, complementary mechanisms are needed.

So long as ethical problems remain clear-cut, the venerable English common law approach which relies on precedent-based judicial decisions may suffice. Nonetheless, today's issues often assume more subtle form, creating gray areas that require different treatment.

Codes of Ethics

While no one mechanism can ensure that governmental actions will be ethical, strong ethics codes and boards for rendering advisory opinions represent a critical first step.[18] Such codes establish essential guidelines for governmental officers, facilitate self-regulation, and bolster public confidence. Publication of advisory board opinions, with appropriate deletions to preserve the privacy of those making the requests, will in time build a case inventory to guide other elected governmental personnel contemplating similar actions.

Sunshine Laws

Sunshine laws are designed to throw light on governmental actions, the decision-making process, and attempts by individuals and interest groups to influence it. They include mandatory financial disclosures by public officers, open meetings of public bodies, and citizen access to public records.

Financial Disclosure. Requirements that public officers publish information about their personal and family finances are related closely to conflict-of-interest laws and codes of ethics. Manditory disclosure preferably should be restricted to a listing of income sources rather than specific amounts, and also might be limited to specified sources of income exceeding a stipulated amount. The required statement should contain the name and address of each creditor to whom a minimum amount is owed, due date, interest rate, date and original amount of the debt, existing special conditions, and a statement indicating whether or not the debt is secured. Mortgage debt on a personally occupied home and retail installment debt might be exempted from the disclosure requirement.

3. CITIZENS AND GOVERNMENT: Referenda, Initiatives, and Recalls

A thorny question is whether financial disclosure should apply to all part-time citizen officers in small municipalities who serve without compensation or receive only minor stipends. There is no denying that service on a non-paid board of commission represents a sacrifice of time and money, and may also subject the officers to abuse and criticism by the public. A mandatory disclosure requirement for all officers might discourage candidacies—something to be avoided when the aim is to encourage wider participation by qualified individuals. Thus, in the case of part-time positions, it seems wise to limit disclosure requirements to candidates for bodies with regulatory powers such as planning boards.

A thorny question is whether financial disclosure should apply to all part-time citizen officers in small municipalities who serve without compensation or receive only minor stipends . . . A mandatory disclosure requirement for all officers might discourage candidacies—something to be avoided when the aim is to encourage wider participation by qualified individuals.

Open Meetings. Informed citizen participation is hindered by *in camera* decision-making. Many local governments and state legislatures have enacted open meeting laws designed to throw light on the policy process while, at the same time, permitting closed-door executive sessions for certain sensitive issues as property acquisition, disciplinary action, salary negotiations, or matters that could prejudice a government's position in a law suit.

Care must be exercised in defining the term "meeting" when adopting such laws. The Council of State Governments recommends that the concept refer to "the convening of a governing body for which a quorum is required in order to make a decision or to deliberate toward a decision on any matter."[19] It is also important to require that adequate public notice be given to interested persons and organizations of the place and time of meetings, and to specify exceptions to the open meeting requirements. In addition, complete and accurate records of meetings should be kept so that citizens unable to attend can examine proceedings.

Freedom of Information. A third type of "sunshine" law attempts to ensure that citizens will have ready access to most official records of government. Such devices are desirable because excessive confidentiality can shield unethical or prejudicial actions from cure. Yet the matter of what information should be released and under what conditions raises delicate questions which should not be addressed haphazardly. In 1977, the New York State Legislature addressed this problem by creating the Committee on Public Access to Records, charged with developing guidelines for the release of official information by state and local government agencies, and providing advice in cases of disputes.[20] The Committee's performance of its duties has been excellent.

A conflict can exist between freedom of information and privacy laws. The Federal Privacy Act of 1974, for example, requires executive agencies to keep confidential personal information, yet the Federal Freedom of Information Act requires agencies to make executive branch records available for inspection or duplication except "to the extent required to prevent a clearly unwarranted invasion of personal privacy."[21]

Balancing these two elements is a challenge for which no universal solution exists, indicating that communities must experiment with alternatives within the current legal framework until they find one which serves local needs.

Local Discretionary Authority

As suggested earlier, citizen participation tends to increase as communities gain greater control over their own public policy process. Historically, the legal relationship between states and their political subdivisions was governed by the *Ultra Vires* (beyond powers) concept, also know as Dillon's Rule, which denied inherent powers of local self-government and emphasized the plenary authority of the state legislature.[22] Fortunately, most states have modified the *Ultra Vires* Rule and provided for increased local discretionary authority by the adoption

of provisions for an *Imperium in Imperio* (empire within an empire). New York State employs the three approaches simultaneously, thereby producing considerable confusion relative to the legal powers of various local jurisdictions.

Clearly, local governments that deliver most public services and operate on a relatively small scale offer greater participatory opportunities. When these institutions lack substantial autonomy, citizen interest obviously wanes.

Retention of broad powers over local governments makes the state legislature a target of interests unable to achieve their goals at the grass roots. In general, state legislatures have been responsive to such demands, enacting many laws that mandate courses of action for more accessible political subdivisions.

The only national survey of this phenomenon reveals that most states have imposed numerous mandates upon their local governments, with New York in the lead. There, the legislature imposed its will in 66 of the 76 functional areas studied.[23] In contrast to the national government which still provides most financial assistance to subnational units with conditions attached, New York State is generous in sharing its income tax revenues with its political subdivisions with few conditions attached. However, the separate enactment of state mandates by the New York State Legislature over the years has reduced significantly the discretionary authority of the local units.

To what extent do states reimburse local governments for mandated expenditures? Currently, 12 provide full or partial support. California's Initiative Proposition 4 of 1979 and Massachusett's Initiative Proposition 2-1/2 of 1980 make this a requirement.

Mandates fall into 11 categories: entitlement; structural; service level; tax base; personnel; due process; equal treatment; ethical; good neighbor; informational membership; and record-keeping. A strong case can be made that the states should not be forced to reimburse costs associated with the last six types, since these are relatively inexpensive functions which (in spite of state intervention) should remain under maximum local control.

Conclusion

This review reveals that a substantial range of formal, participatory instruments have been devised to make state and local governments more responsive and accountable to their electorates. Unfortunately, not all of these mechanisms are everywhere available. Moreover, legal and other impediments often prevent their best use to overcome widespread feelings of political impotence and achieve "dynamic" democracy.

Given their greater authority and scope, state legislatures remain the prime key to establishing broader participatory "rights." They are still in the best position to initiate statutes and constitutional amendments for corrective devices to expand potential citizen influence on the governance process. They can increase the discretionary authority of local governments and establish general mechanisms for furnishing ethical advice to public officials. While not sufficient by themselves, such democratizing actions would set the stage for enlarged, more satisfying citizen participation.

Notes
[1]For details, see Joseph F. Zimmerman, "Electoral Systems and Direct Citizen Law Making." A paper presented at the University of Wurzburg, Federal Republic of Germany, July 1, 1987.
[2]Joseph F. Zimmerman, *The Federated City: Community Control in Large Cities* (New York: St. Martin's Press, 1972), pp. 65-79.
[3]*The Acts and Resolves of the Province of the Massachusetts Bay* (Boston: Wright and Potter, 1874), vol. II, p. 30, and *Constitution of South Dakota*, art. III, I (1898).
[4]Joseph F. Zimmerman, *Participatory Democracy: Populism Revived* (New York: Praeger Publishers, 1986), pp. 91-95.
[5]Nathaniel B. Shurtleff, ed. *Records of the Governor and Company of the Massachusetts Bay in New England* (Boston: From the Press of William White, Printer to the Commonwealth, 1853), vol. I, p. 293.
[6]*Constitution of South Dakota*, art III, I (1898).
[7]*Ibid.*
[8]*Constitution of the Commonwealth of Massachusetts*, Articles of Amendment, art. XLVIII, The Referendum, 2.

⁹*Articles of Confederation and Perpetual Union,* art. V.

¹⁰Frederick L. Bird and Frances M. Rayan, *The Recall of Public Officers: A Study of the Operation of the Recall in California* (New York: The Macillan Company, 1930), p. 22.

¹¹Alaska, Arizona, California, Colorado, Georgia, Idaho, Kansas, Louisiana, Michigan, Nevada, North Dakota, Oregon, Washington, and Wisconsin.

¹²*Town of Billerica* (Massachusetts) *Charter,* art. VI, pp. 6-4.

¹³*Town of Oxford* (Massachusetts) *Charter,* chap. VII, p. 6.

¹⁴For details on signature requirements, see *The Book of the States* (Lexington, Kentucky: The Council of State Governments, latest edition).

¹⁵*Constitution of California,* art. II, p. 14 (b) and *California Elections Code,* p. 27211 (b).

¹⁶For details, see Zimmerman, *Participatory Democracy: Populism Revived,* pp. 122-26.

¹⁷Benjamin Jowett, trans., *Artistotle's Politics* (New York: Carlton House, n.d.), p. 288.

¹⁸Joseph F. Zimmerman, "Preventing Unethical Behavior in Government," *Urban Law and Policy,* vol. VIII, 1987, pp. 335-56.

¹⁹*Guidelines for State Legislation on Government Ethics and Campaign Financing* (Lexington, Kentucky: The Council of State Governments, 1984), p. 4.

²⁰*New York Laws of 1977,* chap. 933 and *New York Public Officers Law,* pp. 84-90.

²¹*Freedom of Information Act,* 88 Stat. 1986, 5 U.S.C. p. 552 (a) (2).

²²For details on the legal relations existing between state and local governments today, see Joseph F. Zimmerman, *State-Local Relations: A Partnership Approach* (New York: Praeger Publishers, 1983), pp. 15-48.

²³Joseph F. Zimmerman, *State Mandating of Local Expenditures* (Washington, D.C.: United States Advisory Commission on Intergovernmental Relations, 1978).

Is the initiative process a good idea?

Point ▶▶▶▶▶▶▶▶▶▶

◀◀◀◀◀◀◀ Counterpoint

Douglas P. Wheeler

Douglas P. Wheeler is the California secretary for resources.

When Hiram Johnson was elected governor of California in 1910, he promised to rescue state government from special interests, especially the Southern Pacific Railway Co., and to "restore absolute sovereignty to the people."

After his election, Johnson called for establishment of the initiative, referendum and recall. California voters agreed with him and approved the measures in a special election in 1911.

Initiatives, especially in recent years, have had a profound effect on the course of California's — and in some cases the nation's — history by providing a means for frustrated voters to speak out when entrenched political forces and the legislative process failed to respond to their needs.

In 1972, California voters passed an initiative to protect the coastline from excessive development when it seemed that coastal resources otherwise would be unprotected. Six years later, when state legislators failed to respond to their needs, voters passed Proposition 13, putting a lid on rapidly spiraling property taxes and setting off a national trend on tax limitations.

Recently, however, we have seen a spate of initiatives that represent not so much a response to failures of the Legislature or other officeholders to act in the public interest, but an attempt by special interests to bypass traditional legislative processes.

In a media age, the initiative process is prone to abuse, substituting sound bites and billboard advertisements for reasoned debate on the merits of the issue. The initiative's format calls for an aye or nay without benefit of constructive interaction among legislators, voters and interest groups.

Not only is there no opportunity for rational debate and sensible give-and-take in the pre-election stage of an initiative campaign, initiatives once enacted often are difficult or almost impossible to modify.

The result can mean that unreasonable, shortsighted or unwieldy concepts are established in law. The laws tie the hands of administrators, lock in spending requirements regardless of need and fail to provide for changing times.

Bill Owens

Sen. Bill Owens served three terms in the Colorado House prior to his election to the Senate in 1988.

Like most of my legislative colleagues, I used to be a critic of initiatives. I felt the initiative process threatened our system of representative government. I have changed my mind. A properly structured initiative process results in increased responsiveness by government to the will of the people, greater citizen participation and a better-informed electorate. Legislatures recognize this by passing legislation under the threat of initiative. This fear of being bypassed by the people was at least partially responsible for the passage of acid rain legislation in Massachusetts, abolition of the sales tax on food in Arizona and Wyoming's minimum stream flow legislation.

Initiatives also lead to a better-informed electorate as well as to greater voter participation. Surveys show that the voter has a better understanding of most initiative proposals than of the platforms of the candidates they elect. Turnout also improves when initiatives are on the ballot — not to mention the beneficial effect of involving in the political process the 500,000 citizens who circulate petitions and the 25 million citizens who sign them during each two-year election cycle.

Initiatives often spark lively public debate, much needed during a time when incumbency and attack ads stifle substantive policy discussion. They also allow the public to better understand the political candidate's position on issues since the candidates usually are forced to disclose their views on the ballot questions.

The initiative represents an important safeguard against undue concentration of political power. American history is no stranger to accounts of the abuse of power — and even honest government can be concentrated too much in the hands of a few at the expense of the people. California Speaker Willie Brown was taught this lesson last November when California voters limited legislative terms and rolled back legislative perks, despite the multimillion dollar campaign against the initiative. The initiative allows for new ideas to be placed on the political agenda. Through the initiative, the people can play a direct role in making policy, joining legislators, judges and the media in defining public debate.

Critics claim that the initiative leads to "ballot clutter" — yet legislators place four times as many proposals

Point

The legislative process often is time-consuming and cumbersome, but it provides a forum in which all sides of an issue can be debated and fine-tuned to accommodate a range of interests. In addition, it is subject to the careful scrutiny of the governor. Finally, there is a continuing legislative oversight, both to assure compliance with original intent and to modify laws and policies as circumstances change.

There are few written works of any kind — novels, short stories, newspaper articles and even op-ed page pieces — that would not benefit from review, deliberation and debate.

Legislation benefits from this process, but initiatives don't. What you see is what you get. And what the public gets all too often is a bad law, a law that could not have survived the open debate, critical review and modification provided by the legislative process.

The initiative process too often results in bad laws by forgoing debate.

In California, environmentalists recently have encountered growing voter resistance to the initiative process. Confronted last fall by a plethora of pro- and anti-environmental measures, including the nationally publicized "Big Green," voters rejected them all.

That defeat lead to speculation that Californians had abandoned their environmental sensitivity and left important capital programs, which routinely require voters' approval, without adequate funding. A more accurate assessment would reveal that the defeat of "Big Green" was evidence of growing awareness of the perils of "government by initiative."

I'll continue to defend the initiative process as a necessary last resort of the people when our elected representatives fail to act responsibly. But a far better strategy is to elect responsible public officials and to insist that they fulfill the trust we place in them.

Counterpoint

on the ballot than do citizens. Since 1900, about 700 initiatives have passed in the United States — less than one-half of 1 percent of the hundreds of thousands of laws passed by our 50 state legislatures. Skeptics claim that initiatives "confuse" the electorate — yet the initiative questions on a ballot garner more votes — pro and con — than do most candidate races.

Critics charge that many initiatives are poorly drafted — yet of the 40 passed during two election cycles in the early 1980s only two have been held unconstitutional.

Opponents usually cite California when arguing against the initiative, and sometimes with good reason. I am not about to defend how the initiative is used in California. I would suggest that the safeguards built into the political process by California legislators designed to protect their incumbency has forced California's citi-

The people are the winners when the initiative process works properly.

zens to use the initiative to bypass their self-perpetuating Legislature. Common Cause reports that in 1986 California Senate incumbents outspent their challengers 75 to 1, while Assembly incumbents built up a 39 to 1 fundraising advantage. And guess what? No incumbent was defeated in 1986.

Combine this overwhelming spending advantage with safe, gerrymandered seats and large staffs — and it's no wonder the voters in California choose to influence public policy directly through the initiative rather than by running against entrenched incumbents.

The same is true in other states. The fact is that our political system is designed — with incumbents as the architects — to re-elect incumbents. And if you doubt that, just look around your legislature to see how many of your colleagues have been defeated recently. The initiative is a healthy response to the structural problems present in today's political process. While the initiative can be overused, or abused, it nevertheless provides a critical check on the powers of the three branches of government.

Government Institutions and Officeholders

- Legislatures (Articles 17–20)
- Executives (Articles 21–23)
- Courts (Articles 24–27)
- Other Institutions and Related Matters (Articles 28 and 29)

Government institutions are to state and local political systems what skeletons are to people. They shape the general outlines of policy processes in the same way that bones shape the outlines of human bodies. For state and local governments, as well as for the national government and most governments everywhere, institutions are critical factors in the governing process.

There are important variations among the states in executive, legislative, and judicial structures and in the degree to which citizens have access to the policy-making process. In "strong governor" states, chief executives hold substantially greater appointive, budgetary, and veto powers than in "weak governor" states. The roles of parties, committees, and leaders differ among state legislatures, as does the degree of "professionalization" among legislators themselves. The roles of state court systems vary according to the contents of state constitutions as well as state political and judicial traditions. In some states, the state's highest court plays a role that may be roughly comparable to that of the United States Supreme Court at the national level. The highest courts in most states, however, are generally less prominent. States also differ in whether judges are elected or appointed. With respect to policy-making and government as a whole, some states allow for direct citizen involvement through the devices of initiative, referendum, and recall, while others do not. Many of these structural details of state governments are spelled out in each state's written constitution, although state constitutions generally do not play as prominent or symbolically important a role in state government as the United States Constitution does in national government.

Local governments do not incorporate the traditional three-branch structure of government to the extent that state and national governments do. Legislative and executive powers are often given to a single governing body, with the members choosing one of themselves to be the nominal chief executive. For example, school boards typically elect their own board "president" to preside over meetings, but they hire a professional educational administrator, called a superintendent, to manage day-to-day affairs. What is true of school districts also applies to many other local governments. In contrast, the structures of some "strong mayor" cities do resemble the executive-

legislative arrangements in national and state governments. The traditional notion of an independent local judiciary as a "third branch" does not easily apply at the level of local government. Local courts, to the extent they exist, do not restrain the other branches of local government in the way that state and national courts are empowered to restrain their respective legislative and executive branches. As with state judges, some local judges are appointed and some are elected.

This unit on institutions is organized along traditional legislative, executive, and judicial lines. The first section treats state and local legislatures, which include town meetings, city and town councils, school boards, and, of course, state legislatures. The second section turns to governors and local government executives. The third section treats state and local courts, and the last section considers miscellaneous institutions and related matters that appear on the state and local landscape.

Looking Ahead: Challenge Questions

Compare and contrast the positions of president of a school board, elected chief executive of a small town, city manager, mayor of a large city, state governor, and president of the United States.

Compare and contrast the positions of school board member, member of a town meeting, town council member in a small town, city council member in a large city, state legislator, and member of the United States House of Representatives.

Get a copy of your state constitution and read it. How does it compare and contrast with the United States Constitution—in length, subjects covered, ease of reading, and familiarity?

Attend a meeting of your local school board. What was the meeting like? Did the meeting seem to consist of formally enacting decisions already made or of genuine give-and-take before board members actually made up their minds?

How many state governors and state legislators can you name? Do you feel you know enough about your own state governor and your representatives in your home state legislature to evaluate their performance?

Is it better to have well-paid and prestigious elected

positions as in the national government, or less well paid, part-time elected posts as are common in local governments and many state legislatures? Which makes for better government?

Do you think that it is a good idea to let citizens participate directly in the policy process by means of initiatives, referenda, or town meetings? Or is it better to leave legislating to elected representatives? Why?

In 1990, three states—Oklahoma, California, and Colorado—passed referenda establishing "term limits" for their state legislatures. In 1992, more than a dozen other states followed suit. What effects on the functioning of the state legislatures in these states do you expect term limits to have? Do you think it is a good idea to limit the number of terms or length of years that individuals can serve in one house of a state legislature? What about term limits for members of town councils, city councils, county councils, school boards, and other such elected bodies at the local level? Do you think that term limits will be put into operation in still more states? Why or why not?

The Legislature 2010: Which Direction?

Legislatures have made significant advances in the past 20 years. While some still have a ways to go, others are grappling with the question of whether they've gone too far.

Rich Jones

Rich Jones is NCSL's director of legislative programs.

Will legislatures in the 21st century be just like the U.S. Congress—full-time, professional bodies with long sessions, large personal staffs, career politicians and expensive media campaigns? Or will they be the more traditional, part-time legislatures with shorter sessions, smaller central staff organizations and members who hold down other jobs?

As is the case today, there are apt to be some of each. But lawmakers—and citizens—are more likely to decide consciously on a direction for their institution by taking stock of how the reforms of 20 years ago are affecting them today.

To a large extent, the modern state legislature is a product of reforms advocated by the legislative modernization movement in the mid-1960s. At that time, a series of studies conducted by universities, foundations and the Citizens Conference on State Legislatures characterized legislatures as ineffective, "sometime governments" that played little if any role in the development of state policy. They were not representative of the citizenry as a whole, met infrequently, experienced high rates of turn-

over among the members and depended for information almost exclusively on lobbyists and the executive branch. Partly because they were part-time bodies—in 1966, 30 states held biennial sessions—governors pretty much ran the show.

To correct these shortcomings, reformers advocated transforming state legislatures into more professional institutions. They recommended expanding the amount of time legislatures spent in session, providing legislatures with staff, improving legislative facilities, increasing lawmakers' pay, passing open meeting laws to make it easier for the public to participate in the process, improving legislative budget procedures to provide greater oversight of the executive branch and adopting statutes governing ethics and conflicts of interest.

The reformers succeeded; state legislatures are stronger. In 1988, there were over 33,000 staffers working in state legislatures, 40 percent of them full-time professionals. In 1990, all but seven states met in annual sessions. Legislative compensation has been increased in most states (although barely keeping pace with inflation) and legislators in 42 states are eligible for retirement benefits and in 46 states receive various insurance benefits such as health and hospitalization. The turnover in state legislatures has declined

from almost 40 percent in state houses during the 1950s to 28 percent in the early 1980s. In 1988, almost one out of every five legislators viewed the legislature as a career.

As a result of these changes, legislatures have been able to develop innovative state policies in areas as diverse as education reform, economic development, health care and the delivery of social services. The Kentucky General Assembly, for example, adopted a sweeping education reform and finance bill in 1990, and while Congress is at a stalemate, legislatures in Arizona, Iowa and Oregon have passed comprehensive groundwater protection statutes. During the coming decade, legislatures are likely to build upon their current policymaking capability to take on even more responsibilities. As they do, the already substantial demands on their time and attention will increase. How legislatures deal with these growing demands will determine the type of institutions they will become in the 21st century.

Legislators, political scientists and other observers point to current trends that suggest legislatures are on the path to becoming full-time, professional bodies like the U.S. Congress. Alan Rosenthal, director of the Institute of Politics at Rutgers University, observes

From *State Legislatures*, July 1990, pp. 22-24. Copyright © 1990, National Conference of State Legislatures.

that "state legislatures are entering an era of congressionalization. If legislatures do not attend to the drift in where they are going institutionally, legislatures in a majority of the states will resemble mini–congresses." Rosenthal cites as evidence of this trend the growing number of full-time legislators, the rising costs of campaigns, the amount of time lawmakers must devote to fund raising and the decentralization of power within state legislatures, with individual members getting stronger and legislative leaders getting weaker.

Lawmakers such as Representative John Martin, speaker of the Maine House, and Kansas Senate Majority Leader Fred Kerr feel that pressures on modern legislatures are pushing them toward full-time status. "Kansas is in a free fall toward a full-time legislature," says Kerr. "You cannot have a commitment to a family and a complicated business and still serve in the legislature."

This trend toward full-time legislatures is not affecting all states uniformly. States can be grouped into three broad categories based on their level of professionalization such as time spent in session, legislative compensation, the amount of staff and turnover among the members. Using these criteria California, Illinois, Massachusetts, Michigan, New York, Ohio, Pennsylvania and Wisconsin are currently considered to be full-time, professional legislatures. There are 17 states that have purely part-time legislatures—New Hampshire, Nevada, Vermont and Wyoming, for example. Because such states have relatively small, rural, homogeneous populations with traditions of limited government, these legislatures are not likely to become full-time in the near future. In between are the 25 states whose legislatures have some full-time characteristics but not all.

"Over the next decade, the most interesting legislatures to observe will be those that fall in the vast middle between the professional and amateur extremes," writes Burdett A. Loomis, political science professor at the University of Kansas. "It is in these bodies where the tensions between the full-time legislature and the citizen legislature will play out most dramatically."

And these tensions are likely to run high. The notion of a full-time professional legislature is diametrically opposed to the traditional model in which citizens from all walks of life come

to the Capitol to conduct the people's business and then return to their other jobs.

Sentiment is strong among many legislators and some political scientists that the traditional, citizen-based legislature works best and should be preserved. They argue that these bodies are more representative of the general population, contain members who bring "real world" experience to the legislature and, because these members have to go back and live in that real world, provide a valuable, pragmatic perspective on issues. In addition, because their livelihood does not depend on their legislative salaries, members in traditional legislatures are more likely than their full-time colleagues to take greater risks by supporting responsible but unpopular positions that might cost them re-election.

At a recent conference on the future of state legislatures cosponsored by the National Conference of State Legislatures and the Eagleton Institute of Politics, the participants—current and former legislators, political scientists and media representatives—generally agreed that legislatures should try to avoid becoming highly professional bodies like the U.S. Congress. These observers thought the inability of congressional leaders to forge consensus on important issues such as the budget deficit, sky-high campaign costs, a heavy reliance on staff, and career members who become entrenched incumbents, make Congress a less than enviable model to follow. "There is a growing fear that the problems in Congress are moving into our own general assemblies," says Senator Steve Johnson of Indiana. "We need to find ways to avoid following the congressional model." One of the recommendations that came out of the conference was for legislators to consider closely any changes that would have the effect of increasing the professionalization of their legislatures.

But have the issues grown too complex and the time demands on legislators increased to the point that part-time service is unworkable in many states? Budgets in several states exceed those of some countries. As state bureaucracies have grown, so has the public's need for assistance in getting services. Difficult issues such as how to provide affordable health care to all the

people who need it, how to protect workers and the environment from hazardous pollutants while balancing the need to protect jobs, and how to finance and repair our aging infrastructure will require lawmakers who have the time, expertise and savvy to craft imaginative solutions. Will legislatures comprised of part-time members who meet for 30, 60 or 90 days a year be up to these tasks? If not, it is likely that the public will look to the governor, the courts or the initiative process to address their concerns.

"The central problem remains today what it was, in many ways, 20 years ago," writes Loomis, "how to balance the value of a citizen legislature against the need for enhanced expertise and experience in dealing with the increasingly large, difficult and complex problems facing the states."

Because of the strong emotional and philosophical commitment to the traditional part-time model, it is likely that legislatures will resist the trends pushing them toward full-time status. During the 1990s, legislatures are likely to experiment with various ways to improve the efficiency of their operations in an attempt to be effective without devoting any more time to legislative business.

Since 1985, studies aimed at improving legislative operations have been conducted in Alaska, Florida, Kansas, Minnesota, Nevada and Washington. A central focus of these studies was the question of time and how state legislatures can best use it. They emphasized the broad support for the traditional citizen legislature, recommended eliminating inefficient and ineffective procedures and advocated improving committee scheduling, holding more joint meetings between house and senate committees, strengthening interim committees and handling noncontroversial bills more efficiently as ways to make the legislature more effective.

In addition to streamlining and improving their procedures, legislatures in the 1990s are likely to use technology to increase their productivity. One of the objectives of the study of the Florida House of Representatives was to establish state-of-the-art technological solutions to problems of organization, administration and operations. The Michigan Senate has recently installed computers on the floor for every senator who wanted one. They can vote through the computer, review the bill being considered, as well as proposed amendments, send and receive messages through an electronic mail system and access the computer system in their offices to draft correspondence and communicate with their staff. California and New Jersey link computer systems in district offices with the main information system at the Capitol. A special task force in the Delaware House of Representatives is examining the use of fax machines, improved telecommunication systems and computers linking the legislators' homes to the Capitol as ways of increasing the effectiveness of their mostly part-time members.

But legislatures can only squeeze so much wasted time from the current process. The trends pushing legislatures toward becoming full-time institutions are strong and, as issues become more complex, are likely to get stronger.

"Legislatures have made considerable progress with respect to their competence in policymaking and the power they exert," says Rosenthal. "They want to continue to be professional as a legislature while avoiding complete careerism as legislators."

Although they want to resist this movement, it will be hard, because the problems confronting the states are not always open to quick solutions. Legislatures that meet in short regular sessions often must hold special sessions to complete their work. In Colorado and Oklahoma, for example, voters adopted constitutional amendments in 1988 shortening their legislative sessions. Both legislatures met in special session in 1989 to resolve issues left over from the regular session. Texas, which technically meets in regular session for 140 days every other year, has been in session over 270 days in 1989-90, holding three special sessions in 1989 and at least three in 1990.

When sessions convene in the year 2011 there are likely to be more full-time legislatures than in 1990, and fewer purely part-time bodies. The states in the middle of these two extremes, while not yet full-time, will likely be headed in that direction.

AN EMBATTLED INSTITUTION

Alan Ehrenhalt

There is no better symbol for the irony of the modern legislature than the mugging that it got in Orlando last August.

For six days, 1,500 state legislators—nearly a quarter of all the legislators in America—gathered there for a series of speeches and workshops and panel discussions whose titles themselves tell us just how specialized and technical the work of their institutions has become: The Potential Effects of Federal Financial Regulatory Overhaul; States' Rights and Insurance Antitrust; Automating a Clerk's Office; Legislative Cutback Management.

While they were slogging through those sessions, a horde of reporters who had followed them from home did what they could to turn the meeting—the 17th annual meeting of the National Conference of State Legislatures—into a scandal.

A Tennessee TV station caught the state House speaker at a Sunday morning golf game, shot pictures of members' families relaxing around a swimming pool, and returned to broadcast a report labeling the whole affair as one long party at taxpayers' expense. A Minnesota reporter went undercover to find out what her state's House speaker ordered for dinner at an Orlando hotel, then reported every detail of food, wine and expense.

The New York *Daily News* ran the words "Disney World" in screaming letters on its front page, with a story inside accusing the legislators of "slipping a Mickey to taxpayers" by spending six days in Orlando at public expense. The delegation from Pennsylvania could have predicted that; the previous week, they had been taunted in the capitol by disgruntled state workers chanting the Mickey Mouse club theme song.

It was all a political nightmare. And yet it was one that none of the legislators had to work very hard to understand. They were meeting in the middle of a very embarrassing legislative year, one in which nearly every state faced painful budget cuts and/or tax increases, and sev-

eral—including Pennsylvania—had to endure weeks of angry bickering past the mid-year fiscal deadline before approving budgets that few leaders even bothered to defend. It was also a year in which voters all over the country read about the antics of legislators in Arizona and South Carolina who advertised their corruption and greed on tape to undercover agents of the FBI.

For America's legislatures, 1991 was a year only a cynic could love. When the members took off for Orlando in August, accompanied by more than 6,000 staffers, lobbyists and relatives and financed by taxpayers' money, they might have known what was coming. True, the location was what set it off. Had the NCSL met in Cincinnati, where they are gong next year, or in Tulsa, where they went two years ago, there would have been no Mickey Mouse headlines and few accusations of junketing. Still, nearly everyone who went to Orlando came back acknowledging that there was a problem. It was a simple problem: As a group, the country was sick of them.

In the weeks after the Mickey Mouse debacle, Karl T. Kurtz, the NCSL state services director, provided figures to document the extent of the problem. In 1968, asked about the job their legislature was doing, a cross-section of people surveyed in six states had responded positively 50 percent of the time. By 1990, in seven states, the number had fallen to 30 percent. Early returns from 1991 placed it at 28 percent. "The hard fact," Kurtz concluded, "is that legislatures as institutions do not rate well in the public's eye."

That conclusion isn't likely to knock anyone out of his chair. In the past 20 years, public confidence in virtually all public institutions has declined. Legislatures, in fact, do considerably better than Congress in most surveys. The erosion of public support is no surprise. What is interesting is the irony. Of all the institutions under attack, only legislatures can seriously claim to have reformed away most of the specific weaknesses critics confronted them with a generation ago.

To say that is to invite disbelief from millions of voters who have watched their legislators wallow in scandal and stalemate over the past year. The only way to challenge that skepticism is to invite people to consider what legislatures used to be like. A tour of American legislatures in 1961, as opposed to 1991, would have found some stories disturbing enough to make a week at Disney World lose significance very quickly.

A tourist in Alabama in those days would have found a legislature managed and all but owned by the state's timber companies and big farm owners, refusing to create any new programs or establish any new services that would result in increased taxes on land. At the capitol, he would have watched legislators as they ate, drank and misbehaved in public in the House and Senate chambers, each body forced to do all its business in one noisy, raucous room because there was no such thing as office space. The most powerful legislators, all of whom were white, came from overwhelmingly black counties, where a handful of white voters decided the election because blacks were not allowed to vote, let alone hold office.

In Colorado, the same tourist would have watched a different corps of rural members systematically deprive the state's growing cities of the rights they were entitled to by population. As late as the mid-1960s, blatant malapportionment allowed this clique to steal Denver's highway money and restrict its authority to tax railroads. There was a crowd like this in every legislature: It was the "cowboys club" in Colorado; the "Pork Chop Gang" in Florida. It was a flat denial of equal protection.

In Connecticut, the tourist would have encountered an assemblage of docile, fearful party hacks, beholden to the party chairman for patronage and renomination and unwilling to cast a vote or say a word that might place either one in jeopardy. But there was little to see in Connecticut, since most of the important decisions were made in small private meetings to which the public, like most of the rank-and-file members, was not invited.

California offered the spectacle of an institution in which huge combines of lobbyists made and unmade legislative careers, and money was known to change hands on the chamber floor. Everyone knew the stories about the legendary Arthur Samish, who proclaimed, "I am the governor of the legislature; to hell with the governor of California." Arthur Samish was a liquor lobbyist.

Those were, more or less, the legislatures of a generation ago. They were, to put it bluntly, racist, sexist, secretive, boss-ruled, malapportioned and uninformed. But there was no great public outcry against any of those conditions. The Alabama legislature, ranked in a Ford Foundation study in 1971 as 50th out of 50 in independence, 50th in accountability and 48th overall performance, had been judged favorably just three years earlier by 65 percent of the respondents to a statewide poll. In 1990, freed of its racism, secrecy and malapportionment, fully equipped to gather information and operating in a new, state-of-the-art legislative facility, it got an approval rating of 24 percent.

It might seem that the public is somehow attempting to repudiate a generation of reforms it once believed in. But the truth is that the public was not all that heavily involved in the reforms of the 1970s. Legislatures changed not through popular disgust but through the proposals of their own reformist leaders and elite critics. Jesse M. Unruh, speaker of the California Assembly in the early 1960s, inaugurated the movement by raising salaries (to attract a core of dedicated and serious members) and bringing in a professional staff (to gather the information that could compete with that supplied by lobbyists and the executive branch). Larry Margolis, a one-time Unruh aide, took this movement national by creating the Citizens' Conference on State Legislatures, and the Ford Foundation provided the money for its efforts. By 1971, rating every legislature in the country on five standards of effectiveness, the reform movement was gaining influence almost everywhere.

To read *The Sometime Governments* today is to come to one inescapable conclusion: Virtually everything it recommends has been done. Salaries, staffing, information, better facilities, open meetings, public access—by the mid-1980s just about all of it was in place.

And what was the public reaction to all of this change? An NCSL report summarized it in 1985: "The modern full-time legislature envisioned by the reformers of the 1960s and 1970s has not fulfilled its promise," the report concludes. "A lack of trust has created a gap between legislatures and the public."

That was six years ago. Since then, reform has continued to spread: It has reached some of the smaller and less sophisticated state capitols that its first wave did not penetrate. Meanwhile, however, the public image of the legislature has grown worse.

The incongruity of it all is not lost on those who participated in the original reform effort, such as Alan Rosenthal, political scientist and director of the Eagleton Institute at Rutgers University. "Legislatures really did transform themselves," he says. "They are an institutional success story, in terms of where they were 20 years ago and where they are now. . . . It's quite ironic."

None of the people who pushed for reform 20 years ago dreamed that it would make legislatures less popular rather than more. But looking back on the whole period, it is not all that difficult to explain. Legislatures have gotten better in the context of a much more intrusive law enforcement network and an overall political system that was steadily growing pettier, more quarrelsome and more troubling.

The voters who gave legislatures a 50 percent positive rating in 1968 had not, for example, been subjected to a full decade of news stories reporting the indictment of state legislators on corruption charges, accompanied in many cases by transcripts of incriminating conversations recorded on tape. Some may attribute this to the superior virtue of that generation; others to the primitive quality of tape technology. Much more important, though, is the fact that it was very difficult to prosecute a state legislator in those days, especially for federal prosecutors, who have created most of the sensational cases of the 1980s.

In order to be convicted of mail fraud, the most potent charge in the U.S. attorney's arsenal, a public official had to be shown to have used the mails to deprive individual citizens of money or property. It was only in 1969 that the law was expanded to cover deprivation of "intangible rights," and only in the 1970s that the new weapon came into widespread use. Similarly, the Racketeer Influenced and Corrupt Organizations Act, passed in 1970, was not applied successfully to political corruption cases until the closing years of the decade.

In those early years, the idea of a tape-recorded sting operation against a whole collection of legislators was implausible legally as well as technologically. A 1978 Supreme Court ruling made it possible for prosecutors and investigators to ensnare public figures in stings without having any hard evidence of prior criminality on their part. All the nationally known political sting cases, starting with the Abscam investigation of members of Congress in 1980, would have been impossible without this 5–4 decision.

Whatever one thinks of the propriety of these intrusive law enforcement efforts, it seems safe to argue that they have been a disincentive to corruption. As one prosecutor in Oregon said last year, "It can have a deterrent effect on someone who's teetering on edge. The fact that they know there may be a local or federal law enforcement agency looking at it . . . can have a positive effect." (*See* GOVERNING, *June 1991, page 26*).

But the voter does not read about the crimes that this sort of prosecution prevents, however many they may be; he reads only about the crimes it exposes. The new impression, unsupported by common sense or solid evidence of any sort, is of a much more corrupt institution. In a 1989 survey by the *Los Angeles Times*, 53 percent of the respondents said they thought bribe-taking was a routine legislative occurrence.

If prosecutors had less capacity to discredit legislators a generation ago, the legislators had less willingness to discredit each other. Negative campaigning has a long and colorful history in American politics, but 20 years ago, the prolonged attack-and-response media barrage had not made its presence felt even in congressional elections, let alone those at the state legislative level. The voters of 1968 had not witnessed the spectacle of a candidate accusing his opponent of corruption in TV commercials one night, followed by the opponent reversing the charges the next night, with the result that one of them wins the election, but both candidates and the institution itself sustain lasting damage.

Even today, most state legislative contests do not generate this sort of televised name-calling, or any sort of television coverage at all. But it is impossible to separate the poisonous effects of negative campaigns at the congressional and statewide level from the legislatures that people see correctly as part of the same political system. Last year, when the Kettering Foundation conducted its now-famous study of the mood of the American voters, one of the most frequent complaints dealt with the name-calling that they see as pervading the entire political system. A man in Richmond, Virginia, explained the whole system in very simple terms: "Whoever slings the most mud wins." There is no way to prevent judgments like those from coloring perceptions of the institution that candidates sling mud in order to join.

Most of the voters of the 1960s lived in states where one party controlled both the executive and legislative branches at a given time. This did not preclude a fair amount of public bickering, but it was an amount that has been vastly multiplied in the years since then by the growing American preference for divided government. Through most of the 1980s, more than two-thirds of Americans lived in states where one party held the governorship and the other controlled at least one legislative chamber. This is a recipe for public squabbling, as Maine, Pennsylvania, Michigan and a host of other states demonstrated in 1991. When, as in Maine, the democratic speaker labels the Republican governor an unprincipled opportunist, and the governor makes it clear he considers the speaker an arrogant autocrat, the natural tendency of many voters is to believe both of them—and to think less of the legislature in the bargain.

Taken together, these three changes in the political system—divided government, negative campaigning and recurring scandal—might well be enough to explain the declining reputation of legislatures in the 1990s.

But they are not its only causes. Besides being victims of an altered political and legal system, legislatures are casualties of long-term economic decline. They are having to contend with problems that did not exist in the days when they themselves were sick but the economy was relatively healthy. "Maybe we're getting better," says John Brandl, a veteran Minnesota legislator who retired this year, "but the problems are getting worse faster than we are getting better."

The legislatures of the 1960s demonstrated conclusively that they were ill-equipped to handle the issues of that decade. Had the issues stood still, the reformed legislatures of the 1990s might reasonably be expected to be able to deal with them. But of course the issues have not stood still. The legislator of 1991 is operating in the context of a stagnant economy, declining real income for most working-class and middle-class citizens, a discredited public school system and a drug epidemic in nearly every large city.

Voters expect legislatures to solve those problems—candidates promise to solve them—and yet the basic intractability of the problems makes it hard to imagine any vote of confidence for legislators in the foreseeable future, no matter how earnestly any of them might be attempting to work on solutions. "Legislatures reflect society," argues William Pound, executive director of NCSL, "and what they reflect now is a confused and frustrated and angry society." At its deepest level, the anger that has erupted against legislatures and politicians in the past few years has been an anger against the conditions of life in the 1990s. It is hard to think of a legislative reform that would dissolve that.

But it is possible to think of reforms that might make it worse. What gnaws at many of the most thoughtful legislators these days—including those who organized a rather somber NCSL conference in Annapolis, Maryland, in November on "State Legislatures in the 21st Century"—is the idea that their institutions are unpopular not so much in spite of the reforms of the past two decades, but because of them.

This is the "careerism" argument: that as legislatures have evolved into full-time professional bodies, they have produced members whose obsession with politics and holding office collides with sensible long-term public policy. John Brandl likes to tell the disturbing story of a senior colleague in the Minnesota legislature, eager to retire in middle age but lacking any work credentials or experience in private life, who hangs on term after term and is an easy mark for special interests that threaten him with a campaign challenge if he does not vote their way.

Brandl was one of a surprising number of respected legislators at that Annapolis meeting who didn't dismiss term limits as a crazy idea. He likes the notion of a two-house legislature in which one chamber features strict limits on the number of terms a member can serve while the other chamber imposes none at all. Barry Keene, the majority leader of the California Senate and one who will eventually be forced to retire by that state's term-limit law, has made his own peace with the term-limit concept. He now argues that term limits will break the monopoly control exercised by safe-seat veterans, and that newcomers elected in more competitive districts will be forced to respond to a more diverse array of interests.

For all that debate and speculation, however, the fact remains that term limits are not a reform most members or most students of American legislatures are interested in. Nor do many of those who are willing to consider them believe that they would have much effect on the public perception of the institution. So when it comes to improving the long-term legislative image, they are forced to turn elsewhere for solutions.

Ideas are floating around. There is, for example, old-fashioned public relations. Individual members burnish their reputations by promoting themselves in the media. Entire legislatures could do the same. The speaker of the Tennessee House, if he is concerned about bad institutional publicity, could commission a series of television ads outlining all the positive things the legislature has been up to over the course of the year. Money could be raised to pay for them. This notion comes up at least half-seriously a few times in any sustained discussion of the image problem.

It is difficult, however, to find legislators who believe such a paid media campaign would have much credibility with the voters. A legislature that needs to spend money touting its accomplishments is inherently suspect in most people's eyes.

There remains, of course, the news media. Every conference on the subject of legislatures and their future includes at least one impassioned plea from an elected official to his colleagues to do a better job of educating reporters on the way legislatures work and the complexity of the whole process. Some states have been doing this quite well for a long time. Throughout the 1980s, the Minnesota legislature held periodic "media days" in which legislators and reporters discussed their mutual needs and problems in a setting removed from the pressure of daily business. Pennsylvania House Speaker Robert O'Donnell tells his legislators that they must learn to think like reporters if they expect to get anything useful out of the relationship.

At bottom, however, these are exercises in damage control. The adversarial relationship between press and politician has become deeply entrenched in nearly every state capitol in the past two decades and is not going to go away. Years of sensitivity sessions between legislators and the media in Minnesota did not prevent a reporter from that state from splashing the story about the speaker's Orlando convention dinner expenses all over the front pages last summer.

However shrewd legislators may become in their dealings with the press, the vast majority of them agree with Robert O'Donnell when he says that the media are "one of the most destructive forces in American society." It is hard to see how, given that attitude of mutual suspicion, the press can be much of a partner in the rehabilitation of the institutional image.

One aspect of the public relations problem is changing, however: Technology is creating ways in which legislators can take their case to the public without benefit of the media or old-fashioned advertising. Martin Linsky, who has been both a Massachusetts legislator and a newspaper editor and now teaches government at Harvard, is a crusader on this subject. He wants legislators to go around the media with cable TV programs, hot lines, satellite town meetings, interactive computer hookups and every other new communications device that can be harnessed to public-relations use. A decade or so of this, Linsky believes, and the understanding of legislatures—if not necessarily the approval—will be much higher than it is now.

Even fully wired for the 21st Century, however, legislatures need to have something to take to the public besides the story of their institutional processes. Some of the experiences of 1991 suggest what the most effective public relations weapon might be: some simple and not very subtle moves in the direction of ethics reform.

Early in the 1991 session of the Wisconsin Assembly, Speaker Walter Kunicki—never identified as an outspoken reformer before—took the conspicuous step of banning lobbyists from the Assembly chamber. The response was overwhelming, both in the press and among the public. Legislators from all over the state returned to Madison reporting that voters had sought them out to tell them what a good job they thought Kunicki was doing.

A little later in the year, the Kansas legislature created a new ethics commission and stipulated that no one who had held public office in the state for the previous three years would be allowed to serve on it. Most veteran officials made fun of the newly created body, some referring to it in public as the "eunuchs only" commission. But the citizens loved it.

It seems clear that changes like those really do have an effect on the image of a legislature. The drawback, of course, is that they wear off very quickly and possess very little substantive significance. But they lead quite a few members to speculate that some form of meaningful campaign finance reform, reducing the role of private money in the election process, might have an impact that would last for years. "If we had meaningful campaign finance reform," says Representative Elliott Naishtat of Texas, "we wouldn't be talking about term limits right now."

No doubt some combination of public relations devices and conspicuous reform efforts could be found that would boost the public image of American legislatures closer to where it was a generation ago.

But all the outreach in the world is not going to make citizens love their legislatures anytime soon—not when people are so hostile to the entire political system and skeptical of its ability to solve deepening public problems. So while legislators debate ways to restore public confidence, it might make sense for them to devote equal attention to how they can best function in its absence. Quite a few of them are doing that.

The normal comity of New Mexico's easygoing legislative institution was shattered last year by a war involving members and the media that stunned politicians used to much friendlier treatment. The image of the legislature itself suffered. Rather than launch a program to turn reporters into allies, members turned inward for what they described as "survival exercises"—mutual support sessions at which leaders urged colleagues to bolster each other and the institution, rather than scoring individual political points by joining the media in attacking the institution.

This concept of survival training for besieged legislators has attracted interest all over the country, and there is certain to be more of it in the coming months. "Bonding is the in-word," Alan Rosenthal says. In many ways, it is the opposite of looking to the public for support. It is a way of seeking a substitute.

Beyond the bonding idea is the notion that what legislators need most in a time of public distrust is someone willing to set an example of political courage by taking a correct but unpopular stand and damning the consequences. That is, of course, easier said than done. But Tom Loftus, former Wisconsin Assembly speaker and 1990 gubernatorial candidate, startled legislators from all over the country in November by challenging them to "take a dive" for something they believe in. "I think it is now time," Loftus said, "for good people to lose—purposely—so good things happen. Someone needs to take a dive because they showed courageous leadership on an issue that counts."

There is no reason to expect any large-scale diving exhibitions in American legislatures anytime soon. People who work hard for election are unlikely to throw their seats away in pursuit of lost causes, however noble. Still, the fact that Loftus issued his challenge—and that the audience took it seriously—suggests the sort of frustration some of the brightest legislators are feeling at a moment when problems seem intractable and voters uniformly unsympathetic.

John Brandl sympathizes with Loftus. An economist by training, he helped to found the Hubert H. Humphrey Institute of Public Affairs at the University of Minnesota, left it in the 1970s to run for the legislature, then returned to it this year after serving in both the state Senate and the state House. Brandl retired from politics convinced that the way for legislatures to earn respect in the long run is to stop being so parochial. "The problem," he says, "isn't corruption, it's narrow-mindedness."

When Brandl was a member of the Senate leadership, and members used to seek his advice, he urged them to ask themselves what James Madison would have done. "What if we just didn't accept the argument that you vote your district?" he likes to ask. What if every state senator somehow could be made to keep his eye on the good of the state?

Well, what if that happened? What if today's parochial careerist legislators somehow turned into statesmen? What if legislatures finally started to work the way Jesse Unruh believed they could? Would the voters finally learn to love the legislatures?

No, Brandl says. "Not in America."

Running a Town the 17th-Century Way

Government by town meeting may be obsolete. But be careful when you say that in New England.

Shirley Elder

Shirley Elder, who used to spend her days in the U.S. Capitol covering Congress, now attends the town meeting in Center Sandwich, New Hampshire.

In hundreds of New England towns this month, in the chill and the bluster of late winter, men and women in bulky jackets and sturdy boots will be stomping onto the wooden floors of small frame buildings, keeping intact a thread of representative democracy that runs all the way back to colonial America. They will be going to town meeting.

It is a tradition worth celebrating. Every few years, a panel of experts somewhere pronounces the imminent death of the town meeting as obsolete, archaic, unworkable. It is, after all, a system of government that depends on decisions by local citizens meeting once a year, nearly always in March and only in New England, and thrashing out critical issues such as when to plow roads and how much to spend on recycling at the dump. It is decidedly unprofessional.

But the system lives on, remarkably resilient. More than 1,300 towns in the six New England states will do their civic business in town meetings this month in a process that dates to the Massachusetts Bay Colony in the

mid-1600s. In those days, attendance was open only to men. It was also mandatory, and absentees were fined. Thomas Jefferson, whose home state of Virginia did not use the town meeting, nevertheless hailed it as "the wisest invention ever devised by the wit of man for the perfect exercise of government."

Perfection, of course, is a lot to ask, especially over time. In recent years, some towns, in a nod to the complexities of modern life, have been changing the process. Nearly half the towns in Vermont open the polls a day after town meeting to give people a chance to vote on the budget. It's called the "Australian ballot": no discussion, just a vote.

For many New England towns that cling to the town meeting tradition, it represents much of what they consider best in their community life.

Larger towns—one in Maine, one in Vermont, six in Connecticut and 46 in Massachusetts—have shifted to a "representative" town meeting, where delegates are elected to attend

the meeting instead of inviting the whole town. Most of Connecticut's 169 towns limit their meetings to budget questions and leave other policy decisions to selectmen. All in all, though, a remarkable number of places still operate in something resembling the old-fashioned way. Even in sophisticated, computer-driven Massachusetts, where most municipal government options have been tried somewhere at some time, 80 percent of the towns still follow the old colonial open-meeting tradition.

Where the system has changed, the reason has usually been growth. As towns grow larger, issues become more complex and the percentage who turn out for the meeting falls. Frank Bryan, a political scientist at the University of Vermont, has found that average attendance, in towns under 2,500, drops by 2 or 3 percentage points with each increase of 100 registered voters.

And there is a point somewhere, an elusive point, where a town meeting, assembled only once a year, simply can't handle the essential business without professional help. John B. Andrews of the New Hampshire Municipal Association has his own way of defining when the old way is no longer practical. "If you get to the point where the budget is complex enough you can't figure it on the back of an envelope," he says, then it may be time to think about more professional government.

Towns tend to fight those realities as long as they can. For many of them, town meeting represents a great deal of what they consider best in their community life. That is as true of naturalized New Englanders as it is of the natives. "I'm biased," says Edmund Jansen, an economist who lives in the town of Rollinsford, New Hampshire (population 2,629). "I'm a Midwesterner who came here and became enamored with the town meeting form of government. It gives people a chance to be involved, and all it takes is time. . . . If you're interested in participatory de-

mocracy, then this is one of its purest forms."

Jansen liked the system so much he became part of it, serving as selectman in Rollinsford for 16 years and now as president of the New Hampshire Municipal Association. "With town meetings," he says, "you vote issue by issue. I can vote liberal on one issue and conservative on another, and get my voice heard. If I vote only for a representative, I have to take whatever comes."

Jansen, too, concedes there is a time when town meetings in more populous communities begin to be unworkable. "Once you get to 10,000 people or so," he says, "you have to

go professional." But in the environment of village New England, he insists, the town meeting approach is as practical as ever. Distances are short and people run into each other so frequently that most questions are fully discussed long before the gavel falls on that one day in March.

John Andrews concedes that, amid all the complications of modern society, town meetings may eventually fade away. But if so, he predicts, they will fade away at a comfortingly slow pace. "I think reports of the death of town meetings are premature. Maybe people like them as an historical artifact. I don't know. But town meetings will be with us for a long, long time."

Practicing Political Science on a Local School Board

Gerald M. Pomper

*Eagleton Institute, Rutgers University
Gerald Pomper is professor of political science at Rutgers and director of the Center on Political parties at the University's Eagleton Institute of Politics. Normally engaged in research on American politics, including* The Election of 1984 *(1985), he is now preoccupied with the most critical current campaign—winning voter approval of the annual school budget.*

If politics is the art of the possible, political scientists have much to learn through the practice of government. Accepting this premise, many political scientists, following the example of Charles Merriam, have taken on political and governmental jobs. In this informal article, I want to report on my own experience.

My involvement is minor—one member of a nine-person school board, in a small community of 14,000 people and 1,600 students, with an annual budget of $8 million. The scope is relatively small, but I still find the lessons I have learned widely applicable. I have been particularly gratified to find that political science *is* relevant. The small matters that constitute the work of a small political entity have been illuminated by the generalizations of the discipline. In turn, these experiences have deepened my knowledge of political science—and provided good illustrative material for my courses.

I will briefly deal with four subjects: elections, interest groups, bureaucratic politics, and the political community. Inevitably, this is a personal report, but still, I hope, one that will be of more than parochial interest.

Getting Elected

School boards are voluntary and unpaid bodies. There are few "self-starters" and political parties usually refrain from involvement. "Recruitment," in this case, is not only a category of analysis, but a reality. Probably like most candidates, I was asked to run, and had to be persuaded.

Once committed to the race, however, the campaign becomes as personally absorbing and important as a contest for offices with far greater power and personal rewards. It almost seemed as if I were running for president—but in an alternate universe in which every political variable had been compressed to microscopic size. Fundraising and spending limits were important, even though the legal limit on expenditures was only $1,000. We considered gender balance, and concluded that I had an advantage over my female opponent when five of the other eight positions on the Board were already filled by women. Discussions of means to attract the "black vote," the "Catholic vote," etc. were as earnest as any in the Democratic National Committee. The difference was that we were talking about how to win support from 50 blacks, or 500 Catholics, not millions.

Once sworn into office, I found myself in still another universe, a pluralistic world apparently designed by David Truman.

These small numbers underlined the truth of the old adage, "All politics is local." One of my unofficial "campaign managers" persuasively argued that every campaign is an effort to establish a personal tie between the candidate and each voter. Presidential candidates must do this artificially, by bogus personal letters and media messages. In a school board campaign, where 800 ballots would probably win, I could realistically hope to reach every voter. On the strategic level, this fact meant targeting specific individuals. Tactically, it led to an hour of telephoning every night for a month, holding

20 informal coffees for groups of as few as three people and no more than 15, and shaking hands for hours at the local supermarket, our functional equivalent of the traditional general store.

Personal contact is more important than I had believed. Early in the campaign, I went to a meeting of parents favoring an all-day kindergarten, one of the most visible school issues. By attending and declaring my support, I hoped to win the support of this group of voters—and to counter the appeal of my opponent, who had been one of the prime advocates of the program. The next day, however, I learned that I had lost rather than won votes, despite my being scored "right" on the issues. My mistake was in leaving the meeting at its formal end. What the parents had wanted was not only my programmatic support, but personal contact, the opportunity to "schmooz," and "press the flesh." After that, I never left a meeting until the hostess began yawning.

In these meetings, I deepened my understanding of the impact of issues on voting behavior. Educational issues are quite specific, proximate, and personal. Parents are often the true experts when it comes to the needs of their children, and parents of schoolchildren (and resident teachers) are the essential constituency in a school election. As a result, public opinion is highly informed, and a candidate must be both knowledgeable and ready to learn. At the same time, the voters I met seemed to me to be realistic in their expectations. They knew that no elected official could solve even the small problems of one school district and were willing to allow discretion and to follow leadership. In short, I found no "democratic distemper" but a healthy dialogue.

The effective place for citizen control is the budget.

Most generally, I came to value elections in a personal way that reinforced

Reprinted from *PS*, Vol. XVII, No. 2, Spring 1984, pp. 220-225. Copyright © 1983 by The American Political Science Association. Reprinted by permission.

my academic appreciation. We have long known about the "arrogance of power," and academicians often have inflated egos. But in the voting booth, all women and men are equal—and you, as a candidate eagerly want their approval. I spent four hours one evening listening to three people tell me about the decline of morality in contemporary society (i.e., beer bottle on the high school football field) and the extravagance of government (i.e., the cost of lettuce for home economics classes). Yet, despite the fact that I held a Ph.D. and have taught for 25 years, I listened respectfully to them. Once elected, I was eager to support policies to bar drinking from school grounds and to reduce food purchasing bills. On large as well as trivial matters the dependence of elected officials on their constituents makes them responsive to their democratic masters. Mill, I found, was right: "Rulers and ruling classes are under a necessity of considering the interests of those who have the suffrage; but of those who are excluded, it is in their option whether they will do so or not."

Interest Group Politics

Once sworn into office, I found myself in still another universe, a pluralistic world apparently designed by David Truman. Decisions often depended on the resolution of conflicts between self-interested groups. Intensity and proximity made some groups more influential than their numbers warranted, but considerations of the general public interest did have an impact.

One example is provided by our biennial negotiations for a teacher contract. Despite the decline in the national rate of inflation and despite a comparatively high salary schedule, the premise of our negotiations was that a settlement would require at least an annual seven percent increase in teacher salaries. The teachers were the only organized interest group involved. Moreover, many of their members were local voters, and their cooperation was obviously central to any improvement in the schools. Parents, the only other obvious interest group, typified Walter Lippmann's "phantom public"—wanting a resolution of the conflict and unwilling to deal with specific issues in dispute. The "general interest" may have been that of the taxpayers, who were already typically paying $3,000 annually in property taxes for the schools, but it was not represented specifically. Speaking for this interest, the Board was able to win some concessions that would effect future economies—but at a price.

A second case involved the sale of a school building closed as the result of declining enrollment. Two alternatives were possible—selling to a developer who would convert the building to condominium apartments or tearing it down and selling subdivided lots for single-family homes. The first option would produce the most revenue for the schools, but the loudest demands came from a handful of persons near the school, who favored single-family homes on many grounds, including the resultant increase in the value of their own property. A majority of the Board was prepared to listen to this limited public, until—following Schattschneider—the "scope of conflict" was changed. A federal mandate to equalize girls' athletic facilities suddenly required the Board to find a large new source of revenue. Forced to concentrate on the schools' own needs, the Board decided to sell to the highest bidder.

Bureaucratic Politics

Most of a school board's time is spent with professional administrators. Working full-time, versed in the educational lore and jargon, regulated and protected by state laws their colleagues often have drafted, the staff has immense advantages in any conflict with a volunteer and amateur Board. Not surprisingly, scholarly studies have found that these boards exercise relatively little real authority over the professionals. School governance sometimes is undiluted symbolic politics, a la Edelman, as boards go through impotent rituals of power. All appointments are formally made by roll-call votes, even when they involve tenured personnel who could be removed only for the most flagrant moral abuses. Similarly, each new course and each financial transaction requires a roll-call, even though the members must necessarily follow staff recommendations in almost all details.

The effective place for citizen control is the budget. As representatives of the taxpayers, who in many states vote directly on the school budget, Board members attempt to hold down spending to limit tax rates. School bureaucrats have their established routines to counter these economy drives, many of them resembling the techniques used by the Pentagon to resist cuts in defense spending. "We can't fall behind the Russians" is a slogan that can be employed to buy either multi-warhead missiles or the newest science texts. "Most of the increase is due to inflation" can explain expensive tanks or new $45 basketballs. As we know from Wildavsky, bureaucrats build budgets incrementally, assuming that past expenditures are unquestionable, and that only new spending for the coming fiscal year requires discussion.

The best technique to use in this situation is to make the professional educators directly aware of the tradeoffs inherent in any social policy, including a school budget. This cannot be done by asking abstractly, "Which programs are of lower priority?" The answer will inevitably be that everything is indispensable, whether it is sewing in the fourth grade, calculus for a handful of advanced students, or separate whirlpools for girl and boy athletes. Instead, there must first be a total limit placed on spending, forcing prioritizing among programs and, not incidentally, providing a defense against the many particular interests that will want a "small" increase for their pet programs. Seeing the process at work, I am now far more sympathetic to such proposals as mandatory ceilings on taxes. Imposing real, even seemingly arbitrary, limits prods administrators to think creatively and to question past assumptions. When there is no new money for math courses, an additional secretary becomes less indispensable. In the end, school administrators will usually make the choices that are best for the children—but they can use some encouragement.

This strategy is particularly necessary in education policy, for school spending is likely to rise annually, whatever the level of inflation or the school enrollment. Spending groups are identifiable and organized. The basic object of this spending, our children, are the embodiment of our dearest hopes. The natural generosity we feel toward their education inherently cannot be tested against any measures of cost-effectiveness. Still more is this the case when the nation has become alarmed over "a rising tide of mediocrity" (or at least a "rising tide of reports") in the schools.

Budgets have the advantage for the citizen Board member of being tangible and precise. More difficult to control are the curriculum and administrative matters that come before the Board. On such matters, professors are likely to be misled by analogies to higher education. They believe that universities are, or at least ought to be, governed and collegial, while public schools are administered and hierarchical. Other Board members' experience may be even less relevant. In their efforts to improve the schools, most representatives follow two very different strategies—suggesting "grand ideas" ("back to basics") or dealing with very specific grievances ("Why do the buses come late on Third Avenue?"). These interventions can be very valuable, but they typically miss the middle range of activity, such as program development and implementation that comprises most of the actual management of any bureaucracy, including schools.

This pattern leaves school administrators free to shape most policy, unless a school board member is unusually pointed and persistent. (But, as Neustadt asked of presidents, how often does a Board member ask three times about the same issue?) Even then, it is hard to "command" such desired outcomes as "creative thinking" (and Neustadt reminds us how rarely direct command is used). If challenged, administrators use some common bureaucratic defenses. Delay, as I have just suggested, is one. A second is to argue that law or practice will not allow innovation, e.g., "the state (union/commissioner/insurance company) won't permit it." Lacking expertise and time for research, the Board member must usually accept the answer. Another defensive technique is over-compliance. A new policy is followed to a logical absurdity, so that the Board member learns to mind his own business. A request for information is dutifully answered by reams of paper, the mass of detail burying the Board member's original thought. In dealing with academicians, like myself, a particular variant is to cite the research literature in education. As you might guess, the reference is not necessarily enlightening.

Political science suggest some ways to deal with these problems. Here are a few recommendations. Create competing interests within the bureaucracy. Thus, if dissatisfied with the results of English instruction, establish a new "writing across the curriculum" program. Provide incentives, such as competitive awards for new teaching techniques. Rotate administrators, so that undesirably entrenched patterns are necessarily disrupted. Define issues so that the Board sets the terms of agenda, rather than the school hierarchy. For example, reduce the time devoted to woodworking by emphasizing additional language instruction, rather than debating the merits of ripsaws. Perhaps most important, remember that organizations are not simply goal-oriented groups, but are natural systems in which individual needs and interpersonal relationships must be nurtured.

The Political Community

Much of this essay suggests that school

board membership is frustrating and that the idealistic goal of educating our children faces great obstacles in voter resistance, interest group parochialism, and administrative routines. All of that is true.

Nevertheless, it is a rewarding experience, and I suspect the rewards are even greater in positions of greater responsibility. It is a learning experience, and professors can and should always learn. It is a real experience, more so than most of what we do in the classroom or research center. In our academic work, we may talk about the relative desirability of spending public money for an MX missile or a food stamps program, but we are only talking theoretically. It is quantitatively much less important, but qualitatively more meaningful, actually to find means to reduce the cost of health insurance by $50,000, so that you can begin to teach computer literacy to 1,600 students who are your friends' children and your neighbors. It is also an enlarging experience. The office-holder necessarily becomes conscious of acting, however inexpertly and bounded, on behalf of larger interests, and this feeling may be most satisfying when acting for a powerless group, such as children.

The benefits of political involvement go beyond these personal satisfactions, toward the discovery of public life in a deeper sense. As de Tocqueville warned us early, the greatest defect in American life is likely to be the lack of community, the absence of personal ties which gain meaning in common enterprises. That defect is even more apparent today, when we have necessarily delegated much of the work of government to distant sites, when we live in transient communities, when material and emotional demands force a concentration on our personal well-being.

Political life counteracts this absence of community. In holding even a minor public office, your relationships to others in the community change. Conversations are more likely to be on the general issues with which you deal. Neighbors talk not only about the weather or the grocery prices, but about the desirability of revis-

ing the science curriculum. The relationship is not less friendly or less egalitarian (there is no "power" involved), but it is more *public*, more concerned with your common lives.

That talk educates both the public official and his or her constituents. After my election, I fulfilled a campaign pledge to go back monthly to some of the homes where I had campaigned and to discuss school developments. It is a sad commentary on the trust voters have in politicians that my hosts were surprised that I bothered to return, and one assumed, incorrectly, that I was running for a new term. Otherwise, these were heartening evenings. We discussed not theories of education, but classroom instruction in the fourth grade. While I tried to explain our new program budget, I also was taught the realities of raising children in single-parent families. Amid the fun and the coffee cake, all of us learned. Madison was right in thinking that the election of representatives would "refine and enlarge the public views," but he neglected to mention the same effect of community activity upon the representatives themselves.

My experience has convinced me that there is still great potential for a public life, at least in small localities. Residents have a vast reservoir of knowledge about their towns; on one occasion, I found that there was cumulative local experience of over 200 years among ten householders on a single street. Schools—and other issues—do matter to the voters, whether they view them as past or present students, parents or grandparents, or taxpayers. And there is a desire, inexpert but warm, to "do good," for children and for the community.

Democratic political theorists have based their philosophies on such optimistic premises. In current political dialogue, however, they are often forgotten, as both academicians and electoral candidates stress self-interest and group competition. As political scientists, we might do better to teach these other lessons, not only in our schools, but to our national leaders.

Gubernatorial Styles:
Is There a Right One?

In governing, a leader's management style is less important than the ability to communicate values. There is no single management style that ensures a successful administration.

Chase Riveland

Chase Riveland is secretary of the Washington Department of Corrections. He previously served as executive director of the Colorado Department of Corrections and as deputy director of the Wisconsin Division of Corrections. He also has been a Gates Fellow at the Kennedy School of Government of Harvard University.

Leader, manager, chief executive officer, policymaker, politician, negotiator, "keeper of the vision" and chief of ceremony are roles that must be performed by the governor of a state. A governor must fulfill these roles while keeping a wary watch on political adversaries, assuring appropriate accommodation of supporters, consuming enormous amounts of written information and digesting advice from staff, legislators, interest groups and family. The governor must set an agenda, establish priorities, manage crises, assure recognition of a range of individuals, groups and causes — all while being constantly scrutinized by the media. Governors are frequently blamed publicly for all that goes wrong in a state; yet, when something goes right, legislators and others scamper to take the credit.

The governor must manage a breadth of issues and subjects that would startle the private-sector chief executive. The typical responsibilities of the business executive — financial management, labor relations, marketing and personnel management — also are core responsibilities of the governor. In addition to these core responsibilities, however, the governor must function under the constant surveillance of a large board of directors — legislators — many of whom inevitably are philosophically, politically and personally adversarial. Further complexity is added by the plethora of commissions, advisory groups and boards that inevitably help manage state government.

Frequently, one or both houses of the legislature are not controlled by the governor's political party, creating an environment of philosophical differences as well as political agendas that are more focused on the next election than on statesmanly development of sound public policy and law. Because elected state officials must run for office every two or four years, the next election is always near and the desire for political success omnipresent in the politically partisan mind. In these circumstances, political opposition to the governor may reflect more of a power struggle than an honest difference over policy. Indeed, the governor's basic responsibility to manage government often is questioned, challenged and threatened.

Public and Private Management

In most states, the number of persons appointed by and reporting to the governor would challenge the most liberal span-of-control theories. It is not at all unusual to have more than 20 prime cabinet members and a similar number of minor cabinet positions all reporting to the governor. For example, in Colorado in the early 1980s, the cabinet included at least 16 agency heads. Washington state today includes at least 20. Executive authority often is diffused intentionally by the legislature — for example, by making an executive agency responsible to a commission rather than to the governor. Such actions, while often for good cause, mitigate the executive's ability to manage.

If to manage is to control or direct, how then does a governor ensure that his or her policies, priorities, expectations and agendas are carried out? How does a governor discourage individual agendas or agency competition for funds? Concurrently, how does a governor encourage a sense of unity or direction, create a collegial approach to priorities, and take advantage of the variety of talents, perspectives and ideas that a cabinet and staff bring to bear on developing policy and managing government? Is there a singular best style?

Management theories abound suggesting a variety of successful techniques for managing organizations, both simple and complex. Objective setting, participatory involvement, walking around, explicit mission statements, public agency business plans and matrix management are but a few of the techniques offered by trainers, textbooks and consultants. One can undoubtedly find examples where each of these techniques, as well as others, have been used successfully or have failed.

Should a newly elected governor simply adopt the most current or popular management theory in the private sector? Unless that particular technique is in keeping with the governor's personality and interests and is comfortable, the governor may not be well-served by simply borrowing private-sector strategies and styles.

For the last several years, the media, the public and politicians have chanted religiously about inept, inefficient, nonresponsive government and bureaucracy. Normally, in the same breath, they also have suggested that the simple infusion of private-sector management skills and techniques would provide obvious solutions. But before making too many campaign promises based on dedication to private-sector management, gubernatorial candidates should reassess such popular slogans. They also should discuss their practical potential with present or former governors.

The drafters of state constitutions had objectives that were different from those of the creators of corporate organizations. Although large corporations may rival the complexity of government, pure corporate organizational design generally is intended to promote accountability as measured in sales, production and profit and a crispness of management. In contrast, the writers of state constitutions ensured inevitably (if only implicitly) that governors would not be aided by crisp organizational design. Rather, state constitutions force governors to negotiate, anticipate, ameliorate, bargain, threaten, withdraw, entice, promise, reward, punish, ignore and apologize — simply to perform as the chief executive officer of the state. As if the checks and balances of its executive, legislative and judicial triumvirate were not enough, most constitutions ensure further diffusion and limitations of executive power. And then there is the electorate.

Government by its structural nature is not designed for strong executive action. It is designed to encourage negotiation, influence, input and adversarial relationships. Still, the governor op-

erates in a public environment that expects crisp executive management. Consequently, a governor must attempt to perform accordingly (or at least to be perceived so) while fulfilling all other roles symbolically and politically essential to survival.

But before making too many campaign promises based on dedication to private-sector management, gubernatorial candidates should reassess such popular slogans.

Indeed, it may be that the ability of a governor to transmit expectations, values and priorities to the staff, cabinet and public may be of great importance to the actual managing of government. The nurturing of strong allegiances and confidence may well be the best that can be expected given the complexity of governance today.

Because I have worked for two governors who had many similarities but different styles, it may be useful to briefly examine their approaches to managing government.

Richard Lamm: A Hands-On Style

Richard Lamm, governor of Colorado from 1975 to 1987, enjoyed enormous popularity among the electorate. Initially gaining office after walking the state and campaigning on a risky pro-environmental stance to keep the Winter Olympics out of Colorado, Lamm entered office as a surprising upstart and political unknown. A Democrat running for re-election during a time when most of Colorado's state and national offices were dominated by Republicans, he easily was returned to office twice, choosing in 1986 not to seek a fourth term. An attorney, certified public accountant and former legislator, Lamm was a governor whose personal characteristics and management style were integrated closely. As an individual, he is bright, inquisitive, energetic, a voracious reader and intrigued by creative solutions to problems.

As governor, Lamm was involved in the management of executive agencies to a level few governors are. He presided over monthly cabinet meetings that were attended by 15 to 20 cabinet members, key gubernatorial staff and the media. The presence of journalists not only provided the governor with a pulpit, but reinforced to all — including the public — that he was actively managing state government. Indeed, cabinet members often witnessed a new policy direction set spontaneously in the midst of whirling cameras. Cabinet members learned not to be surprised when the governor paged through a stack of correspondence and briefing memos and randomly asked for their spontaneous reaction to a question he had about the subject matter. His subsequent directives for action or follow-through dramatized to newspaper readers, television viewers and those present that he was in charge.

The cabinet also was broken down into two working subgroups, with human-service agency directors generally assigned to one group and the remainder of the cabinet to a second. Attendance at an assigned group was required; attendance at the second was optional. At monthly group meetings, the governor dealt with policy or strategy from an agenda of three to five issues. Lamm was involved in all discussions, and the others in attendance were encouraged and expected to participate regardless of whether the subject was relevant to their responsibilities. On a given day, the agenda might contain a discussion of vouchers for K-12 education, health care cost containment, prison population projections and alternatives to the federal welfare program of Aid to Families with Dependent Children.

Lamm inevitably surprised new cabinet members with his depth of knowledge about a wide variety of topics and with his willingness to consider the opinions of everyone present. The interchange not only allowed the governor to hear a variety of opinions and to test his own views, but it also educated cabinet directors about the issues confronting other agencies. Further, these discussions built commitment among the cabinet to the governor's solutions, direction and priorities. These sessions promoted a collegial style in the administration as cabinet members worked towards cross-agency solutions. In addition, they helped cabinet members develop values on issues beyond their specific area of responsibility; many cabinet members formed their own opinions about greenways and greenbelts, sugar beet farming, the oil-shale industry and variety of other topics.

Two or three times annually, Lamm held cabinet retreats at a variety of locations throughout Colorado. The governor, cabinet directors, key gubernatorial staff and advisers attended. Typically, the agenda included dinner with local officials the first evening followed by a day-and-a-half of meetings covering topical issues on legislative and agency agendas. Often, the governor focused on establishing short- and long-term direction.

Again, Lamm's involvement allowed the cabinet to participate in the development of administration policies and positions while cabinet heads learned of the governor's views on a variety of subjects. An ethos developed that generally discouraged agencies from competing against each other in policy or budget areas. The contact and interchange among the governor and cabinet members at these retreats was enhanced during the social time; at a Steamboat Springs retreat, Lamm cooked supper featuring his own recipe for peanut-butter-laced hamburgers.

Finally, Lamm held regular one-on-one sessions (sometimes including his chief of staff) with cabinet members. During these meetings, the governor covered the agency's problems, initiatives and successes, and developed with the agency director goals and directions. Given the number of executive agencies reporting directly to the governor and the numerous time-consuming items on his agenda, this was almost a herculean effort.

Booth Gardner: The CEO

Booth Gardner has been a state legislator, the chief executive officer of a Fortune 500 company, a county executive and a business-school dean. After a surprise primary victory in 1984, Gardner defeated the incumbent to become the chief executive of Washington. As governor, Gardner has continued many of his outside activities — such as coaching a girl's soccer team — and is accurately perceived by the public as particularly sensitive to the future of the state and its residents. In 1988, Gardner was re-elected governor with 63 percent of the vote.

Known as a walk-around manager who frequently appears unannounced at agency offices around the state, Gardner possesses an unpretentious management style. His management philosophy is to hire good managers and then empower them to lead their agencies. He and his staff delegate to cabinet members authority for day-to-day agency operations and policy development. Regular cabinet meetings generally are chaired by the governor's chief of staff, as are the day-long cabinet retreats. In addition, Gardner has created two subcabinet groups consisting of five or six of the 20 cabinet members; one deals with management issues while the other handles policy questions.

The subcabinet management group addresses issues that affect all agencies: personnel practices, efficiency initiatives, affirmative action, management development and labor relations. This subcabinet also deals with issues that it identifies itself, are assigned by the governor and are referred by cabinet members. Subgroups charged with making recommendations to the governor on particular topics may draw from other cabinet members, outside resources and the governor's staff.

The policy subcabinet committee identifies emerging or unaddressed issues that require policy decisions or direction. In the past, this policy group has handled issues such as growth management, state and local relationships and the growing underclass of people in poverty. Generally, this subcabinet develops policy or strategy recommendations for the governor. In contrast, the governor's own policy staff concentrates on the more ongoing, agency-oriented policy issues. Again, ad hoc cabinet groups are formed to address specific initiatives that cross agency lines. For example, seven cabinet directors formed a year-long working body to provide leadership for creating a state economic development plan.

Gardner enjoys larger policy and budget staffs than Lamm had in Colorado, and he uses these people to ensure consistency in state policies and continuity in state budgets. But it is Gardner who sets the tone for his administration. To cabinet members and gubernatorial staff alike, Gardner makes it clear that efficiency, effectiveness and a service-orientation are expected of every state agency. Those agency directors who assimilate and put into operation the governor's message are rewarded with greater independence, autonomy and trust.

Is There a "Correct" Model for Gubernatorial Management?

These profiles of two governors with opposite management styles suggest that there is no model to mimic, no formula to follow. Lamm and Gardner enjoyed political success and popularity; both generally are acclaimed as serious and effective managers. Yet they are different. And there is little to suggest that the style or technique of one is more likely than the other to produce success. Still, there were some important similarities in how Lamm and Gardner sought to influence the behavior and performance of their cabinet and department heads:

• Both Lamm and Gardner respected public service and imparted that view to their cabinets. Their commitment to responsible public stewardship — as well as their expectation that cabinet members live up to their commitment — was evident to staff and cabinet members.

• Both were accessible to individual cabinet members. Lamm and Gardner made it clear that the views and concerns of individual cabinet directors were important.

• Both governors articulated an expectation that public agencies should be managed well. Efficiency and effectiveness were their bywords.

• Lamm and Gardner placed a premium on appointing well-qualified leaders — rather than simply political supporters — to cabinet positions.

Indeed, the specifics of the management style selected by a governor may be of limited consequence. Much more important may be the values transmitted by the governor to the cabinet. The governor's objective is for cabinet members to put into practice the governor's values. The clarity and intensity with which a governor sets the administration's central values will have a much greater impact on managing the cabinet — and thus state government — than will any particular combination of management techniques. The process selected for developing the budget, the governor's attitude toward internal organization and support for agency directors who manage prudently are just some of the gubernatorial actions that transmit important operating values.

To state cabinet and department heads, every governor articulates — explicitly or implicitly — a set of management values. For Lamm and Gardner, important baseline values were intolerance of corruption and ethical conflicts combined with the presumption of caution in public expenditures. Yet, these were but minimal expectations. By selecting cabinet members for managerial abilities and recognizing success in achieving the stated objectives, a governor can further reinforce an administration's values.

For Lamm's administration, a key phrase was "hard choices." These words were popularized by the governor's "duty to die" speech, in which he questioned the expenditure of large sums of money to prolong life for the terminally ill or those sustained by life-support systems. (The implication was that the money might be better spent on other quality-of-life problems.) But the hard choices phrase often was bandied about in cabinet meetings, reinforcing the recognition that a finite amount of state funds existed. The message was that cabinet members needed to measure agency needs against the overall priorities — and budget — of the administration.

"Efficiency and effectiveness" is more than a slogan to the Gardner administration. The governor acted to reinforce this central value. Each year, Gardner recognizes 10 individuals for their success in promoting efficient and effective government by naming them the "Governor's Distinguished State Managers-of-the-Year." Gardner also chairs an Efficiency Commission that involves the private sector in partnership with government employees in improving public services while saving money. And he regularly rewards with cash bonuses state employees who develop innovative ways to save state money.

Lamm and Gardner publicly have articulated the core values of their administrations. Using opposing styles, they have reinforced these values to their cabinet — and through them large numbers of state employees.

Is there a right or best style for a governor?

Clearly not. The style that works for a governor — as is true with any leader — depends upon individual character. The governor's personality, background and interests must be blended with the strengths and weaknesses of the gubernatorial staff and the political environment.

Public expectations run high — higher than any governor can possibly achieve. The governor who can articulate and reinforce personal values may be doing as much as can be done.

Wisconsin's 'quirky' veto power

*Wisconsin legislators, outraged by the governor's
veto power, plan to fight their battle in the
U.S. Supreme Court.*

Michael H. McCabe

*Michael H. McCabe is assistant director of CSG's Mid-
western office.*

Chalk up another victory for Wisconsin Gov. Tommy
G. Thompson in an ongoing battle with Democratic lawmakers over the scope of his authority to
veto spending bills.

Thanks to a recent decision by a federal court of
appeals, the Republican governor remains free to exercise
one of the most unusual veto powers in the nation—at least
for now.

At issue is a provision in the Wisconsin Constitution
that empowers Thompson to approve or veto any appropriations bill "in whole or in part." Like similar measures
in other states, this provision enables the governor to
remove individual line items from a large spending bill
without resorting to a full veto.

The result is a revised bill that automatically becomes
law unless the governor's action is overridden by a two-
thirds vote of the Legislature. There's nothing unusual
about that, but in practice, Wisconsin's "partial veto" has
been used in ways unimaginable in other states.

Thanks to the silence of the state constitution on this
point, Wisconsin's governors have, over the years, taken it
upon themselves to define the scope of their partial veto
authority. Not surprisingly, they have taken full advantage
of this license by vetoing whole sections of spending plans
as well as individual sentences, words, parts of words,
single letters, digits, spaces and even the drafting symbols
that appear in enrolled bills.

In 1987, the governor used the partial veto power to
substitute the Legislature's language that certain juveniles
could be detained for "not more than 48 hours," with
language that said they could not be detained for more than
"10 days."

Equally unsurprising is the fact that the creative use
of this power doesn't always sit well with the Legislature.
By stringing together the remnants of a partially vetoed
bill, the governor can effectively create new language,
sometimes thwarting the express intent of the General
Assembly.

Though lawmakers retain the power to override such
measures, the constitutional requirement of a two-thirds
majority to do so can leave smaller legislative majorities frustrated. Here again, Wisconsin is not alone.

Override provisions requiring super majorities are
fairly common and serve to magnify the voting power
of legislative minorities in any state. The difference is
that a creative partial veto combined with a legislative
failure to override can result in the enactment of a law
that has never been approved by a legislative majority.

In this respect, Wisconsin is unique.

Disgruntled lawmakers have repeatedly challenged
the governor's creative use of the partial veto, claiming
it infringes upon their legislative authority. But state
courts in Wisconsin have consistently sided with the
governor.

The Wisconsin Supreme Court has acknowledged
that the partial veto originally was intended to curb the
General Assembly's habit of attaching controversial substantive measures to omnibus spending bills to secure
their passage. But the court has specifically rejected the
contention that the partial veto only may be used to
eliminate rather than create language. In fact, the only
judicially-imposed limitation on the governor is that the
result of a partial veto must be a complete and workable law that is germane to the subject of the original bill.

In the spring of 1990, Wisconsin voters narrowed the
governor's power by approving a constitutional amendment that prohibited the rejection of individual letters
to create new words in a bill. But according to Senate
President Fred Risser, the so-called "Vanna White veto"

Governors' Powers to Veto Appropriations Bills

State or other jurisdiction	May Veto Amount	May Veto Language	State or other jurisdiction	May Veto Amount	May Veto Language
Alabama	Y	Y	New Hampshire	N	N
Alaska	Y(a)	N	New Jersey	Y(a)	N
Arizona	Y	N	New Mexico	Y	N
Arkansas	Y	N	New York	Y	N
California	Y(a)	N	North Carolina	N	N
Colorado	Y	Y	North Dakota	Y	Y
Connecticut	Y	N	Ohio	Y	Y
Delaware	Y	N	Oklahoma	Y	N
Florida	Y	Y	Oregon	Y	Y
Georgia	Y	N	Pennsylvania	Y(a)	N
Hawaii	Y(a)	N	Rhode Island	N	N
Idaho	Y	N	South Carolina	Y	Y
Illinois	Y(a)	N	South Dakota	Y	Y
Indiana	N	N	Tennessee	Y(a)	N
Iowa	Y	Y	Texas	Y	N
Kansas	Y	N	Utah	Y	N
Kentucky	Y	N	Vermont	N	N
Louisiana	Y	Y	Virginia	Y	Y
Maine	N	N	Washington	Y	Y
Maryland	Y	N	West Virginia	Y(a)	Y
Massachusetts	Y(a)	Y	Wisconsin	Y	Y
Michigan	Y	Y	Wyoming	Y	N
Minnesota	Y	N	American Samoa	Y	N
Mississippi	Y	Y	Guam	Y(a)	N
Missouri	Y	N	No. Mariana Islands	Y	N
Montana	Y	Y	Puerto Rico	Y(a)	Y
Nebraska	Y(b)	N	U.S. Virgin Islands	Y	Y
Nevada	N	N			

Y — Yes   N — No

(a) Governor also can reduce amounts in appropriations bill. In Hawaii, governor can reduce items in executive appropriations measures, but cannot reduce nor item veto amounts appropriated for the judicial or legislative branches.

(b) No appropriation can be made in excess of the recommendations contained in the governor's budget except by a 2/3 vote. The excess is not subject to veto by the governor.

The Book of the States, 1990-91 Edition, published by The Council of State Governments

was only "the most outrageous form of partial veto," because individual letters can be changed. Even without it, a creative governor can subvert legislative intent by crafting new provisions within a bill.

Risser continues to spearhead efforts to limit the partial veto. Last year, he and Assembly Majority Leader David Travis took the Legislature's case into federal court. There the two Democrats alleged that Republican Gov. Thompson's exercise of the partial veto in 20 recent instances violated federal constitutional safeguards. But in June 1990, District Court Judge John C. Shabaz, a former Republican leader in the Wisconsin Assembly, ruled in favor of Thompson.

The plaintiffs appealed, but to no avail. Last April, the 7th Circuit Court of Appeals affirmed the district court's decision, leaving little room for the plaintiffs to maneuver. In an opinion written by Circuit Judge Richard Posner, the court held that Wisconsin's partial veto provision was not unconstitutional because, "the federal Constitution does not fix the balance of power between branches of state government."

In denying the lawmakers' charges, the court noted the availability of a political remedy for their grievance — "amend the Wisconsin Constitution" — and concluded that there is "no need to involve the federal courts in this affair and no legal basis for doing so."

"A modest shift of power among elected officials is not a denial of republican government or even a reduction in the amount of democracy."
— Wisconsin 7th Circuit Court

The plaintiffs, according to Travis, remained "absolutely convinced of the righteousness of our cause" and quickly petitioned the court for a rehearing. That request was denied in May, but by mid-June, the lawmakers were preparing to take their case to the U.S. Supreme Court.

Risser believes the 7th Circuit failed to address the plaintiffs' main point — namely, that "laws should only be made by a majority." Risser contends that when a new law is created by partial veto, the fundamental principles of republican government are undermined.

Although the plaintiffs are pursuing their case, the Circuit Court's opinion offers little hope for success.

While conceding that Wisconsin's partial veto may well alter the balance of power in favor of the governor, the court concluded that "a modest shift of power among elected officials is not a denial of republican government or even a reduction in the amount of democracy." That the partial veto is "unusual, even quirky, does not make it unconstitutional."

To make matters worse, from the plaintiffs' perspective, the appellate court noted that lawmakers' grievances were compounded by their own actions, since the partial veto power is limited to appropriations bills. While the governor has partially vetoed non-appropriations items, it is only because legislators continue to attach substantive provisions to spending bills.

While the governor is reportedly pleased with the court's decision, the plaintiffs remain unconvinced — and undaunted. Travis "felt all along that the issue would have to be decided one way or another by the U.S. Supreme Court."

Risser agrees and was unmoved by the Circuit Court's admonishment that legislators upset with the governor's veto power should change the state constitution. "There's a political remedy to just about every issue the Supreme Court deals with," said Risser. "The courts should act to protect the basic philosophies at stake in this case."

Failing a reversal by the Supreme Court, lawmakers may be forced to reconsider their options. A constitutional amendment is possible, but the amendment process in Wisconsin is a lengthy one requiring legislative consent to any proposed language in two consecutive sessions of the General Assembly. Then the voters have the final say.

In the meantime, the governor's "quirky" power remains safe.

"City Managers Don't Make Policy": A Lie; Let's Face It

DAVID N. AMMONS and CHARLDEAN NEWELL
David N. Ammons is a Research Associate at the Carl Vinson Institute of Government at the University of Georgia. Charldean Newell is Professor of Public Administration and Associate Vice President for Academic Affairs at North Texas State University.

Spoils, graft, and corruption in U.S. cities had 19th century reformers clamoring for change. In 1899 the National Municipal League adopted "A Municipal Program" (soon dubbed the *Model City Charter*) as a blueprint for reform.

Model City Charter: Democracy + Management

Now in its sixth edition with a seventh in preparation, the League's model charter has been broadly distributed and widely adopted, though commonly with local modifications. The purpose of the model is to provide a plan of municipal government that is "(1) democratic—that is to say responsive to the electorate and the community—and at the same time (2) capable of doing the work of the city effectively and translating the intentions of the voters into efficient administrative action as promptly and economically as possible."[1]

Since 1913, that prescription has been interpreted by the League as a call for the council-manager plan. That plan assigns to the city council responsibility for municipal legislation and policy formulation and to the city manager, appointed by and answerable to the city council, responsibility for carrying out policy directives and managing the delivery of municipal services. In a single stroke, the reformers believed they had preserved democracy in local government while removing undue political influence and enhancing managerial expertise in the "business" of local government.

The six versions of the *Model City Charter* reflect the concerns of their times and, to a lesser degree, the concerns of the times that came before. Remedies designed to address issues in the era of one edition became embedded in the next. Over the years the focus has moved from the elimination of blatant corruption and political spoils, and the introduction of scientific management practices and local "home rule," to professionalizing the public service, instituting modern budget procedures and state-of-the-art planning and zoning practices, and enhancing positive intergovernmental relations.[2]

Changing Attitudes in the Model Charter

Although the model charter has continued to prescribe the council-manager form of local government, its most recent versions, as well as deliberations for the seventh edition, suggest an increasing willingness to accept the "strong mayor" alternative. In part, such disposition is no doubt attributable to the passing of time since the worst excesses of turn-of-the-century political machines. More favorable consideration of the strong mayor alternative may also be attributable to the recognition that, in practice, city managers are less insulated from politics and more active in policy processes than originally envisioned. In other words, the idea that administration can be divorced completely from policy and politics is a myth...a lie.

The fact is, the politics vs. administration dichotomy presumed to be established through the council-manager plan has proven to be far less absolute than at least some of the reformers had originally thought.[3] Furthermore, anecdotal evidence regarding more than a few strong mayors suggests that even elected officials may be managerially as well as politically progressive and that many, in fact, concern themselves with managerial issues more commonly than caricatures of the mayor as a perpetually wheeling-and-dealing political broker would suggest.

This article explores the evolving roles of chief executives in reformed and unreformed cities (i.e., city managers in council-manager cities and mayors in mayor-council cities). The implications of that evolution are examined not only as they relate to the philosophical underpinnings of the council-manager plan but also more concretely as they relate to the prescriptions of the *Model City Charter.*

Mayors vs. Managers: Perceptions vs. Reality

A role-perception and time-allocation survey of chief executives in the 418 U.S. cities having 1980 populations of 50,000 or greater was completed during the spring of 1985. Responses were received from 226 executives for a response rate of 54 percent. The total included 153 city managers and 73 mayors.[4]

Respondents were asked to indicate the amount of their time that they devote to each of three roles identified by Deil Wright in his pioneering work on the role perceptions of city managers, published two decades ago.[5] The three roles identified by Wright are the "management role," the "policy role," and the "political role." Mayors and city managers were asked to report how their time was spent, and which role they perceived to be most important to their job success.

As expected, city managers reported devoting higher percentages of their time to the management role than did mayors. Surprisingly, however, given the rationale of the council-manager plan and the assumptions of its proponents regarding strong mayors, the management role commanded less of the city managers' time and more of the mayors' time than expected. City managers reported spending 51 percent of their time on the management role—much less than might be expected of an administrative technician. By comparison, mayors reported 44 percent—much more than expected of a politician (Table 1).

Reprinted by permission from the March/April 1988 issue of *National Civic Review,* pp. 124-132. National Civic Review, 1601 Grant Street, Suite 250, Denver, CO 80203.

TABLE 1
Mean Percentage of Time Devoted to the "Management," "Policy", and
"Political" Roles by Chief Executives in City Government

	Mayors[a]			City Managers[b]		
	Management Role	Policy Role	Political Role	Management Role	Policy Role	Political Role
Jurisdiction Population (1980)						
50,000 - 74,999	48.6%	24.6%	26.8%	51.7%	30.1%	18.2%
75,000 - 100,000	48.8	24.2	26.9	49.5	34.1	16.4
Greater than 100,000	37.8	27.2	35.0	50.6	33.4	16.0
Mean	44.2	25.6	30.2	50.8	32.2	17.0

[a]Mayor-council or commission form of government.
[b]Council-manager form of government.

Average time allocations to the management role differ little across the mayor and city manager groups from cities of 50,000 to 100,000 population. Among chief executives of larger cities, those greater than 100,000 population, substantial differences in role expectation become evident. While city managers in large cities report devoting 51 percent of their time to the management role on average, their mayoral counterparts report devoting only 38 percent of their time to that role.

City Managers: 32 Percent Policy Makers

Perhaps even more surprising to the council-manager purist expecting the overwhelming allocation of time by city managers to the management role is their substantial involvement in the policy-making process in local government. City managers reported devoting 32 percent of their time on average to the policy role, clarified on the survey instrument to include council relations, compared to a reported 26 percent average allocation by mayors.

Stereotyped views of the mayor and city manager would suggest heavy allocation of time to the political role by strong mayors and virtually none by city managers. Neither expectation is borne out by the survey results. Mayors report spending an average of 30 percent of their time on the political role, associated on the survey instrument with community leadership; city managers, 17 percent.

Images Behind the Mayor vs. Manager Dichotomy

These results suggest a rather clear break from the images supporting local government distinctions promulgated by naive partisans of one form of government or another. Somewhat paradoxically, the images conveyed by each camp are fundamentally similar. Both pretend that the strong mayor is a political leader unencumbered by managerial minutiae—a condition viewed by one group as positive (i.e., "providing political leadership") and by the other as negative (i.e., a management "amateur" whose guiding principle is political gain). The city manager, on the other hand, is imagined to be an expert administrator unencumbered by policy responsibilities or political incursions—again, viewed positively by one camp (i.e., free to make rational decisions regarding the "business" of local government) and negatively by the other (i.e., "insulated," "unresponsive," "insensitive").

What differ, of course, are the values assigned to particular roles. Advocates of the council-manager plan consider the management role most essential and base their support of that plan on the assumption of greater expertise in and devotion to the management role by the city manager. Advocates of the mayor-council form place a higher priority on political leadership—i.e., the political role and the policy role—and suggest that the city manager is ill-equipped to fulfill that need, and moreover is precluded by city charter from doing so.

Reality: A Mix of Roles

Reality suggests something much different from stereotyped images. Although degrees of emphasis differ substantially, mayors *do* manage and city managers *do* engage in policy and political roles. This assertion is not to suggest that mayors and city managers are indistinguishable from each other; such an assertion would be far from truth, as city managers tend to emphasize the management role, and even the policy role, to a greater degree than strong mayors, while mayors tend

to emphasize the political role to a greater degree than do the city managers.

But suggesting that the approaches taken in fulfilling their obligations are so different as to have virtually nothing in common would be just as inaccurate. Differences exist and they are perceptible; but they are differences in emphasis and degree, not absolutes.

Mayors who ignore their management responsibilities are rarely reelected. Their background may be partisan politics and they may perceive themselves to be local visionaries, but somebody has to cope with service problems and somebody has to resolve the interdepartmental quarrels.

Similarly, the city manager cannot and should not be insulated from the policy processes of local government. Policy proposals, expert advice, and policy interpretation and implementation are all crucial aspects of the policy process that often turn on the talent, shrewdness, and integrity of the chief executive. The maintenance of council relations is interwoven in that role. Without policy adeptness, the city manager may also have a short tenure. Even the political role, when its meaning is softened to exclude partisan involvement and instead to imply community leadership, has been territory occupied by many city managers, perhaps to the degree that elected officials left it vacant or even overtly encouraged city managers to assume it.

Although they differ in time allocations, mayors and city managers acknowledge involvement in all three of Wright's roles. Each of the three roles, in fact, is designated by some members of each fraternity as most important to job success. That is an important finding for those who fail to see any common ground between the jobs. For others the evolving perspective of city managers and the contrasting perceptions of mayors are equally important.

In 1965 Wright surveyed 45 city managers in cities of greater than 100,000 population and found that 37 percent perceived the management role as most important to their job success, while 22 percent accorded that status to the policy role and 33 percent to the political role (Table 2).[6] City managers form cities of similar size surveyed in 1985 placed similar priority on the management role but substantially different priority on the other two. The management role was considered most important to job success by 39 percent of the 1985 city managers, the policy role by 56 percent, and the political role by only 6 percent. In contrast, only 23 percent of the mayors thought the management role was most important to their success; 35 percent, the policy role; and 42 percent, the political role.

TABLE 2
City Managers and Mayors' 1985 Designation of Most Important Role
Compared with Wright's 1965 Findings (Populations Greater than 100,000)

Role Perceived as Most Important to Job Success	Wright's Study of City Managers 1965[a]	City Managers 1985[a]	Mayors 1985[b]
Management Role (administrative activities)	37%	38.5%	23.1%
Policy Role (and council relations)	22%	55.8%	34.6%
Political Role (community leadership)	33%	5.8%	42.3%

[a]Council-Manager form of government.
[b]Mayor-council or commission form of government.

Implications for the Model City Charter

The *Model City Charter* informs and influences choices affecting fundamental aspects of local governance across the country. Reliance on the model by countless city charter commissions bears out that point. However, as its drafters have acknowledged, the model is influenced by its times. It molds views on good government, but its drafters have also attempted to reflect prevailing sentiment and realities. Insistence on a particular city council size, at-large elections, explicit procedures for planning and budgeting have already, or will eventually, give way to more flexible prescriptions and language. The model in its current form even attempts to accommodate the possibility of an elected chief executive, albeit as an appendix to the prescription of the preferred local-government structure.

A model charter informs and influences, but it does not, and should not be expected to, dictate what local government structures will be adopted across the nation and what division of responsibilities will be deemed acceptable. The role of local government itself has changed dramatically since the sixth edition of the *Model City Charter* was adopted. Local officials, in wrestling with complex policy issues such as environmental pollution, civil rights, and welfare services, have inevitably seen more blurring of traditional lines of responsibility. Role changes among city managers from 1965 to 1985 have occurred during an era covered by only one edition of the model charter, and the increasing "policy role" priority of modern city managers is hardly prescribed by that model. It is safe to assume that actual roles and activities commonly depart at least to a degree from those prescribed in actual, adopted city charters. Still, copies of the *Model City Charter* are in considerable demand; the model does appear to influence the intent, at least, of those who would reform their local government.

Differences in form of government are important. The selection of a particular form says something about the values of a community — the aspects of governance that it thinks most important, that it wishes to have emphasized. The selection of a particular form should not exclude the chief executive from roles necessary for functioning — regardless of formal declarations in the city charter. Perhaps as important as any of the formal effects is the influence that the choice of a particular form of government has on the types of people — their orientations, backgrounds, and specialties — that are drawn to the key offices in one form or another. Communities that want their government to be managed by a person with an extensive background in municipal management, a graduate degree in public administration, and a "passion for anonymity"[7] are more likely to get their wish by adoption of the council-manager form of government. That adoption, however, does not mean that the chief executive officer (i.e., city manager) will have no role in the policy process.

Drafters of the seventh edition of the *Model City Charter* would be well advised to consider the reality of the policy, if not the political, role of city managers. Many of the modifications contemplated or already made in the model charter would have the effect of heightening the political environment of local government.[8] Allowances for district election of council members and direct election of the mayor are two prominent examples. To survive in such an environment and to pro-

vide the policy assistance that councils increasingly demand, city managers must be more than mere technocrats. The survey results reported in this article suggest that city managers are making the necessary changes. It is time that the model charter recognize and legitimize this evolution, specifying among the powers and duties of the city manager the obligation to provide policy assistance as required by the council.

Notes

[1] Luther H. Gulick, "The New Model," NATIONAL CIVIC REVIEW, vol. 52 (December 1963), p. 584.

[2] A New Model City Charter," NATIONAL CIVIC REVIEW, vol. 74 (June 1985), p. 256.

[3] James H. Svara, in what is perhaps a more accurate depiction of reality, posits the existence of a four-category continuum depicting both the sharing and separation of responsibilities. Elected officials dominate "mission," share responsibility with managers for "policy and administration," and yield "management" to the managers. See: Svara, "Political Supremacy and Administrative Expertise," *Management Science and Policy Analysis,* vol. 3 (Summer 1985), pp. 3-7, and "Dichotomy and Duality: Reconceptualizing the Relationship Between Policy and Administration in Council-Manager Cities," *Public Administration Review,* vol. 45 (January/February 1985); *A Report to the Profession from the ICMA Committee on Future Horizons,* (Washington, D.C.: ICMA, 1979), which notes that the always fuzzy distinction between politics and administration has reached the point "at which both elective and administrative officials should concede that they have a shared stake in both policy and administration" (p. 17).

[4] For a more complete description of the study and its findings, see Charldean Newell and David N. Ammons, "Role Emphases of City Managers and Other Municipal Executives," *Public Administrative Review,* vol. 47 (May/June 1987), pp. 246-253.

[5] Deil S. Wright, "The City Manager as Developmental Administrator," Chapter Six in *Comparative Urban Research,* Robert T. Daland, ed. (Beverly Hills: Sage Publications, 1969), pp. 203-248.

[6] Wright, "The City Manager as a Developmental Administrator," p. 236. The data were gathered in 1965.

[7] *A Passion for Anonymity* is the title of Louis Brownlow's autobiographical account of his career as a public servant (Chicago: University of Chicago press, 1958).

[8] See "Working Paper III," unpublished working document of the Model Charter Revision Project, National Civic League, 1987.

The New Judicial Federalism:
The States' Lead in Rights Protection

A lot of attention is given to the rights afforded American citizens by the Bill of Rights amendments to the U.S. Constitution. But state constitutions are equally important, often expanding upon federal protection. Many times, state courts have interpreted state constitutional guarantees liberally. This trend, sometimes referred to as the new judicial federalism, can serve as an example to developing democracies as a means of protecting and supporting their ethnic diversity.

John Kincaid and Robert F. Williams

John Kincaid is executive director of the U.S. Advisory Commission on Intergovernmental Relations, Washington, D.C. Robert F. Williams is professor of law at Rutgers University, Camden, N.J.

Claus von Bulow, whose trial was popularized in the film *Reversal of Fortune*, might not be a free man today but for the protection afforded individual rights in Rhode Island's Constitution.

Incriminating evidence in his wife's death was thrown out by the state court under the state's exclusionary rule. That decision hinged on the state high court's interpretation of search-and-seizure provisions in Rhode Island's constitution. The U.S. Supreme Court later declined to review the state ruling because the decision was based on independent and adequate state grounds.

Rhode Island is not alone in going farther than the U.S. Supreme Court in protecting individual rights. The emergence since 1970 of many state high courts as assertive protectors of individual rights comes as a surprise to many people. The fact that state courts are expanding protections beyond those guaranteed by the Bill of Rights is even more surprising. This development, called the new judicial federalism, defies traditional theories of American federalism, which saw the states being eclipsed by the federal government in every field.

The new judicial federalism generally refers to the authority of a state court to interpret its state constitution so as to provide broader rights protections than those recognized by U.S. Supreme Court interpretations of the federal Constitution.

As in the von Bulow case, such state decisions are immune from Supreme Court review when they are based on "independent and adequate" state constitutional grounds.

In a 1970 decision, for instance, the Alaska Supreme Court wrote:

> While we must enforce the minimum constitutional standards imposed upon us by the United States Supreme Court's interpretation of the Fourteenth Amendment, we are free, and we are under a duty, to develop additional constitutional rights and privileges under our Alaska Constitution. . . . We need not stand by idly and passively, waiting for constitutional direction from the highest court of the land.

The Power of Interpretation

It is one thing for the Supreme Court to hold that people have certain rights under the federal Constitution. It is quite another for the Court to hold that people do not have certain rights. Because both kinds of decisions come from the "highest court in the land," we tend to believe that both should have the same force in every court, police precinct and state and local office throughout the land. But, just because a government action is not prohibited by the federal Constitution does not mean that it is automatically permitted under a state's constitution. A state constitution is the supreme law of a state, so long as it does not contradict the U.S. Constitution.

The new judicial federalism allows state courts and legislatures to set rights standards that are higher, but not lower, than those established under the U.S. Constitution. States also may recognize rights such as privacy and victims' rights that are not even found, at least not explicitly, in the U.S. Constitution. As such, the new judicial federalism conforms to an old principle of American federalism: that states may act where the U.S. government has elected not to act, so long as state action does not violate the U.S. Constitution or federal law.

Actually, the new judicial federalism is no longer new. Since 1970, state courts have rendered at least 700 decisions providing broader rights than those recognized by the U.S. Supreme Court or new rights not found in the Bill of Rights. Partly in response to this development, the U.S. Advisory Commission on Intergovernmental Relations in 1988 issued *State Constitutional Law: Cases and Materials*, the first textbook of its type ever published.

Examples of new rights protections can be found in Florida whose constitution contains a privacy provision approved by voters in 1980. It reads: "Every natural person has the right to be let alone and free from governmental intrusion into his private life except as otherwise provided herein." Under this rule, the Florida Supreme Court struck down a state law that required minors to obtain parental consent before ending a pregnancy, and it voided a municipal ordinance prohibiting people from sleeping in their automobiles. The Florida court also used the provision to uphold a 1990 law that broadened the "right to die" for citizens of the state.

State vs. Federal

However, most state court decisions under the new judicial federalism involve interpretations of state constitutional provisions that are very similar or identical to provisions in the U.S. Bill of Rights. A state court may interpret its state provision more broadly than the U.S. Supreme Court interprets the companion federal provision. Thus, state courts can choose to follow federal precedent or take a higher road and expand rights protections.

For example, in 1988 the U.S. Supreme Court ruled in *California vs. Greenwood* that police do not need a warrant to search trash put out for collection. In 1990, however, the New Jersey and Washington high courts ruled that their state constitutions do require police to obtain a warrant to search curbside trash. If no warrant is obtained, then evidence gleaned from the search will not be admitted in state court.

However, federal agents operating under U.S. rules need not obtain warrants to search curbside trash in New Jersey and Washington. This revival of dual federalism in the judicial arena raises interesting intergovernmental issues. For example, will federal agents deliver evidence gathered without warrants to state police? Probably. Will such evidence be admitted in state courts? Possibly.

The New Jersey Supreme Court recently held in split decisions that such evidence can be admitted in state court so long as there was no active cooperation "between the officers of the two sovereigns." Thus, after decades of cooperative federalism, during which great emphasis was placed on getting states to cooperate with federal rights laws and rulings, state courts now are talking about "uncooperative federalism," and about the need to protect their citizens' rights against federal action. This development could disturb intergovernmental cooperation in law enforcement.

State constitutions offer opportunities to entrench rights for which there is no national consensus.

Another question is whether states can nullify federal action. If states can set rights standards that are stricter than federal standards, can they apply those standards to federal agents within their borders — despite the supremacy clause of the U.S. Constitution? If states cannot abridge rights protected by the U.S. Constitution, can the federal government come into a state and abridge rights protected by the state constitution? Must the federal government explicitly preempt a state rights protection in order to immunize itself from state nullification?

These kinds of questions were raised by Thomas Jefferson and James Madison against the Alien and Sedition Acts passed by Congress in 1798. Their Virginia and Kentucky Resolutions triggered a debate over state nullification and interposition thought to have been settled by the Civil War.

Until recently, the new judicial federalism generally was viewed as a liberal movement. Indeed, former Justice William J. Brennan Jr. helped spur the movement in a now famous *Harvard Law Review* article in 1977. Critics charge that the new judicial federalism is little more than a reflex liberal reaction to the conservative Burger and Rehnquist Courts. The activism of the Warren Court years (1954-69) is being kept alive by numerous "little Warren courts" in the states.

But conservatives have also had victories in state courts. In 1991, the Pennsylvania Supreme Court produced a conservative ruling based on a liberal reading of the "takings" clause in Pennsylvania's Constitution. The court struck down Philadelphia's historic preservation ordinance on the ground that its application in this case constituted a "taking" of the owner's property without just compensation. The decision sent shock waves through the historic preservation and environmental protection communities because of its constraining implications for government regulation of private property. The decision is being reconsidered, though, because several concurring justices believe the court went overboard.

The U.S. Supreme Court has upheld other preservation and environmental laws against challenges under the "takings" clause of the Fifth Amendment to the U.S. Constitution. However, the court is hearing several new "takings" cases this term.

Looking Ahead

The future of the new judicial federalism is hard to predict. If the U.S. Supreme Court resumes an activist rights role, it may again move ahead of state courts. Also, given that most state high court justices must face the voters periodically, activist justices may be unseated by a disgruntled electorate. In addition, state constitutions can be amended more easily than the U.S. Constitution. In 1982, for instance, Florida voters nailed their supreme court to the federal rights floor by approving a constitutional amendment requiring the court to adhere to the U.S. Supreme Court's view of the exclusionary rule under the Fourth Amendment. By 1982, the Court had narrowed its view of the Fourth Amendment compared to the view of the Warren Court. Thus far, however, voters have expanded rights as much as they have restricted them through state constitutional amendments.

Finally, the new judicial federalism revives some basic questions about rights. If rights are universal, should they not apply equally everywhere? If not, what rights are universal, and what rights can vary among states? Just as women once crossed state lines to obtain abortions, will ambulances carry people across borders to states with more liberal right-to-die laws? Will some ambulances go in the opposite direction, carrying patients away from relatives eager to "pull the plug" under liberal state rules?

Although universal rights may seem to be the natural order, independent state constitutions offer opportunities to entrench certain rights, at least in some places, when the nation or its highest court cannot agree on applying these rights. We have already seen signs of this with regard to privacy, victims' rights, women's rights and environmental rights provisions in some state constitutions. In this way, states can also serve as laboratories for rights experimentation.

The new judicial federalism may have implications for emerging democracies worldwide, as well. Often, ethnic, religious and linguistic hostilities preclude consensus on common rights. However, entrenching even a few common rights in the national constitution is a step in the right direction that can foster the trust needed to break down barriers to the recognition of more universal rights.

View From the Bench: A Judge's Day

Judge Lois G. Forer

Lois G. Forer is a judge in the Philadelphia Court of Common Pleas. This article is adapted from her book, The Death of the Law.

At 9:30 the court personnel begin to assemble. The crier opens court. "All rise. Oyez, oyez, all persons having business before the Court of Common Pleas Criminal Division come forth and they shall be heard. God save this honorable court. Be seated and stop all conversation. Good morning, Your Honor." The crier calls out the names of the defendants. Most of them are represented by the public defender. He checks his files. One or two names are not on his list. A quick phone call is made to his office to send up the missing files.

On one particular day when I was sitting in criminal motions court, three cases had private counsel. One had been retained by the defendant. The other two had been appointed by the court to represent indigents accused of homicide. Where are these lawyers?

As is customary, the court officer phones each of them and reminds his secretary that he has a case listed and he must appear. Several of the defendants are not present. The prison is called to locate the missing parties. The judge, if he wishes to get through his list, must find the lawyers and litigants and order them to come to court.

Frequently the prosecutor cannot find his files. When he does, he discovers that a necessary witness has not been subpoenaed. The case must be continued to another day. The other witnesses, who are present and have missed a day's work, are sent home. The defendant is returned to jail to await another listing. Often cases are listed five and six times before they can be heard.

On this day there were three extra-ditions. Amos R. is wanted in South Carolina. Seven years ago he had escaped from jail and fled north. Since then he has been living in Philadelphia. He married here and now has two children. His wife and children are in the courtroom. He is employed. Amos has not been in trouble since leaving South Carolina, where 10 years ago he was convicted of stealing a car and sentenced to nine to 20 years in prison. He had no prior record. In Pennsylvania, for the same crime, he would probably have been placed on probation or at most received a maximum sentence of two years.

Now he testifies that he didn't steal the car, he only borrowed it. Moreover, he didn't have a lawyer. When he pleaded guilty he was told he would get six months. This is probably true. Also, he was undoubtedly indicted by a grand jury from which Negroes were systematically excluded. All of these allegations would be grounds for release in a postconviction hearing, for they are serious violations of constitutional rights. But they are irrelevant in extradition hearings. The only issues that the judge may consider before ordering this man to leave his family and shipping him off to serve 18 more years in prison are whether he is in fact the Amos R. named in the warrant and whether the papers are in order. There is little judicial discretion. One is often impelled by the system to be an instrument of injustice.

This is the dilemma of a judge and of many officials in the legal system. Following the rule of law may result in hardship and essential unfairness. Ignoring the law is a violation of one's oath of office, an illegal act, and a destruction of the system. Some choose to ignore the law in the interests of "justice." Others mechanically follow precedent. Neither course is satisfactory. The judge who frees a defendant knows that in most instances the state cannot appeal. Unless

there is an election in the offing and the prosecutor chooses to use this case as a political issue, there will be no repercussions. But it is his duty, as it is that of the accused, to obey the law. If the judge is not restrained by the law, who will be? On the other hand, it is unrealistic to say, "Let the defendant appeal." In the long period between the trial judge's ruling and that of the higher court, if it hears the appeal, a human being will be in jail. One does not easily deprive a person of his liberty without very compelling reasons. Almost every day, the guardians of the law are torn between these conflicting pulls.

After hearing the life story of Amos R., as reported by the prosecutor, the young defender said, "Mr. R. wishes to waive a hearing."

I looked at the lawyer. "Mr. R., do you know that you have a right to a hearing?"

"Yes."

"Have you consulted with your attorney about waiving a hearing?"

"My attorney?" R. looks bewildered.

"Your lawyer, the defender," I pointed to the young man.

"Oh, him," R. replies. "Yes, I talked to him."

"How long?"

" 'Bout two minutes."

"Your Honor," says the defender, "I have spoken to the sheriff. There is no question that this is the Amos R. wanted. The papers are in order."

I search through the official-looking sheaf of documents with gold seals and red seals and the signatures of two governors, hoping to find a defect, a critical omission. At last I discover that Amos R. was arrested in New Jersey on a Friday night. He was not taken to Pennsylvania until the following Monday. It is 89 days that he has been in jail in Pennsylvania. The extradition hearing must by statute be held within 90 days of arrest. By adding on the three days he was in custody in New Jersey, I conclude that the 90-day time limit has not been met. Amos R. is once again a free man. This happy ending is unusual. Bureaucratic inefficiencies seldom redound to the benefit of the individual.

Prisoners of Bureaucracy

The next four matters are bail applications. All the defendants fit the stereotype. They are black males under the age of 30. Only one is in the courtroom. The others are in the detention center. It is too much trouble and too expensive to transport them to court for a bail hearing. I must decide whether to set free or keep locked up men whom I cannot see or talk to. If I don't release them, they may be in jail for as long as a year awaiting trial. The law presumes that they are innocent. I look at the applications. This is not the first arrest for any of them. For one there are records going back to age nine, when he was incarcerated for truancy.

"The defendant's juvenile record may not be used against him in adult court," I remind the prosecuting attorney.

"I know, Your Honor," he replies apologetically, "but the computer prints out all the arrests."

"How many convictions?"

The computer does not give the answer to that question.

One man is accused of rape. The record shows that his prior offenses were larceny of an automobile and, as a child, running away from home. The police report indicates that when the police arrived the defendant was in the complainant's apartment with his clothes off. He left so quickly that he abandoned his shoes and socks. The complainant admitted knowing him and gave his name and address to the police. No weapon was involved.

My usual rule of thumb is a simple one: "If he had time to take off his shoes, it wasn't rape."

Before releasing an alleged rapist from jail, possibly to prey on other victims, I want to speak with the accused. Although Lombroso's theory that one can tell a criminal by his physical appearance is out of fashion, I still want to see him, but he is not in the courtroom. Perhaps his lawyer, the defender, can give some helpful information. The defender, however, has never seen the accused. Someone else interviewed him on a routine prison visit. No one knows whether he has a family, a job, a home.

"Please have this defendant brought to court tomorrow and get me some information on him," I tell the defender.

He replies, "I'm sorry, Your Honor. I'll be working in a different courtroom tomorrow. There is no way I can find out about this man."

"We're dealing with human beings, not pieces of paper," I expostulate. "You are his lawyer. You should know him."

The young defender sadly shakes his head. "Your Honor, I work for a bureaucracy."

So do I, I remind myself, as I look at the clock and see that it is past 11:00 and there are 14 more matters to be heard today.

Four Up, Four Down

I refuse bail for a 14-year-old accused of slaying another child in a gang rumble. Will he be safer in jail than on the street, where the rival gang is lying in wait for him? I do not know. The boy is small and slender. The warden will put him in the wing with the feminine homosexuals to save him from assault. I mark on the commitment sheet that the boy is to attend school while in prison awaiting trial. But if the warden does not honor my order, I will not know.

A 23-year-old heroin addict tells me that there is no drug treatment program in prison. "It's just like the street. Nothin' but drugs," he says. I try to move his case ahead so that he can plead guilty at an early date and be transferred to the federal drug treatment center. He, like so many others up for robbery and burglary, is a Vietnam veteran. He acquired his habit overseas and now must steal in order to pay for his daily fix.

The next matter is a petition to suppress a confession. Court appointed counsel alleges that the defendant did not make a knowing and intelligent waiver of his rights when he confessed three murders to the police. Cornelius takes the stand and describes his life. His history is typical. He was sent to a disciplinary school at 11, ran away at 12, and spent a year in juvenile jail. At 17, there was a conviction for larceny and another period of incarceration. He is married, two children, separated from his wife. He is vague about the ages of the children. Cornelius works as an orderly in a hospital earning $80 a week take-home pay. At the end of each week he divides his money in two parts: $40 for living expenses and $40 for methadrine, which costs $20 a spoon.

Where does he buy it? On any corner in the ghetto. He steals the syringes from the hospital. His expenses are minimal except for the precious methadrine. He is riddled with V.D. He seldom eats.

While on a high, he shot and killed three strangers. Why did he do it?

"There are these voices I hear. They're fightin'. One tells me to kill; the other tells me not to. Sometimes I get so scared I run out into the street. That's when I'm in a low. But when I'm in a high, I feel I can walk in the rain without getting wet. I don't feel sad, I ain't lonely. When I'm comin' down from a high, I got to get another shot."

Now he is in a low—sad, soft-spoken, withdrawn, disinterested in his own fate. I see his skinny brown arms pocked with little needle scars. The psychiatrist says that when Cornelius is on drugs he cannot gauge reality. He could not understand the meaning of the privilege against self-incrimination and make a knowing and intelligent waiver of his rights.

The earnest psychiatrist explains patiently. I watch Cornelius, wraith-thin, sitting in withdrawn disinterest, lost in some dream of flight. Is he mad or are we—the prosecutor, the defense lawyer, the psychiatrist, and the judge? After five hours of testimony, I rule that the confession must be suppressed. There are dozens of eye-witnesses. The confession is not necessary to convict Cornelius. After this hearing, and before trial, a psychiatrist for the defense will testify that Cornelius is not mentally competent to stand trial; he cannot cooperate with his lawyer in preparing his defense. A psychiatrist for the prosecution will testify that when Cornelius has withdrawn from drugs he will be able to participate intelligently in his defense. The motion to defer trial will probably be denied. At the trial itself, one psychiatrist will testify that at the time of the shootings Cornelius did not know the difference between right and wrong and the nature and quality of his act. Another will testify that he did. Neither psychiatrist saw Cornelius at the time of the crimes. Both of them examined him in prison months later. They are certain of their opinions.

A middle-aged, white, epicenely soft man is next on the list. His face is a pasty gray. He mutters under his breath. He is accused of committing sodomy on three teenaged boys. Most of his meager salary he spent on these boys, and now they have turned on him. I order a psychiatric examination simply because I don't know what else to do. A month later the report is sent to me. It follows a standard format: facts (gleaned from the accused), background, diagnostic formulation and summary, and recommendation. This report states: "Probable latent schizophrenia. We recommend a full examination 60-day commitment." At the end of 60 days and the expenditure of hundreds of dollars, the doctors will decide that he is or is not schizophrenic, possibly sociopathic. A long period in a "structured environment" will be recommended. But what will the judge do? There are only two choices: prison, where he will be tormented and perhaps beaten by strong young thugs, or the street.

Lost in the Jailhouse

Most of the prisoners brought before me are young—under 30. I also see children who are charged with homicide. They are denied even the nominal protections of the juvenile court and are "processed" as adults. The 14-year-old accused of slaying another child in a gang rumble; the 16-year-old dope addict who, surprised while burglarizing a house, panicked and shot the unwary owner; the girl lookout for the gang, who is accused of conspiracy and murder. Many of these children are themselves parents. Can they be turned back to the streets? I refuse bail for an illiterate 15-year-old accused of murder and note on the bill of indictment that he be required to attend school while in detention. I ask the court-appointed lawyer to check with the warden and see that the boy is sent to class. But is there a class in remedial reading at the detention center? Who would pay for it? Not the overburdened public schools or the understaffed prisons. It is not a project likely to find a foundation grant.

A perplexed lawyer petitions for a second psychiatric examination for his client. The court psychiatrist has found him competent to stand trial but the lawyer tells me his client cannot discuss the case with him. Randolph, who is accused of assault with intent to kill, attacked a stranger in a bar and strangled the man, almost killing him. Fortunately, bystanders dragged Randolph away. I ask to speak with Randolph. A big, neatly dressed Negro steps up to the bar of the court. He speaks softly, "Judge," he says, "I'm afraid. I need help."

Randolph is out on bail. This is his first offense. He has a good work record. He is married, has two children, and lives with his family. It is Friday morning. I fear what may happen to him over the weekend. The court psychiatric unit is called.

"We've got people backed up for a

month," the doctor tells me. "Even if I took Randolph out of turn I couldn't see him until next week." When he does see Randolph it will be a 45-minute examination. A voluntary hospital commitment seems to be the only safeguard. But at least he will be watched for ten days. Gratefully, Randolph promises to go at once to the mental health clinic. What will happen to him after the ten-day period?

There is no time to wonder. The next case is waiting.

It is a sultry day. When the ancient air conditioner is turned on we cannot hear the testimony. When it is turned off the room is unbearable. At 4:45 p. m., I ask hopefully, "Have we finished the list?" But no, there is an application for a continuance on an extradition warrant. The papers from the demanding state have not arrived. It is a routine, daily occurrence.

I look around the courtroom. By this hour only the court personnel and a few policemen and detectives are present. "Where is the defendant?" I inquire. The prosecutor does not know. He is not responsible for producing him. The defender does not have him on his list. "Is he in custody?" I ask. We all search the records and discover that he was arrested more than five months ago. There is no notation that bail has ever been set. No private counsel has entered an appearance. A deputy sheriff checks and reports that he has not been brought up from the prison. The computerized records show that this man has never had a hearing. Hardened as we are, the prosecutor, the defender and I are horrified that someone should be sitting in jail all this time without ever having had an opportunity to say a word. Is he, in fact, the person wanted for an offense allegedly committed years ago and hundreds of miles away? Was he ever there? Is he a stable member of society? Has he a family, a job, a home? Is he a drug addict? No one knows. The papers do not indicate. No one in the courtroom has ever seen him. Each of us makes a note to check on this forgotten prisoner whom the computer may or may not print out for appearance on some other day in some other courtroom.

Nobody Waived Good-bye

The scene in criminal trial court is similar. Most of the cases are "waivers" and guilty pleas. The accused may waive his constitutional right to be tried by a jury of his peers and be tried by a judge alone. Fewer than five per cent of all cases are tried

by jury. In most cases, the accused not only waives his right to a jury trial but also to any trial and pleads guilty. Before accepting a waiver or a plea, the accused is asked the routine questions. Day after day defense counsel recites the following formula to poor, semiliterate defendants, some of whom are old and infirm, others young and innocent. Read this quickly:

"Do you know that you are accused of [the statutory crimes are read to him from the indictment]?

"Do you know that you have a right to a trial by jury in which the state must prove by evidence beyond a reasonable doubt that you committed the offenses and that if one juror disagrees you will not be found guilty?

"Do you know that by pleading guilty you are giving up your right to appeal the decision of this court except for an appeal based on the jurisdiction of the court, the legality of the sentence and the voluntariness of your plea of guilty? [The accused is not told that by the asking and answering of these questions in open court he has for all practical purposes also given up this ground for appeal.]

"Do you know that the judge is not bound by the recommendation of the District Attorney as to sentence but can sentence you up to —— years and impose a fine of ——— dollars? [The aggregate penalty is read to him. Judges may and often do give a heavier penalty than was recommended. They rarely give a lighter sentence.]

"Can you read and write the English language?

"Have you ever been in a mental hospital or under the care of a psychiatrist for a mental illness?

"Are you now under the influence of alcohol, drugs, or undergoing withdrawal symptoms?

"Have you been threatened, coerced, or promised anything for entering the plea of guilty other than the recommendation of sentence by the District Attorney?

"Are you satisfied with my representation?"

All this is asked quickly, routinely, as the prisoner stands before the bar of the court. He answers "Yes" to each question.

The final question is: "Are you pleading guilty because you are guilty?" The defendant looks at the defender, uncertainly.

"Have you consulted with your lawyer?" I inquire.

"Right now. 'Bout five minutes."

"We'll pass this case until afternoon. At the lunch recess, will you please confer with your client," I direct the defender.

In the afternoon, the accused, having talked with the lawyer for another ten minutes, again waives his right to a trial. He has been in jail more than eight months. The eight months in jail are applied to his sentence. He will be out by the end of the year—sooner than if he demanded a trial and was acquitted.

The plea has been negotiated by the assistant defender and the assistant prosecutor. The defendant says he was not promised anything other than a recommendation of sentence in return for the guilty plea. But the judge does not know what else the defendant has been told, whether his family and friends are willing to come and testify for him, whether his counsel has investigated the facts of the case to see whether indeed he does have a defense. The magic formula has been pronounced. The judge does not know what the facts are. Did the man really commit the offense? Even if there were a full-scale trial, truth might not emerge. Many of the witnesses have long since disappeared. How reliable will their memories be? The policeman will say he did not strike the accused. The accused will say that he did. Friends and relatives will say that the accused was with them at the time of the alleged crime. The victim, if he appears, will swear that this is the person whom he saw once briefly on a dark night eight months ago.

The lawyers are in almost equal ignorance. The prosecutor has the police report. The defender has only the vague and confused story of the accused. The judge is under pressure to "dispose" of the case. There is a score card for each judge kept by the computer. The judges have batting averages. Woe betide those who fail to keep pace in getting rid of cases. A long trial to determine guilt or innocence will put the judge at the bottom of the list. The prosecutors and public defenders also have their score cards of cases disposed of. Private defense counsel—whether paid by the accused or appointed by the court and paid by the public—has his own type of score card. For the fee paid, he can give only so many hours to the preparation and trial of this case. He must pay his rent, secretary and overhead. All of the persons involved in the justice system are bound by the iron laws of economics. What can the defendant afford for bail, counsel fees, witness fees, investigative expenses? All of these questions will inexorably determine the case that is presented to the court.

The National Conference on Criminal Justice, convened in January 1973 by Attorney General Kleindienst, recommends that plea bargaining be abolished within five years. What will replace it?

At the end of a day in which as a judge I have taken actions affecting for good or ill the lives of perhaps 15 or 20 litigants and their families, I am drained. I walk out of the stale-smelling, dusty courtroom into the fresh sunshine of a late spring day and feel as if I were released from prison. I breathe the soft air, but in my nostrils is the stench of the stifling cell blocks and detention rooms. While I sip my cool drink in the quiet of my garden, I cannot forget the prisoners, with their dry bologna sandwiches and only a drink of water provided at the pleasure of the hot and harried guards.

Was Cottle really guilty? I will never know. Fred made bail. Will he attack someone tonight or tomorrow? One reads the morning paper with apprehension. It is safer for the judge to keep them all locked up. There will be an outcry over the one prisoner released who commits a subsequent offense. Who will know or care about the scores of possibly innocent prisoners held in jail?

This is only one day in a diary. Replicate this by 260 times a year, at least 15,000 courts, and 10 or 20 or 30 years in the past. Can one doubt that the operation of the legal system is slowly but surely strangling the law?

I must sit only three and a half more weeks in criminal court. But there is a holiday. So with relief I realize that it is really only 17 more days that I must sit there this term. Next year I shall again have to take my turn.

I am reminded of Ivan Denisovich. Solzhenitsyn describes Ivan's bedtime thoughts in a Soviet prison. "Ivan Denisovich went to sleep content. He had been fortunate in many ways that day—and he hadn't fallen ill. He'd got over it. There were 3,653 days like this in his sentence. From the moment he woke to the moment he slept. The three extra days were for leap years."

WATCHING THE BENCH

Justice by Numbers

Mandatory sentencing drove me from the bench

Lois G. Forer

Lois G. Forer, a former judge of the Court of Common Pleas of Philadelphia, is the author, most recently, of Unequal Protection: Women, Children, and the Elderly in Court.

Michael S. would have been one of the more than 600,000 incarcerated persons in the United States. He would have been a statistic, yet another addition to a clogged criminal justice system. But he's not—in part because to me Michael was a human being: a slight 24-year-old with a young wife and small daughter. Not that I freed him; I tried him and found him guilty. He is free now only because he is a fugitive. I have not seen him since the day of his sentencing in 1984, yet since that day our lives have been inextricably connected. Because of his case I retired from the bench.

Michael's case appeared routine. He was a typical offender: young, black, and male, a high-school dropout without a job. The charge was an insignificant holdup that occasioned no comment in the press. And the trial itself was, in the busy life of a judge, a run-of-the-mill event.

The year before, Michael, brandishing a toy gun, held up a taxi and took $50 from the driver and the passenger, harming neither. This was Michael's first offense. Although he had dropped out of school to marry his pregnant girlfriend, Michael later obtained a high school equivalency diploma. He had been stead-

ily employed, earning enough to send his daughter to parochial school—a considerable sacrifice for him and his wife. Shortly before the holdup, Michael had lost his job. Despondent because he could not support his family, he went out on a Saturday night, had more than a few drinks, and then robbed the taxi.

There was no doubt that Michael was guilty. But the penalty posed problems. To me, a robbery in a taxi is not an intrinsically graver offense than a robbery in an alley, but to the Pennsylvania legislature, it is. Because the holdup occurred on public transportation, it fell within the ambit of the state's mandatory sentencing law—which required a minimum sentence of five years in the state penitentiary. In Pennsylvania, a prosecutor may decide not to demand imposition of that law, but Michael's prosecuting attorney wanted the five-year sentence.

One might argue that a five-year sentence for a $50 robbery is excessive or even immoral, but to a judge, those arguments are necessarily irrelevant. He or she has agreed to enforce the law, no matter how ill-advised, unless the law is unconstitutional.

I believed the mandatory sentencing law was, and like many of my colleagues I had held it unconstitutional in several other cases for several reasons. We agreed that it violates the constitutional principle of separation of powers because it can be invoked by the prosecutor, and not by the judge. In addition, the act is arbitrary and capricious in its application. Robbery, which is often a simple purse snatching, is covered, but not child molestation or incest, two of society's

From *The Washington Monthly,* April 1992, pp. 12-14, 16-18. Copyright © 1992 by Lois G. Forer. Reprinted by permission of Curtis Brown, Ltd.

most damaging offenses. Nor can a defendant's previous record or mental state be considered. A hardened repeat offender receives the same sentence as a retarded man who steals out of hunger. Those facts violate the fundamental Anglo-American legal principles of individualized sentencing and proportionality of the penalty to the crime.

Thus in Michael's case, I again held the statute to be unconstitutional and turned to the sentencing guidelines—a state statute designed to give uniform sentences to offenders who commit similar crimes. The minimum sentence prescribed by the guidelines was 24 months.

A judge can deviate from the prescribed sentence if he or she writes an opinion explaining the reasons for the deviation. While this sounds reasonable in theory, "downwardly departing" from the guidelines is extremely difficult. The mitigating circumstances that influence most judges are not included in the limited list of factors on which "presumptive" sentence is based—that an offender is a caretaker of small children; that the offender is mentally retarded; or that the offender, like Michael, is emotionally distraught.

So I decided to deviate from the guidelines, sentencing Michael to 11-and-a-half months in the county jail and permitting him to work outside the prison during the day to support his family. I also imposed a sentence of two years' probation following his imprisonment conditioned upon repayment of the $50. My rationale for the lesser penalty, outlined in my lengthy opinion, was that this was a first offense, no one was harmed, Michael acted under the pressures of unemployment and need, and he seemed truly contrite. He had never committed a violent act and posed no danger to the public. A sentence of close to a year seemed adequate to convince Michael of the seriousness of his crime. Nevertheless, the prosecutor appealed.

Michael returned to his family, obtained steady employment, and repaid the victims of his crime. I thought no more about Michael until 1986, when the state supreme court upheld the appeal and ordered me to resentence him to a minimum of five years in the state penitentiary. By this time Michael had successfully completed his term of imprisonment and probation, including payment of restitution. I checked Michael's record. He had not been rearrested.

I was faced with a legal and moral dilemma. As a judge I had sworn to uphold the law, and I could find no legal grounds for violating an order of the supreme court. Yet five years' imprisonment was grossly disproportionate to the offense. The usual grounds for imprisonment are retribution, deterrence, and rehabilitation. Michael had paid his retribution by a short term of imprisonment and by making restitution to the victims. He had been effectively deterred from committing future crimes. And by any measurable standard he had been rehabilitated. There was no social or criminological justification for sending him back to prison. Given the choice between defying a court order or my conscience, I decided to leave the bench where I had sat for 16 years.

That didn't help Michael, of course; he was resentenced by another judge to serve the balance of the five years: four years and 15 days. Faced with this prospect, he disappeared. A bench warrant was issued, but given the hundreds of fugitives—including dangerous ones—loose in Philadelphia, I doubt that anyone is seriously looking for him.

But any day he may be stopped for a routine traffic violation; he may apply for a job or a license; he may even be the victim of a crime—and if so, the ubiquitous computer will be alerted and he will be returned to prison to serve the balance of his sentence, plus additional time for being a fugitive. It is not a happy prospect for him and his family—nor for America, which is saddled with a punishment system that operates like a computer—crime in, points tallied, sentence out—utterly disregarding the differences among the human beings involved.

The mandatory sentencing laws and guidelines that exist today in every state were designed to smooth out the inequities in the American judiciary, and were couched in terms of fairness to criminals—they would stop the racist judge from sentencing black robbers to be hanged, or the crusading judge from imprisoning pot smokers for life. Guidelines make sense, for that very reason. But they have had an ugly and unintended result—an increase in the number of American prisoners and an increase in the length of the sentences they serve. Meanwhile, the laws have effectively neutralized judges who prefer sentencing the nonviolent to alternative programs or attempt to keep mothers with young children out of jail.

Have the laws made justice fairer—the central objective of the law? I say no, and a recent report by the Federal Sentencing Commission concurs. It found that, even under mandatory sentencing laws, black males served 83.4 months to white males' 53.7 months for the same offenses. (Prosecutors are more likely to demand imposition of the mandatory laws for blacks than for whites.)

Most important, however, as mandatory sentencing packs our prisons and busts our budgets, it doesn't prevent crime very effectively. For certain kinds of criminals, alternative sentencing is the most effective type of punishment. That, by the way, is a cold, hard statistic—rather like Michael will be when they find him.

Sentenced to death

In the past two decades, all 50 state legislatures have enacted mandatory sentencing laws, sentencing guideline statutes, or both. The result: In 1975 there were 263,291 inmates in federal and state prisons. Today there are over 600,000—more than in any other nation—the bill for which comes to $20.3 billion a year. Yet incarceration has not reduced the crime rate or made our streets and communities safer. The number of known crimes committed in the U.S. has increased 10 percent in the last five years.

How did we get into this no-win situation? Like most legislative reforms, it started with good intentions. In 1970, after the turmoil of the sixties, legislators were bombarded with pleas for "law and order." A young, eager, newly appointed federal judge, Marvin Frankel, had an idea.

Before his appointment, Frankel had experienced little personal contact with the criminal justice system. Yet his slim book, *Fair and Certain Punishment*, offered a system of guidelines to determine the length of various sentences. Each crime was given a certain number of points. The offender was also given a number of points depending upon his or her prior record, use of a weapon, and a few other variables. The judge merely needed to add up the points to calculate the length of imprisonment.

The book was widely read and lauded for two main reasons. First, it got tough on criminals and made justice "certain." A potential offender would know in advance the penalty he would face and thus be deterred. (Of course, a large proportion of street crimes are not premeditated, but that fact was ignored.) And second, it got tough on the "bleeding heart" judges. All offenders similarly situated would be treated the same.

The plan sounded so fair and politically promising that many states rushed to implement it in the seventies. In Pennsylvania, members of the legislature admonished judges not to oppose the guidelines because the alternative would be even worse: mandatory sentences. In fact, within a few years almost every jurisdiction had both sentencing guidelines and mandatory sentencing laws. Since then, Congress has enacted some 60 mandatory sentencing laws on the federal level.

As for unfairnesses in sentencing—for instance, the fact that the robber with his finger in his jacket gets the same sentence as the guy with a semiautomatic—these could have been rectified by giving appellate courts jurisdiction to review sentences, as is the law in Canada. This was not done on either the state or federal level. Thus what influential criminologist James Q. Wilson had argued during the height of the battle had become the law of the land: The legal system should "most definitely stop pretending that the judges know any better than the rest of us how to provide 'individualized justice.' "

Hardening time

I'm not sure I knew better than the rest of you, but I knew a few things about Michael and the correctional system I would be throwing him into. At the time of Michael's sentencing, both the city of Philadelphia and the commonwealth of Pennsylvania were, like many cities and states, in such poor fiscal shape that they did not have money for schools and health care, let alone new prisons, and the ones they did have were overflowing. The city was under a federal order to reduce the prison population; untried persons accused of dangerous crimes were being released, as were offenders who had not completed their sentences.

As for Michael, his problems and those of his

family were very real to me. Unlike appellate judges who never see the individuals whose lives and property they dispose of, a trial judge sees living men and women. I had seen Michael and his wife and daughter. I had heard him express remorse. I had favorable reports about him from the prison and his parole officer. Moreover, Michael, like many offenders who appeared before me, had written to me several times. I felt I knew him.

Of course, I could have been wrong. As Wilson says, judges are not infallible—and most of them know that. But they have heard the evidence, seen the offender, and been furnished with presentence reports and psychiatric evaluations. They are in a better position to evaluate the individual and devise an appropriate sentence than anyone else in the criminal justice system.

Yet under mandatory sentencing laws, the complexities of each crime and criminal are ignored. And seldom do we ask what was once a legitimate question in criminal justice: What are the benefits of incarceration? The offenders are off the streets for the period of the sentence, but once released, most will soon be rearrested. (Many crimes are committed in prison, including murder, rape, robbery, and drug dealing.) They have not been "incapacitated," another of the theoretical justifications for imprisonment. More likely, they have simply been hardened.

Sentence structure

Is there another way to sentence criminals without endangering the public? I believe there is. During my tenure on the bench, I treated imprisonment as the penalty of last resort, not the penalty of choice. And my examination of 16 years' worth of cases suggests my inclination was well founded. While a recent Justice Department study found that two thirds of all prisoners are arrested for other offenses within three years of release, more than two thirds of the 1,000-plus offenders I sentenced to probation conditioned upon payment of reparations to victims successfully completed their sentences and were not rearrested. I am not a statistician, so I had my records analyzed and verified by Elmer Weitekamp, then a doctoral candidate in criminology at the Wharton School of the University of Pennsylvania. He confirmed my findings.

The offenders who appeared before me were mostly poor people, poor enough to qualify for representation by a public defender. I did not see any Ivan Boeskys or Leona Helmsleys, and although there was a powerful mafia in Philadelphia, I did not see any dons, either. Approximately three fourths of these defendants were nonwhite. Almost 80 percent were high school dropouts. Many were functionally illiterate. Almost a third had some history of mental problems, were retarded, or had been in special schools. One dreary day my court reporter said plaintively, "Judge, why can't we get a better class of criminal?"

Not all of these offenders were sentenced to probation, obviously. But I had my own criteria or guidelines—very different from those established by most states and the federal government—for deciding on a punishment. My primary concern was public safety. The most important question I asked myself was whether the offender could be deterred from committing other crimes. No one can predict with certainty who will or will not commit a crime, but there are indicators most sensible people recognize as danger signals.

First, was this an irrational crime? If an arsonist sets a fire to collect insurance, that is a crime but also a rational act. Such a person can be deterred by being made to pay for the harm done and the costs to the fire department. However, if the arsonist sets fires just because he likes to see them, it is highly unlikely that he can be stopped from setting others, no matter how high the fine. Imprisonment is advisable even though it may be a first offense.

Second, was there wanton cruelty? If a robber maims or slashes the victim, there is little likelihood that he can safely be left in the community. If a robber simply displays a gun but does not fire it or harm the victim, then one should consider his life history, provocation, and other circumstances in deciding whether probation is appropriate.

Third, is this a hostile person? Was his crime one of hatred, and does he show any genuine remorse? Most rapes are acts of hostility, and the vast majority of rapists have a record of numerous sexual assaults. I remember one man who raped his mother. I gave him the maximum sentence under the law—20 years—but with good behavior, he got out fairly quickly. He immediately raped another elderly woman. Clearly, few rapists can safely be left in the community, and in my tenure, I incarcerated every one.

Yet gang rape, although a brutal and horrifying crime, is more complicated. The leader is clearly hostile and should be punished severely. Yet the followers can't be so neatly categorized. Some may act largely out of cowardice and peer pressure.

Fourth, is this a person who knows he is doing wrong but cannot control himself? Typical of such offenders are pedophiles. One child abuser who appeared before me had already been convicted of abusing his first wife's child. I got him on the second wife's child and sentenced him to the maximum. Still, he'll get out with good behavior, and I shudder to think about the children around him when he does. This is one case in which justice is not tough enough.

By contrast, some people who have committed homicide present very little danger of further violence—although many more do. Once a young man came before me because he had taken aim at a person half a block away and then shot him in the back, killing him. Why did he do it? "I wanted to get me a body." He should never get out. But the mandatory codes don't make great distinctions between him and another murderer who came before me, a woman who shot and killed a boy after he and his friends brutally gang-raped her teenage daughter.

I found this woman guilty of first-degree murder, but I found no reason to incarcerate her. She had four young children to support who would have become wards of the welfare department and probably would have spent their childhoods in a series of foster homes. I placed her on probation—a decision few judges now have the discretion to impose. She had not been arrested before. She has not been arrested since.

Of course, the vast majority of men, women, and children in custody in the United States are not killers, rapists, or arsonists. They're in prison for some type of theft—a purse snatching, burglary, or embezzlement. Many of these criminals can be punished without incarceration. If you force a first-time white-collar criminal to pay heavily for his crimes —perhaps three times the value of the money or property taken—he'll get the message that crime does not pay. As for poor people, stealing is not always a sign that the individual is an unreasonable risk to the community. It's often a sign that they want something—a car, Air Jordans—that they are too poor to buy themselves. Many of them, if they are not violent, can also be made to make some restitution and learn that crime doesn't pay.

Of course, to most of us, the idea of a nonprison sentence is tantamount to exoneration; a criminal sentenced to probation has effectively "gotten off." And there's a reason for that impression: Unless the probationer is required by the sentencing judge to perform specific tasks, probation is a charade. The probationer meets with the probation officer, briefly, perhaps once a month—making the procedure a waste of time for both. The officer duly records the meeting and the two go their separate ways until the probationer is arrested for another offense.

When I made the decision not to send a criminal to prison, I wanted to make sure that the probation system I sent them into had teeth. So I set firm conditions. If the offender was functionally illiterate, he was unemployable and would probably steal or engage in some other illegal activity once released. Thus in my sentencing, I sent him to school and ordered the probation officer to see that he went. (I use the masculine pronoun deliberately for I have never seen an illiterate female offender under the age of 60.) I ordered school dropouts to get their high school equivalency certificates and find jobs. All offenders were ordered to pay restitution or reparations within their means or earning capacity to their victims. Sometimes it was as little as $5 a week. Offenders simply could not return to their old, feckless lifestyles without paying some financial penalty for their wrongdoing.

Monitoring probation wasn't easy for me, or the probation officers with whom I worked. Every day I'd come into my office, look at my calendar, and notice that, say, 30 days had passed since Elliott was let out. So I'd call the probation office. Has Elliott made his payment? Is he going to his GED class? And so on. If the answer was no, I'd hold a violation hearing with the threat of incarceration if the conditions were not met within 30 days. After I returned a few people to jail for noncompliance, both my offenders and their probation officers knew I meant business. (Few probation officers protested my demands; their jobs were more meaningful and satisfying, they said.)

Of course, probation that required education and work and payment plans meant real work for criminals, too. But there was a payoff both the probation officers and I could see: As offenders worked and learned and made restitution, their attitudes often changed dramatically.

Time and punishment

My rules of sentencing don't make judgeship easier; relying on mandatory sentencing is a far better way to guarantee a leisurely, controversy-free career on the bench. But my rules are, I believe, both effective and transferable: an application of common sense that any reasonable person could follow to similar ends. What prevents Americans from adopting practical measures like these is an atavistic belief in the sanctity of punishment. Even persons who have never heard of Emmanuel Kant or the categorical imperative to punish believe that violation of law must be followed by the infliction of pain.

If we Americans treated crime more practically—as socially unacceptable behavior that should be curbed for the good of the community—we might begin to take a rational approach to the development of alternatives to prison. We might start thinking in terms not of punishment but of public safety, deterrence, and rehabilitation. Penalties like fines, work, and payment of restitution protect the public better and more cheaply than imprisonment in many cases.

Mind you, sentencing guidelines are not inherently evil. Intelligent guidelines would keep some judges from returning repeat offenders to the streets and others from putting the occasional cocaine user away for 10 years. Yet those guidelines must allow more latitude for the judge and the person who comes before him. While some states' sentencing laws include provisions that allow judges to override the mandatory sentences in some cases, the laws are

for the most part inflexible—they deny judges the freedom to discriminate between the hardened criminal and the Michael. Richard H. Girgenti, the criminal justice director of New York state, has long proposed that the legislature give judges more discretion to impose shorter sentences for nonviolent and noncoercive felonies. This common-sense proposal has not been acted on in New York or any other state with mandatory sentencing laws.

Current laws are predicated on the belief that there must be punishment for every offense in terms of prison time rather than alternative sentences. But when it comes to determining the fate of a human being, there must be room for judgment. To make that room, we must stop acting as if mathematic calculations are superior to human thought. We must abolish mandatory sentencing laws and change the criteria on which sentencing guidelines are based.

Why not permit judges more freedom in making their decisions, provided that they give legitimate reasons? (If a judge doesn't have a good reason for deviating—if he's a reactionary or a fool—his sentencing decision will be overturned.) And why not revise the guidelines to consider dangerousness rather than the nomenclature of the offense? If we made simple reforms like these, thousands of nonthreatening, nonhabitual offenders would be allowed to recompense their victims and society in a far less expensive and far more productive way.

You may be wondering, after all this, if I have a Willie Horton in my closet—a criminal whose actions after release privately haunt me. I do. I sentenced him to 10 to 20 years in prison—the maximum the law allowed—for forcible rape. He was released after eight years and promptly raped another woman. I could foresee what would happen but was powerless to impose a longer sentence.

And then there are the other cases that keep me up nights: those of men and women I might have let out, but didn't. And those of people like Michael, for whom justice shouldn't have been a mathematical equation.

The High-Tech Court Of the Future

**It holds the promise of cheaper, fairer, quicker justice.
But there will be a few hurdles along the way.**

STEVE POLILLI

Steve Polilli is a Dallas-area freelance writer.

A criminal-court judge sitting in her chambers mulls over a difficult fraud case. She picks up a pen-like device attached to a computer to select a case from an on-screen list. The computer displays videotaped trial testimony with captioned text. Using the computer pen, the judge writes a key phrase onto the screen and the computer fast-forwards to that portion of the testimony. After reviewing the video passage, the judge switches to a criminal records database before calling up an artificial-intelligence-based software program to determine the appropriate punishment.

Downstairs, several citizens ready to plead to traffic citations insert credit cards into slots in automatic teller-style kiosks. After viewing a computer likeness of the ticket, each offender is told by an on-screen narrator the cost of a guilty plea.

At the same time, lawyers across the county transmit filings in civil cases to a courthouse computer from their firms' desktop computers. Other attorneys use touch-tone phones to access a voice-response docketing information system.

Meanwhile, a suspect at a rural jail some 40 miles distant is brought before a video conferencing console connected through telephone lines to a similar device at the county courthouse, where a judge conducts remote arraignment hearings.

Welcome to the courthouse of the future.

While all of the individual components of this high-technology scenario are available now and in use in government or the private sector, no courthouse yet embodies them all, or the range of other technologies that also promise to make the judicial process more efficient. In fact, judicial automation lags behind the other branches of government.

Many courts, for example, still shun the use of credit cards for payments of fees and fines, according to Phil Atkisson, president of a Bakersfield, California, information systems development firm. That, Atkisson thinks, will have to change. "Courts cannot continue doing business as they have," he says. "They must change their ways and look at things as businesses do, and technology is part of that."

Take collections, for example. Larry Webster, director of technology programs for the National Center for State Courts, tells of one jurisdiction that saw its collections from default judgments increase from $3 million to $7 million during the first year it began using computers to track them. Even after the court caught up with some long-overdue accounts, collections in subsequent years were still running about $5 million annually.

Success stories like that are a big part of the reason for the increasing interest in automating the judicial process. Another reason is the growing role and size of the court systems. "Courts haven't gotten a lot of attention in the technology arena until now because they didn't have the big payrolls and the big budgets as did the executive and legislative branches," says Fred Dugger, a past president of the National Association of State Information Resource Executives. "That's all beginning to change, particularly for civil courts."

The flow of paper, a prime target for the high-tech approach, is greater in the civil courts, and the number of related agencies to be integrated is fewer. In addition, high-tech equipment vendors have surely noted that civil-court budgets are bigger.

Technologically speaking, criminal courts are a tougher nut to crack. They must interface seamlessly with computers and databases at a number of agencies, including those of law enforcement, corrections and prosecutors. Adding a further layer of difficulty are the largely unanswered questions about how to secure sensitive data when access is widespread.

DESPITE THE BARRIERS, THE FULL-scale automation of the courts is getting under way. While it may be years before some technologies, such as automated speech recognition and artificial intelligence, will yield great benefit, others offer immediate help.

For most court administrators, the most immediate need is for ways to cope with the mountains of paper that clog the court systems. That's why many court systems are getting into imaging technology, in which paper documents are optically scanned and stored on laser disks.

The Los Angeles County Municipal Courts have installed an imaging system valued at over $1 million. A central site has an optical storage system with laser disk "jukeboxes," and several courts have terminals to access within seconds any of the more than 60,000 traffic citations issued monthly. Scores of file cabinets have been eliminated.

"Phone inquiries and various transactions can be handled much more quickly and easily, and the processing time for tickets is greatly reduced," says Peggy Mitchell of the court's information systems division.

But while captured images may be viewed or printed out, the information those images contain cannot be used as traditional computer data—searched, manipulated by database software, or compiled into reports. One solution is the use of optical character recognition systems. Like imaging systems, OCR systems scan in the image of a document, but a computer program then "reads" the data contained by the document bit by bit to convert it to a digitized format.

Documents including court proceedings, penal codes and state statutes can be scanned, digitized and stored on either optical or magnetic media in a central statewide computer. "The biggest payback on this is if a rule of law is changed. Instead of sending out replacement pages and instructions for making the change, the change is made centrally and everyone has immediate access to it," says Mary Lu Holter, IBM's Baltimore-based senior adviser for justice applications.

Of course, the courts would be better served if all of the raw material of justice—traffic tickets, filings, motions and other documents—didn't exist on paper at all. There have already been steps in that direction. Most large police departments already create offense reports from data keyed into a computer system. Hand-held citation computers and legal papers created and filed by computer could eliminate a lot of the burden on the court.

The process of creating such an integrated judicial automation scheme is highly specific to each jurisdiction, which must cope with data coming in from agencies that use incompatible computers and data formats. A nationwide judicial standard for an electronic data interchange format and access techniques would eliminate much of the work involved. An effort to create such a universal format is under way under the auspices of the American Bar Association and the American National Standards Institute.

MEANWHILE, THE RAPIDLY declining cost of computing power is making increasingly viable many once-exotic technologies. Among those that the courts are beginning to put to use are multimedia computing, computer-aided transcription and video conferencing.

Multimedia is a series of computer programs and powerful hardware that when combined allow integration of computer data, colorful graphics, voice and video signals. The Long Beach Municipal Court in California uses multimedia for its automated court clerk kiosk system. The kiosks, located at the court building, look much like an automated bank teller machine, with a screen, credit card slot and keypad. Attached to a personal computer and a video disk

player, the color video monitor shows a narrator, speaking in either English or Spanish, advising the user of options on a given traffic offense. The citizen presses a touch-sensitive screen to choose a plea, method of payment or other options.

The courts would be better served if all of the raw material of justice didn't exist on paper at all.

Video conferencing is particularly useful in rural areas or anywhere a courthouse is physically remote from the jail. Video conferencing units, some as small as a briefcase, include a television screen, camera and microphone. A judge might sit before one unit while another is put in the jail. These devices are typically used in pretrial hearings.

Computer aided transcription hasn't moved legal stenographers from their familiar position in front of the bench, but it does eliminate the need for translation of the stenographic record. With CAT, the recording keypad is linked to a small computer that has been programmed to translate the keystrokes into text. The text, which on some available systems annotates a video recording, can be searched for keywords; when a jury asks to review certain testimony, the system scans the data and replays the video or prints a partial transcript.

Other, still-evolving technologies hold a lot of promise for the courts. Voice recognition computers have a

considerable development process ahead of them before they can recognize different speakers at one time, but such systems are now fairly adept at responding to a single speaker who has given speech samples. Within a decade, experts predict, voice recognition systems may replace court stenographers entirely.

Artificial intelligence, in which a computer replicates the knowledge and reasoning of a skilled professional, may someday assist judges in sentencing or attorneys in selecting jurors. While development of those applications is just beginning, a number of courts are already using a sophisticated computer program to evaluate the likelihood of substance abuser rehabilitation.

Substance Abuse Life Circumstance Evaluation, or SALCE, is a computerized questionnaire that provides judges and social workers with a tool for sentence recommendations. Bryan Ellis, president of Clarkston, Michigan-based ADE Inc., is a psychologist who used his background in substance abuse treatment to develop the personal computer-based program. He said SALCE has been used in 26 states to evaluate 300,000 substance abusers with a 98 percent degree of accuracy. "The program isn't perfect, but it's a much more sophisticated and accurate evaluation than a human can perform," Ellis says. "The computer has absolutely no biases that a human can bring to an evaluation of this sort."

SALCE is an example of the effort under way to bring the promise of information technology to bear on the problems and needs of the courts. The bottom line is that the public will be better served by increased use of technology in the courtroom. Justice will be cheaper, fairer and quicker in the automated court.

"The bulk of the work of the courts is mindless and repetitive," says Larry Webster, the National Center for State Courts technology director. "That is exactly what the computer is good at. Technology makes the court more effective."

Charter Reform in the 1990s

Recent release of the new Seventh Edition of the Model City Charter *has heightened awareness of the need for substantive charter review in many municipalities. The new* Model—*with its emphasis on simplicity and brevity—is truly a charter for the 1990s, in that it fosters citizen understanding of local government structure and (ultimately) broader participation in local governance. Administrative specifics on which the Charter is silent can readily be provided through legislative ordinance appropriate for unique local conditions.*

Joseph F. Zimmerman

Joseph F. Zimmerman is professor of political science, Graduate School of Public Affairs, State University of New York at Albany. He is also editor of the National Civic Review *Metro Trends Department.*

Issuance of the Seventh Edition of the *Model City Charter* by the National Civic League in 1989 focuses attention upon the need for a review of the typical local government charter by concerned citizens and public officials. A municipal charter is the fundamental law of the municipal corporation and is the local equivalent of a state or national constitution. The charter establishes the government, structures the legislative and executive branches, allocates power to the two branches, and contains provisions to ensure that the government will remain under the control of the voters.

A carefully drafted charter promotes democratic control of the government by providing citizens with a readily available source of information on the structure, powers, and procedures of the government and the roles that citizens can play in the governance system. In addition, a good charter helps ensure that city resources are employed in the most efficient, economical, and ethical manner.

Unfortunately, many charters are old and highly detailed, and not attuned to the special environments within which many local governments operate today. The older charters were drafted prior to the municipal reform and professional management movements that were active at the turn of the century and influenced the development of the *Model City Charter*.

Citizens in a non-chartered general purpose local government experience great difficulty in obtaining complete and accurate information on the structure, powers, and procedures of their government because such information is buried in various general and special state laws, and many of these laws are archaic and technically confusing. Hence, a strong case can be made for enactment of a state constitutional or statutory requirement that every general purpose local government must operate under a charter.

TYPES OF MUNICIPAL CHARTERS

Cities in the United States operate under special, general, optional, and "home rule" charters. In addition, counties, towns, and villages in a number of states also have charters or are authorized to draft and adopt charters. In New York State, for example, nineteen of the fifty-seven counties outside New York City have charters. Units without a charter are governed by state general laws.

Special charters. Historically, the city was the only form of municipal corporation in the United States and originally operated under a charter granted by the colonial legislature or a royal charter issued by the Lieutenant Governor-in-Council. Subsequent to the Revolutionary War, all cities were created by the state legislature by issuance of a special charter.

In theory, a special charter is custom-tailored to the city, granting it precisely the type of government organization and powers the unit needs. The special charter system in practice suffers from two major disadvantages:

• The state legislature often acts capriciously, forcing upon cities unwieldy or burdensome governmental structures and imposing severe limitations on city action; and

• The excessive time expended by state legislatures on city problems leads to a neglect of state problems. For these reasons, the constitutions of many states have been amended to prohibit the granting of special charters.

General charters. Under the general charter system, each type of local government, large or small, is granted an identical charter. In theory, the system provides for equal corporate privileges for all cities and no distinctions are made in the structure of the cities. In practice, a general charter has grossly uneven effects because it burdens small cities with administrative paraphernalia they do not need or want, and deprives large cities of urgently needed powers and facilities.

Classified charters. In an effort to avoid the defects associated with special and general charters, a number of states have adopted the classified charter system. Under it, cities are classified according to populations, and a uniform charter is provided for all cities within the same population class.

Unfortunately, classification often has been utilized by the state legislature to evade constitutional prohibitions against the issuance of special charters. By creating a large number of classes of cities, a legislature in effect can impose a special charter upon each or most cities.

Even if the legislature adopts a reasonable classification system, classified charters suffer from two defects:
• The charter fails to take account of different environment characteristics of cities with similar populations; and
• The system requires a change of charter—no matter how satisfactory the existing one is—if a city's population increases or declines beyond the limits of its class.

Optional charters. The optional charter system has the advantages of securing a degree of uniformity while permitting a degree of local self-determination. Although considered by many observers to be superior to the special, general, and classified charter systems, a consensus of opinion exists that citizens should be granted greater discretionary authority in determining the structure and powers of their local governments.

"Home rule" charters. A "home rule" charter system allows voters in a local government to draft, adopt, and amend a municipal charter. The 1875 Missouri Constitution was the first state constitution to authorize a local government to draft and adopt a charter.[1]

Alabama, Indiana, Illinois, Kentucky, North Carolina, and Virginia do not allow the adoption of a locally drafted charter. In the other states, the power to adopt such a charter is limited to specific types of political subdivisions (counties in Georgia) and in still other states the power is restricted to units with a specified minimum population size (cities with a population of 3,500 or more in Arizona and cities exceeding 5,000 in Texas). The constitutional grant authority to local governments to draft, adopt, and amend charters specifies the matters that are subject to local control. The New York State Constitution, for example, grants general purpose local governments authority relative to their property, structure of government, and local affairs.[2] A major problem that arises involves distinguishing between local and state or general affairs, and the courts are called upon to make the distinction.

The "home rule" charter system has four major advantages:
• The system eliminates or reduces greatly state legislative interference in local affairs.
• Citizens are permitted to determine the form and administrative organization of their local government.
• The state legislature is relieved of the time-consuming burden of special legislation and can devote its full attention to state problems.
• Citizens have a greater voice in the determination of local governmental policies and thus are encouraged to become more interested and active in local affairs.

THE MODEL CITY CHARTER

The Model City Charter traces its origin to the first draft of the charter presented at the 1898 National Conference on Government in Indianapolis and the first edition adopted by the National Municipal League (now the National Civic League) in 1900. The purpose of the *Model* is to provide interested citizens and public officials with guidance relative to the best provisions that should be included in a municipal charter. As a model, it is anticipated that adopting municipalities will make a number of changes in its provisions to accommodate special conditions within cities. Recognizing this fact, the *Model* contains several carefully drafted alternative provisions that have functioned successfully in various municipalities.

A municipal charter is the fundamental law of the municipal corporation and is the local equivalent of a state or national constitution.

Based upon the devolution of powers method of allocating political power to municipalities, the *Model* stipulates that "the city shall have all powers possible for a city to have under the constitution and laws of this state as fully and completely as though they were specifically enumerated in this charter." By adopting this method of determining powers of the city, the charter is kept short because there is no need to list the specific powers the city may exercise. Special charters, in contrast, are long because they *do* contain a listing of the powers the city may exercise.

The electoral system. Recognizing the critical importance of the electoral system employed to elect members of the city council, the *Model City Charter* offers five alternative methods. There are two additional electoral systems—limited voting and cumulative voting—not included in the *Model City Charter.*[3] While space limitations preclude a discussion of all the trade-offs involved in choosing one electoral system over another, the principal considerations are summarized in the following paragraphs:

- **Election at-large.** Under this alternative, each voter may cast a ballot for as many candidates as there are seats on the council. All seats may be elected at each election, or staggered terms may be employed. This alternative is the one favored by the early municipal reformers who were convinced that large "invisible" city councils were controlled by corrupt political machines which were the product of a ward electoral system that failed to provide fair representation.[4]

In cities with a sizable minority population, at-large elections may result in the underrepresentation of minority groups because only candidates who command wide support throughout the city generally will be elected.

- **Election at-large with residency requirements.** This system is designed to ensure that members of the city council elected at-large reside in the various sections of the city. If a minority group is geographically concentrated in a district, the system may facilitate the election of a minority member of the council, but does not guarantee that the group will be represented by someone of their choice.

- **Mixed at-large and single-member district system.** This system recognizes that at-large systems may not provide proper representation for all groups, and that ward or single-member district elections in the past have had undesirable consequences.

By employing a mixed system, it is hoped that a number of members of the council will have a city-wide perspective and concern for what is best for the city as a whole, while other members will have a special concern for the problems of their respective districts.

- **Single-member district system.** Originally known as the ward system, the single-member district system is a form of limited voting, in that each voter may cast a ballot only for one candidate for city council.

Although discredited in the past, the Federal Voting Rights Act of 1965, as amended, has promoted the employment of this system to help racial and ethnic minorities gain direct representation on city councils. Where minority groups 1) are concentrated geographically and 2) vote as blocks, the system helps ensure the election of representative members of the city council. Nevertheless, the system suffers from defects, such as the opportunity for gerrymandering of district lines and failure to provide direct representation of any minority that is so evenly distributed that it cannot elect a candidate in any district, even though its voting strength throughout the city is large enough to warrant direct representation.

- **Proportional representation.** This system of preferential voting is designed to alter the basis of representation by ensuring that sizable parties and groups are represented approximately in proportion to their voting strength.

With the exception of New York City and Cleveland, where multi-seat districts were used, proportional representation has always been employed on an at-large basis in the United States. The principal advantage of proportional representation is that it ensures majority rule while guaranteeing minority representation. This system is based upon the recognition that in a modern city there are numerous factional and ethnic divisions; proportional representation makes it impossible for any political party or faction with a slight voting majority or plurality to elect all or most members of a legislative body.

- **Limited voting.** This semi-proportional system is traceable in origin to the failure during the nineteenth century of the single-member district system in England and the United States to provide fair representation of minority parties. Under limited voting, each elector must vote for fewer candidates than there are seats on the city council; the plurality rule determines the winners. Limited voting ensures that a sizable minority group cannot be excluded from the legislative body. For example, if voters are limited to voting for a maximum of five candidates for a seven-member council, the largest party typically will win five seats and the other party will win two seats.

- **Cumulative voting.** As a semi-proportional system, cumulative voting has the same objective as limited voting: allocating seats approximately in proportion to votes. Each voter has the same number of votes as there are seats on the legislative body and the voter may give all votes to one candidate or apportion them among several candidates according to preference. Provided it is politically cohesive and informed, a minority party or group can concentrate its votes on one candidate or a few candidates with the expectation that the candidate(s) will be elected.

In cities with large councils, limited voting, cumulative voting, and proportional representation may be combined with multi-seat districts.

The chief executive. Special city charters issued in the nineteenth century suffer from a number of defects, including lack of a strong executive, as the mayor typically is weak in terms of formal powers. Council domination and decentralization of administration are prominent characteristics of this form of municipal government. In general, cities with this form are not operated in the most efficient and economical manner.

To remedy this problem, the *Model City Charter* directs the city council to appoint a professional city manager for an indefinite term. Subject to removal by a majority vote of the council at any time, the manager is the chief administrative officer of the city. The council is responsible for establishing municipal policies with the advice of the manager who appoints and supervises all subordinate administrators and employees, prepares and submits the budget to the council, implements ordinances, and performs other duties as directed by the council.

The council-manager plan has four major advantages:

• The direction of the city's administration is centered completely in one professionally trained individual.

• The plan is simple and the governmental processes are followed readily by all voters.

• Responsibility may be enforced, by citizens upon the council, and by the council upon the manager.

• The deadlocks and delays encountered in other forms of municipal government are avoided.

Other provisions. The *Model City Charter* authorizes the city council to create and reorganize departments and offices, and requires that all appointments and promotions of city officers and employees be made in accordance with the merit principle.

In addition to presenting an annual budget message and balanced current budget to the council, the manager is directed to prepare and submit the five- or six-year capital-improvement program listing all needed capital improvements in priority order, with cost estimates and proposed methods of finance.

If district elections are employed, the *Model City Charter* provides for council appointment of a five-member districting commission responsible for redrawing district lines subsequent to the decennial United States Census of population to comply with the U.S. Supreme Court's "one-person, one-vote" dictum. To prevent or reduce gerrymandering, the *Model* contains districting criteria which must be employed by the commission, to the extent practicable, in establishing district lines. The criteria include equally populated districts, districts composed only of contiguous territory, no division of a city block between districts, and the shortest possible aggregate length of all district boundaries.

The *Model* also reserves to the voters the powers of the initiative and the referendum, subject to the provisions of the state election laws. The former allows voters, by means of a petition containing the signatures of a specified number or percentage of voters, to place a proposed ordinance on the ballot. The petition or protest referendum allows voters, by means of petitions containing the signatures of a required number or percentage of voters, to suspend implementation of an ordinance until a referendum election is held to determine whether the ordinance should be repealed.

Although not included in the *Model City Charter,* local governments may wish to include in their charters a provision for recall. This device allows voters to petition for a special election to determine whether a public official should be removed from office prior to the expiration of his or her term.[5] The recall can be employed for any reason, including inefficiency or disappointment with the official's conduct or program. The purpose of the recall is to enforce a continuing responsibility of public officers to the electorate.

The *Model City Charter* prohibits conflicts of interest on the part of the municipal officers and employees, and also directs the city council to create an independent board of ethics. The latter administers and enforces the conflict of interest and financial disclosure ordinances, and also issues advisory opinions in response to the requests of officers and employees for guidance on ethical matters.

Amendments to the city charter may be proposed by the city council or by a charter commission created by ordinance. Amendments become effective if ratified by a majority of the voters casting ballots on the amendments.

LARGE CITIES

Although the *Model* contains excellent provisions for inclusion in the charter of a typical city or other general purpose local government, the largest cities have special problems; the unitary governmental structure proposed by the *Model* is perceived to impede effective citizen participation in decision making. The discontent, which emerged in large cities in the 1960s, was attributable in part to 1) the development of a ponderous municipal bureaucracy, 2) the "unrepresentativeness" of city councils, and 3) the inability of traditional municipal institutions to solve the multitudinous problems of citizens, especially poor ones. In particular, many minority group members have become convinced that they are being shortchanged by a closed decision-making process.

The fact that we lack government by consent in a number of large city neighborhoods cannot be denied. Charter drafters in these cities should give serious consideration to including in their documents provisions for neighborhood government and administrative decentralization.

A good charter is a relatively short document that can be understood readily by citizens.

A two-tier governmental system for large cities could be based upon the metropolitan Toronto model where the upper-tier unit is responsible for area-wide functions as water supply, major roads, and sewage treatment, and lower-tier units are responsible for functions closest to the people, such as health and social services.[6] Certain functions—roads are an example—would be the responsibility of both levels. A number of functions could be performed on a wholesale/retail basis. Solid waste, for example, could be collected by the lower-tier units (retail) and disposed of by the upper-tier unit (wholesale).

An alternative or supplement to political decentralization is administrative decentralization: the division of the city into unifunctional or multi-functional service-delivery districts. In contrast to a neighborhood government, the director of each administrative district reports to a superior in city hall.

In New York City, the charter directs the President of each of the five Boroughs to appoint up to 50 members to serve on each community board within the Borough. Each board appoints a district manager, who serves at the board's pleasure, to monitor service delivery by city agencies.[7] To coordinate service delivery within each district, the manager is directed to form and chair a service cabinet composed of a representative of the Department of City Planning and the head of each service-delivery agency in the district. [For more information on New York City's community board system, see Robert F. Pecorella, "Measured Decentralization," NATIONAL CIVIC REVIEW, 78:3, May–June 1989, pp. 202–08—Ed.]

CHARTER AND STATE LAWS REVIEW

Periodic review of a charter is essential to ensure that it is responsive to changing conditions. Events may necessitate the creation of new offices or departments, granting of additional authority to the council or chief executive, a change in the electoral system or the size of the council, and administrative reorganization of the executive branch.

A charter should provide for a mandatory referendum each decade on the question of creating a charter review commission composed of citizens or a combination of public officials and citizens. The charter also should authorize the voters at any time by petition to call for a referendum on the question of appointing or electing a charter review commission.

Surveys by the author reveal that the municipal laws in several states are in need of recodification and removal of obsolete and conflicting provisions. These statutes allow officials with long experience to take advantage of the divergent provisions in various general laws in deciding which statutes to operate under for a given purpose. One undesirable consequence is citizen lack of understanding of the local governance system.

A careful recodification of the municipal laws of a state, undertaken in conjunction with the enactment of a code of restrictions upon local government powers, would facilitate greatly citizens' and local government officials' understanding of the extent of local discretionary authority.

SUMMARY AND CONCLUSIONS

Democratic theory is premised upon citizens playing an active and informed role in the governance system. The Seventh Edition of the *Model City Charter*—in contrast to antiquated and long municipal charters diffusing political power and responsibility—promotes citizen understanding and participation, and cooperation among municipal officials.

A good charter is a relatively short document that can be understood readily by citizens. A desirable supplement is an administrative code, enacted by the governing body, containing many details of the administrative organization and procedures of the municipal corporation. Traditionally, municipal charters could be amended only with the approval of the electorate. The need to implement administrative changes in response to new conditions suggests that details of administrative organization and procedure belong in an administrative code that can be amended by the local legislative body without a referendum.

A final recommendation is the amendment of state constitutions and state laws, where needed, to grant authority to citizens of all general purpose local governments to draft, adopt, and amend charters. Adoption of a charter will permit a reorganization of the local government to improve performance, public officials' responsiveness to the citizenry, and public understanding of the governance system.

NOTES

1. *Constitution of Missouri*, Art. IX, § 19 (1875). Only St. Louis met the threshold requirement of a population exceeding 100,000. For more information on the general concept of home rule, see also *Guide for Charter Commissions* (Denver: National Civic League, 1989).

2. *Constitution of New York*, Art. IX, § 2(c).

3. For details on all alternative electoral systems, see Joseph F. Zimmerman, *The Federated City: Community Control in Large Cities* (New York: St. Martin's Press, 1972). Relative to criteria that can be employed to judge the desirability of various electoral systems, see Joseph F. Zimmerman, "A 'Fair' Voting System for Local Governments," *National Civic Review*, 68:9, October 1979, pp. 481–87, 507. See also Bernard Gofman and Arend Lijphart, Eds., *Electoral Laws and their Political Consequences* (New York: Agathon Press, Inc., 1986).

4. See, for example, Richard S. Childs, *The First Fifty Years of the Council-Manager Plan of Municipal Government* (New York: National Municipal League, 1965), p. 37.

5. For detailed information on the initiative, referendum and recall, see Joseph F. Zimmerman, *Participatory Democracy: Populism Revisited* (New York: Praeger Publishers, 1986), pp. 35–134.

6. For details on the two-tier system, see Zimmerman, *The Federated City: Community Control in Large Cities*.

7. *New York City Charter*, § 2800.

Bringing Government Back to Life

It can be depressing to watch the governmental process at work in America in the 1990s. But it can be exciting, too. And there are signs of hope all around us.

David Osborne
and Ted A. Gaebler

David Osborne was the author of Laboratories of Democracy, *a 1988 book
on innovation in the states during the
previous decade. In the past year, he
has been an adviser to the governors of
Florida and Massachusetts. His column on the subject of management will
begin appearing in the March 1992
issue of* GOVERNING.

*Ted A. Gaebler spent more than 20
years as a city manager and local official in California, Oregon, Ohio and
Maryland, and is now a consultant to
state and local government, specializ-
ing in the budget and tax processes.*

As the 1980s drew to a close, *Time* magazine asked on its cover: "Is Government Dead?" As the 1990s unfold, the answer—to many Americans—appears to be "yes."

Our public schools are the worst in the developed world. Our health care system is out of control. Our courts and prisons are so overcrowded that convicted felons walk free. And many of our proudest cities and states are virtually bankrupt.

Confidence in government has fallen to record lows. By the late 1980s, only 5 percent of Americans surveyed said they would choose government service as their preferred career. Only 13 percent of top federal employees said they would recommend a career in public service. Nearly three out of four

Americans said they believed Washington delivered less value for the dollar than it had 10 years earlier.

And then, in 1990, the bottom fell out. It was as if all our governments had hit the wall, at the same time. Our states struggled with multibillion-dollar deficits. Our cities laid off thousands of employees. Our federal deficit ballooned toward $350 billion.

Since the tax revolt first swept the nation in 1978, the American people have demanded, in election after election and on issue after issue, more performance for less money. And yet, during the recession of 1990 and 1991, their leaders debated the same old options: fewer services or higher taxes. In disgust, the voters threw out incumbents from coast to coast.

Today, public fury alternates with apathy. We watch breathlessly as Eastern Europe overthrows the deadening hand of bureaucracy and oppression. But at home we feel impotent. Our cities succumb to mounting crime and poverty, our states are handcuffed by staggering deficits, and Washington drifts through it all like 30 square miles bounded by reality.

Yet there is hope. Slowly, quietly, far from the public spotlight, new kinds of public institutions are emerging. They are lean, decentralized and innovative. They are flexible, adaptable, quick to learn new ways when conditions change. They use competition, customer choice and other non-bureaucratic mechanisms to get things done as creatively and effectively as possible. And they are our future.

Visalia, California, is the prototypic American community. A leafy oasis of 75,000 people in California's hot, dry San Joaquin Valley, it is the county seat of rural, conservative Tulare County. It is an All-American city: the streets are clean, the lawns are mowed, the Rotary Clubs are full.

In 1978, the Proposition 13 property tax initiative cut Visalia's tax base by 25 percent. With financing from one final bond issue that slipped through on the same day as Prop. 13, the school district managed to build a new high school. But as the years went by, it could never scrape together the money to put in a swimming pool.

One hot Thursday in August of 1984, a parks and recreation employee got a call from a friend in Los Angeles, who told him that the U.S. Olympic Committee was selling its training pool. The employee immediately called the Visalia school district, and two days later he and an assistant superintendent flew down to take a look. They liked what they saw: an all-aluminum, Olympic-size pool that would likely survive an earthquake. To buy one new, they would have had to spend at least $800,000; slightly used, they could buy it, transport it and put it in the ground for half that amount.

Like any other government agency, the school district needed at least two weeks to advertise the question, hold a board meeting and get approval for a special appropriation. But on Monday, the parks and rec employee got a second call. Two colleges wanted the pool, and they were racing each other to get the $60,000 deposit together. So he got in his car and took a check from the city down that afternoon.

How could a third-level parks and recreation employee get a check for $60,000, with no action by the City Council and no special appropriation? The answer is simple. Visalia had adopted a radically new "expenditure control" budgeting system, which allowed managers to respond quickly as circumstances changed. Invented in the 1970s by Oscar Reyes, a local official in Fairfield, California, this system made two simple changes. First, it eliminated all line items within departmental budgets—freeing managers to move resources around as needs shifted. Second, it allowed departments to keep what they didn't spend from one year to the next, so they could shift unused funds to new priorities.

Normal government budgets encourage managers to waste money. If they don't spend their entire budget by the end of the fiscal year, three things happen: They lose the money they have saved, the budget director scolds them for requesting too much, and they get less next year. Hence the time-honored government rush to spend all funds by the end of the fiscal year. By allowing departments to keep their savings, Visalia not only eliminated this rush, but encouraged managers to save money. The idea was to get them thinking like owners: "If this were my money, would I spend it this way?"

Under the new budget system, Visalia's Parks and Recreation Department had managed to save $60,000 toward a new pool. Arne Croce, an assistant city manager who had worked on the problem, knew that both the school district and the city council wanted a pool. Between them, he was sure, they could find $400,000. Although the Olympic pool was an unexpected opportunity, he had no qualms about seizing it. "It's something you'd find in private enterprise," the school superintendent said afterward. "You don't have the bureaucracy you have to deal with in most governments."

E ast Harlem is not the prototypic American community. It is one of the poorest communities in America. Single mothers head more than half of its families; 35 percent of

its residents are on public assistance; median income is $8,300. Dilapidated public schools—their windows covered by protective grilles—co-exist with crack houses. East Harlem is precisely the sort of community in which public schools normally fail. Yet it has some of the most successful public schools in America.

New York City has 32 school districts. Twenty years ago, Community School District 4, in East Harlem, was at the bottom of the barrel: 32nd out of 32 in test scores. Only 15 percent of its students were reading at grade level. Attendance rates were pathetic. "It was totally out of control," says Michael Friedman, now director of a junior high called the Bridge School.

In 1974, out of sheer desperation, then-superintendent Anthony Alvarado, an assistant principal named John Falco, and several teachers decided they had to get the "incorrigible, recalcitrant, aggressive kids" out of the schools, so that others could learn. They created an alternative junior high for troubled students.

The task was so daunting that Alvarado told Falco and his teachers to do whatever it took to get results. They created a very non-traditional school, which worked. They began adding others: an East Harlem Career Academy, an Academy of Environmental Sciences, an Isaac Newton School of Science and Mathematics, a traditional school in which children wore uniforms.

In 1983, the district converted all its junior high schools to schools of choice, doing away with assignment by zone. By 1990, District 4 boasted 21 junior high schools, plus six alternative grade schools. Under the new system, schools are no longer synonymous with buildings; many buildings house three or four schools, one on each floor. Schools are small—from 50 to 300 students— and education is personal. "Kids need to be dealt with personally," says Falco, who now administers the choice program. "The downsizing of the schools has been a tremendous plus."

Authority is decentralized: Teachers manage their own schools. Principals still administer school buildings, but actual schools are run by "directors"— most of whom also teach—and by teachers. If a teacher wants to create a new school or move to an alternative school, the opportunity is often there. This has released tremendous energy.

"There are teachers who were burned out—they were going nowhere," says Falco. "We put them in an alternative setting, and they flowered."

Before long, the junior highs were competing for students. District leaders began closing schools that were not attracting enough students, or replacing directors and staff. "If you're not operating a program that kids want to come to, you're out of business," says Falco. "You just can't rest on your laurels. You have to continually strive for ways to meet the needs of these kids."

Just as important as competition is the ownership students and teachers feel for their schools. They are allowed to choose the style of education they prefer. "There's ownership in that choice," says Robert Nadel, assistant director of a junior high called the Creative Learning Center. "There's also ownership on the part of the parent and ownership on the part of the teachers."

The results of District 4's experiment have been startling. Reading scores are up sharply: In 1973, 15 percent of junior high students were reading at grade level; by 1988, 64 percent were. All told, more than a quarter of District 4's graduates are earning places in elite public and private high schools—schools that were virtually off-limits to them 15 years ago.

District 4 is smack in the middle of one of America's most renowned ghettos. Yet it has a waiting list of teachers who want to work there. Perhaps the most telling statistic is this: Out of 14,000 students in District 4, close to 1,000 come in from outside the district. "On any given day, I receive at least four or five calls from parents requesting admission from outside the district," says Falco. "I just have to turn them away."

V isalia and East Harlem are not alone. Look almost anywhere in America, and you will see similar success stories. We believe these governments represent the future.

Our thesis is simple: The kind of governments that developed during the industrial era, with their sluggish, centralized bureaucracies, their preoccupation with rules and regulations, and their hierarchical chains of command, no longer work very well. They accomplished great things in their time, but somewhere along the line they got away from us. They became bloated, wasteful, ineffective. And when the world began to change, they failed to change with it. Hierarchical, centralized bureaucracies designed in the 1930s or 1940s simply do not function well in the society and economy of the 1990s. They are like luxury ocean liners in an age of supersonic jets: big, cumbersome, expensive and extremely difficult to turn around. Gradually, new kinds of public institutions are taking their place.

Similar transformations are taking place throughout American society. Corporations have spent the last decade decentralizing authority, flattening hierarchies, focusing on quality, getting close to their customers—all in an effort to remain competitive in the new global marketplace. Our voluntary, non-profit organizations are alive with new initiatives. New "partnerships" blossom overnight—between business and education, between for-profits and non-profits, between public sector and private. It is as if virtually all institutions in American life were struggling to adapt to some massive sea change—striving to become more flexible, more innovative and more entrepreneurial.

It is hard to imagine today, but 100 years ago the word "bureaucracy" meant something very positive. It connoted a rational, efficient method of organization—something to take the place of the arbitrary exercise of power by authoritarian regimes.

A century ago, our cities were growing at breakneck speed, bulging with immigrants come to labor in the factories thrown up by our industrial revolution. Boss Tweed and his contemporaries ran these cities like personal fiefdoms: In exchange for immigrant votes, they dispensed jobs, favors and informal services. With one hand they robbed the public blind; with the other they made sure that those who delivered blocs of loyal votes were amply rewarded. Meanwhile, they ignored many of the new problems of industrial America—its slums, its sweatshops, its desperate need for a new infrastructure of sewers and water and public transit.

In reaction to the machines and their abuses, the Progressive movement was born. Over the next 30 years, it transformed government in America. To end

the use of government jobs as patronage, the Progressives created civil service systems with written exams, lockstep pay scales and protection from arbitrary hiring or dismissal. To keep major construction projects out of the reach of politicians, they created independent public authorities. To limit the power of political bosses, they split up management functions, took appointments to important offices away from mayors and governors, created separately elected clerks, judges, even sheriffs. To keep the administration of public services untainted by the influence of politicians, they created a profession of "city managers"—professionals, insulated from politics, who would run the bureaucracy in an efficient, business-like manner.

Thanks to Boss Tweed and his contemporaries, in other words, American society embarked on a gigantic effort to *control* what went on inside government—to keep the politicians and bureaucrats from doing anything that might endanger the public interest or purse. This cleaned up many of our governments, but in solving one set of problems it created another. In making it difficult to steal the public's money, we made it virtually impossible to *manage* the public's money. In adopting written tests scored to the third decimal point to hire our clerks and police officers and fire fighters, we built mediocrity into our work force. In making it impossible to fire people who did not perform, we turned mediocrity into deadwood.

The product was government with a distinct ethos: slow, inefficient, impersonal. This is the mental image the word "government" invokes today; it is what most Americans assume to be the very essence of government. Even government buildings constructed during the industrial era reflect this ethos: they are immense structures, with high ceilings, large hallways and ornate architecture, all designed to impress upon the visitor the impersonal authority and immovable weight of the institution.

For a long time, the bureaucratic model worked—not because it was efficient, but because it solved the basic problems people wanted solved. It provided security—from unemployment, during old age. It provided stability, a particularly important quality after the Depression. It provided a basic sense of fairness and equity. And it

delivered the basic, no-frills, one-size-fits-all services people needed and expected during the industrial era: roads, highways, sewers, schools.

But the bureaucratic model developed in conditions very different from those we experience today. It developed in a slower-paced society, when change proceeded at a leisurely gait. It developed in an age of hierarchy, when only those at the top of the pyramid had enough information to make informed decisions. It developed in a society of people who worked with their hands, not their minds. It developed in a time of mass markets, when most Americans had similar wants and needs.

Today all that has been swept away. We live in an era of breathtaking change. We live in a global marketplace, which puts enormous competitive pressure on our economic institutions. We live in an information society, in which people get access to information almost as fast as their leaders. We live in a knowledge-based economy, in which educated workers bridle at commands and demand autonomy. We live in an age of niche markets, in which customers have become accustomed to high quality and extensive choice.

In this environment, bureaucratic institutions developed during the industrial era—public *and* private—increasingly fail us.

Today's environment demands institutions that are flexible and adaptable. It demands institutions that deliver high quality goods and services, squeezing ever more bang out of every buck. It demands institutions that are responsive to their customers, offering choices of non-standardized services; that lead by persuasion and incentives rather than commands; that give their employees a sense of meaning and control, even ownership. It demands institutions that *empower* citizens rather than simply serving them.

Bureaucratic institutions still work in some circumstances. If the environment is stable, the task is relatively simple, every customer wants the same service, and the quality of performance is not critical, a traditional public bureaucracy can do the job. But most government institutions perform increasingly complex tasks, in competitive, rapidly changing environments, with customers who want quality and choice. These new realities have made

Our fundamental problem today is not too much government or too little government. It is that we have the wrong kind of government.

life very difficult for our public institutions—for our public education system, for our public health care programs, for our public housing authorities, for virtually every large, bureaucratic program created by American governments before 1970.

In some ways, this is a symptom of progress—of the disruptive clash that occurs when new realities run headlong into old institutions. Our information technologies and knowledge economy give us opportunities to do things undreamed of 50 years ago. But to seize these opportunities, we must pick up the wreckage of our industrial-era institutions and rebuild. "It is the first step of wisdom," Alfred North Whitehead once wrote, "to recognize that the major advances in civilization are processes which all but wreck the society in which they occur."

The first governments to respond to these new realities were local governments—in large part because they hit the wall first. On June 6, 1978, the voters of California passed Proposition 13, which cut local property taxes in half. Fed by the dual fires of inflation and dissatisfaction with public services, the tax revolt spread quickly. In 1980, Ronald Reagan took it national—and by 1982 state and local governments had lost nearly one of every four federal dollars they received in 1978. During the 1982 recession, the deepest since the Depression, state governments began to hit the wall.

Under intense fiscal pressure, state and local leaders had no choice but to change the way they did business. Mayors and governors embraced "public-private partnerships" and developed "alternative" ways to deliver services. Cities fostered competition between service providers and invented new budget systems. Public managers began to speak of "enterprise management," "learning organizations" and "self-reliant cities." States began to restructure their most expen-

sive public systems: education, health care and welfare.

Phoenix, Arizona, put its Public Works Department in competition with private companies for contracts to handle garbage collection, street repair and other services. St. Paul, Minnesota, created half a dozen private, nonprofit corporations to redevelop the city. Santa Clara, California, launched the nation's first solar energy utility.

Indianapolis Mayor William Hudnut described the phenomenon as well as anyone. "In government," he said in a 1986 speech, "the routine tendency is to protect turf, to resist change, to build empires, to enlarge one's sphere of control, to protect projects and programs regardless of whether or not they are any longer needed." In contrast, the "entrepreneurial" government "searches for more efficient and effective ways of managing."

"It is willing to abandon old programs and methods. It is innovative and imaginative and creative. It takes risks. It turns city functions into money-makers rather than budget-busters. It eschews traditional alternatives that offer only life-support systems. It works with the private sector. It employs solid business sense. It privatizes. It creates enterprises and revenue-generating operations. It is market-oriented. It focuses on performance measurement. It rewards merit. It says, 'Let's make this work,' and it is unafraid to dream the great dream."

Over the past five years, as we have journeyed through this landscape of governmental change, we have sought constantly to understand the underlying trends. We have asked ourselves: What do these innovative, entrepreneurial organizations have in common? What incentives have they changed, to create such different behavior? What have they done which, if other governments did the same, would make entrepreneurship the norm and bureaucracy the exception?

The common threads were not hard to find. Most entrepreneurial governments promote *competition* between

service providers. They *empower* citizens by pushing control out of the bureaucracy, into the community. They measure the performance of their agencies, focusing not on inputs but on *outcomes*. They are driven by their goals—their *missions*—not by their rules and regulations. They redefine their clients as *customers* and offer them choices—between schools, between training programs, between housing options. They *prevent* problems before they emerge, rather than simply offering services afterward. They put their energies into *earning* money, not simply spending it. They *decentralize* authority, embracing participatory management. They prefer *market* mechanisms to bureaucratic mechanisms. And they focus not simply on providing public services, but on *catalyzing* all sectors—public, private and voluntary—into action to solve their community's problems.

We believe that these 10 principles are the fundamental principles behind the new form of government that we see emerging: the spokes that hold together this new wheel. Together they form a coherent whole, a new model of government.

The old ideas still embraced by most public leaders assume that the important question is *how much* government we have—not *what kind* of government. Most of our leaders take the old model as a given, and either advocate more of it (liberal Democrats), or less of it (Reagan Republicans), or less of one program but more of another (moderates of both parties).

But our fundamental problem today is not too much government or too little government. We have debated that issue endlessly since the tax revolt of 1978, and it has not solved our problems. Our fundamental problem is that we have *the wrong kind of government*. We do not need more government or less government, we need *better* government. To be more precise, we need better *governance*.

Governance is the process by which we collectively solve our problems and meet our society's needs. Government is the instrument we use. The instrument is outdated, and the process of reinvention has begun. We do not need another New Deal, nor another Reagan Revolution. We need an American *perestroika*.

Regionalism and Variations Among Regions and States

The 50 state and approximately 83,000 local governments in the United States share many characteristics. They also differ in important respects. Diversity among regions and states is the subject of this unit.

The states and localities are all part of an overarching system of government whose center lies in Washington, D.C. Most state and local governments depend on higher levels of government for significant portions of their operating revenues. All operate in the context of a common national political culture and a common national economy.

The states share a common status in the American federal system. Each has a three-branch structure of government based on a written constitution and a system of local government that serves, in effect, to decentralize state governmental authority. Local governments have similar formal relationships with their state governments in that they are all "creatures" of their states.

For all their similarities, states and localities vary greatly. Alaska, the largest state in area, is nearly 500 times larger than Rhode Island, the smallest. California, the most populous state, has more than 60 times the population of Wyoming, the least populous state. The city of New York, with about 7 million residents, provides a great contrast with those local government jurisdictions in rural areas in which the residents all know one another. The states and localities also vary in their economic activities and well-being; the ethnic, racial, and religious makeup of their populations; their history; their policies; and the voting habits and partisan attachments of their citizens. Thus, when we talk about "the states" or "local governments"—their problems, activities, capabilities, and weaknesses—we must bear their differences in mind.

Differences in state and local jurisdictions are often regionally based. That is, clusters of neighboring states (or localities) often exhibit common characteristics that vary from those characteristics held in common by other clusters of neighboring states (or localities). For example, the adjacent, oil-producing states of Texas, Oklahoma, and Louisiana have problems and opportunities different from those faced by states without substantial oil reserves such as Connecticut, Massachusetts, and Vermont. And the three cold-weather states just mentioned have sometimes found themselves in a situation quite different from such warm-weather southeastern states as Georgia, South Carolina, and Alabama that also lack sizable oil deposits. Sparsely settled Rocky Mountain neighbors such as Montana, Idaho, and Wyoming differ in significant ways from highly urbanized, densely populated Middle Atlantic states such as New York and New Jersey.

Local governments also vary regionally. For example, as James Bryce observed in the nineteenth century (see unit 1), structures of local government differ significantly among New England, Middle Atlantic, and Southern states. Another example involves party organizations, which typically play more important roles in local and state governments in Middle Atlantic states than they do in West Coast states.

Not all differences among states and localities are regionally based, of course. Governments of populous states such as California, New York, and Texas have substantially more capabilities and responsibilities than governments of less populous states such as Vermont, Alaska, and Wyoming. The former have enormous tax bases and huge populations to service; the latter have smaller sources of revenue as well as responsibility for fewer people. It is one thing to design and administer programs to serve a state with 15 to 30 million people and quite another to handle programs for a state with only about a half-million inhabitants. The same point applies when cities with a million or more residents are contrasted with local governments serving only a few hundred citizens.

Selections in this unit convey some important differences among states and regions. Whether these differences outweigh common features of states and regions is a question of perspective, and reading the selections should help provide a basis for a more informed judgment on the matter.

Looking Ahead: Challenge Questions

What characteristics of your home state make it different from neighboring states? What characteristics does it have in common with its neighbors?

What region(s) of the country face(s) the biggest opportunities and biggest problems in the next 20 years? Why?

What distinguishes the locality in which your school is located from neighboring localities? What different problems are posed for the various local governments?

All in all, do you think that the differences among regions and states are more significant than the similarities? Or vice versa? Why?

Is there a region of the country to which you would like to move? If so, what is different about that region from the region in which you now live?

Legacy of the '80s: Richer Rich and Poorer Poor

In the 1980s income disparities between the rich and poor widened, and so did income gaps among the states.

Steven D. Gold

Steven D. Gold is the director of the Center for the Study of the States at the State University of New York's Nelson A. Rockefeller Institute of Government.

The rich got richer and the poor got poorer. That is the major finding of a recent report by the U.S. Department of Commerce, tracing changes in income levels among the regions of the United States in the 1980s. This is not the way it used to be. For half a century, from 1929 to 1979, regional differences in income levels narrowed in the United States. But that long-term trend halted in the past decade.

It has been widely reported that inequality of income among families increased considerably in the 1980s. The proportion of personal income received by the richest 20 percent of the population during that decade was greater than at any time since 1954, and correspondingly, the share of income going to the poorest fifth of the population was smaller. While these income disparities were widening, the income gaps among the states were also growing.

The Commerce Department study focuses on per capita income, that is, the total personal income received by residents of a state divided by the state's population. Nationally, per capita income rose 83 percent between 1979 and 1988, from $9,033 to $16,489. (After taking inflation into account, the increase was 12 percent.) For comparative purposes, the best way to analyze these statistics is in relative terms—that is, if

per capita income rose faster than the national average, a state was a "winner"; if per capita income increased slower than average, it was a "loser" in the sense that its residents did not fare as well as most other people in the United States.

The big winners in the period from 1979 to 1988 were New England states, where per capita income jumped from 104 percent to 122 percent of the national average, and the Mid-Atlantic states, where the corresponding increase was from 106 percent to 115 percent of the national average. Connecticut and New Jersey, which ranked first and third in 1979 income, enjoyed the biggest relative increases in income of any states. Their economies, along with those of their neighbors, boomed as a result of strong service, high technology and defense industries.

The laggards were the Southwest and Rocky Mountain states, hit hard by the depression in the energy sector. The Southwest region dipped from 95 percent to 87 percent of the national average, and the states in the Rocky Mountains fell from 96 percent to 87 percent of the average.

The Southeast region was one of the two major exceptions to the general pattern of widening disparities. Traditionally the poorest section of the country, the Southeast rose from 85 percent to 88 percent of the national average. Increases were particularly strong in Georgia and Virginia. But prosperity was not evenly distributed: five of the 12 states in the Southeast slipped further behind the na-

tional average, including Mississippi, which stayed at the bottom.

Surprisingly, the per capita income of the Far West states did not increase as rapidly as the national average. California, Nevada, Oregon and Washington all had relative declines in per capita income, although only Oregon is below the average. Their large population increases exerted a "drag" on their average income levels, offsetting the strong growth of their economies.

All 12 of the Great Lakes and Plains states had per capita incomes that fell relative to the national average. The Great Lakes states slipped from above to below average, while the Plains states fell from 99 percent to 93 percent of the average. Note that these decreases are relative, not absolute. Their per capita income rose, but not as fast as it did for the country as a whole. The economies of these states generally depend more heavily than average on heavy manufacturing and agriculture.

Alaska and Wyoming suffered the biggest declines in relative per capita income of any states. Excluding those two, North Dakota, Iowa, Montana, Oklahoma, Oregon and South Dakota had the biggest decreases. The culprits varied from state to state, with energy, farming and forest products the big problem in various places.

Increasing disparities in income among states represent the Achilles heel of the Reagan administration's New Federalism policy of cutting back federal aid and

 From *State Legislatures*, August 1990, pp. 31, 33. Copyright © 1990, National Conference of State Legislatures.

turning more responsibilities over to state governments. The implicit assumption of such federal policies is that states have the resources to deal adequately with problems. While this may be true for some states, it is certainly not true for the poorest states, many of which have been losing ground as their economies sputter.

The differing growth rates of per capita income go a long way in explaining how state governments fared in the 1980s. Until the last few years, the state budgets of the New England and Mid-Atlantic states were in good shape, with larger than average increases in spending between 1983 and 1988. The Rocky Mountain and Southwest states were at the other end of the spectrum, many of them undergoing considerable fiscal stress. In the mid-1980s, many Northeastern states were cutting taxes while many Western states were raising them.

The last couple of years have seen a turnaround, with the economies of many Northeastern states lagging behind the national average and quite a few of the formerly depressed states doing much better than five years ago.

According to DRI Inc., a leading econometric consulting firm, the New England and Mid-Atlantic regions have the weakest economies in the country. From the second quarter of 1989 to the final quarter of 1990, DRI predicts an absolute decrease in non-farm employment in New England and a tiny increase in the Mid-Atlantic region.

The budgets of the New England and Mid-Atlantic states are in bad shape for two reasons. Their revenue growth has plummeted because of the weakness in employment and income. Their fiscal troubles have been exacerbated in some cases by egregious forecasting errors. After their state economies outperformed the national economy year after year in the mid-1980s, state officials in some cases assumed that this superior performance would continue. They were whipsawed when their economies not only failed to do as well as the national average, but actually did worse.

How Incomes Compare

	Per-Capita Personal Income 1988	% of U.S. Average (100) 1979	% of U.S. Average (100) 1988
United States	$16,489	100	100
New England	20,191	104	122
Connecticut	23,059	119	140
Maine	15,106	81	92
Massachusetts	20,816	105	126
New Hampshire	19,434	96	118
Rhode Island	16,892	93	102
Vermont	15,302	86	93
Mid-Atlantic	18,959	106	115
Delaware	17,661	102	107
Dist. of Colum.	21,389	126	130
Maryland	19,487	107	118
New Jersey	21,994	114	133
New York	19,305	107	117
Pennsylvania	16,233	100	98
Great Lakes	16,239	104	98
Illinois	17,575	112	107
Indiana	14,924	96	91
Michigan	16,552	106	100
Ohio	15,536	99	94
Wisconsin	15,524	100	94
Plains	15,398	99	93
Iowa	14,662	101	89
Kansas	15,759	103	96
Minnesota	16,674	102	101
Missouri	15,452	95	94
Nebraska	14,774	98	90
North Dakota	12,833	93	78
South Dakota	12,755	89	77
Southeast	14,462	85	88
Alabama	12,851	78	78
Arkansas	12,219	77	74
Florida	16,603	97	101
Georgia	15,260	84	93
Kentucky	12,822	82	78
Louisiana	12,292	85	75
Mississippi	11,116	71	67
North Carolina	14,304	81	87
South Carolina	12,926	76	78
Tennessee	13,873	82	84
Virginia	17,675	96	107
West Virginia	11,735	80	71
Southwest	14,350	95	87
Arizona	14,970	92	91
New Mexico	12,488	83	76
Oklahoma	13,323	93	81
Texas	14,586	98	88
Rocky Mountain	14,363	96	87
Colorado	16,463	105	100
Idaho	12,665	87	77
Montana	12,866	90	78
Utah	12,193	82	74
Wyoming	13,609	113	83
Far West	18,111	114	110
Alaska	19,079	139	116
California	18,753	117	114
Hawaii	16,753	105	102
Nevada	17,511	116	106
Oregon	14,885	102	90
Washington	16,473	109	100

Source: Daniel Garnick, "Accounting for Regional Differences in Per Capita Personal Income Growth: An Update and Extension," *Survey of Current Business* (January 1990).

One lesson comes out loud and clear from recent economic history: What goes around, comes around. Today's strong may be tomorrow's weak, and vice versa. There are already signs of rejuvenation in the farm belt that went from boom in the 1970s to bust in the 1980s. Higher oil prices likewise improve the outlook in the energy sector. Heavy industry could also do well if the United States continues to reduce its trade imbalance (as it sooner or later will have to, if our massive foreign debts are to be paid off).

But short-term forecasting is precarious. The fortunes of different industries and the state budgets that depend on them are strongly influenced by international economic forces, which determine the exchange rate of the dollar and the price of oil. Lucky are the legislators or governors with the wind at their back: Their economies and hence their budgets will be healthy. Woe to their counterparts in the opposite situation.

Interstate Cooperation:

Resurgence of Multistate Regionalism

More states are working together on a regional basis to solve tough problems and many are saving tax dollars as a result.

Keon S. Chi

Keon S. Chi, Ph.D., is a senior policy analyst at The Council of State Governments.

Multistate regionalism, a persistent phenomenon of the American political tradition, is re-emerging as a viable strategy to deal with a multitude of state problems, ranging from economic development and social services to environment and education. The resurgence of regionalism is due in part to the gradual devolution of federal responsibilities, states' mutual interest in better planning and communication, and the desire to improve state management and programs.

Trends in Regionalism

The history of multistate regionalism is as old as the nation itself. Regionalism has been used over the years as a geographic, economic, planning, administrative and political concept. Since the creation of the Tennessee Valley Authority in 1933, the federal government has continuously used regional mechanisms to provide selected public services. And during the 1960s regionalism gained prominence with the creation of multistate commissions such as the Appalachian Regional Commission. In the past few years, state policy-makers have taken the lead in creating mechanisms for regional cooperation.

The resurgence of regionalism posits several significant trends. First, despite federal pre-emption of state programs and uniform state laws, "nationalization of American politics has not proceeded so far as to obliterate the regions," as political scientist Ira Sharkansky says. Regional differences persist and are sharper than ever in some respects. Also, state interests in regional activities remain strong. Record attendance at recent regional conferences of The Council of State Governments, for example, may be attributed to state policy-makers' interest in regional approaches to problems.

Second, unlike multistate regional mechanisms initiated and administered by the federal government during the 1960s and 1970s, states are developing regional strategies to tackle common problems without federal mandate or involvement. Moreover, some regional programs have been initiated by states without creating additional layers of bureaucracy.

Third, although the number of interstate compacts has declined to less than 10 in the 1980s compared to 50 in the 1960s and 20 in the 1970s, recent compacts tend to be more regional in scope. This is evidenced in the Great Lakes Interstate Sales Compact, Middle Atlantic Governors' Compact on Alcohol and Drug Abuse, Northeast Interstate Low-level Radioactive Waste Compact and proposed compacts such as the Northwest compact for the Pacific Marine Resources Commission and the Midwestern Higher Education Compact.

Fourth, states are initiating regional innovations in policy and management areas without using the traditional form of interstate compact. These interstate regional innovations do not require congressional approval and can be implemented more easily. Over the years, individual states have been management and policy innovators within the American federalism system. Today states are contemplating regional innovations as well.

And, fifth, developments in multistate regionalism extend beyond national borders. States and provinces in the U.S.-Canadian and U.S.-Mexican border areas have initiated regional approaches. One example of such "borderless" cooperation is the Pacific Northwest Legislative Leadership Forum, established to explore greater regional unity for economic development. The forum consists of representatives from Alaska, Idaho, Montana, Oregon, Washington, Alberta and British Columbia. CSG's Eastern and Midwestern regional conferences also have begun cooperative programs with several Canadian provinces.

Regional Innovations

States are using non-traditional regional innovations and interstate compacts for efforts in economic development, social services, environment, education, management and regional trends analysis.

The South and the West are taking the lead in regional economic development efforts. The Southern Growth Policies Board, uniting 13 states, has been an effective vehicle for regional planning and cooperation as well as public-private partnership building. The group has been in the forefront in alerting state officials to economic development issues. Its publications have included "Foresight: Model Programs for Economic Development" and "SGPB: Analysis of Emerging Issues." At its 1989 annual meeting, the Board adopted a strategic plan for technology-based economic development in the South. The plan was prepared by the Southern Technology Council, which studies the interrelationship of science and technology and economic development. The regional plan, "Turning to Technology — A Strategic Plan for the Nineties," set goals, objectives and specific strategies for implementation.

The Southern region also is implementing a 10-year economic development plan completed in 1990 by the Lower Mississippi Delta Development Commission. The plan takes a comprehensive approach to economic challenges facing the South.

A strong case for regional cooperation for international trade was made by the Western Governors' Association in 1988 when the group adopted a regional plan, "Going Global: A Strategy for Regional Cooperation." The rationale for regional cooperation on international trade, investment and tourism is to create jobs in a more effective and less costly manner than states can do independently. The plan pointed out that "programs that are rational when viewed state-by-state can be seen as redundant or ineffective from a regional viewpoint." According to the plan, benefits of regional cooperation in export trade include: "cost reductions and economies from consolidation of efforts, increased impact from a more massive presence of the states when operating in combination, increasingly knowledgeable state officers as a result of pooling of experience; greater and more rational global coverage at little extra cost; and an effective presence for Western interests in Washington and overseas."

The Pacific Northwest Legislative Leadership Forum, another Western regional innovation, is a fresh approach for border states to compete more effectively in the world market, especially in the Pacific Rim and the European Community. The forum was sponsored by the Washington Legislature and the Northwest Policy Center at the University of Washington Graduate School of Public Affairs to explore regional economic unity. In 1990, delegates to the forum agreed that unified regional actions are necessary because each state or province is too small to compete effectively in the changing market. They also agreed to appoint two delegates each to a 14-member group to coordinate activities.

The creation of the Center for the New West in 1989 also is indicative of the desire for closer regional economic cooperation. A non-profit private organization, the center provides information on economic development for 19 Western states.

States are cooperating to improve social services. The Southern Governors' Association and the Southern Legislative Conference conducted the much publicized Southern Regional Project on Infant Mortality in an effort to improve infant health. By sharing information on state innovations, the groups seek to reduce the South's high infant mortality rate.

To improve child support collection, 10 Southern states are tracking delinquent parents through an interstate computerized information system. Because the system shares information from state employment offices, corrections systems and drivers' license agencies, it can track absent parents by name or a previous employer as well as Social Security number. The Electronic Parent Locator has found absent parents in three of every four attempts.

Regional efforts also have been launched to fight drug abuse. In 1988, the Southern Governors' Association created the Southern Regional Drug Prevention Network, the first of its kind, to better address state and regional drug problems. A steering committee of the Mid-Atlantic Governors' Drug and Alcohol Abuse Conference drafted a compact to establish a regional approach to substance abuse. The primary goal of the committee is sharing information on new laws and education and training programs. In 1989, the Midwestern Governors' Conference followed suit by adopting the Midwestern Compact on Drug Abuse.

In addition, the environment is the focus of several regional efforts. The Council of State Governments' Eastern Regional Conference created the Northeast Recycling Council in 1988 to share information on ideas and provide for policy implementation. Composed of the state recycling directors from 10 Northeastern states, the council focuses on the development and stimulation of markets for recycled products. The council recently sponsored forums with the region's newspaper publishers and state purchasing officials to promote purchase of recycled papers for newsprint.

An interstate agreement for hazardous waste management became effective in 1990 in the Southern region. Alabama, Kentucky, South Carolina and Tennessee agreed to use regional facilities to treat and dispose wastes generated by industry within their borders. Other Southern states, including Florida, Georgia, Mississippi and North Carolina, are expected to join the regional agreement. Eastern states are considering an interstate compact on radioactive waste.

The Chesapeake Bay is being restored through a cooperative effort involving the District of Columbia, Maryland, Pennsylvania, Virginia and the U.S. Environmental Protection Agency. Following the success of the 1983 agreement, a more detailed agreement was signed in December 1987. The agreement has led to the return of rockfish and an upsurge in osprey and eagles, as well as cleaner Bay waters. The regional program is used as a model for protecting other bays and estuaries.

Regional cooperation in higher education has proved advantageous in the Southern, New England and Western regions. The Western Interstate Commission for Higher Education, the agency created by the Western Regional Education Compact, is regarded as a model for regional cooperation in strengthening higher education. The Council of State Governments' Midwestern Legislative Conference is exploring regional cooperation in higher education through a similar compact.

Recently, administrators in several states have initiated multistate management programs to conduct state business more efficiently. One area that has attracted attention is purchasing. In 1989, an interstate agreement was reached among Colorado, Minnesota and Wisconsin to jointly purchase pharmaceutical products. The DELMARVA cooperative was formed in June 1989 by Delaware, Maryland and Virginia to purchase items such as pursuit vehicles, road salt, light fixtures and insecticide. States also have discussed purchase of heavy equipment on a multistate basis. The cooperative has approached other states, including North Carolina, South Carolina, Pennsylvania and West Virginia. Western states also have considered a similar multistate cooperative to purchase recycled paper. In 1990, the National Association of State Telecommunications Directors formed a Joint Procurement Committee to evaluate purchases of telecommunications equipment.

State treasurers in four Southern states have acted to improve financial management. In October 1990, treasurers of Arkansas, Louisiana, Mississippi and Tennessee held their first Quad State Treasurers' Conference to discuss improving cash and debt management and investment policies in an attempt to establish regional cooperative efforts.

The South and West are known for regional arts efforts. The Southern Arts Federation, which consists of nine state art agencies, recently adopted "The Southern Arts Agenda" with specific goals for states. The arts organization focuses on the relationship between culture and economic development.

The Rural Public Transit Consortium provides technical support services to transit systems in nine Southern states. Since 1984, the consortium has coordinated services among so-cial service transportation agencies and local public transit operators. No other region has such a multistate rural consortium in public transit.

Individual states are taking a look at how regional, national and global events affect them. The Washington Legislature in 1989 launched an initiative to inject long-range thinking into the legislative process. The Washington 2000 project calls for long-range goals and objectives before legislation is drafted.

The Southern Growth Policies Board and The Council of State Governments' Western Legislative Conference are known for their regional trends analysis projects. The SGPB has conducted regional futures projects by creating futures commissions with the help of members of the committees on Southern Trends. Participants in the futures projects have included governors, legislators, private sector representatives and academics. The widely publicized strategic plan for economic development, "Halfway Home and a Long Way to Go," was adopted by the Commission on the Future of the South in November 1986. The document is seen as a blueprint for action for the Southern states.

In 1989, the Western Legislative Conference released its Westrends group's first report, "The Dynamic West: A Region in Transition." It identified 10 trends shaping the West as the 1980s drew to a close. Those trends defined ways in which the West is distinguishable from the rest of the nation. In particular, it showed that rapid change in demography, the economy and politics was a distinguishing regional characteristic. The Westrends study and report are worthy efforts that assist state policy-makers in recognizing major forces in the Western region and the ways in which these forces influence each other.

As a result of the Westrends project, the Idaho Legislature recently considered establishing a task force to study regional trends affecting the state.

Regional Mechanisms and Prospects

Multistate regional cooperation can be initiated and implemented by federal agencies and individual states through interstate compacts or agreements. State policy-makers can use existing mechanisms as well as new vehicles for regional cooperation.

Major regional organizations of state officials are listed in Table 1. In addition, there are regional organizations with rotating secretariat offices in state agencies. These organizations can be used to launch and administer new regional initiatives.

States gain several advantages when taking a regional approach as compared to working alone. First, a regional approach allows state officials to pool their expertise and experience. Second, a regional approach raises policy issues more effectively and, as a result, has a greater impact. Third, such an approach helps states better deal with crisis situations by sharing resources and facilities. Fourth, a regional approach can exert

---

Table 1
Selected Regional Organizations

Eastern Region
Caucus of New England State Legislatures
Coalition of Northeast Governors
Eastern Regional Conference*
New England Governors' Conference
New England Board of Higher Education
Northeast Recycling Council*
New England Council

Midwestern Region
Midwestern Legislative Conference*
Midwestern Governors' Conference*
Council of Great Lakes Governors
Great Lakes Commission
Missouri Basin State Association
Upper Mississippi River Basin Commission
Great Lakes States Recycling Officials

Southern Region
Southern Art Federation
Southern Legislative Conference*
Southern States Energy Board
Southern Regional Education Board
Southern Growth Policies Board
Southern Technology Council
Southern Governors' Association*
Southern Association of State Departments
  of Agriculture
South/West Regional Energy Council

Western Region
Center for the New West
Foremost West
Northwest Power Planning Council
Old West Trails Foundation
Pacific Basin Development Council
Western Attorneys General*
Western Governors' Association
Western Interstate Commission for
  Higher Education
Western Interstate Energy Board
Western Legislative Conference*
Western States Arts Foundation
Western States Water Council
Western United States Agricultural
  Trade Association

Staffed by The Council of State Governments

---

more influence and enhance state visibility in Washington and overseas. And, fifth, it is cost effective.

The cost argument, however, is most appealing. While it is difficult to document cost savings from regional programs, a few examples are available. In the case of interstate child support collection, the 10 Southern states found the computerized system saved more than it cost to operate. Purchasing officials participating in the multistate cooperatives have reported savings for their states.

The greatest savings may come from reduction or elimination of duplicate programs in individual states. An example is the Western Regional Education Compact. The Western Interstate Commission for Higher Education's professional student exchange program has saved states from spending large sums on duplicate educational programs, especially those in health related areas. Because of the interstate compact, the Western region needs only three schools of veterinary medicine, one of which trains veterinarians for 10 states. The 15-state region has only 16 medical schools and eight dental schools.

Regionalism is not a panacea, however. Multistate regional mechanisms initiated by the federal government have raised legal, administrative and fiscal questions. Some questions relate to the authority, jurisdiction and accountability of regional mechanisms. Whether regional approaches should be based on a permanent or ad hoc basis also is an issue. Moreover, sources of interstate conflict must be dealt with to launch an effective regional approach. Interstate conflicts stem from policy differences, poor communication, competition for jobs and investment, and in-state politics. The success of regional approaches depends on policy and program initiatives by state policymakers who are determined to look beyond short-term interests of individual states in favor of cooperative solutions to area problems on a long-term basis.

References

Advisory Commission on Intergovernmental Relations (1972). *Multistate Regionalism*. Washington, D.C.: U.S. Government Printing Office.

Daniel J. Elazar (1972). *American Federalism: A View from the States*. Second Edition. New York: Thomas Y. Crowell Company.

David C. Nice (1987). *Federalism: The Politics of Intergovernmental Relations*. New York: St. Martin's Press.

Ira Sharkansky (1970). *Regionalism in American Politics*. Indianapolis: Bobbs-Merrill.

____ (1972). *Maligned States: Policy Accomplishments, Problems, and Opportunities*. New York: McGraw-Hill Company.

The Delta Looks Up

A new generation of leaders in the poverty-stricken Mississippi Delta rises above the old politics of race that spelled economic doom for blacks and whites alike.

DICK KIRSCHTEN

JONESTOWN, MISS.—A slat is missing from the sun-faded sign that welcomes a traveler to this rundown hamlet about five miles east of U.S. 61, the highway that parallels the Mississippi River from Memphis south to New Orleans. Missing also are the whites who once made up half the town's population and ran most of the businesses.

In the 101-degree heat of a late-summer afternoon, Jonestown looked like a snapshot from the Depression-era 1930s. In the center of town—a single, shabby block of storefronts—few cars or trucks were in sight. A handful of people congregated in front of the liquor store.

Mayor Bobbie Walker recalled that when she came to Jonestown as a 9-year-old orphan in 1948, there were 12-15 stores in the community; now, there are 4. "The whites sold out and moved out about 1968, after the schools were desegregated," she explained. Only blacks attend Jonestown's elementary and middle schools now.

The town's clinic shut down two years ago. Residents without cars pay $6-$10 to be driven to nearby Clarksdale to get medical attention. The nuns who first came to Jonestown in 1984, to offer tutoring and other social services, still find the water here undrinkable.

But Jonestown's biggest problem is the lack of jobs. Walker estimated that only one in four of the town's adults work full-time. "Three-fourths of the people here draw checks, either social security or AFDC [aid to families with dependent children]," she said.

Even in the state that has had the nation's lowest per capita income since that statistic was first calculated in 1929, Jonestown is an embarrassment. In a recent interview in Jackson, Democratic Gov. Ray Mabus declared that "if you've got the Jonestowns, if you have pockets of despair and hopelessness, then we'll never be the country we ought to be."

Mabus—along with his fellow governors from Arkansas, Illinois, Kentucky, Louisiana, Missouri and Tennessee—has decided that the time has come to call attention to, rather than hide, the shameful poverty that afflicts the portions of their states where plantations once farmed by slaves and sharecroppers are now cultivated largely by machines.

"We have disrobed ourselves for the people of the nation to see our problems," said Wilbur F. Hawkins, executive director of the Lower Mississippi Delta Development Commission, which recently completed a congressionally mandated study of 219 counties that cut a swath of

economic and social backwardness across the nation's midsection. *(See map.)*

No one expects the commission's report to prompt major infusions of cash from the deficit-laden federal government, however. "I can't think of anything coming about at a worse possible time, from Washington's standpoint," Sen. Dale Bumpers, D-Ark., author of the bill that created the commission, conceded.

Nonetheless, Bumpers said, from the Delta's standpoint, the time is right. "There is a school of thought that one of the reasons this pervasive poverty has existed up and down both sides of the river for so long is because the white power structure found it to their liking," he said. "If that ever was the case, it isn't now."

A week of travel through Delta communities in Arkansas, Mississippi, Missouri and Tennessee showed what Bumpers meant. Thanks in large part to the hard-won civil rights victories of the 1960s, a new generation of leaders has emerged that keenly senses that the old politics of race spells economic doom for blacks and whites alike.

The 1988 bill creating the Delta commission was quarterbacked in the House by Mike Espy, D-Miss., who in 1986 became the first black Member of Congress since Reconstruction to represent the fertile area between the Mississippi and Yazoo Rivers that gives this region its name. Espy's district is 53 per cent black and includes 22 of the 45 Mississippi counties covered by the study.

"The urgency has always been here, but not the constituency," Espy said in an interview. The Delta, with its disenfranchised blacks, was bypassed by earlier regional attacks on poverty, the Tennessee Valley Authority in the 1930s and the Appalachian Regional Commission in the 1960s, which focused on areas where the impoverished populations were largely white, he said.

The 1965 Voting Rights Act has led to more than the empowerment of blacks who are now voters and elected officials. It also has produced a new generation of racially sensitive white leaders, typified by Arkansas Democratic Gov. Bill Clinton, who chaired the 18-month Delta study; Mabus, the commission's vice chairman; and Louisiana Democratic (now Republican) Gov. Buddy Roemer.

New leaders in both the political and business sectors are seeking to raise this region out of the slough of the Deep South's segregationist past so that it can compete as an equal in national and international markets. As Mabus put it: "In the past, we sold the South and Mississippi to the nation and the world by saying, 'Come on down, we can do it cheaper.' We don't do that anymore. Now it's, 'If you want it done better, come to the South.' "

Such declarations of self-respect are music to the ears of black leaders such as Vicksburg (Miss.) Mayor Robert M. Walker, a former state field director for the NAACP. In an interview in the exquisitely preserved Victorian-style city hall perched above the confluence of the Yazoo and the Mississippi Rivers, the mayor said: "In a whole lot of ways, people from the Delta have seen themselves as they have been perceived by others outside the region. That is changing."

NEW LEADERS

Walker credits the efforts of the new breed of Deep South governors who have attracted attention on the national political stage. He said of Mabus, whose 1987 election was lauded in a *New York Times Sunday Magazine* cover story, "Nobody has done more to change the way outsiders see us than he has."

But it isn't just Delta politicians who have learned how to gain national notice. In his office in a converted correctional facility outside of Brinkley, Ark., Calvin R. King, a black farmer and social activist, discussed his recent receipt of a $240,000 "genius" grant from the John D. and Catherine T. MacArthur Foundation. The 11th child of an Aubrey (Ark.) minister and farmer, King still tills the soil of his family's land in Lee County, a jurisdiction cited in the Delta report for a per capita income 50 per cent below the national average. A member of the first integrated graduating class of the county's public high school, King went on to college and has since founded a corporation that helps black farmers stay in business.

In Humphreys County, Miss., which bills itself "The Catfish Capital of the World," Henry Reed Jr. of Belzoni has become director of Aquaculture Technologies Inc., a multistate corporation founded in 1983 by a group of blacks with backing from a Wall Street investment group.

Reed, now in his second term as an elected county supervisor, works closely with white colleagues in business and government; he noted that the county road crew that he oversees "has a white foreman." He said, however, that racial separation continues to be the local norm and that whites who send their children to private academies fiercely oppose higher taxes for public schools. "They say they are strapped because they are supporting two [school] systems," he explained.

Other examples of emerging black leadership abound in the Delta. In Mound Bayou, Miss., a major health facility that treats blacks and whites is run by a sharecropper's daughter, former high school dropout L.C. Dorsey, who returned to her birthplace after earning the equivalent of a doctorate in social work.

Fifty miles south, in Rolling Fork, Miss., ex-nurse Annie Brown organized a widely acclaimed, two-county adult literacy program. Now part-owner of the local black funeral home, Brown told of former nursing patients who died because they couldn't read instructions on prescription drugs.

The great irony of the Delta is the striking contrast between the bubbling impatience of upwardly mobile blacks and the complacency of the landed white aristocracy.

Even in Jonestown, there is talk of growth. Walker, now in her second year in office, is trying to turn things around. Thanks to a $130,000 federal grant, work is under way to bring Jonestown's water supply into compliance with federal health standards, and the town's sewage treatment capacity will be expanded. That could lead to construction of low-cost housing units, a facility for the elderly and maybe even an industrial plant, Walker said.

In presenting the commission's findings to Congress in May, Clinton used deceptively modest language to make a huge request. He asked, simply, that the residents of the Delta be included as "a full partner in America's future."

The commission's report, however, contains an audacious wish list—more than 160 pages of recommendations for federal, state, local and private-sector actions—that makes clear just how far the Delta has to go to achieve economic political tool. *(See box, next page.)*

Despite major education policy reforms enacted in Arkansas, Mississippi and, more recently, Kentucky, the region's schools remain badly underfinanced and of inferior quality. According to the commission, per capita student expenditures in the Delta are 20 per cent below the national average.

The region also has the country's highest rates of teenage pregnancy, high school dropouts and adult illiteracy. And the Delta suffers a severe shortage of doctors and nurses.

The commission's objectives include access for all to an effective health care system; a 90 per cent high school graduation rate; student performance levels equal to the national average; elimination of substandard housing and a 4 per cent increase in home ownership; diversified agricultural activity, with local processing and marketing jobs; and a flourishing tourist industry boosted by improved highways and a new concern for environmental values.

As mechanization has eliminated labor needs for the Delta's staple crops—cotton, soybeans and corn—pressure has built to find jobs for displaced farm workers.

The commission noted that most of the region's produce is shipped out in raw form, diverting jobs and profits to other areas. The advent of large-scale catfish-farming operations, which require local cleaning and packing, has opened eyes to the economic potential of diversified crops and home-based processing in the Delta region.

The most revolutionary aspect of the report, a 10-year development plan for the Delta, is its sense of expectation that a region that historically neglected to invest in its human resources will change its ways.

The report offers a vision of a region that by the year 2001 no longer will be the butt of outsiders' jokes about the decadent South. One goal is "in the year 2001, racial incidents and ethnic polarization will cease to characterize life in the Lower Mississippi Delta region and will no longer serve as impediments to regional economic development."

PRICE OF NEGLECT

The shortest way from Mound Bayou to Tutwiler, Miss., is the county road that crosses the 16,000-acre penitentiary at Parchman, where more than half of Mis-

DELTA'S LEGACY: POVERTY AND RACISM

John Jordan Crittenden was a lousy prophet. A 19th-century politician who served for more than four decades as U.S. Senator, U.S. Attorney General and governor of Kentucky, Crittenden badly misread the future of his home region. In an 1850 message to his state's legislature, he declared, "Kentucky and the other western states of the Valley of the Mississippi . . . occupy the most fertile region of the world, . . . and in no long time must become the most populous and productive portion of the United States."

Nearly a century-and-half later, a federal commission reports that the rich topsoil of the valley has produced instead "a legacy of poverty and racism." The commission said that a dismal pattern of outmigration and under-achievement marks sections of seven states that border the Mississippi River, from its confluence with the Ohio River south to the Gulf of Mexico.

Established by Congress in 1988, the Lower Mississippi Delta Development Commission undertook an 18-month study of a 219-county area that the group's chairman, Arkansas Democratic Gov. Bill Clinton, described as "the poorest region in the United States."

Poverty has always been more pervasive in the flatlands of the Delta than in the hills of Appalachia, the region targeted for special federal assistance in the 1960s, commission executive director Wilbur F. Hawkins said.

The Delta is home to 8.3 million people, about 3.5 per cent of the nation's population. But the region contains 6 per cent of America's poor and 6.7 per

cent of its substandard housing. Of the nation's 282 most distressed counties, 89 are in the Delta.

What most sets the Delta apart from Appalachia and the country as a whole is its high concentration of blacks. The

region is 30 per cent black, compared with a national average of 12.5 per cent. The generation that will make up the Delta's work force of the future, those 19 and under, is 40 per cent black; the national average is 19 per cent.

In the 1980 census, the poverty rate for the Delta's blacks was measured at 41.6 per cent, double the rate for the region as a whole. Predominantly black Tunica County, Miss., with a poverty rate of 52.9 per cent, was rated the poorest county in the nation.

Blacks contribute disproportionately to the region's other dismal social indicators: an infant mortality rate 1.8 points higher than the national rate, unemployment 3.3 points higher and per capita income that is $3,400 a year lower. Adult illiteracy and teenage pregnancy also abound in the Delta.

Welfare benefits within the region tend to be meager. For example, six of the Delta states—Arkansas, Kentucky, Louisiana, Mississippi, Missouri and Tennessee—rank among the bottom eight states in the country in benefit levels for the aid to families with dependent children program, Isaac Shapiro of Washington's Center on Budget and Policy Priorities said.

Despite recent reforms, education spending also lags. According to the U.S. Education Department, per-pupil expenditures in elementary and secondary schools in six of the seven Delta states are lower than the U.S. average.

The Delta has attracted little outside help. Targeted Research Associates, a Sikeston (Mo.) firm, found that Delta counties lost at least $79 million in potential welfare payments in 1988 because states were reluctant to put up more matching money. The commission also contended that the Delta's 104 institutions of higher learning get short shrift in the distribution of federal research and development grants: $268 million in 1985, compared with $448 million that year for a single institution, the Johns Hopkins University in Baltimore. At the commission's urging, a consortium of regional universities is being formed to concentrate on teacher training and economic development.

Organized philanthropy also overlooks the region. The commission reported that the region has a below-average number of charitable foundations and that over-all foundation giving within the 219-county area averages $82 per resident per year. That's less than a fifth of the national average, $431.

sissippi's 8,000 convicts are confined. The drive through Parchman offers an unsettling perspective on Delta sociology.

Seven of 10 Parchman inmates are black—about double the proportion of blacks in Mississippi's population. The sprawling, unshaded Parchman complex is dotted with watchtowers, fenced compounds and athletic fields. Prisoners wear color-coded uniforms: red for death row,

yellow for maximum security and various combinations of blue and white for other classifications. Near the main gate is a vocational technology center.

At the Delta Health Center in Mound Bayou, executive director Dorsey spoke of "the unbelievable waste of human potential" that can be traced to the inadequacies in Mississippi's schools. "If you spend your money on education, you'll

have to spend less money later on in crime prevention, court procedures, incarceration, even the woes of neglected health," Dorsey said.

Dorsey vented her frustration over the Legislature's rejection this year of a lottery to raise additional funds for education. She attributed the vote to "lingering racism" among legislators "who can't see the broad picture" or decline to support education because they are "afraid" that blacks will benefit. "It's archaic and ridiculous," she snapped.

The experience of the 51-year-old Dorsey demonstrates the determination within the Delta's black community. After leaving school to get married, and after bearing six children, she "dropped back in" to education with a boost from "the Johnson programs"—the antipoverty initiatives passed by Congress in the 1960s.

In 1965, Mound Bayou became the site of the first rural health pilot project of the federal Office of Economic Opportunity (OEO). Adult education classes, offered in conjunction with the health center, lured Dorsey back to earn certification as a high school graduate. She later studied at the State University of New York (Stony Brook) and Howard University in Washington.

Unlike many high school classmates who "took the Greyhound to Chicago," Dorsey returned to where she started. Now chief administrator of the successor to the OEO's pilot clinic, she oversees a modern outpatient facility (which is saddled with a "hefty mortgage"). The center serves a four-county area and has an annual budget of $3.2 million. Her biggest problems: recruiting physicians (the center currently has only four, one a part-timer) and finding competent support staff. "Even when people have credentials, the skills aren't there," she complained, returning to her criticism of the schools.

A late bloomer of another sort is Sister Anne Brooks, who, at age 40, persuaded her religious order to send her to medical school. Now 50, she is the lone physician in Tutwiler (pop. 1,381), and one of only four physicians in all of Tallahatchie County (pop. 9,264).

Like many other human services centers in the Delta, the Tutwiler Clinic dispenses more than health care. The staff of 18, 6 of them nuns, provides a variety of services to the predominantly black community. These range from a preschool play program and classes for high-school-equivalency certificates to quilting bees.

As members of the Sisters of the Holy Names of Jesus and Mary, the Tutwiler nuns have been able to obtain tax-exempt status for the clinic, but they have to do their own fund raising to help meet the $400,000-a-year budget. Two-thirds of the money comes from charitable solicitations; the rest, from third-party medical payments, mostly medicare and medicaid. Brooks and a social worker colleague, Sister Joann Blomme, have worked in poor neighborhoods in big cities. Both said that the poverty they have encountered in rural Mississippi is more damaging to the human spirit, as evidenced by the cases of

physical and emotional abuse that they see.

"It's amazing to me how people survive in the face of the enormous hopelessness and frustration that come from being deprived of economic means to improve their lives," Blomme said.

30 YEARS TOO LATE?

"The Delta remains the No. 1 economic problem in the country; it has been all along," former (1980-84) Mississippi Democratic Gov. William F. Winter said during a recent visit to Washington. "Let's just say this candidly: Because so much of the population consisted of black people without any real political clout, there was no great push [during the 1960s] to do for the Lower Delta what was done for Appalachia, where everybody voted."

Winter, regarded by many as the guiding light of the new breed of progressive politicians in his state, added, "It's 30 years too late" to expect a response to the Delta's problems akin to the big-spending, public-works-oriented approach of the Appalachian Commission program enacted in 1965 as the first of President Johnson's Great Society initiatives.

"I do not see any federal programs that are going to materially change the pattern of life and certainly no enhanced programs, given today's fiscal facts of life," Winter said. He added that "the states can't do it either: Mississippi is running a deficit, and Arkansas and Louisiana are both having problems."

To rise from the morass, Winter said, the Delta will need "a commitment on the part of the private sector to become involved in a more extensive way than they ever have before." Toward that end, and with the help of a $1 million "challenge grant" from the Entergy Corp., a regional holding company for electrical utilities, he has helped launch a philanthropic organization, the Foundation for the Mid South.

Winter said the foundation is raising $2 million in matching donations from the region and will then branch out to try to build a broader base of support. Its goal is to spur economic development, educational and family support activities in Arkansas, Louisiana and Mississippi.

At least one major outside charity already is working in the Delta. Save the Children, based in Westport, Conn., which sponsors community development programs in 33 Third World countries, started an eight-county project in eastern Arkansas in 1979. It has since expanded into Mississippi and currently spends $400,000 a year in the region, $100,000 of which comes from grants from the Winthrop Rockefeller Foundation in Little Rock, Ark., and the Levi Strauss Foundation in San Francisco.

Save the Children helped MacArthur prize-winner King found his Arkansas Land and Farm Development Corp. King said he gets great satisfaction from working to improve his native region. "There are others who don't want to go back to their roots, who go after big bucks," he said. "My desires are different."

Another Save the Children grantee is the Marvell (Ark.) social services center directed by Beatrice Clark Shelby, a veteran of the OEO-sponsored community action organization movement of the 1960s and '70s. Operating out of an old shirt factory with a hard-to-miss new coat of pink paint, the Boys, Girls, Adults Community Development Center shares space with a state public health clinic.

The facility provides recreational, educational and preventive health services for families in 12 communities. It also operates a diner, primarily as a means of providing jobs to women who otherwise would be unemployed.

Shelby said that heavy emphasis is placed on a counseling program aimed at reducing the region's high rate of teenage pregnancies and in cooperating with local schools in an antidrug alliance. It is also involved in seeking financing for 37 new units of low-cost housing.

Shelby said of the center's work, "All of our programs are about prevention, whether it's drugs, pregnancy or just plain failure."

The board chairman of the Marvell community center, Gertrude Jackson, a teacher in the local Head Start program, is another "graduate" of the Great Society programs. To teach preschoolers, she had to go back to school herself, to earn a high school certificate and then to amass college credits in the field of early childhood learning.

The Kaiser Family Foundation in Menlo Park, Calif., this year awarded Mississippi a three-year, $450,000 grant to launch a grass-roots program to promote improved health care.

Winter said that not nearly enough has been accomplished. "There have been some local and spasmodic efforts to do some things," he acknowledged. "But still, we find ourselves in the final decade of the 20th century with this huge pocket of poverty, with educational, economic and social needs largely unmet."

EAGER FOR ACTION

In Sunset, Ark., the city hall's air-conditioning was on the fritz as dashiki-clad Mayor James Wilburn Jr. talked about the medical costs incurred when a local youngster recently was bitten in the face by a snake that had entered the bedroom of his rain-damaged home.

Located 15 miles west of Memphis, tiny Sunset—population 610 by census count, 1,150 by the mayor's—has an average family income of $5,300 a year. It doesn't seem a likely launching pad for a political career, but Wilburn, 38, is a flamboyant personality who knows how to attract the news media's interest.

He garnered publicity by organizing a citizens' fund-raising drive to purchase a fire truck (a used model from the state forestry department) and by his efforts to instill black pride in local youngsters. Unopposed when he first ran for mayor, he now faces opposition for a second term. "I got some recognition, and now everybody wants to be mayor," he laughed.

Wilburn is one of a growing cadre of black elected officials whose rise to power helps explain the Delta's increasing recognition of the need to deal with, rather than ignore, the problems of its poor. Clarksdale (Miss.) Mayor Henry Espy, brother of the House Member, and Mayersville (Miss.) Mayor Unita Blackwell, recently elected president of the National Conference of Black Mayors, are two examples.

Another is Vicksburg's Walker, a Winter protégé, who has won election twice in a community where there are equal numbers of blacks and whites. Walker's idea of affirmative action in city hiring is to give preference to the best-educated. To take the examination for a job on the Vicksburg police force, an applicant must have successfully completed 40 hours of college work.

"The message going out to folks in this community is that if you have the training, the chances of getting a decent job are good," Walker said. "If you refuse to see the importance of schooling, you are going to face difficulties."

Area institutions of higher learning, meanwhile, are reexamining their roles within their communities. The University of Tennessee (Martin), for example, earlier this year persuaded an expert on malnutrition, Dr. Norman L. Betz, to accept an endowed chair. Betz has since teamed up with the lone physician in isolated Lake County, Tenn., to run a supplemental nutrition program for preschoolers.

Betz, a former research director for the St. Louis-based Ralston Purina Co., also

is involved in a nutrition project in Mexico. He said there are striking similarities between the two activities. The 30 families in his Tiptonville (Tenn.) project live in circumstances that are "about as Third World as you can get," he said.

In Sikeston, Mo., on Aug. 27, Rep. Bill Emerson, R-Mo., hosting a public hearing on the Delta commission's report, argued that new federal cost-sharing requirements for water projects confront the states in the Delta with an unjust and untenable burden. The river, he said, serves the entire nation. Without a special break for Delta jurisdictions, he said, "it will be impossible to complete" the final 20 per cent of the Lower Mississippi Valley's flood protection program.

Emerson is vice chairman of the House's Lower Mississippi Delta Caucus, a bipartisan (17 Democrats, 7 Republicans) group formed this summer to push for congressional action to assist the region. A similar group is being organized by Bumpers in the Senate.

The House Delta Caucus is chaired by Espy, who, Winter said, has "proven to be one of the most effective spokespersons for the whole area, including the white landowners." One of Espy's coups has been getting the Defense Department to boost its purchases from the Delta's catfish industry.

Espy said the Delta Caucus already has chalked up some victories. It has adopted a strategy of seeking special legislative consideration for distressed areas in general, not just this one. "The idea is that if you target poor counties everywhere, you will of necessity hit the Delta," he said.

Espy, Emerson and Rep. Carroll Hubbard Jr., D-Ky., sponsored an amendment that in July was added to the 1990 Housing and Community Development Act, which is now in conference with a Senate bill. The amendment would increase by $109 million the funds set aside for the nation's neediest counties: including 35 in the Delta.

Other initiatives in the pipeline, according to Espy, include an amendment to the pending 1990 farm bill that would authorize $10 million in technical assistance for

disadvantaged minority farmers; legislation calling for a tourism-oriented three-year study of the "heritage" of the entire Mississippi River corridor; and a teacher enrichment program.

To sustain momentum after the Delta commission expires (its last official day was Sept. 30), the governors of the seven states have been asked to ante up $50,000 apiece to support an interim body, the Lower Mississippi Delta Center. Espy said that Congress may be asked to augment the group's budget next year.

Hawkins, the commission's executive director, said that the ultimate goal is to set up a regional economic development bank, a public-private entity that would be financed by commercial banks, insurance companies and utilities and government agencies.

"Mississippi is not going to wait for the federal government," Mabus declared. Despite his recent setback in the Legislature on his plan to establish a state lottery and earmark the proceeds for education, he said that the state is committed to improving its schools. "We had a disagreement over how to finance school reforms, not whether to," he declared.

Mabus said his optimism stems from the belief that race relations, the issue that once divided the region and held it back, has become an asset. "The civil rights revolution and the voting rights revolution freed us from the politics of race, so that we can now concentrate on the things that are important," he said. "I would make an argument that we are the most progressive, open, integrated society you will find." Indeed, one of the Delta commission's more provocative recommendations was that Congress designate the region as a "national laboratory" for the study of race relations.

Bumpers, who gave the Delta study its initial push, said that it will be tough for the region to make up for lost time, but not as tough as it once might have been. "One of the beautiful things about this whole proposal is that everybody, black and white, rich and poor, are all enthusiastic about it. Twenty years ago, that would have been unthinkable."

S T A T E
S T A T S

A Comparative Ranking of Economic Entities

Rank	Name	Gross Product or Sales (in millions of dollars)
1	United States	5,237,707
2	Japan	2,920,310
3	Germany	1,272,959
4	France	1,000,866
5	Italy	871,955
6	United Kingdom	834,166
7	California	697,381
8	Canada	500,337
9	New York	441,068
10	China	393,006
11	Brazil	375,146
12	Spain	358,352
13	Texas	340,057
14	India	287,383
15	Illinois	256,478
16	Australia	242,131
17	Netherlands	237,415
18	Pennsylvania	227,898
19	Florida	226,964
20	Ohio	211,545

↓ (Rankings 21 through 31 include 5 states)

Rank	Name	Gross Product or Sales (in millions of dollars)
32	Georgia	129,776
33	General Motors	126,974
34	Finland	109,705
35	Indiana	105,263

↓ (Rankings 36 through 148 include 33 states)

Rank	Name	Gross Product or Sales (in millions of dollars)
149	North Dakota	11,231
150	South Dakota	11,135
151	Wyoming	11,115

Source: National Governors' Association

School days' primer

Elaine S. Knapp

Higher and lower math

State and local governments nationwide spend nearly a quarter of their budgets on elementary and secondary education. States with the highest annual dollar spending through high school are:

- California $23.5 billion
- New York $19.6 billion
- Texas $13.5 billion
- Pennsylvania $ 9.8 billion
- Illinois $ 9.0 billion

Education budgets total one-half billion dollars or less in South Dakota, North Dakota and Wyoming.

But a more revealing figure is how much states spend per pupil a year. Based on average daily attendance, the biggest spenders are:

- New Jersey $8,439
- New York $7,917
- Connecticut $7,876
- District of Columbia $4,427
- Alaska $7,252

The lowest are:

- Utah $2,720
- Mississippi $3,119
- Arkansas $3,272
- Alabama $3,314
- Oklahoma $3,439

Who pays?

The state share of education is highest in:

- Hawaii   91 percent
- New Mexico   76 percent
- Washington   74 percent
- Kentucky   70 percent
- Alabama   68 percent

The local share is highest in:

- New Hampshire   90 percent
- Nebraska   71 percent
- Oregon   67 percent
- South Dakota   63 percent

Prescription for trouble

- *Low birth weight* — 33 percent of children who weighed less than 4 pounds at birth had to repeat a grade or take special classes, compared to only 13 percent of newborns who weighed more than 5.5 pounds.
- *Smoking* — Nearly 11 percent of children born to mothers who smoked more than two packs a day during pregnancy, failed in school.
- *Lead levels* — 24 percent of children with high lead levels dropped out of high school and 39 percent had reading disabilities.
- *Child abuse* — Abused or neglected children have IQs averaging 20 points below those of other children.

Testing, testing

High schoolers rank the highest on college entrance exam scores (SAT and ACT) in:

- New Hampshire
- Wisconsin
- Iowa
- Oregon
- Maryland

Public education is a major enterprise in dollars and sense.

One more day

Extending the school year could prove expensive in some states. The daily cost of running all schools is $121 million in California, $116 million in New York and $50 million or more in Pennsylvania, New Jersey and Florida.

But daily school costs total $3 million or less in Delaware, Wyoming, Vermont, South Dakota and North Dakota.

It's black and white

Pollster Louis Harris reports:
• 37 percent of whites believe most black children cannot be motivated to learn.
• Seven in 10 Americans say the U.S. will lose its competitive edge if minorities and poor are not educated.
• 11 percent say blacks have less intelligence than whites, down from 39 percent in 1963.
• 55 percent feel the poor and minorities do not receive as good an education as most white children receive.
Based on a May 9-15, 1991, survey of 1,250 adults.

Teacher salaries, average 1990-91

Highest
Alaska	$43,861
Connecticut	$43,847
District of Columbia	$42,228
New York	$41,600
California	$39,358

Lowest
South Dakota	$22,363
Arkansas	$23,040
North Dakota	$23,578
Mississippi	$24,443
Oklahoma	$24,649

Graduation rates

Highest (90-85 percent)
1. Minnesota
2. North Dakota
3. Wyoming
4. Iowa
5. Nebraska

Lowest (58-61 percent)
46. Louisiana
47. Arizona
48. Georgia
49. District of Columbia
50. Florida

The most and the least

Out of the nation's 40 million public school children, the most live in:
• California	4.7 million
• Texas	3.3 million
• New York	2.5 million
• Florida	1.8 million
• Illinois	1.8 million

The fewest live in:
Delaware, Vermont and Wyoming, which each have less than 100,000 pupils.

Not ready to learn

Not all kids enter school ready to learn:
• One in eight children has a learning impairment that could have been prevented by better health care or nutrition.
• One in five children lives in poverty.
• Half the kindergarten children in some districts cannot say their names or speak in complete sentences.

Top education govs

While George Bush proclaims himself the "education president" and other politicians follow suit, who really deserves the honor? When polled by *USA TODAY*, governors picked as education leaders: Bill Clinton of Arkansas, Wallace Wilkinson of Kentucky, Booth Gardner of Washington, Carroll Campbell of South Carolina and Roy Romer of Colorado.

Education reform was called for by most of the 37 governors responding to the newspaper poll, who saw as barriers lack of parental involvement, poverty, unemployment, drug abuse and poor health care.

The governors favored day care and social services in schools, alternative teacher certification and parental choice in public schools.

Sources: Research by Melodye Bush, Education Commission of the States, Denver, Colo., unless specified.

Cities and Suburbs

More than three-quarters of Americans live in cities or in surrounding suburban areas. In these densely populated settings, local governments face great challenges and opportunities. One challenge is to provide a satisfactory level of services such as policing, schooling, sanitation, water, and public transportation at a cost that taxpayers can and will bear. An accompanying opportunity is the possibility of helping to create a local setting that improves the lives of residents in meaningful ways. The challenges and opportunities occur amid a formidable array of urban and suburban problems: crime, violence, drugs, deterioration of public schools, racial tensions, financial stringencies, pollution, congestion, aging populations, decaying physical plants, breakdown of family life, and so forth.

Cities are the local government jurisdictions that generally exist where there is high population density. Major metropolitan areas generally have a large city at their center and a surrounding network of suburbs under a number of smaller local government jurisdictions. Smaller cities may be part of suburban rings, or they may exist independently of major metropolitan areas, with their own smaller network of surrounding suburbs.

Cities of all sizes generally provide more services to local residents than other kinds of local government jurisdictions. Thus, city residents generally expect their city governments to provide water, a sewerage system, public transportation, a professional firefighting force, public museums, parks and other recreational areas, and various other amenities associated with city life. By contrast, local governments in rural areas are not expected to provide such services. Local governments in suburban areas typically provide some but not all of them. With the greater range of services provided in cities come higher taxes and more regulatory activities.

Like cities, suburbs come in various shapes and sizes. Some are called bedroom or commuter suburbs because people live there with their families and commute to and from the central city to work. Others have more of an independent economic base. Local governments in suburbs have often emphasized "quality education" (i.e., good schools), zoning plans to preserve the residential character of the locale, and keeping property taxes within tolerable limits. Generally speaking, suburbs have a greater proportion of whites and middle-class people than cities have.

One problem facing suburban governments today stems from aging populations. Older people need and demand different services than the young families which used to occupy suburbia in greater proportions. It is not always easy to shift policy priorities from, for example, public schooling to public transportation and recreational programs for the elderly. A second problem is structural in nature and relates to the overlapping local government jurisdictions in suburban areas—school districts, sanitation districts, townships, counties, villages, boroughs, and so forth. The maze of jurisdictions often confuses citizens and sometimes makes coordinated and effective government difficult.

The goals of suburban local governments and the central city government in a single metropolitan area often come into conflict in such policy areas as public transportation, school integration, air pollution, highway systems, and so forth. Sometimes common aims can be pursued through cooperative ventures between suburban and city governments or through creation of metropolitan-wide special districts. Sometimes, through annexation or consolidation, a larger unit of general-purpose local government is formed in an attempt to cope with metropolitan-wide issues more easily.

Selections in this unit treat city and suburban governments and the problems and opportunities faced in metropolitan areas. Cities and suburbs, of course, typically face different sets of problems. Even so, it is important to note that not all cities face similar problems; nor do all suburbs.

Looking Ahead: Challenge Questions

Do you live in a city or suburb? If so, do you like city or suburban life? If not, what do you imagine are the key differences between city and suburban life?

Many people are pessimistic about the ability of local governments in major urban areas to cope with contemporary urban problems. Do you share their pessimism? Why?

Big city mayors are often highly visible politicians on the national scene. Have you heard of Mayors Richard Daley (Chicago), David Dinkins (New York), Coleman Young (Detroit), Frank Jordan (San Francisco), Raymond Flynn

(Boston), and Maynard Jackson (Atlanta)? Have you formed any impressions of the abilities of those mayors whose names you recognize? If so, what are your impressions?

Would it be desirable for suburban local governments to raise property taxes and provide better public transpor-

tation, more frequent garbage collections, and better recreational facilities? Why?

Would major metropolitan areas be better served if they each had only one metropolitan-wide local government, instead of the large number of local governments that currently exist in each metropolis? Why or why not?

■ WHERE GOOD JOBS GO

Business Flees to The Urban Fringe

CHRISTOPHER B. LEINBERGER

Christopher B. Leinberger is managing partner of Robert Charles Lesser & Co., a Los Angeles–based real estate advisory and metropolitan public policy firm with offices around the country.

As a direct result of the postindustrial economy that America has been creating over the past couple of decades, the locations of the best-paying new jobs are changing radically. These jobs are now overwhelmingly concentrated in obscure crossroads like King of Prussia (Philadelphia metropolitan area), Newport Beach (Los Angeles area), Tyson's Corner (Washington, D.C., area) and Schaumburg (Chicago area). These new suburbs are fourteen, forty, sixteen and twenty-five miles, respectively, from the central business district.

There are three distinct types of employment in our metropolitan areas, two generally well paying and a third almost always at the bottom of the wage scale. About one-third of metropolitan jobs are with companies that "export" goods and services outside the metro area. These are the highest-paying jobs, injecting fresh cash into the local economy. In Los Angeles, for example, those jobs are in aerospace, defense, software development, entertainment, international trade, oil refining and a number of other industries. In Seattle, the export industries are aerospace, software development and international trade; in Philadelphia they include pharmaceuticals, higher education, oil refining and computer hardware development.

Export jobs in turn create demand for the second type of employment, regional-serving jobs, which include finance, real estate, utilities, the local news media and professional services of various kinds. These represent about a quarter of all jobs in most metropolitan areas and on average pay slightly less well than export jobs. It is important to note that export and regional-serving jobs tend to locate in a few concentrations, variously referred to as urban villages, edge cities or urban cores. Most large metropolitan areas have ten to thirty urban cores, the downtown being just one of them.

The third category is local-serving jobs, representing about half of all employment and paying the least well. These jobs are located near where people live and include such occupations as schoolteacher, store clerk, police and local professionals such as neighborhood doctors and "storefront" lawyers. Virtually every job in South Central Los Angeles is—or was—local serving. Following the Watts riots in 1965, most of the export jobs, generally in manufacturing, abandoned the area, leaving only low-wage, local-serving employment.

The export and regional-serving jobs in every metropolitan area in the country have followed the same pattern over the past twenty years. In any metro area in late twentieth-century America, if one knows the layout of the freeway system; where the existing white, upper middle class lives and where the new white middle-income housing is; and where minority populations are concentrated, one can determine where 80 to 100 percent of the new upwardly mobile export and regional-serving jobs are located. With few exceptions, these high-paying jobs have concentrated in the predominantly white upper-middle- and middle-income sections of the metropolitan region, generally on the opposite side of the metro area from the highest concentration of minority housing. Low-income residents and the new high-paying, upwardly mobile export and regional-serving jobs are now located farther apart than ever.

 From *The Nation*, July 6, 1992, pp. 10-12, 14. Copyright © 1992 by The Nation, Inc. Reprinted by permission.

For example, nearly all new export and regional-serving jobs moved north of Atlanta during the 1980s; the vast majority of low-income, black neighborhoods are on the south side of town. In Dallas, nearly all new jobs have been created in the north and northwest quadrants of the metropolitan area; the black and Hispanic populations are concentrated to the east and south. In the Philadelphia metropolitan area, from 1970 to 1990 the number of export and regional-serving jobs that located in the high-income Main Line to the northwest of the city, as well as in the white middle-income areas of lower Bucks County to the northeast and New Jersey to the east, increased by more than 50 percent. The number of these types of jobs in the increasingly black and Hispanic city dropped by 15 percent over the same time period. In Los Angeles—an extremely complex metropolitan area because of its immense size (more than 14 million people) and because it has more growth paths than other metropolitan areas—nearly all new export and regional-serving jobs were created to the west, northwest and southeast during the 1980s. The largest black neighborhood, south of downtown, and the largest Hispanic concentration, to the east, are located very close to the center city and quite far from the emerging new job centers in West Los Angeles, Warner Center (northeast) and Newport Beach (southeast).

The reason for this geographic shift in upwardly mobile jobs is that over the past two decades all metropolitan jobs in the country—with Los Angeles leading the way—have been undergoing a transformation as profound as the metamorphosis of eighteenth-century trading towns into nineteenth-century industrial cities. The shape and size of our metropolitan areas have changed from what, in retrospect, looks like a relatively compact industrial city in the 1950s into the sprawling conurbations of today. The population of the Los Angeles area increased more than four times during the past fifty years, but its geographic size increased by a factor of twenty. Metropolitan Chicago's population increased by just 4 percent in the past two decades, but its size increased by 46 percent.

In the 1990s, the trend of the vast majority of the new export and regional-serving jobs moving to what will soon look like near-in suburbs appears to be ending. The few corporate relocations that have occurred in these recessionary times have been to the even more extreme fringe of our metropolitan areas, generally close to the newest housing developments. J.C. Penney, which left midtown Manhattan in 1988 for several temporary sites in near-in suburban Dallas, is now building a campus-style headquarters in Plano, Texas, at the outermost exurban edge of that metropolitan area, twenty-five miles from downtown and eight miles from its current suburban location. U.S. Borax's headquarters (Los Angeles); I.B.M.'s software development facility (Dallas); the R&D facilities for Rohm and Haas, Sterling Drugs and SmithKline Beecham (Philadelphia); and Chrysler's new R&D facility (Detroit) have all been built in equally distant, fringe locations.

The reasons for these moves to the periphery include the need to be near mid-level employee housing during the com-

ing decade because of the projected shortage of skilled labor once the economy revives. A second reason is that the commute for the bosses, who will probably still live in the upper- and upper-middle-income housing areas, such as Philadelphia's Main Line or L.A.'s Newport Beach, will be against traffic, minimizing their inconvenience. A third reason for the move to the fringe is the tremendous difficulty of obtaining government approvals for the large, campus-style office and business parks in near-in suburbs.

But a fourth reason is the desire to escape the crime and the minority work force in the center city, which are now reaching the near-in suburbs as well. In Chicago, Sears is moving its merchandising division to Hoffman Estates, which is unreachable by public transit—twelve miles beyond Schaumburg and thirty-seven miles from the Sears Tower, where it is now located. Although Sears has proposed a van-pool program for employees living in the city, a number of leaders in the Chicago real estate community have privately commented that one of the primary reasons for the move is that the company wants to rid itself of its predominantly black work force in the downtown. This, the theory goes, would allow Sears to hire better-educated employees, probably predominantly white, who live near the 1.9 million square foot campus-style complex. The same motivation may have been behind the other recent corporate moves to the extreme fringe. The trend will only accelerate in Los Angeles as a result of the riots.

If, as many indicators suggest, jobs in the 1990s, particularly the high-paying ones, become available in the extreme fringe of the metropolitan area in the same proportion as they did in the near-in suburban locations over the past two decades, many inner-city residents will be too far away to commute daily to the new exurban ones. In the 1970s and 1980s the new jobs in relatively close-in suburban locations were at least within commuting distance for many city dwellers. The new relocation trend to the extreme fringe will certainly continue, and could accelerate, the post–World War II exodus of the middle class from the center cities, leaving poorer residents behind.

These trends affecting the location of export and regional-serving jobs are firmly imbedded in the economy and real estate market. Short of massive federal and state intervention in the marketplace (an unlikely event that would undoubtedly produce as many problems as it would solve), the trends must be viewed as something that can be influenced but not reversed. However, here are four ideas, tried and proved in this country and Europe, that might ameliorate some of the intended and unintended consequences of the decentralization of our metropolitan areas.

§ The first is to try to slow down the trend through a kind of holding action by center-city economic development agencies and public/private partnerships, working with those institutions and corporations that have a commitment to the center city. Targeting the existing concentration of export and regional-serving sections of the center city, particularly downtown, these groups must launch programs that increase job training opportunities and enhance security. A well-trained work force and freedom from fear of crime are prerequisites to maintaining the existing job base.

An example of this effort is provided by the more than twenty public/private partnerships in New York City. The Grand Central Partnership, for instance, supplements municipal services in the fifty-three-block section of Manhattan surrounding Grand Central Terminal with its own fifty-person security force, a forty-person sanitation force that sweeps the sidewalks and streets twelve hours a day, and a $2-million-a-year program for the homeless at a former Catholic boys' school. Hundreds of these "business improvement districts" are now operating in cities throughout the country.

§ The second strategy is to encourage a regional approach to government, particularly toward tax-sharing. This strategy requires a recognition that the center city cannot—and should not have to—bear the cost of serving the bulk of the metropolitan area's needy. The growing fiscal and social problems of our center cities have been ignored too long by the suburban jurisdictions. Violent and property crime, homelessness and drug trafficking know no political boundary. These problems have not been magically confined within the center city limits and have resulted in a new trend of declining property values and quality of life for close-in suburbs throughout the country. An example of the kind of tax-sharing needed can be found in the Minneapolis-St. Paul metro area, where 60 percent of new commercial property tax revenues go to the local municipality and 40 percent go to the other metro area jurisdictions.

In addition, a regional approach could allow for the establishment of an urban growth boundary around the metropolitan area, beyond which jobs and suburban housing could not go, as Portland, Oregon, and nearly every European metropolitan area have done. This would force jobs back closer to, and possibly back into, the center cities as well as protect the rural land around our metropolitan areas from sprawling development. While growth boundaries are not without flaws—they can artificially inflate land prices and thus rents and home prices, for example—they do seem to slow lopsided growth toward predominantly white neighborhoods while maintaining the integrity of downtown.

Los Angeles has already created a de facto regional government in the form of the South Coast Air Quality Management District. This body also increasingly regulates traffic congestion, job growth and land use. Even five years ago, regional government in the Los Angeles area was considered a fantasy. Today, most metropolitan-area leaders do not question that it is a reality. The next step would be to add social issues to the regional agenda.

§ A third approach is to encourage affordable and public housing in the near-in and fringe suburbs, enabling low-income residents to live closer to the new jobs. Orange County, California, has in the past required that 20 percent of all new residential projects be set aside for affordable housing. Columbia, Maryland, recently issued a taxpayer-supported bond to build low-income housing for minorities. While these measures are unlikely to be widely adopted, the business community could be a powerful ally. Many companies had a hard time filling lower-level jobs in the near-in suburbs during the 1980s, and this situation will be exacerbated in the 1990s. One promising approach is for corporations to team up with nonprofit affordable-housing organizations, such as the Bridge Housing Corporation in San Francisco and Habitat for Humanity, based in Americus, Georgia. An interim measure is the organizing of car pools and setting up of van pools to bring city residents to distant corporate jobs.

§ Fourth, we must improve the efficiency of central city public services. The cost of maintaining existing infrastructure and providing services in the center city is higher than the cost of building new infrastructure and providing services in the fringe suburbs, even if the extra cost of delivering social services to the needy is subtracted. The trade-off many companies face is either moving to a suburb with lower costs and fewer social problems or staying in the high-cost center city with overwhelming social problems. It is not hard to see that moving out makes more sense economically.

If present trends continue, the center city's future—and the future of many of the close-in suburbs—is likely to be similar to the present-day fate of Camden and Newark, New Jersey; of Chester, Pennsylvania; or of South Central Los Angeles. The "Camdenization" of our major cities, resulting in their being populated primarily by an underclass in an environment of hopelessness, has obviously begun. It is probable that the 1990s offer the last chance to reverse this trend, because if most of the 24 million new jobs that the Labor Department estimates will be created between 1990 and 2005 are located at the fringe of our metro areas, the downward spiral of the center cities may become irreversible.

As a nation we are used to moving away from our problems, striking out to new frontiers. If the market is allowed to take job growth to the extreme fringe of our metropolitan areas, our center cities may well require full-time military occupation. The fires in Los Angeles are a warning that an escapist strategy no longer works. The costs are too steep and the stakes are too high.

Snow White and the 17 Dwarfs: From Metro Cooperation to Governance

DAVID B. WALKER

David B. Walker is professor of political science, University of Connecticut, and former assistant director, Advisory Commission on Intergovernmental Relations. This article is adapted (with the editor's assistance) from his remarks to the November 1986 National Conference on Government in Kansas City. © 1987 by the National Municipal League.

SNOW White nearly lost her heart. But she overcame the hostility of her stepmother and was kept alive in the forest by a family of dwarfs.

Metro America is Snow White. Migration to suburban areas nearly took the heart out of her. Federal hostility toward taking a role in metro governance has driven metro America into a temporary disappearance from public view. The good news is that she is being kept alive by 17 distinct types of interlocal approaches, on a spectrum from intergovernmental cooperation to full regional governance.

Some view this spectrum as a path out of a dark forest of problems, toward a regional Camelot.

Increasing Need for Metro Approaches

The nation's metro areas are growing, and their problems along with them. Substate regionalism seeks to address problems that spill over the artificial boundaries of central city limits. As metro America expands, the substate regional drama is being played out in more arenas. Note these seven current trends:

1. More Metro Areas. More metro areas exist today (1982 data) than ever before, with a more than two-thirds increase since 1962.

2. More People in Metro Areas. Three-quarters of our total population is located there, compared to 63% in 1962. More people also live in suburban jurisdictions than previously—some 45% of total population compared to 30% two decades earlier.

3. Continued Metro Government Fragmentation. Growth in metro areas hasn't meant consolidation. More of the nation's local governments are located in metro areas now: over 36% of the 82,000 total as against 27% in 1972. The average metro area still encompasses about 100 governmental units, despite the slight increase in the percentage (48% of the total) of single county and presumably jurisdictionally simpler metro areas.

4. Increased Metro Diversity. Compared to their situation in the 1960s, metro areas are now more diverse in (a) population and territorial size, (b) the mix of private economic functions and the range of public services offered, (c) the respective position of central cities vis-a-sis outside central city jurisdictions, and (d) the kinds of jurisdictional complexity.

5. Advisory Disharmony. For officials seeking guidance from governmental gurus, theoretical harmony is more elusive than ever. More theories are in vogue as to how metro areas should be run. No wonder actual practice is more eclectic than ever before.

6. Reduced Federal Aid. Direct Federal aid to localities, from day care funds to revenue sharing, has been cut back year by year without a concomitant reduction in Federal regulations.

7. Reduced State Aid. Because non-educational state aid has been reduced without changes in state mandates and conditions, metro (and, though not the focus of this article, rural) communities' budgets have suffered a double whammy.

These metro area trends point to regionalism as a solution because it can (a) handle certain functions (usually of a capital-intensive or regulatory nature) on a multi-jurisdictional basis, (b) achieve economies of scale in providing various services by broadening the basis of fiscal support and the demand for certain services, (c) handle "spillover" servicing problems caused by rapid urban population growth and sometimes decline, and (d) confront the necessity for retrenchment by seeking more effective ways of rendering public services.

The 17 Approaches to Regionalism

Regionalism is a gold mine for officials seeking to solve local problems, and 17 different miners may be put to work to extract the gold. These 17 approaches to regional service problems can be arrayed on a spectrum from the easiest to the hardest—from the most politically feasible, least controversial, and sometimes least effective to the politically least feasible, most threatening to local officials, and sometimes most effective, at least in the opinion of many in jurisdictions that have made these fairly radical reforms (see box).

Easiest Eight

The first eight approaches are the easiest:

1. Informal Cooperation. For many up against the wall, this is the easiest of them all. This approach is clearly the least formal, and the most pragmatic of the 17. It generally involves collaborative and reciprocal actions between two local jurisdictions, does not usually require fiscal actions, and only rarely involves matters of regional or even subregional significance. Although reliable information on the extent of its use is generally absent, anecdotal evidence suggests that informal cooperation is the most widely practiced approach to regionalism.

2. Interlocal Service Contracts. Voluntary but formal agreements

Reprinted by permission from the January/February 1987 issue of *National Civic Review,* pp. 14-28. National Civic Review, 1601 Grant Street, Suite 250, Denver, CO 80203.

```
┌─────────────────────────────────────────────────────┐
│          Regional Approaches to Service Delivery      │
│                                                       │
│   Easiest                                             │
│                                                       │
│    1. Informal Cooperation                            │
│    2. Interlocal Service Contracts                    │
│    3. Joint Powers Agreements                         │
│    4. Extraterritorial Powers                         │
│    5. Regional Councils/Councils of Governments       │
│    6. Federally Encouraged Single-Purpose Regional Bodies │
│    7. State Planning and Development Districts         │
│    8. Contracting (Private)                           │
│                                                       │
│   Middling                                            │
│                                                       │
│    9. Local Special Districts                         │
│   10. Transfer of Functions                           │
│   11. Annexation                                      │
│   12. Regional Special Districts and Authorities      │
│   13. Metro Multipurpose District                     │
│   14. Reformed Urban County                           │
│                                                       │
│   Hardest                                             │
│                                                       │
│   15. One-Tier Consolidations                         │
│   16. Two-Tier Restructuring                          │
│   17. Three-Tier Reforms.                             │
└─────────────────────────────────────────────────────┘
```

between two or more local governments are widely used. Some 45 states now sanction them broadly. Survey data suggest a slight decline (4%) between 1972 and 1983 in their use, but well over half the cities and counties polled in 1983 had used such contracts to handle at least one of their servicing responsibilities. Metro central cities, suburbs, and counties generally rely on them to a greater extent than non-metro municipal and county jurisdictions.

3. Joint Powers Agreements. These agreements between two or more local governments provide for the joint planning, financing, and delivery of a service for the citizens of all the jurisdictions involved. All states authorize joint service agreements, but 20 still require that each participating unit be empowered to provide the service in question. Surveys indicate that the number of cities and counties relying on joint services agreements for at least one service rose from 33% in 1972 to 55% in 1983, making then slightly more popular than interlocal contracting, although usage closely parallels interlocal servicing contracts.

4. Extraterritorial Powers. Sanctioned in 35 states, extraterritorial powers permit all or at least some, cities to exercise some of their regulatory authority outside their boundaries in rapidly developing unincorporated areas. Less than half the authorizing states permit extraterritorial planning, zoning, and subdivision regulation, however, which makes effective control of fringe growth difficult. Because a number of states do not authorize extraterritorial powers, and because this approach does not apply to cities surrounded by other incorporated jurisdictions, this approach is less used than other techniques.

5. Regional Councils/Councils of Governments. In the 1960s, no more than 20 or 25 jurisdictions had created wholly voluntaristic regional councils. That figure had soared to over 660 by 1980, thanks largely to Federal aid and especially to Federal requirements (notably Section 204 of the Model Cities legislation) that required a regional review and comment process in all metro areas for certain local grant applications. Title IV of the Intergovernmental Cooperation Act of 1968 built on the Section 204 base to create a "clearinghouse" structure at the rural and urban regional as well as state levels. Local participation in regional councils still remained primarily voluntary, however, with jurisdictions resisting any efforts at coercion.

Regional councils, also known as Councils of Government (COGs) which rely so heavily on interlocal cooperation, assumed far more than a clearinghouse role in the late 1960s and 1970s. Thirty-nine federal grants programs with a regional thrust sometimes utilized COGs for their own integral parts of a strong state-established substate districting system, as well. Rural COGs tended to take on certain direct assistance and servicing roles for their constituents, while the more heavily urban ones usually served a

role as regional agenda-definer and conflict-resolver.

With the advent of Reagan federalism a reduction in the Federal role in substate regionalism occurred. Reagan's Executive Order 12372 put the prime responsibility for the A-95 clearinghouse role with the states, while providing a back-up Federal role (48 states picked up the challenge). Twelve of the 39 Federal regional programs were scrapped, 11 were cut heavily, nine lost their regional component, and six were revised substantially; only one was left fully intact.

To survive, COGs had to adapt and the overwhelming majority did so; less than one-fifth (125) of the 660 regional councils shut their doors. Some got greater state support both in funding and in power. Many others sought more local fiscal contributions and became a regional servicing agency for constituent local units. A majority of regional councils now serve as a chief source of technical services and provide certain direct services under contract to their localities. Some state functions have been transferred to regional council and many serve as field administrator of certain state-planned and fund services. All still perform some type of clearinghouse function and some assume specialized regional planning and other related functions under at least 11 Federal single-purpose grants and loan programs as of FY 1983.

Most COGs, then, reflect a greater "nativism," "pragmatism," and service activism than their predecessors of a decade ago.

6. Federally Encouraged Single-Purpose Regional Bodies. Single-purpose regional bodies came into being when institutional strings were attached to some 20 Federal aid programs (as of 1980). According to the 1977 Census of Local Governments, these federally encouraged special-purpose regional units numbered between 1,400 and 1,700 depending on definitions and classifications. A less rigorous, private, and meagerly funded survey identified more than 990 such bodies in 1983. Although the actual number as of 1983 was probably higher, by 1986 the total was probably a lot less, given the number of regional program revisions, budget cuts, and eliminations during the 1983-86 period. Single-purpose regional bodies now exist only in a few Federal aid programs (notably economic development, Appalachia, Area Agencies on Aging, Job Training, and metro transportation). Continued Federal fundings make them easy to establish and they play a helpful, non-threatening planning role.

7. State Planning and Development Districts (SPDDs). These districts were established by the states during the late 1960s and early 1970s to bring order to the chaotic proliferation of Federal special purpose regional programs. A state's own substate regional goals were a prominent part of the authorizing legislation (19 states) or gubernatorial executive orders (24 states) that established SPDDs. By 1979 18 states had conferred a "review and comment" role on their SPDDs for certain non-federally aided local and state projects. Sixteen conferred such authority for special district projects and 11 authorized SPDDs to assume a direct servicing role, if it was sanctioned by member governments or the regional electorate.

As a matter of practice, practically all SPDDs adhere to the confederate style of regional councils/COGs. Many regional councils have been folded into the SPDD system, although boundaries have sometimes changed. Approximately the same number of SPDD systems (43) exist today as in the late 1970s, although in the hard-pressed midwest funding problems have rendered some moribund. All of these states took on the devolved responsibilities under Reagan's Executive Order 12372 for the "clearinghouse function," as did five others. Over half fund their SPDDs but only five in a respectable fashion.

Although feasible, SPDDs are somewhat difficult because special authorizing legislation is required, state purposes and goals are involved, and the establishment of a new statewide districting system can at least initially appear threatening, especially to counties.

8. Contracting (Private). Contracting with the private sector is the only form of public-private collaboration analyzed here and is the most popular of all such forms. Service contracts with private providers are now authorized in 26 states—far fewer than their intergovernmental counterparts and usually with far more detailed

procedural requirements. Their use has clearly increased from the early 1970s to the present with scores of different local services sometimes provided under contracts with various private sector providers. Joint powers agreements and inter-local service agreements, however, are both more popular than contracting with private firms.

This approach rounds out the cluster of interlocal approaches that we term easiest. Contracting with private organizations has been placed last because authorizing legislation, especially non-re-

> "Metro America is being kept alive by 17 distinct types of interlocal approaches, on a spectrum from intergovernmental cooperation to full regional governance."

strictive statutes, may be difficult to obtain. Moreover, the fears of public sector unions as well as certain public employees are aroused when local officials seek to contract services privately.

Middling Six

The middle cluster in the spectrum includes four institutional and two tough procedural approaches for new and usually broader territorial service delivery systems. These approaches present somewhat greater hurdles than those in the prior group but each is a more stable way to effectively align governmental and service delivery boundaries.

9. Local Special Districts. These districts are a very popular way to provide a single service or multiple related services on a multi-jurisdictional basis. Three-quarters of all local special districts serve areas whose boundaries are not coterminous with those of a city or country, a situation that has prevailed for at least two decades. Forty-one percent of all special districts were found within metro areas, making special districts the most numerous of the five basic categories of local government in metro America.

10. Transfer of Functions. This procedural way to change permanently the provider of a specific service jumped by 40% in a decade, according to a 1983 survey of counties and cities. The larger urban jurisdictions were much more likely to transfer functions than the smaller ones. Over three-fifths of the central cities reported such transfers compared to 37% of the suburban cities and 35% of the non-metro municipalities. Among counties, 47% of the metro-type counties transferred functions compared to only 29% in the non-metro group. Cities were likely to shift services, first to counties, then to COGs and special districts.

Despite its increased popularity, the difficulties involved in transfer of functions should not be overlooked. Only 18 states authorize such shifts (eight more than in 1974) and in half these cases voter approval is mandated. In addition, the language of some of the authorizing statutes does not always clearly distinguish between a transfer and an interlocal servicing contract.

11. Annexation. The dominant 19th century device for bringing local jurisdictional servicing boundaries and expanding settlement patterns into proper alignment remains popular. The 61,356 annexations in the 1970s involved 9,000 square miles and 3 million people. The 23,828 annexations in the first half of the 1980s affected one million citizens and 3 million square miles. Although the vast majority of these annexations involved very few square miles, they are an incremental solution to closing the gap between governmental servicing boundaries and the boundaries of the center city.

A look at the larger-scale annexations of the past four decades highlights a dozen municipalities that serve almost as de facto regional governments: Phoenix, Houston, Dallas, San Antonio, Memphis, San Jose, El Paso, Huntsville, Concord (Cal.), Ft. Worth, Omaha, and Shreveport. Most large-scale annexations have occurred in the southwest and west, thanks to the large amounts of unincorporated land on municipal peripheries and to pro-city annexation statutes. Students of public finance point out that central cities that were able to annex substantial land are usually in good fiscal shape since they have escaped the "hole in the doughnut" problems of central cities in the older metro areas of the east and midwest.

Annexation is limited by the nature of state authorizing laws

(most do not favor the annexing locality); its irrelevance in most northeastern states, given the absence of unincorporated turf in their urban areas; and a reluctance to use the process as a long-range solution to eliminating local jurisdictional, fiscal, and servicing fragmentation. Annexation, then, has limited geographic application and is usually used incrementally but when it is assigned a key role in a city's development, it can transform a municipality from a local to a regional institution.

12. Regional Special Districts and Authorities. These big areawide institutions comprise the greatest number of regional governments in our 304 metro areas. Unlike their local urban counterparts, these Olympian organizations are established to cope on a fully areawide basis with a major urban surviving challenge such as mass transit, sewage disposal, water supply, hospitals, airports, and pollution control. Census data show there were approximately 132 regional and 983 major subregional special districts and authorities in 304 metro areas in 1982, compared to 230 and 2,232, respectively, in non-metro areas.

Relatively few large, regional units have been established because they (a) require specific state enactment and may involve functional transfers from local units; (b) are independent, expensive, professional, and fully governmental; and (c) are frequently as accountable to bond buyers as to the localities and the citizen consumers.

13. Metro Multipurpose Districts. These districts differ from the other regional model in that they involve establishing a regional authority to perform diverse, not just related regional, functions. At least four states have enacted legislation authorizing such district, but they permit a comparatively narrow range of functions.

This option clearly ranks among the most difficult to implement, with metro Seattle the only basic case study. While multipurpose districts have a number of theoretical advantages (greater popular control, better planning and coordination of a limited number of areawide functions, and a more accountable regional government), political and statutory difficulties have barred their widespread use.

14. The Reformed Urban County. Because it transforms a unit of local government, a move frequently opposed by the elected officials of the jurisdiction in question, new urban counties are difficult to form. As a result, though 29 states have enacted permissive county home rule statutes, only 76 charter counties (generally urban) have been created.

In metro areas, however, three-quarters of the 683 metro counties have either an elected chief executive or an appointed chief administrative officer. The servicing role of these jurisdictions has expanded rapidly over the past ten decades or so. Since 1967, outlays for what used to be traditional county functions (corrections, welfare, roads, and health and hospitals) have declined, with expenditures for various municipal-type, regional and new federally encouraged services have risen commensurately. Overall, the range of state-mandated and county-initiated services have risen rapidly in metro counties, during the past two decades, which has necessitated a better approach to fiscal and program management.

> "Informal cooperation is the easiest and probably the most widely practiced approach to regionalism. It generally involves collaborative and reciprocal activities, but not fiscal transactions."

In the 146 single-county metro areas this reform county option is excellent. However, since county mergers and modification of county boundaries are almost impossible, in the 159 multi-county metro areas the option is less valuable. It can only provide a subregional solution to certain service delivery problems, not a fully regional approach.

The Tough Trio

The hardest approaches to metro regionalism are the three general governmental options: one-tier or unitary, two-tier or federative, and three-tier or super-federative.

All three involve the creation of a new areawide level of government, a reallocation of local government powers and functions, and, as a result a disruption of the political and institutional status quo. All three options involve very rare and remarkable forms of interlocal cooperation.

15. One-tier consolidations. This method of expanding municipal boundaries has had a lean, but long history. From 1804 to 1907, four city-county mergers occurred, all by state mandate. Then municipalities proliferated but city-county mergers virtually stopped for 40 years. From Baton Rouge's partial merger in 1947 to the present there have been some 17 city-county consolidations, most endorsed by popular referendum. Among the hurdles to surmount in achieving such reorganizations are state authorization, the frequent opposition of local elected officials, racial anxieties (where large minorities exist), an equitable representational system, concerns about the size of government, and technical issues relating to such matters as debt assumption. Only one out of every five consolidation efforts has succeeded in the past 25 years.

Most consolidations have been partial, not total, with small suburban municipalities, school districts and special districts sometimes left out but the new county government generally exercises some authority over their activities. In addition, the metro settlement pattern in some cases has long since exceeded the county limits, so

---

"The hardest approaches to metro regionalism are complex consolidations and restructurings, which create new areawide levels of government, reallocate local government powers and functions and disrupt the political and institutional status quo."

---

that the reorganized government may be the prime service provider and key player, but not the only one. This, of course, is another result of rigid county boundaries.

To sum up, one-tier consolidations have generally been most suitable in smaller non-metro urban areas and in smaller and medium (ideally uni-county) metro areas.

16. Two-Tier Restructurings. These seek a division between local and regional functions with two levels of government to render such services. These and other features, notably a reorganized county government, are spelled out in a new county charter that is adopted in a county wide referendum. The Committee for Economic Development advanced one of the most persuasive arguments for this approach in the 1970s. Metro Toronto, which created a strongly empowered regional federative government to handle areawide functions and ultimately led to some local reorganization by the merger of some municipalities, is a model for this approach.

The prime American example of this federative approach is Metro Dade County (Miami-Dade). Unlike the incremental reform approach of the modernized or urban county, a drastically redesigned county structure and role emerged from a head-on confrontation over the restructuring issue. Narrowly approved in a countywide referendum in 1957, the new Metro government's cluster of strong charter powers and its authority to perform a range of areawide functions were steadily opposed until the mid-1960s. Since then, its powers have grown and it is widely considered a success. Witness the extraordinary responsibilities Metro Dade assumed during the various waves of immigration since the early 1960s. The level of metro-municipal collaboration is better now than it was a generation ago, but tensions and confrontations are still part of the relationship—as they are in most federative systems. In my opinion, however, its survival is assured.

17. The Three-Tier Reforms. This is a rarely used approach, with just two U.S. examples. However, it deals with the special problems of multi-county metro areas.

The first example is the Twin Cities (Minneapolis-St. Paul) Metropolitan Council. Launched as a metro initiative and enacted by the state legislature in 1967, the Council is the authoritative regional coordinator, planner, and controller of large-scale development for its region which includes seven counties and a dozen localities.

It is empowered by the state to review, approve, or suspend projects and plans of the area's various multi-jurisdictional special districts and authorities; it is the regional designee under all federally

sponsored substate regional programs for which the area is eligible, and has the right to review and delay projects having an adverse areawide impact. Direct operational responsibilities do not fall within its purview but it directly molds the region's future development. Like any body that possesses significant power over other public agencies and indirectly over private regional actors, the Council has become somewhat politicized in recent years but its rightful place in the governance of the Twin Cities is not questioned.

The other three-tier experiment is the Greater Portland (Oregon) Metropolitan Service District (MSD), a regional planning and coordinating agency that serves the urbanized portion of three counties. Approved by popular referendum in 1978, the MSD supplanted the previous COG, and assumed the waste disposal and Portland Zoo responsibilities of the previous regional authority. The enabling legislation also authorized the MSD to run the regional transportation agency and to assume responsibility for a range of the functions, subject to voter approval, but these options have not been utilized. A 1986 referendum on a new convention center did pass and this task was assigned to the MSD. Unlike the Twin Cities' Council, the MSD has an elected mayor, an appointed manager, and an elected council of 12 commissioners, which provides a popular accountability that the Met Council has yet to achieve.

Both three-tier examples suggest how other multi-county metro areas might approach areawide service delivery and other metro challenges but they are arduous to achieve and not easy to sustain.

Summary Analysis

This probe of metro Snow White's current status suggests that she is alive and well, and is being looked after by her 17 regionable dwarfs:

1. Overall Growth in Regionalism. Virtually all of the various approaches have been on the increase. Since the early 1970s, the use of the eight easiest approaches has seen a net increase despite a reduction in the number of regional councils and federally supported substate districts. Meanwhile five of the six middling approaches grew markedly (the exception was the metro multi-purpose authority). Even the three hardest approaches have grown in use.

2. Multiple Approach Use. Very few metro areas rely on only one or two forms of substate regionalism.

3. The easier procedural and unifunctional institutional types of service shifts tend to be found more in larger metro areas while the harder restructurings usually take place successfully within the medium-sized and especially the small metro areas.

4. The expanded use of at least ten of the 14 easiest and middling approaches is largely a product of local needs and initiatives, as well as of a growing awareness of their increasingly interdependent condition.

5. Jurisdictional fragmentation has not been reduced as a result of restructuring successes, but even incomplete forms of cooperation are useful. Such approaches are used extensively; in a majority of metro areas they are the only feasible forms of regional and subregional collaboration.

6. Like much else in the American system of metro governance, the overwhelming majority of interlocal and regional actions taken to resolve servicing and other problems reflect an ad hoc, generally issue-by-issue, incremental pattern of evolution. However, most of the major reorganizations were triggered, at least in part, by a visible crisis of some sort.

7. The intergovernmental bases of substate regional activities remain as significant as ever. The states, which always have played a significant part in the evolution of their metro areas, must move into a new primary role if the federal role in this arena continues to erode.

Our Snow White would be ever so happy if her Prince Charming would gallop up soon, wake her from the slumber induced by her stepmother, take her out of the forest and—please—make room in the palace for 17 hard-working dwarfs!

Bibliography

Advisory Commission on Intergovernmental Relations, *Intergovernmental Service Arrangements for Delivering Local Public*

Service: Update 1983 (A-103). Washington, D.C., October, 1985.

————, *Pragmatic Federalism: The Reassignment of Functional Responsibility (M-105)*. Washington, D.C., July, 1976.

————, *Regional Decision Making: New Strategies for Substate Districts (A-43)*. Washington, D.C., October, 1973.

————, *State and Local Roles in the Federal System (A-88)*. Washington, D.C., April, 1982.

Bollens, John C. and Schmandt, Henry J., *The Metropolis, Fourth Edition*, New York, N.Y., 1982.

Florestano, Patricia and Gordon, Stephen, "County and Municipal Use of Private Contracting for Public Service Delivery," *Urban Interest*, April, 1984.

Hatry, Harry P. and Valente, Carl F., "Alternative Service Delivery Approaches Involving Increased Use of the Private Sector," *The Municipal Year Book—1983*. International City Management Association, Washington, D.C., pp. 199-207.

Henderson, Lori, "Intergovernmental Service Arrangements and the Transfers of Functions," *Municipal Year Book—1985*. International City Management Association, Washington, D.C., pp. 194-202.

Jones, Victor, "Regional Councils and Regional Governments in the United States," paper presented at the Annual Meeting of the American Society for Public Administration, Detroit, 1981.

Marlin, John Tepper, ed., *Contracting Municipal Services: A Guide for Purchase from the Private Sector*, Ronald Press, John Wiley & Sons, New York, 1984, pp. 1-13.

McDowell, Bruce D., "Moving Toward Excellence in Regional Councils," based on a paper presented at the New England Regional Council Conference in Portland, Maine on October 26, 1984.

————, "Regional Councils in an Era of Do-It-Yourself Federalism," a paper presented to the Regional Council Executive Directors of the Southeastern States," March 20, 1986.

————, "Regions Under Reagan," a paper presented at the National Planning Conference, American Planning Association, Minneapolis-St. Paul, Minnesota, May 8, 1984.

National Association of Regional Councils, *Directory of Regional Councils, 85-86*, Washington, D.C.

————, *Matrix of Regional Council Programs, 1985-86*, Washington, D.C.

————, *Special Report—No. 91*. Washington, D.C., January, 1984.

U.S. Bureau of the Census, *Local Governments in Metropolitan Areas* (1982 Census of Governments, Vol. 5-GC82 (5)). Washington, D.C.

U.S. Senate, Committee on Governmental Affairs, Subcommittee on Intergovernmental Relations, *Metropolitan Regional Governance*, Hearing, February 6, 1984. Washington, D.C.

Wikstrom, Nelson, "Epitaph for a Monument to Another Successful Protest: Regionalism in Metropolitan Areas," *Virginia Social Science Journal*, Vol. 19, Winter 1984, pp. 1-10.

Wirt, Frederick M., "The Dependent City: External Influences upon Local Autonomy," paper delivered at the 1983 Annual Meeting of the American Political Science Association, September 1-4, 1983.

A tale of two suburbias

*The decline of blue-collar suburbs and growth of 'edge cities' create
a new kind of isolation*

James Adamek, mayor of the Village of Posen, recalls his childhood 30 years ago in the blue-collar community south of Chicago as being "like 'The Wonder Years.'" Dads would gather on Saturdays at the lumber yard on Western Avenue, moms at the flea market on 147th Street, teenagers at the roller rink or the Dog 'n' Suds. At night, Adamek and his friends would climb to the top of his backyard slide and watch cartoons on the screen of a nearby drive-in movie.

Today, Posen isn't doing so well. Though its three-bedroom ranch houses are still mostly well kept, the roller rink, flea market and lumber yard are vacant lots, part of a larger decline brought on by the devastation more than a decade ago of the steel and manufacturing industries where most Posen men worked. While those industries have bounced back, wages have not: Real median household income in Posen dropped nearly 12 percent in the 1980s, even as wives went to work. Meanwhile, the crime rate rose, and home prices, already low, failed to keep pace with inflation.

Driving through town, the mayor eagerly points out signs of vitality—houses with new siding and front porches. But these are mostly do-it-yourself jobs, he admits. Many Posen homeowners are carpenters and electricians who commute to jobs in places like Hoffman Estates, 20 miles northwest of Chicago, a onetime middle-class community that is becoming upper middle class. Incomes and property values soared there in the 1980s as gleaming office towers sprouted from cornfields even during the recent recession. Says Hoffman Estates Mayor Michael O'Malley: "We're a pro-development community."

Not a monolith. Pundits and political seers this year declared the suburbs the dominant—and near monolithic—voting bloc. They seemed to believe the suburbs uniformly prospered in the 1980s while the cities declined. But the divergent paths of Posen and Hoffman Estates reveal a more accurate and disturbing picture. According to a *U.S. News* survey of census data from six representative metropolitan areas, 35 percent of

American suburbs saw real declines in median household income from 1979 to 1989. During the same period, 33 percent saw incomes rise more than 10 percent.

The suburbs, in short, are becoming more riven by class. The widening gap between communities like Posen and Hoffman Estates parallels the growing income disparities between individuals. Municipalities that were already affluent in 1979 saw their fortunes rise in the decade that followed; those of more modest means experienced further decline. In the process, many suburbs that have served for decades as stepping stones for the working class found themselves in the same downward spiral as urban areas. "The nation that invented the throwaway city," notes real-estate consultant Charles Lockwood, "is now creating the throwaway suburb."

This growing gap between suburbs, together with the continuing flight of the middle and working classes from the city, is producing a nation in which people of different incomes live in ever greater isolation from each other. In a study for *U.S. News* of 1990 census data for 240 metro areas, Paul Jargowsky of the University of Texas at Dallas found that American neighborhoods became increasingly class-segregated in the 1980s. Indeed this trend, already evident in the 1970s, accelerated in the 1980s at a far faster rate of 22.5 percent. And it was evident virtually everywhere and among both blacks and whites.

Snob values. In their choice of neighborhoods, Americans have always tried to segregate themselves by class. "It's the dark side of the fluid system of status here," notes British-born geographer Brian Berry, also at the University of Texas at Dallas. As a result, the suburbs of most American cities can be divided into sectors that roughly correspond to the paths different income and occupational groups took out of the city.

In Chicago, the corporate and professional elite headed north along Lake Michigan and northwest along the commuter train lines into Du Page County. Working-class families, meanwhile, settled the "inner ring" suburbs just over the city line and the areas farther south, near the steel mills of Northern Indiana. Those divisions weren't much of a problem in the '50s and '60s, when everybody had rising incomes and worked in the city. But in the 1980s, they became crucial as the blue-collar suburbs declined and the white-collar suburbs blossomed (see map). A similar pattern of clustered growth and areas of decline appears in other cities, such as Atlanta, St. Louis, Minneapolis and Dallas. With their low housing costs, these suburbs attracted the majority of black families who were escaping the city. And some worry that as these suburbs decline, the same forces that drove these aspiring black families out of the city will catch up to them in their new homes, as it has in the poorest black suburbs.

In addition to their older housing stock, the biggest reason for the deterioration of working-class suburbs is that the post-industrial economy passed them by. For two decades, most American job growth has been in and around the shopping malls, office towers and light industrial parks that have sprouted along suburban interstate highways–places journalist Joel Garreau calls "edge cities." Typical is the I-90 corridor between Schaumburg, Ill., 15 miles northwest of Chicago, and Hoffman Estates. It has attracted everything from the new corporate headquarters of Sears Merchandising Group to Medieval Times, a giant dinner theater that boasts jousting tournaments and parking for 600 cars.

Once, the captains of industry built smelly factories near the homes of unskilled workers. Today's corporate managers aim to locate offices near their best-educated "knowledge workers"–those involved in finance, engineering, marketing and computer specialties–while at the same time reducing the bosses' own commuting times. Sears chose Hoffman Estates, says Mayor O'Malley, in part because many of its senior executives live nearby in towns like South Barrington and Inverness, where most homes could pass for "Stately Wayne Manor" of Batman fame. "Show me the highway system and where the upper-middle and middle-class whites live," says real-estate consultant Christopher Leinberger, "and I'll show you where the 'edge cities' are."

The result, says economist John Kasarda of the University of North Carolina at Chapel Hill, is that "in the post-industrial economy, good housing begets good housing, white-collar jobs beget white-collar jobs." The flip side is that edge cities almost never grow near blue-collar suburbs like Posen, which is virtually all white, and black communities like neighboring Harvey. Posen has plenty of undeveloped land and sits at the crossroads of two interstates. Yet at the interstate 57 interchange, where a glass office tower might be expected, there is only an abandoned Ford dealership.

Country club. As their commercial tax bases erode, working-class suburbs "can't offer the kind of services

that businesses and higher-income residents want," says sociologist John Logan of the State University of New York at Albany. Posen has had to raise taxes and hustle federal grants just to rebuild its sidewalks. In contrast, Hoffman Estates has been able to cut tax rates and still build a lavish municipal golf and country club.

Edge-city prosperity fuels class isolation in another way: It boosts land prices, which in turn force landlords to raise rents and developers to build higher-end properties. Soon, edge-city waitresses and security guards can't afford to live very near their jobs. That is exactly the dilemma faced by many lower-level Sears employees, who must make two-hour commutes to Hoffman Estates from the south suburbs, where median-priced homes are half as expensive.

Communities nudge this "suburban gentrification" along with zoning ordinances, such as large lot-size requirements, that drive up housing costs. Hoffman Estates has its own method of keeping lower-income people out. Flush with cash, the city has hired 15 more building inspectors to clamp down on owners of low-rent apartments. "A cancer on the community," Mayor O'Malley calls these buildings. "I'll pave them over before I let them become slums."

Over the years, policy makers have devised plenty of plans to reconnect growing suburbs to declining cities and older communities. None is flawless. One solution is "reverse commute" bus services like those run by Suburban JobLink, a nonprofit agency that shuttles workers from Chicago's West Side to suburban factories, where entry-level, low-skill jobs are still plentiful. Unfortunately, edge-city jobs keep moving farther away. Metropolitan Chicago has grown geographically by 46 percent in 20 years, even though population is up only 4 percent. Covering that much sprawl would make commuter bus runs, with their multiple drop-offs and pickups, unbearably long, admits Suburban JobLink director John Plunkett.

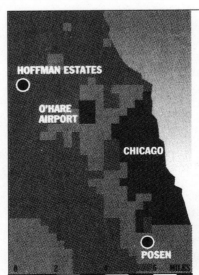

Chicago's boom and bust

■ The growth and decline of Chicago's suburbs typifies the pattern in many U.S. metro areas in the 1980s. Suburbs near the city, especially those to the south, saw real median incomes decline. But income grew in "edge city" suburbs farther out, particularly those north and northwest.

Change in median household income, 1980-90 (adjusted for inflation)

■ Incomes increased
□ Incomes decreased

COMPILED BY DORIAN FRIEDMAN

If the working poor can't get to edge-city jobs, many politicians argue that jobs should be lured back to the city through programs like enterprise zones, with generous tax breaks for firms locating in poor neighborhoods. Unfortunately, they have never been shown to generate many new jobs in impoverished communities. A related solution was pioneered by Portland, Ore., which in 1973 limited sprawl by drawing a boundary at the edge of the suburbs. The path of development thus moved back toward the city. However, such growth controls can boost land costs and hurt the poor.

More housing. Another solution is to build more low-cost housing in the growing suburbs. Children who have been through the Gautreaux Project, which relocates Chicago welfare families to private apartments in suburbs like Hoffman Estates, are twice as likely to go on to college and land good jobs as their peers who stay behind. But building affordable apartments in affluent suburbs, even for working families, is extremely difficult because of local opposition.

Some say a more sensible reform is for states to make it illegal for municipalities to stop homeowners from fixing up their basements and garages and renting them. Legalizing "granny flats" could open up millions of relatively low-cost rental units, at no taxpayer cost, throughout existing suburbs. It might also allow people with modest incomes who otherwise could not afford "nicer" suburbs the chance to subsidize their mortgages with rental income, the way generations of immigrants built wealth by owning three-flat apartments.

A number of urban geographers see the decline of older working-class suburbs as a benign and natural part of the succession of cities that is useful in providing somewhat better neighborhoods for city refugees. What these experts don't see is the suffering of those refugees, many of them black, who have sunk retirement nest eggs into suburban homes, only to watch their investments wither and their neighborhoods decline. Nor do they see the damage that increasing class isolation may be doing to the national character. "The less citizens of different classes mix in neighborhoods and schools, the greater the chance that a snobbish European class structure will take hold," argues author Mickey Kaus in "The End of Equality." To many, that doesn't seem very American.

BY PAUL GLASTRIS WITH DORIAN FRIEDMAN

HEALTH PROBLEMS OF INNER CITY POOR REACH CRISIS POINT

ILLNESS RATES SKYROCKET

Experts Say Rise in Poverty and Deteriorating Medical Services Are to Blame

Elisabeth Rosenthal

While Americans elsewhere are living longer, healthier lives, residents of the inner cities inhabit islands of illness, epidemics and premature death. After decades of gradual improvement, the health of the urban poor took a turn for the worse in the late 1980's and has now reached critical condition.

Experts blame new depths of urban poverty and inadequate medical services for the situation. Struggling for day-to-day survival, people have little time for niceties like doctor's visits. Poor nutrition and overcrowded housing create ideal conditions for the spread of disease. The arrival of AIDS and crack pushed chronic hardship into crisis, shattering families and monopolizing scarce health dollars.

In the past three years, cities have reported skyrocketing rates of tuberculosis, hepatitis A, syphilis, gonorrhea, measles, mumps, whooping cough, complicated ear infections and, of course, AIDS. The number of cases is still often small, but most of these diseases were considered on the verge of eradication only five years ago after steadily declining since the beginning of the century. Many of them are virtually unknown in middle-class or wealthy neighborhoods.

'I've Seen Horrible Things'

Dr. David Wood, a pediatrician at Cedars-Sinai Medical Center in Los Angeles, called 1990 a "gangbuster year" for inner city epidemics. "If you look at maps of measles outbreaks in Los Angeles and where the poverty is, they are the same."

Studies also show that poor city dwellers with serious conditions like cancer and heart disease die far more quickly and often than their middle-class counterparts. "I never saw a woman die of cancer of the cervix until I

came to the Bronx," said Dr. Carolyn Runowicz, a gynecologist at the Montefiore Medical Center. "On Park Avenue, women get pap smears, which prevent it." In 1988, death rates from diabetes-related illnesses were five times as high in Central Harlem as in the city's wealthier neighborhoods.

But statistics, which at best count deaths and infectious diseases, capture only a glimpse of the big picture. They do not tally unnecessary suffering or the lifelong handicaps that result when treatable conditions like asthma and epilepsy go unrecognized or neglected.

"I've seen horrible things," Dr. Wood said. "Kids who have such frequent seizures that they can't go to school. Kids with asthma who don't get medications and can't play outside because they get coughing fits. It's like years ago when people with unsalvageable conditions were hidden away."

Dr. Harold P. Freeman, chief of surgery at Harlem Hospital in New York, caused a stir earlier this year when he reported in the New England Journal of Medicine that a black man in Harlem was less likely to reach 65 years of age than a man in Bangladesh. While violent crime is part of the problem, the paper said high rates of disease were the primary cause.

"When 67 people die in an earthquake in San Francisco, we call it a disaster and the President visits," said Dr. Freeman. "But here everyone is ignoring a chronic consistent disaster area, with many more people dying. And there is no question that things are getting worse."

In Newark, Dr. Beatriz Arpayaglou has learned to be a pessimist. "We're seeing scenes here straight out of underdeveloped countries, diseases that haven't been seen in the United States since the turn of the century," said Dr.

Arpayaglou, a pediatrician with the University Hospital in Newark's Children's Health Project, which sends medical teams to low-income housing projects in vans fitted like medical offices. "It's really very frightening."

In the next room of the medical van at the Stella Wright Apartments, a nurse, Anne Young, was seeing Kisor Chauvers, a 2-year-old boy with anemia from nutritional deficiencies. The day before the team had rushed a 5-year-old girl to the hospital with a life-threatening kidney infection whose symptoms had been neglected for several days. Her grandmother, the stoic guardian to seven children of two daughters who died of AIDS, couldn't get the child to a doctor sooner.

Epidemics of Yesteryear
To Poor, Vaccines Prove Elusive

Different cities have fallen prey to different diseases:

In New York City, 1,017 babies were born with congenital syphilis in 1988, the most recent year for which figures are available, up from only 16 in 1982. New York City accounts for about half the cases nationally.

Newark has had a 35 percent yearly rise in the number of new tuberculosis cases between 1988 and '89, and the pediatric clinic at Newark's University Hospital reports a fourfold increase since 1987. There has been a 15 percent increase in tuberculosis cases in the country as a whole since 1988, largely in urban areas.

In Los Angeles this year several hundred people have been hospitalized for measles, and 30 have died. The number of measles cases nationwide rose to 17,000 last year, from a low of 1,500 in 1983. The city had also played host to an outbreak of rubella, or German measles, which has left at least nine babies with serious birth defects. Rubella is a mild illness in adults but leads to blindness in the offspring of women who catch it while pregnant.

Washington is just recovering from a 3-year mumps outbreak. After seeing less than a half dozen cases a year for a decade, the city had about 200 reported cases a year in 1988 and '89.

"These epidemics are sentinel events for the crumbling of our public health services," Dr. Wood said. Measles, mumps, rubella and whooping cough are entirely preventable with vaccines, but many people do not get the shots.

Nationally, asthma rates have undergone a dramatic and somewhat baffling rise, a rise doctors say is more pronounced among the urban poor. Dr. Michael Wietzman and colleagues at Boston City Hospital found that black children were twice as likely as white children to have asthma.

In many studies, scientists compared black and white rather than rich and poor to eke out information about health care differentials, since it is easier to figure out race than salary from medical records and far more blacks than whites live in the inner city. But most experts say it is primarily poverty, not race, that raises the risk.

"It's mostly the social dimensions of being black," said Dr. Weitzman, now chief of Pediatrics at Rochester General Hospital in Rochester, N.Y. "It's being poor, living in overcrowded housing, having a low birth weight, being exposed to household toxins."

In Need of the Basics
Hazardous Homes, Dangerous Diets

Experts say the growing number of people who live in substandard housing with poor sanitation creates conditions favoring the rapid spread of infectious disease. "Diseases transmit more effectively and rapidly in crowded living conditions," said Dr. Shirley Fannin, associate deputy director of disease control programs for Los Angeles County. " A few years ago we went out to investigate a typhoid case and we found 27 people living in one house sharing a bathroom."

As middle-class people worry about clean air and the ozone layer, many scientists blame indoor pollution for the high rates of asthma and other diseases among the poor. In the Boston study, the factor most tightly linked to a child's risk of developing asthma as smoking by the mother, Dr. Weitzman said. Poor young women from minority groups are the country's fastest growing group of cigarette smokers.

Living in decaying housing, 68 per-

cent of very poor black children and 36 percent of very poor white children in central cities have blood lead levels greater than 15 micrograms per deciliter. The Centers for Disease Control currently defines toxic levels at above 25, but the agency said last week it will advise local health officials to take action when children have lead levels higher than 10.

Diets rich in fat and low in nutrients also take their toll. Many poor children have chronic anemia, a low red blood cell count brought on by a lack of iron in their diet, leaving them perpetually tired.

Once sick, poor people in the inner cities tend to suffer serious complications. Dr. Wood remembers being asked to examine a 9-year-old girl with a facial tic. As he examined her, he discovered 20/200 vision and profound hearing loss from damage done by untreated ear infections. "She was holding her face funny partly because she couldn't see," he said. "Her parents had seen a few doctors and used up their money. No wonder she's failing in school."

Quality of Care
Little Prevention, And Much to Cure

For poor in the cities, access to care is part of the problem. To be treated in a public clinic for sexually transmitted disease in Washington, a patient has to be in the clinic by 9:30 A.M. and often must wait most of the day, said Dr. Reed Tuckson, former Commissioner of Health for Washington and now a senior vice president at the March of Dimes.

The typical wait to schedule a pediatric appointment in inner city clinics was several months, according to a survey done by the New York Children's Health Project, a medical outreach program affiliated with the Montefiore Medical Center in the Bronx.

But many experts say an even greater issue is the quality of care. The Community Service Society of New York polled 248 primary care doctors in poor neighborhoods in the Bronx as to whether they offered 24-hour coverage, had 20 or more regular office hours a week, accepted Medicare and had admitting privileges at a hospital—what the society defined as minimum components of a decent medical practice. Only six met the criteria.

The society's study also found that more than 60 percent of doctors providing prenatal care could not actually deliver babies because they had no hospital affiliation; the mothers were referred to an emergency room.

"The family says yes we're seeing a doctor, but when you look the care is not well organized," said Dr. Karen Burke,

medical director of the New York Children's Health Project. Experts say that clinics in poor neighborhoods focus on acute illnesses and ignore routine care like pap smears, anemia screening and vaccinations, which are generally less profitable.

Pediatricians are particularly worried about how early lives plagued by health problems will affect children as they age. Babies born in Central Harlem are four times as likely to have very low birth weight than babies born in more prosperous New York neighborhoods, a statistic with lifelong consequences since babies under 3.5 pounds are more likely to have seizures, mental retardation, heart problems, asthma, blindness, deafness and learning disabilities. In today's inner cities, drug abuse and poor prenatal nutrition converge to yield tiny babies.

"A kid in a middle-class suburb who has an ear infection gets antibiotics and gets better," said Dr. Irwin Redlener, director of the New York Children's Health Project. "A poor kid with an ear infection doesn't and progresses to chronic infection, hearing loss and language delays."

In both Newark and New York, the majority of preschool children seen in the mobile vans are not fully vaccinated, leaving them vulnerable to serious diseases. But others have been wastefully, though not harmfully, vaccinated over and over again.

Many inner city children have fragmented lives—and no vaccination records—so the vaccines are frequently repeated. At a health van in Harlem, 15-year-old Jewel S. has no records because his life has been a flurry of different welfare homes and schools as he and his mother flee an abusive father.

A surging number of poor children and the rising costs of medicines have stymied vaccination programs, Dr. Woods said. In the early '70s, the total cost of a child's vaccinations was under $5; now it is several hundred dollars.

Contrasts of the Crisis
Determining Death By Money and Race

In a study published in the International Journal of Epidemiology this year, scientists at the Washington, D.C., Commission on Public Health estimated that blacks in Washington were more than four times as likely as whites to die prematurely, before 65, of heart disease, asthma, pneumonia and some cancers. While the death rates for blacks in Washington have climbed steadily since 1982, the rates for whites have not changed.

"We looked at conditions that people

The Inner City and the Rest of the City

Disease rates and infant health statistics for three neighborhoods in New York City: the heavily studied inner-city area of East Harlem, the high-income area of Kips Bay-Yorkville and the middle-income area of Astoria-Long Island City.

Death rate per 1,000 Population (all causes, 1988)	East Harlem	Kips Bay-Yorkville	Astoria-Long Island City
	18.1	10.7	11.7
Disease deaths			
Heart disease	4.34	3.14	5.52
Cancer	3.28	2.24	2.58
Influenza and pneumonia	.66	.38	.53
AIDS	1.22	.40	.15
Cerebrovascular disease	.83	.40	.35
Chronic obstructive pulmonary diseases	.31	.22	.29
Chronic liver disease and cirrhosis	.59	.15	.29
Diabetes	.45	.10	.17
Infant health			
Infant deaths per 1,000 live births 1989	23.4	7.3	14.9
Live births per 100 with late or no prenatal care (Average, 1986-88)	35.8	6.1	10.4
Low-birth weight babies per 100 live births (less than 5.5 pounds, 1989)	18.5	6.0	6.1
Very low birth-weight babies per 100 live births (less than 3.3 pounds, 1989)	3.8	0.87	0.98

Source: Department of Health, City of New York

shouldn't be dying from in the prime of life," said Dr. Eugene Schwartz, the study's first author, and the chief of the Washington Bureau of Cancer Control. "And remember, death is a very crude measure. It's the tip of an iceberg, the end of a long chain of illness and disability that we don't have a handle on."

Dr. Freeman tells of the shock of moving to Harlem Hospital from Memorial Sloan-Kettering Cancer Center, also in Manhattan, but four long miles downtown. "When I came to Harlem Hospital in the late '60s I suddenly found I was seeing extremely advanced cancer, and that hasn't changed," he said. Because they come so late to treatment, only 30 percent of women diagnosed with breast cancer at Harlem Hospital live 5 years, compared to 70 percent of white women and 60 percent of black women overall in the United States. Dr. Freeman has set up free cancer screening at Harlem Hospital two mornings a week.

The fates of blacks and whites, rich and poor are diverging. The National Center for Health Statistics first started comparing black-white infant mortality in 1950, and the difference has never been greater than it is today, with black babies dying at twice the rate before their first birthday. While the life expectancy of whites rose to 75.6 years in 1987, that of blacks fell to 69.2.

Doctors involved in outreach efforts hope they will save a few lives, but know these are frail, jury-rigged solutions.

"We're using Band-Aids and things are getting worse rather than better," Dr. Freeman said. "You have to see disease in the context in which it occurs: poor education, unemployment, homelessness, hopelessness."

Cities Get Into The Game

Glen Macnow

Glen Macnow covers the business of sports for the Philadelphia Inquirer.

It was author Kurt Vonnegut—a native son—who dubbed Indianapolis "Naptown." Indeed, a national survey in the 1970s found that the Hoosier state capital didn't exactly have a bad national image; rather, it had no image at all.

But that was 10 years ago. These days, Indianapolis is nationally known as "Sportstown, U.S.A." Since 1979, when city officials and business leaders began a concerted effort to capitalize on America's infatuation with sports, Indianapolis has hosted more than 200 events, from the Pan American Games to the NBA All-Star Game. The contests have generated an estimated $300 million in direct funds, perhaps double that figure in spinoff revenues, and an incalculable amount in media exposure.

Indianapolis is now home to six national sports-governing bodies. Its $130 million worth of gleaming new facilities—from the 60,000-seat Hoosier Dome to the Major Taylor Velodrome for bicycle races—are among the best in the country. The city has already been chosen to host the 1991 NCAA Final Four basketball championships and the 1991 Professional Golfers Association Championships.

"Sports has created a renaissance in this city," says Susan Conner, spokeswoman for the Lilly Endowment, a private foundation that has bankrolled much of Indianapolis' redevelopment. "There is an esprit de corps that didn't exist a decade ago."

The city's success story stems from a partnership of civic and business leaders who moved in 1979 to form the Indiana Sports Corp., a nonprofit organization created to bring amateur sports events to Indianapolis.

The Sports Corp., which started with one full-time employee and now has 25, was the first in the nation designed to identify, bid for, and host sporting events systematically. It did not remain alone for long. The Indianapolis model has spurred dozens of American cities, large and small, to join in the competition to lure sports dollars to their communities. About $50 billion was spent on all aspects of sports in the U.S. in 1987, and the figure is rising.

To invigorate their economies, dozens of American cities—many inspired by Indianapolis' success—are joining the competition to attract sports dollars to their communities.

Today there are more than 30 commissions—many of them offshoots of their cities' chambers of commerce or tourism divisions—slugging it out for sports events. A few groups are charged solely with seeking major-league franchises or new stadiums, but most are closely copying Indianapolis' methods.

"It's amazing how much competition there is for some of these events now," says David W. Brenner, a former Philadelphia commerce director and now president of the city's Sports Congress. "And it's not just the big ones like World Cup soccer. We bid for [and later got] the 1990 NCAA men's volleyball championships. Ten years ago, maybe one or two cities would have sought that event. This year, there were many, and each city was making a better offer than the last."

Competition for sporting events of all sizes has increased, and no one wants to be left out. Cities with fewer than a half-million people have formed sports commissions, which now bravely march into sports boardrooms seeking to compete against Los Angeles and New York. Florida has no fewer than seven separate sports authorities, which often end up banging heads in trying for the same events. Indeed, a Florida state advisory council was formed last year to try to keep representatives of the various sports groups from disparaging one another.

But why sports? Why are cities vying for events such as the national women's softball finals when there are major industries to compete for?

The answer lies in both economics and image. Sporting events are now regarded much like conventions—they attract affluent tourists who stay in hotels, eat in restaurants, ride in taxis. An economic-impact study in Utah in 1985 concluded that "sporting events have the potential of producing significant revenue for the state."

The economic impact of hosting a Super Bowl is considered to be at least $125 million. An NCAA Final Four is worth $40 million. But even a regional body-building competition flexes some financial muscle.

"We figure that if we can land just 5 percent of the amateur events in the country, we'll get an economic boost of $30 million to $50 million annually," says Mike Millay, executive director of the New Orleans Sports Foundation. Millay's group recently wooed 1990 stops for the U.S. Tennis Association tour, the Miller Lite Pro Beach Volleyball tour, the International Body Building championships, and the Women's National Rugby Championships. "Individually, those small events may not sound like much," he says, "but when you add them up, they really help the city economically."

Beyond that, sports may be the ultimate in light, clean industry. And they can bring more positive exposure to a city in one weekend than a manufacturing plant might in a hundred years. When Buffalo was named last December as U.S. host city for the 1993 World University Games, Mayor Jimmy Griffin predicted: "This ought to bring us more good publicity than anything that has come to Buffalo since the [1901] Pan-American Exposition."

The quote might seem curious, since President William McKinley was assassinated at that event, but the point is well taken. For evidence, look no farther than Indianapolis.

"We had an awful self-image," says Sandy Knapp, president of the Indiana Sports Corp. "People here had been told for so long that Indianapolis was a dying city that they were starting to believe it. But now, we're getting positive national media coverage, and the residents have responded. We had 6,700 volunteers, literally unsolicited, when we hosted the 1982 National Sports Festival. This city has come to believe in itself through sports."

Knapp, perhaps more than anyone, deserves credit for that. She has been president and executive director of the Indiana Sports Corp. since its beginning 10 years ago. "She is an impressive, persuasive, imaginative, and well-organized advocate for this city," says John L. Krausse, Indianapolis' deputy mayor. "She's the best cheerleader Indianapolis could have."

Knapp, 44, shies away from that title, since she began her career in 1970 as a cheerleader for the Indiana Pacers basketball team. "We didn't really dance or cheer," she recalls, "we were more like glorified models."

Within three years, Knapp moved up from modeling, to billing and receiving, to promotions director, and eventually to vice president of promotions and marketing for the Pacers. At the time, she was the only woman holding a management position in the old American Basketball Association.

In 1979, a coterie of Indianapolis business leaders identified five areas in which they felt the city should strive toward excellence and a national reputation—education, arts and culture, health and medicine, food and nutrition, and sports. Out of that planning, the Sports Corp. was born, with Knapp as its only employee.

Today, the Sports Corp. is a self-sustaining, not-for-profit corporation with an annual budget of $700,000. But in the beginning, Knapp had no office, no staff, and no money—until the Lilly Endowment came up with a six-figure start-up grant.

The Lilly Endowment, one of the five largest charitable foundations in the nation, has been crucial to Indianapolis' success in sports. The private foundation was started by three members of the Lilly family; the pharmaceutical manufacturer Eli Lilly and Co. is Indianapolis' largest employer. The foundation has donated more than $300 million to the city. A $25 million grant got the Hoosier Dome started. Other contributions went toward building Market Square Arena, the Indiana University Natatorium, the National Institute of Fitness and Sport, the American College of Sports Medicine, and other facilities for skating, bicycling, and track and field.

Indianapolis business leaders have become involved as well. When the Pan-Am Games came to the city in 1987, developer Michael Browning persuaded local contractors to donate their services at cost, and they built the Pan American Plaza, a 12-story office building that stands as a monument to the role played by amateur sports in the city's revitalization.

The office building, which includes two skating rinks, was then turned over to the Sports Corp., which is housed on the top floor. Thirty percent of the rest of the building is rented on a subsidized basis to the sports-governing bodies headquartered in Indianapolis. The rest is rented—for profit—to private companies.

"I know it sounds as if everything we did involved great planning," says Knapp, "but, to be honest, we never had a five-year plan of any sort. Sometimes we would just throw up a trial balloon to see if it worked."

The first balloon was floated in 1980, when the Sports Corp. bid for the 1982 National Sports Festival, now called the U.S. Olympic Festival. At the time, the city had no track-and-field stadium, no natatorium, no softball fields, no velodrome, and not much image. "We did it with bluster," Knapp admits. "We used a lot of smoke and mirrors."

Whatever the way, it worked. Indianapolis won the bid, and the facilities—funded with city, state, and private money—materialized. Thousands of volunteers helped stage the festival, which set records for ticket sales and attendance. The city's new image as "The Amateur Sports Capital of the United States" took hold.

Since then, more and more hopefuls have sought to mimic the Indiana Sports Corp.'s formula. Recently, Knapp spoke at a Business of Amateur Sports symposium in Orlando, Fla., and found 150 rapt listeners making notes on what she said. "It made me think," she says, "do I really want to give out all our secrets?"

The keen competition has spurred some sports commissions to hire specialists and sports-marketing firms to help cities make their pitches for events. And it has prompted the organizers of events to ask cities for a greater return. The U.S. Gymnastics Federation had three serious bids for its 1984 Olympic trials and 14 bids for the 1988 trials, which went to Salt Lake City. The growing interest enabled the federation to ask for—and receive— production expenses, a minimum $100,000 event fee, and 50 percent of all ticket revenues.

And that, some say, is a dangerous trend. Robert Baade, a professor of economics at Lake Forest College, in Lake Forest, Ill., expresses concern that sports will be overrun by "ruinous competition" among cities "caught up in a captive parity syndrome."

He says: "City leaders argue that they need sports because it brings in dollars, but it has more to do with psychology. To be identified as big-league gives a city a big boost. People see sports as an indication of their worldliness or their city's standing. More than economics, it's an issue of civic monumentalism.

"Indianapolis had a good idea, and it worked for them. But do we really think that every city in the country can copy that idea effectively? There just aren't enough sports events to go around."

Baade says that cities without major sports are now building expensive stadiums just to remain competitive, citing the $170 million Alamo Dome planned for San Antonio, Texas. "I envision a whole string of white-elephant stadiums and white-elephant sports commissions around the country," he says.

Others are not so sure. "Yes, there's only one Super Bowl a year," says Millay, in New Orleans. "But those smaller events can also be very beneficial for a city—and there are enough of them to keep everyone in the game."

And for now, more cities are seeking entry into that game. Baade expects the number of sports commissions to top out at about 60, or about double the current number. Most will have just a few staff members and an annual operating budget of under $250,000. All will seek a piece of the same pie.

"To be honest, I'm surprised more cities aren't getting into this area," says Indianapolis' Knapp. "Some people may feel that many of the events we host are small-time, but each one means more exposure, and most make some money for the city. What more could you ask for?"

HOW TO HOLD A RIOT

EUGENE H. METHVIN

Mr. Methvin is the author of The Riot Makers: The Technology of Social Demolition, *published in 1970.*

ON MAY 12 Los Angeles Police Chief Daryl F. Gates, clad in flak jacket and aided by two hundred FBI agents and cops, personally arrested one of three gang members accused of the televised beating of white truckdriver Reginald Denny.

Gates was only about three hundred hours late.

Los Angeles was still burying its dead (58 and counting), nursing the 226 critically wounded (including Denny), clearing rubble from 3,700 fires, and trying to help thousands whose jobs were destroyed in the holocaust. As always after such social hurricanes, the debate rages: Why? Whose fault was it? What are the causes—proximate causes and "root causes"? How can we prevent recurrences? The causology of riots is not simple, and like the nine blind Hindus debating the shape of the elephant, people with different vantage points dispute furiously. Most black spokesmen yell "racism." White House Press Secretary Marlin Fitzwater blamed LBJ's "Great Society." I'll nominate as my prime scapegoat Daryl Gates, and will prove it to you anon. But first, some basics.

Riots are analogous to avalanches in the Alps. A gentle breeze, a cracking limb, or a zestful yodel shakes loose a tiny handful of snow. Within minutes a thunderous avalanche may bury an entire town. What follows bears no relation in magnitude to the tiny triggering event. We could argue that the heavy winter snowfalls months before "caused" the avalanche. Or we could trace the cause back to the earth's movement around the sun, or whatever force gave our planet a tilted axis, or even to the Big Bang that launched the universe. (And what came before that?)

But the practical Swiss don't go back that far. They have studied the chain to discover where they can most expediently interrupt the process to minimize damage.

We have such specialists for riots. They are called cops. When family, church, and school fail, they are civilization's last line of defense. But sometimes they do not do their jobs, and we need to understand why.

Look at the chronology in Los Angeles on April 29:

1 P.M.: The court notifies the LAPD that the verdict will be announced in two hours.

3:15 P.M.: The acquittals are broadcast live on TV.

4 P.M.: Hundreds of police are released at the end of the eight-hour day shift.

5:25 P.M.: The first report of trouble: juveniles throwing beer cans at cars, at the intersection of Florence and Normandie. More than a dozen police cruisers, with 25 officers, converge. After twenty minutes of skirmishing with a growing mob, Lieutenant Mike Moulin, the field commander, orders everybody out. As the last two cruisers depart the intersection, sirens blaring, the mob beats a *New York Times* photographer who was left behind. Hispanic and white motorists are dragged from their cars and beaten.

6:46 P.M.: Nearly six hours after the LAPD was alerted, Reginald Denny pulls his 18-wheeler into the intersection. Five rioters surround him, yank him out of the cab, beat him savagely. One throws a brick, hitting him a glancing blow in the head. As he attempts to rise, another runs up from behind and clobbers him in the head with a ball-peen hammer. He falls inert.

A TV helicopter overhead broadcasts the whole scene live to millions. A reporter cries, "Where's the police?" Four Good Samaritans who live nearby, all black, leave their homes, drive to the scene, and rescue Denny, who has suffered critical brain damage. In the 77th Street police station cops mill and watch in horror on portable television sets. "Every single blue suit here wanted to go in and save that guy," Officer Robert Frutos, a six-year-veteran, told the *New York Times*. But their commanders refuse to send them in. The televised scene advertises police inaction and commencement of the moral holiday.

About this time another TV crew broadcasts live a few blacks looting a liquor store. "This drink's on the LAPD," a woman yells at the crew as she walks off with a fifth of Chivas Regal. At a command post a mile away Lieutenant Moulin and as many as two hundred other police officers wait as their superiors give contradictory commands.

8:15 P.M.: At Vermont and Vernon a 42-year-old man

emerges from a corner supermarket with milk he has just bought for his two children. Nearby, looters empty a Korean flea market. Gunfire erupts. The father falls, bleeding, and dies in a friend's arms. His last words: "Tell my kids I love them, and tell my wife I said goodbye." Across the street an 18-year-old county-government employee guides two elderly women to a bus stop and tells them to board the first bus "and keep your heads down." A bullet hits him in the forehead, killing him instantly. These were apparently the first two deaths, 7 hours and 15 minutes after the LAPD was notified of the verdicts. Both victims were black.

Three of the cops who were pulled from the riot flashpoint talked anonymously to *Washington Post* reporter Lou Cannon and a colleague. One said: "We thought we were beating a tactical retreat and would return in force. We didn't know we were abandoning the community." Sergeant John Gambill, a motorcycle officer with long experience in the neighborhood, said: "We could have crushed it with a show of force." One cop wept as he told the *Post* what happened: "We weren't allowed to do our job. It's demoralizing to cops to be depicted as cowards, when our leaders wouldn't send us in."

In the 1965 Watts rioting, in which 34 died, the LAPD cordoned off the riot zone and left it to the burners and looters. "That decision may well have been the major cause of the Watts riot," District Attorney Evelle Younger declared in 1969. "Looking back now, all law enforcement in our community is in general agreement that it was a mistake not to apply massive but restrained force . . . immediately." Ironically, the civilian Police Commission probing the new disaster has uncovered a memo that Daryl Gates, an inspector at the time, wrote in 1965 indicating that he and another inspector made the fatal pullout decision.

Reporters dissecting the police inaction this time have found that Chief Gates assured the mayor and others he was ready for any eventuality. But the police high command seems to have made no special preparation at all.

Faces in the Crowd

I ATTENDED my first riot exactly forty years ago this spring, a "panty raid" at the University of Georgia. As a fledgling journalist and campus newspaper photographer, I was in the middle. Since then I have ventured into or done inquests on scores of riots from Tokyo to Washington, and written a fat book on the topic.

In that first riot I saw the first of three faces in the crowd that tell the whole story.

Face #1. As the student mob milled about the quadrangle of girls' dorms, I sneaked off into the bushes to load more film for my vintage 4 × 5 press camera. Hidden in the shadows of my makeshift darkroom, I saw a student come around the corner, look furtively about, and hurl a rock at a window. To me, his act was an in-

conceivable conundrum. What was it deep in his soul that impelled a privileged young WASP collegian to do such a thing?

Face #2. In Newark's 1967 riot, a psychologist saw a 12-year-old boy watching looters with shopping carts empty a store. The boy stood, shifting uneasily. The man put a hand on his shoulder: "What's the matter, son?"

"It's crazy. I don't see no sense in it!" the boy exploded.

The psychologist threw out a shrewd guess, naming a parochial school with strict moral training. "Do you go to St. —— ?"

Wide-eyed, the boy replied, "Yes, sir. How did you know?"

Face #3. As the smoke still choked Los Angeles, a black teacher screamed at *Washington Post* reporter Donna Britt over suggestions that the schools had somehow failed. "Teachers can't fix these kids all by themselves!" the teacher, Larrie Pennington, declared.

She's right. For whatever reasons, American families have delivered vast numbers of children teachers cannot fix to our streets. Consider what you would face if you were the police chief in charge of the Rose Bowl on New Year's Day with an ordinary crowd of 100,000 Americans of all ages. If we project onto that crowd the 1990 U.S. arrest rates, we will find 5,806 people who will be arrested within the year for felonies, 1,203 for serious crimes, 290 of them for violent crimes. We will have 10 murderers, 8 arsonists, 16 rapists, 70 robbers, 176 burglars, and 195 who will commit aggravated assault. Experts tell us one to two thousand will be pure psychopathic personalities, with little empathy for anybody and little control over their violent impulses. With such a population, we would do well to take precautions!

South-Central Los Angeles presents more volatility than the average Pasadena Tournament of Roses. The L.A. County Sheriff's Department had 100,500 names entered in its computer file on gangs late last year. And 775 of the year's more than 1,900 homicides were gang-related, the preponderance of them in the riot zone.

About 15 per cent of youngsters seem congenitally resistant to "aversive learning." That is the psychologists' $3 word for learning the "thou shalt nots" on which all civilization rests. Mothers of criminal psychopaths, the most extreme form of anti-social personalities, uniformly make some variant of the retrospective observation, "I could not seem to teach him the meaning of the word 'no.'"

Clearly, civilization's first lines of defense against savagery—family, church, and school—had failed with the WASP collegian in 1952, and succeeded with the black youngster in Newark in 1967. He had internal controls that prevented him from joining the carnival of looting. Society's interest must be in supporting those families, schools, and churches that still try to inculcate these controls. But when these break down, the police must step in.

Rules for Riots

POLICE SHOULD be well drilled in a wide array of riot-control techniques. A handful of professionals can suppress large mobs. Even untrained cops under good leaders can give a good account, saving lives and preventing much destruction. But cops and the public must accept the rule: "When the looting starts, the shooting starts." It can be done with restraint and precision, but it clears the carnival-goers and lets SWAT teams deal with the hard-core fire-setters and terrorists. Consider two cases:

Newark, 1967. This riot began with two hundred demonstrators bombarding a police station with rocks and bottles. Police who tried to disperse them retreated inside, bloodied, where a second-in-command did not know what to do. The mayor, fearful of "provoking" his city's volatile blacks, had forbidden riot training in anticipation of a "long hot summer."

Precinct commander Captain Charles Zizza, rushing home from an Atlantic City vacation, turned onto the main shopping street two hours after the trouble began. He saw "masses of people, must've been ten thousand over ten blocks, smashing windows, looting, singing, shouting, setting fires." And not a policeman in sight.

At his police station, Zizza found chaos. He yelled: "What the —— are all these cops doing in *here*? Why aren't they out on the street?" It took nearly an hour, but Zizza got his men organized. Some, anticipating trouble, had stored personal shotguns in their lockers. A man with the military habit of command, Zizza ordered out every available shotgun, took a dozen officers to the main street, and marched them in a picket line, driving looters before them without firing a shot. By midnight he had cleared a good part of the avenue, made several arrests, and begun receiving sniper fire from rooftops. Looters simply shifted to other sections. But the police were mobilizing and fighting.

Newark's killing and burning never reached the scale of Watts in 1965. Newark counted 23 dead. Nine days later Detroit tried the pullback strategy and 43 died. As in Watts 1965 and L.A. 1992, most were black bystanders, wholly innocent, or looters caught up and burned in the fires after police inaction advertised the carnival.

Panama, 1964. Two thousand rioters, whipped by Castro-trained agitators, stormed toward American homes in the Canal Zone. A police sergeant and eight men, following their training in riot drills, fired their service revolvers in unison, by command, into the pavement in front of the rioters. Such fire normally ricochets low, into the legs of the crowd, but may hit higher. The crowd backed off; one rioter was killed. A mile away another horde 1,500 strong stormed the Zone. Police fired two volleys over their heads. At each volley the crowd fell back, without apparent casualties. On the third round, when the sergeant gave the standard preparatory command, "Ready on the firing line," the crowd broke and ran. Meanwhile, new supplies of tear gas arrived and police were able to hold until troops relieved them.

Napoleon cowed Paris mobs with "a whiff of grapeshot." A historian later said, "If the commander of the Bastille had not been an imbecile, the Revolution never would have happened."

Americans have a right to expect their police and mayors to read history. Then the debate over "root causes" can proceed, and we can listen to our Robespierres in peace.

After the Los Angeles Riots

In the immediate aftermath of the Rodney King trial and riots in Los Angeles, the country as a whole was shocked by the verdict and terrified to see the social fabric of our cities coming unravelled. Yet within a short time, "order" was more or less restored in Los Angeles and the other cities where rioting broke out. Today, the danger is that, as the images of fire and looting in Los Angeles slowly fade, the public and the press may lose interest in the issues that gave rise to the situation in the first place.

The LA riot was like a bomb, a wrathful wake-up call reminding whites that Blacks are overcrowded in the underclass, the welfare class, the marginal working class, and the full-time working poor class. Even though within African-American communities a relatively solid blue- and white-collar laboring class has grown and a significant professional class has developed, the Great White Fear is still that when a few of the "good" Black types are allowed entry into white neighborhoods, a large number of "bad" types will soon follow. The politics of overt and codified racism are built on this fear, and reflect the institutional fact that whites reside in suburbs and Blacks in our central cities.

Conservative and right-wing Republicans have responded to the wake-up call with a "new line" on inner cities that will likely constitute their side of the debate in this November's elections. William J. Bennett, James Q. Wilson, Lawrence Mead—some of the primary, intellectual architects of the Republican party—have all written "op-eds" recently in the *Wall Street Journal* and *New York Times* on the subject, and were quickly mimicked by Vice President Quayle. Using concepts and phrases they all repeat, a composite picture of the "new" line they are presenting goes something like this: *The urban crisis is a moral crisis. What happened in LA is about moral issues of law and order, safety, growing up without civilizing influences, and without learning the importance of individual responsibility and obedience to the law. What happened in LA symbolizes the corrosive role of popular culture and the spiritual breakdown of the family. The welfare system and dangerous young Black men are the main culprits. To overcome all these corrosive forces that have caused dependency, Blacks must be forced to work like the model immigrant groups who accept low-wage jobs. Whatever rebuilding program might be proposed for the inner-city communities, the first task is to overcome the influence of the liberal anti-incarceration elite and put Black gangs and criminals in jail. If criminals are not imprisoned with long sentences, no inner-city development is possible.*

It is ironic that conservatives talk about the corrosive role of culture in inducing a moral breakdown in our society without noticing that the culture about which they speak is the product of the very "free" and commercialized market system they promote with unrestrained passion. Should the government regulate television? Should government take a more active role in fostering a positive culture? Do conservatives see any contradiction here?

The irony of their position notwithstanding, the conservatives are on the right track, but their train is headed in the wrong direction. Where they are right is in pointing out that we desperately need a moral framework that will bond people and help them understand policies. Where they are wrong is in their vision of what that moral framework should be. The moral posturing we've seen from conservatives so far—and at a heated pace since the riots in LA—is divisive, breeds a flag-waving nationalism that helps nurture hate of "foreigners" in our midst, and encourages fundamentalist exhortations.

The task for those outside the Democratic and Republican mainstream is to develop a public ideology, a clear and coherent moral vision capable of resonating with people's lives and needs. Social justice and fairness, civil discourse and compassion for the impersonal other—if these are to become embedded in the general consciousness, they need continuous cultivation. A laundry list of popular programs and issues is not enough. A new moral framework should embrace a role for government that emphasizes innovation and social development, environmental policies, measures for economic equity and security through the establishment of a universal social wage, an educational philosophy that guides school reform, and ways to revitalize community and family life (with "family" not limited to traditional forms). But most importantly, progressives must show how these issues fit together; the common moral principles that guide our response to all of these issues must be made explicit.

A white backlash against Blacks is one possible outcome of the LA riots—an outcome the Bush administration is actively fostering. That was the reaction of whites to race riots in the 1960s, administration officials are quick to remind us, off the record.

But there is also reason for hope. The situation in 1992 is a new one. In contrast to the period following the civil rights movement and its alleged "excesses," the current stagnation of the economy, the unfairness of the taxation system, diminished confidence in the future and the fiscal impotence of the federal government are not seen as induced by Black protests and demands. White backlash is a possibility, but it hardly seems inevitable. The questions we must ask are: How can we channel the frustration and despair in the land? What will bring people together?

The Los Angeles riot provides us with an opportunity. Let's talk about rebuilding America by revitalizing city life as a start. Our approach should be holistic—not just refurbishing the ghettos, but rebuilding a vital social, cultural, and material environment in our cities. We must

From *Social Policy*, Spring 1992, pp. 2-5. *Social Policy*, published by Social Policy Corporation, New York, NY 10036.

create not only jobs, but jobs with a purpose.

Consider one small example. Suppose we were to develop a rapid-rail system stretching from Maine to Florida, and an efficient urban rail system that would link suburbs to the central city. Such a reconstruction could be designed to reduce reliance on the automobile, revitalize our depots, create socially meaningful jobs all over the country, eliminate the need for short-distance air travel, and, of course, become part of a larger effort to revitalize the central cities.

I do not mean to suggest, of course, that a large-scale rail system would be a panacea for economic and racial divisions. My point is that we must frame our agenda with an integrated purpose. Government projects with large social multipliers are not hard to find; we should be working to develop them as we proceed to address racism directly at work and in communities.

Who is likely to initiate this enlarged urban agenda—one that serves the whole country, as well as meeting specific needs of those trapped in dying cities? One important source will be the large and talented pool of Black leaders, city administrators, and professionals who now run, work, and reside in many of our major central cities. Members of this relatively new Black middle class, more than most people, live in two worlds. They know by experience that any degree of serious and satisfying integration is impossible as long as Blacks are over-represented in the lower classes that are concentrated in the inner cities. If Black leaders who have become central to city life can help, along with others, to create a national movement to rebuild America's urban places, they will once again help America close the gap between its reality and its promise.

—Raymond S. Franklin
Director of the Michael Harrington
Center for Democratic Values and
Social Change; author of *Shadows of
Race and Class*

Rediscovering
the village

Small-town comforts are now the cutting edge of urban planning

Robert Gerloff

Special to Utne Reader
*Robert Gerloff is an associate with Mulfinger, Susanka &
Mahady Architects in Minneapolis.*

**The United States is poised to become the first subur-
ban-majority nation in human history. The 1990 census
showed that nearly as many Americans now live in
suburbs as live in cities, small towns, and rural areas
combined—a fact with all sorts of implications for our
future. We can expect greater environmental woes and
increased social fragmentation as more and more people
are absorbed into the suburban lifestyle of driving all
over the place all the time. But we are also seeing signs
of a counterrevolution. Planners and people everywhere
are pining for the pleasures of the village—a way of life
where people can walk to work and shopping and
perhaps bump into their neighbors in the process.**

Today on my walk home from work I dropped in at
Dave's Dinkytown Hairstylists for a haircut. Dave's
8-year-old son, his 15-year-old daughter, and her
boyfriend were hanging out in the shop after school.
While Mona was snipping away at my hair, Fred, a
Dinkytown institution, came in for his monthly trim. He
told us all about his new great-grandson while Dave
trimmed his hair ("short on the top, just trim the

sides . . ."). Afterward I popped into Biermaier's Books
to see if Bill had a used paperback of *Main Street* (he did)
and stopped in at Ralph & Jerry's Grocery to pick up a
half-gallon of 2% and to flirt with the new checkout
woman (she has a boyfriend).

To me, this relaxing, 20-minute stroll home from work
seems only natural—and far more convenient than bat-
tling traffic on the freeway. But to those who are thinking
about the future of our cities, my 20-minute walk is along
the cutting edge of contemporary urban planning, and
the Dinkytown/Holmes neighborhood of Minneapolis,
where I live, work, eat, shop, and play, is the very
definition of an "urban village." It is the village, that most
ancient of human settlements, that is stirring people's
imaginations today, reinforcing the Swiss architect Luigi
Snozzi's belief that "nothing needs to be invented; everything needs to be rediscovered."

*It is the village that is stirring the
imagination of urban planners.*

The qualities that are being rediscovered in the village
are simple: A village is a compact gathering of houses,
apartment buildings, corner groceries, Main Street shops
and offices. A village is inhabited by people of diverse age
groups and income levels. And a village is friendly to

pedestrians, a place where you can easily walk to work or to the grocery rather than driving a money-hungry, resource-hogging, smog-pumping automobile.

The qualities of the village can be encapsulated in a simple model for urban planning: the city as a collection of villages. In recent decades, this idea has been discarded, and replaced with the modernist model of the city as machine. While the village blends houses with shops, the old with the young, and the rich with the poor, the notion of the city as machine, which is now rigidly enforced in the United States through impenetrable layers of zoning codes, relentlessly and single-mindedly separates the old from the young, the rich from the poor, apartments from town houses, houses from shops, and factories from offices, until the city is so sprawled out that such simple, everyday tasks as getting a haircut, browsing for a novel, and picking up a half-gallon of milk require three separate automobile trips.

According to city-as-machine thinking, all these separate activities would be easily accessible by high-speed freeways, and every citizen would be mobile and independent in his or her private automobile. The machine model of cities promised efficiency, convenience, and the tidy clarity of everything having its own place. Unfortunately, it didn't work—as our downtowns, which are generally lifeless after five o'clock, and modern suburbia, which has become a classic case of there being no there there, can attest.

The village promises a life that is simpler, slower, safer.

The simple city-as-village idea may have the power to reshape our soulless cities and suburbs over the coming decades, for this model has gained adherents all across the ideological spectrum, from the '60s activist roots of California planner Peter Calthorpe to the Ivy League style of Miami architects Andres Duany and Elizabeth Plater-Zyberk; from the Marxist urban theorist Leon Krier to the future king of England, Prince Charles (who hired Krier to design his new showcase village of Poundbury in Dorset); from the golf-cart retirement villages of the Sunbelt to the Birkenstock-style Village Homes development in Davis, California.

Clearly the city as village functions more smoothly as urban design than the city as machine—this is becoming increasingly evident as problems with pollution, traffic, and affordable housing mount. But the strongest appeal of the village model is its tug on human

emotions: The village promises a life that is simpler, slower, and safer; a life where a neighborhood is transformed through social ties into a community; a life more intimately tied to the cycles of nature; a life that seems somehow more honest and genuine.

At its best this emotional tug provides a genuine historical continuity that taps into the spirit of such beloved communities as Aspen, Carmel, Taos, and Bayfield, Wisconsin—tourist villages that are now being loved to death. At its worst this emotional tug is the mindless nostalgia that Christopher Lasch denounces as "the abdication of memory," a nostalgia that many developers are now exploiting with white picket fences and front porch railings lifted from traditional neighborhoods and deposited in otherwise ordinary sprawling suburban developments.

Reshaping the world, of course, is not a simple task. Any attempt to create a new village, or even to build a simple corner store in an existing residential neighborhood, faces a major battle, for the principles of the modernist city-as-machine model are deeply entrenched in the zoning codes of every city, municipality, and county in the nation.

Yet even within this legal superstructure of zoning codes the marketplace is rediscovering the village in unexpected ways: A new SuperAmerica outlet in Burnsville, a suburb that grew up around a freeway exit 15 miles south of my home in inner-city Minneapolis, functions as a grocery store (milk, nachos, sandwich meat), a bakery (bread, cookies, muffins), a service station (gasoline, wiper blades, oil), a bank (automatic teller machines), a hardware store (light bulbs, screwdrivers, snow shovels), a video store (Julia Roberts, Sylvester Stallone, and Woody Allen), a newsstand (newspapers, magazines, paperback novels), a café (sit-down dining on microwave foods), a post office (stamps, a fax machine, a Federal Express drop box) . . . all the commercial institutions of a village Main Street have been compressed into one small convenience store. It's not hard to imagine people bumping into each other here and trading stories about the weather, the traffic, the high school hockey team or maybe even the birth of a great-grandson.

The village was supposed to be dead and buried alongside the covered wagon in our nostalgic memory, but it turned out to be both too practical and too deeply embedded in our imaginations to die.

A village, of course, is far more than a simple physical structure. It is a community of diverse individuals and families. Sinclair Lewis skewered the smug, parochial, small-town way of life in his 1920 masterpiece, *Main Street.* Can we revive the village forms without also reviving the social and moral codes that allowed small-town life to function smoothly? Can we recreate village forms and community without the social strictures Lewis satirized? Perhaps Lewis' own life provides us with an answer. When he fled the stifling provincialism of Sauk Centre, Minnesota, for the sophistication of New York in 1907, he found a home in the bohemian enclave of Greenwich Village, a community perhaps as provincial and literally villagelike as the society he left behind—just one with a different set of values.

Journalist James Fallows argues in his book *More Like Us* that it is America's rejection of Old World village life—where society is static, time is cyclical, and the rhythms of life flow from the natural cycles of birth, death, and rebirth—that has made America a world economic power. The American dream is built on values alien to the village,

on our willingness to tolerate unpredictable disorder, to follow the job market like nomads, and to reinvent our lives with every generation. This economic prowess has come at a cost measured in escalating levels of traffic, environmental damage, rushing around, rootlessness, and alienation—a cost many people are no longer willing to pay.

On the larger scale, questions about what kind of society we really want are daunting. On the smaller scale, the scale of everyday life, they are simple. If I had driven to a trendy hair salon rather than stopping in at Dave's Dinkytown Hairstylists, I never would have shared Fred's joy at the birth of his great-grandson. And Fred's joy made my life just a little bit richer.

In Suburbs, a Stealthy War Against Infiltrating Students

Jonathan Rabinovitz

Special to The New York Times

ELMONT, N.Y., Nov. 2—With the stealth and precision of agents on a drug raid, private detectives and security guards fanned out through this middle-class community in unmarked cars one recent morning.

Their quarry was not crack dealers or violent thugs. It was teen-agers from Queens who had crossed the border into Nassau County in search of a better education.

Faced with a surge of students fleeing the New York City school system, the Sewanhaka Central High School District here is one of many financially strapped suburban school systems that have embraced spying to discover children who are not residents.

$100 Bounties Offered

"I feel for these students," said George Goldstein, the Sewanhaka district's superintendent. "They are simply trying to pursue the American dream. But our taxpayers are paying through the nose and it's just got to be stopped."

Other systems are facing the same pressures. In Fort Lee, N.J., all students are required to register with the borough's housing office, which then investigates whether they are legal residents. Two other New Jersey districts have offered $100 bounties for tips about nonresident students. On Long Island, the Herricks Union Free School District and at least two others have recently hired detective agencies.

The Sewanhaka district, considered one of the most aggressive, removed

more than 150 students in the last school year and at least 77 more since the summer. But some critics wonder whether the district may have gone too far, perhaps terrorizing innocent students and, in the words of one attendance officer, turning the school into a "police state."

Dr. Goldstein estimates that his efforts have saved the Sewanhaka district at least $6 million during the last seven years, if one considers the amount that would have been spent to educate the hundreds of out-of-district children who would have remained. The administrative cost of the program is about $100,000 a year, he said, though this does not include the thousands of hours of staff time.

In Walking Distance of Queens

In addition, Dr. Goldstein said, families of former students have paid about $50,000 to the school system after the district threatened them with lawsuits.

The Sewanhaka district, composed of five high schools, includes the middle-class communities of Elmont, New Hyde Park, Franklin Square and Floral Park. Three of its schools are within walking distance of Queens.

Homeowners pay an annual average of $2,600 in school taxes, and last year the residents approved an increase of about $36 per household. The district is expected to spend about $10,500 educating each of its 6,500 students this year, Dr. Goldstein said, with 20 percent of it from the state.

School officials said the nonresident students were driven by parents or shared taxis, traveling from as far as the South Bronx, Brooklyn and Staten Island. The majority, however, live just

over the border in Cambria Heights, Laurelton and Rosedale, Queens.

Mailboxes and Empty Rooms

To register the students, the parents use tricks that have been practiced for years, school officials said. They find a friend or relative in the suburbs who will list them as tenants or perhaps put up a mailbox with their name on it. Sometimes, officials said, an empty room may be decorated as if the child lived there.

Some school districts have hired detectives.

The students come, Dr. Goldstein and others said, to escape city schools where metal detectors are needed to keep weapons out. Some come from impoverished, troubled families but others simply want to take advantage of schools that spend $3,000 more per student than those in the city.

James S. Vlasto, a spokesman for the New York City Schools Chancellor, said the school system had no way of tracking students who switch illegally to suburban schools, but that it was not a source of great concern. "Our high schools are full," he said, referring to rapidly increasing enrollment during the last three years. "If anything, we need more seats."

On the morning of the sweep at Elmont Memorial High School, 16 school officials, security guards and private detectives, hidden at intersections and inside the school, communicated by walkie-talkie. When a car was spotted crossing the border, officials in the school were informed so they could see if the child was dropped off. Then they would follow the child into the building and get his or her name from a teacher.

In the next few weeks, license-plate numbers were checked, and then investigators followed and covertly photographed those students who they believed had used false addresses to register.

So far, 18 of these students have received letters telling them that they can no longer attend Elmont, and 12 who have not appealed the eviction have been billed for at least $480 each for the instruction they had received.

Jack Dempsey, a retired police detective who serves as a security consultant to Sewanhaka, said he sometimes will "sit on a house" for eight-hour stretches, watching from midnight to 8 A.M. to see if a child spends the night there before going to school. One investigator has been known to camp out in trees, watching the home with binoculars, Dr. Goldstein said. It is also routine to patrol the Queens-Nassau County border and to follow children home from school.

The enforcement procedures start when a student enrolls. All are required to provide notarized documentation, proving that they live in the district with a parent or someone who claims a custodial relationship. During the year, students receive three unannounced home visits to confirm that they are actually living at the address.

If the family cannot be found at the listed address, if mail is returned to the school or if the sweep or a tip suggests that the student is living outside the district, officials will begin a more thorough investigation.

'Double-Stakeout'

In the most serious cases, Mr. Dempsey said, the district may employ a "double stakeout," with an investigator at the questionable address in Elmont and another at what may be the family's true address in New York City. Some-

times an investigator will hide beneath a car to videotape a student leaving the real home, while at other times a specially outfitted van will carry a driver and a camera operator.

The district has two full-time investigators, in addition to attendance officers at each of the schools. It also has hired a detective agency. A lawyer devotes 12 to 15 hours each week to these matters. Dr. Goldstein said that he spends five hours a week on residency issues.

Some students pose as tenants with relatives.

Linda Wain, executive director of the Long Island Advocacy Center, a nonprofit legal services center for students, said the enforcement has been, at times, "overly vigilant." The center has represented students across the Island in 79 cases this year, up from 29 in all of 1991, and most of these have been at Sewanhaka and one other district.

Because of confidentiality requirements, Ms. Wain could not discuss specific cases. But she said Sewanhaka had evicted students who had fled to the district from desperate situations and had moved in with relatives or friends. Dr. Goldstein said he believed many of the students in such situations were using their predicaments as an excuse to attend his schools.

One family, who insisted on anonymity because their daughter was still enrolled in the district, said the schools' investigation had "traumatized" the girl. Officials tried to evict the student, because they did not believe that the family lived in the basement of a friend's home in the district, one parent said. School documents provided by the parent show the district had observed the family in another residence outside the district and taken photos as they entered and left. When the parent tried to explain why the family had stayed there, officials dismissed her story as a lie, the documents show.

Ultimately, state education officials ruled that the girl should remain in the

school, but the experience left the family angry.

"They interrogated me," the parent said. "And when my daughter learned about it, she cried and cried and cried. She still looks over her shoulder when she goes out of the house, wondering if there's anyone behind her."

On a visit to the Elmont cafeteria one day, three boys talked reluctantly about the residency enforcement. "Two of my friends got pushed out," said one. "It's messed up, but if it has to happen, it has to happen. You can't do nothing about it."

State education officials and other school officials said such surveillance is legitimate to gather evidence.

Complicated Cases

But in the last year, several of Sewanhaka's decisions have been overturned by the State Commissioner of Education, as they and others disagree over what constitutes residency.

"There are societal realities that make residency cases more complicated," said Karen Norlander, an assistant counsel in the State Education Department. Because many children are no longer living in traditional families and are sent to live with friends or relatives, the school district is often faced with the sticky question of whether the child is living in the district for legitimate reasons or to take advantage of the school system, she said. In some instances, Ms. Norlander said, "the situation has no easy answer."

Experts in residency said that two criteria determine a student's status: whether the child usually sleeps in the district and whether the person with whom the child lives exerts financial and legal control. For example, Ms. Norlander said, if a child is sent to live with relatives for reasons of financial hardship, but the parents visit on weekends and list the child as an income-tax dependent, residency may be in the parents' district.

Attendance officers say they are often forced to make judgment calls.

Finances and Development

- **Revenues (Articles 44–48)**
- **Development (Articles 49–52)**

Like all governments, state and local governments need financial resources to carry out their activities. State and local governments rely on a variety of revenue sources, including sales taxes, income taxes, and property taxes; user charges (for example, motor vehicle registration fees and college tuition); lotteries; and grants of money from other levels of government. But despite this diversity of funding sources, the overall financial situation of state and local governments is often far from satisfactory.

Conspicuous attempts to curb spending at all levels of government have been made in recent years. Most prominent among such measures was Proposition 13, passed by California voters in a 1978 referendum. Proposition 13 put ceilings on local government property taxes and, in turn, affected the programs that local governments in California could offer. The Proposition 13 tax revolt soon spread to other states. By now, measures designed to limit government spending have come into effect in states and localities across the country. At the national level, a constitutional amendment has been proposed and legislation has been passed in attempts to make it difficult for Congress to pass an unbalanced budget.

Unlike the national government, state and local governments get a sizable portion of their revenues from intergovernmental grants. The national government gives money to state and local governments with various conditions attached. Money can be given with virtually no accompanying strings or with considerable limitations on how it can be spent. Similarly, states provide state aid to local governments under varying sets of conditions. Governments providing financial grants, of course, exercise control over the amount of funds available and the conditions attached to such funds. This, in turn, can cause considerable uncertainty for governments relying on grant money. As should be apparent, intergovernmental relations and state and local finances are areas which overlap considerably.

The financial situation of state and local governments differs from that of the national government in other important respects. The national government has considerable ability to affect the national economy by controlling the money supply and by budgetary deficits or, at least in

theory, budgetary surpluses. By contrast, most state and local governments are legally required to balance their budgets. For those not required to have balanced budgets, it is difficult to borrow money for large and persistent budget deficits. The fiscal crises of New York City and other local governments during the 1970s showed that lenders will go only so far in providing money for state and local governments whose expenditures are consistently greater than their revenues.

Both the national government and state and local governments seek to promote economic development. New industries employ workers who pay taxes and thus increase government revenues. What is new on the state and local scene is the energy and persistence with which states and localities compete with one another to attract industries to their areas.

Finances are a complicated but critical aspect of state and local government. The first section of this unit treats taxes, lotteries, and related revenue-raising matters. The second section focuses on activities of state and local governments related to economic development.

Looking Ahead: Challenge Questions

Approximately how much money do you (or your parents, if you are not a full-time wage earner) annually pay to local, state, and national governments, respectively? Is this an easy question to answer? Why or why not?

Property tax, a tax on the value of real estate and buildings, is a primary source of revenue for local governments. Do you think people who live in rented apartments or houses avoid property taxes? Why or why not?

Why do you think that the national government has assumed more and more of the burden for raising revenues for all three levels of government?

What do you think is the best means for state and local governments to raise revenues: property taxes, income taxes, sales taxes, lotteries, user charges, or something else?

Do you think that measures such as Proposition 13 in California and Proposition 2½ in Massachusetts are desirable? Why or why not?

Revenue-Raising Partners

State and local governments, closest to home, provide the services most visible and most important to taxpayers.

James Edwin Kee and John Shannon

James Kee, associate professor of public administration at George Washington University, is a visiting scholar at The Urban Institute. John Shannon, former director of the U.S. Advisory Commission on Intergovernmental Relations, is a senior fellow at The Urban Institute.

What is the most significant feature of American Federalism? After 200 years, state governments and their local government partners remain vibrant domestic policy leaders in the federal system. This remarkable achievement can be traced largely to one overarching truth: During peacetime, the 50 state-local systems of government possess inherent political advantages over the national government when competing for taxpayer support.

After 50 years of apparent federal government centralization, the nation has entered a new period we call "competitive federalism," where leadership in domestic policy will flow to whichever level of government can persuade its voters to provide the tax revenue for necessary government services.

Most political scientists and economists, as well as the general public, assume that the national government enjoys an enormous competitive advantage in raising money. However, the history of the last 50 years points in just the opposite direction. Since World War II, Washington, D.C., has gradually pulled back, and state and local governments have steadily advanced on the general revenue front. In 1944, the federal government raised nearly five times as much general revenue, excluding Social Security, as state and local governments. Now they are essentially equal.

When raising general revenue, the 50 state-local systems have at least six political advantages over the national government.

The close-to-home advantage. Even during periods of severe national crisis, state and local officials never lose control of "core" domestic programs—police, education, land use, local and regional transportation, economic development, public health and public amenities (parks, museums and libraries).

State and local officials are closer to the people in the sense that they operate programs perceived to have the most direct benefit for the greatest number of citizens—a situation that tends both to lessen taxpayer resistance and to generate public support for additional funding.

By sharp contrast, primary responsibility for many of the nation's necessary but highly controversial domestic tasks now rests with Washington: income redistribution, environmental protection, affirmative action and occupational safety. In addition, federal financing of a wide variety of special interest chores, such as subsidies for small business, hospitals for veterans and price supports for farmers, is not perceived to affect a large number of people and tends to generate taxpayer resistance to higher federal taxes for general government purposes.

Only in the special trust fund areas, such as Social Security and Medicare, has Washington repeatedly pushed through major peacetime tax increases. Why? Because in these areas there is a close connection between the dedicated tax paid and the benefit received.

The balance-or-else advantage. There is an iron law that governs the financing of democratic governments: There can be no major tax rate hike *for general government* purposes without a major crisis. Because they must operate with balanced budgets, states and localities frequently confront crisis. Regional and national recessions, judicial mandates and acute demographic pressures (like the baby boom) are stressful but generate consensus that prompts or forces state and local officials to vote major tax increases that would be politically suicidal without a crisis. The higher taxes usually linger on once the crisis has passed—the upward ratchet effect.

Federal policymakers have a natural revenue-raising advantage only during a major war. In the last 50 years, Congress has enacted a general income tax rate hike on only three occasions, World War II, the Korean War and the war in Vietnam. Once the war is over, conservative demands for tax cuts and liberal urgings to spend the peace dividend on domestic needs create an anti-crisis, a polarizing situation that leads first to a gradual reduction in general federal taxes and then to an enormous run-up of the federal debt.

The divide-and-conquer advantage. More than 80,000 units of government making decisions about revenues and expenditures have been created by the states, all competing for public support. This central feature of the American federal system allows states to match more closely the pain of taxation with the rewards of specific benefits and services. In addition, as the state and local tax load increases, state legislators become willing to give local officials more tax rope.

Required to tax uniformly across the nation, the federal government lacks the crucial ability to disperse decision making to these thousands of local governing units.

 The "big four" advantage. Driven by budgetary realities and competitive concerns, most of our 50 systems now make fairly balanced use of the big four revenue sources: income, sales and property taxes and user fees. For example, when Connecticut was faced with a large deficit, it couldn't further hike its sales tax and corporate income tax rates for fear of damaging its competitive position with neighboring states. Thus, it was forced to enact a broad-based individual income tax.

In addition, states especially have a wide variety of miscellaneous levies–"sin" taxes, lotteries and regulatory fees–to bridge smaller budgetary gaps. Diversification is the incrementalist's dream, allowing state and local governments to make a series of light surgical probes on the taxpayers' pockets. In contrast, raising the federal income tax is akin to amputation.

 The follow-thy-neighbor advantage. Unlike the federal government, states and local governments are constantly forced to upgrade services to keep up with their neighboring jurisdictions. Often unusual allies—liberal reformers and conservative business leaders—come together to argue for greater taxes for education and better roads.

However, in an increasingly competitive world market, the federal government will also find that it too will come under increasing pressure to keep up with its foreign trading partners in education, the environment and fiscal discipline.

 The less-to-lose advantage. State and local officials tend to be less risk-averse than their Washington counterparts. Most are "citizen legislators"; their office is not their whole life and career. If they vote for an unpopular tax increase and are defeated in the next election, it is not the end of the world.

With the decline of political parties,

Revenue as a Percentage of Gross National Product

Year	State & Local General Revenue	Federal General Revenue	Total General Revenue	Federal Social Insurance Revenue	Total Government Revenue
1940	9.1	5.7	14.8	.8	15.6
1944	4.9	23.5	28.4	1.3	29.7
1954	7.1	18.3	25.4	1.6	27.0
1964	9.3	15.6	24.9	2.9	27.8
1974	11.7	14.8	26.5	5.1	31.6
1984	12.1	13.7	25.8	6.1	31.9
est. 1990	13.2	13.7	26.9	6.8	33.7

Source: Bureau of the Census data, selected years. State-local general revenue excludes federal aid, employee pension payments and utility and liquor store receipts. Federal general revenue excludes postal receipts; Social Insurance Revenue includes Social Security, Medicare and certain other federal insurance trust fund receipts.

the rise of PAC funding and the emergence of the independent "political entrepreneur," members of Congress have become increasingly risk-averse. Higher congressional salaries and generous perks of office make federal elected officials ever more fearful of political defeat.

Some of the advantages of raising revenue locally (close-to-home, balance-or-else and divide-and-conquer) are inherent in the current political structure of American federalism. The other three advantages (big four, follow-thy-neighbor and less-to-lose) reinforce the first three, but are more susceptible to political change.

What is the big message for state-local relations? When competition for general revenue is viewed broadly, we have only two basic contestants: Washington, D.C., and the 50 state-local revenue systems. Why? Because local governments are the essential offspring and partners of state government in financ-

ing and delivering most domestic public goods and services; they're not stand-alone units of government.

Over the past several decades, the great advances made in strengthening state revenue systems were driven largely by the need to respond to local concerns, such as property tax relief and school finance reform. The growing diversification of revenue at the local level and the creation of myriad special districts provide convincing evidence that state government recognizes the advantage of using local government to gain political accountability for the financing of specific expenditure demands.

In *The Federalist Papers*, Madison argued that if the states did not exist, the central government would be forced to create them. It is equally true that if local governments did not exist, the states would have had to create them—as their indispensable partners and allies in a highly competitive federal system.

Not Quite the Pot of Gold

Legalized gambling started to look enticing as a revenue source about 10 years ago. Now some spots of tarnish are showing up.

Pam Greenberg

Pam Greenberg tracks gambling issues for NCSL.

You got to know when to hold 'em, know when to fold 'em, know when to walk away, know when to run.

So goes the advice to the gambler in the old Kenny Rogers hit. The same suggestion might be given to state policymakers, who now hold the cards in the business of legalized gambling.

Even though some form of gambling is now legal in all but two states, policymakers continue to confront decisions about how to play their cards—not only whether gambling should be legal, but whether to legalize new forms of gambling, and how to regulate and manage the enterprises. To decide, they must know the risks. States without legalized gambling risk losing income from their own residents, who may spend their money in surrounding states that do offer gambling. Those states that choose to legalize gambling risk becoming dependent on an unstable source of revenue. They also may risk cutting into other sources of income, when citizens gamble instead of spending money on other goods and services. States that legalize new forms of gambling risk sacrificing a diversified economy for a gambling-dominated economy. States that legalize gambling risk encountering social costs associated with compulsive gamblers. And states that wait risk letting others corner the market.

Gambling revenues started to look particularly good to states in the 1980s when the economy deteriorated and citizens became increasingly frustrated with tax increases. Gambling proved lu-

crative. The gambling industry grew faster than the economy at large every year from 1982 to 1990, dropping off for the first time in 1991, according to Eugene Christiansen, a gaming consultant who annually compiles data for *Gaming and Wagering Business* magazine. Gross revenues from legal gambling totaled $26.7 billion in 1991. Christiansen compares that figure to the $4.85 billion in revenues generated by the domestic film box office.

In FY 1991, states received some $7.5 billion in net revenues from lotteries (about 2.4 percent of total state tax collections). Lotteries are particularly profitable for states because close to half of the revenue generated goes to state coffers. Casinos are usually taxed at a much lower rate than lotteries, but still bring in substantial revenues. Casinos in Nevada brought in $428 million in gaming taxes and license fees in 1992. In New Jersey, the state collected $236 million in taxes in 1991. Tiny Deadwood, S.D., brought in more than $1 million in state taxes in each of the last two fiscal years. Reve-

nues to Colorado from three small mountain towns totaled $10.7 million in the first fiscal year of operation. Riverboat casino gambling in Iowa and Illinois created more than $13 million for each of those states in 1991. In addition, local governments receive a portion of gaming revenues. For example, in South Dakota, the state receives 40 percent of Deadwood gaming tax revenues; local governments receive the remainder.

However, gambling has its disadvantages. Former Representative Alan Karcher of New Jersey, author of the 1989 book *Lotteries,* concludes that gaming tax revenues generally, and lottery revenues in particular, are regressive because poor people spend a greater proportion of their income on gambling than do the wealthy. Karcher suggests that lotteries could be made less regressive if the amount paid out as winnings was increased (by reducing the amount going to the state) and if lotteries were marketed toward those with higher incomes. And he proposes that local governments share in the proceeds in direct propor-

The owner of a gift shop in Cripple Creek saw his property assessment jump from $89,000 to $521,000, even though he hasn't changed the building's use to gambling.

tion to the level of lottery participation in each region.

Mary Borg, an economics professor at the University of North Florida who has conducted several studies of gambling, warns about other tradeoffs, as well. By instituting a state lottery, says Borg, "you're probably going to lose some revenue from sales and excise taxes." This is because lottery players forego other purchases that are subject to sales taxes. The amount a state can expect to lose will vary depending on its tax structure. For example, Borg estimates that for every dollar gained from the Florida lottery, the state lost 22 cents that would have been collected from sales and excise taxes. Florida's tax structure makes it particularly vulnerable to this loss, because the state imposes no income tax, but has a high sales and excise tax rate. Borg thinks other states won't lose quite as much of the lottery dollar, perhaps 10 percent to 15 percent.

Legalizing new forms of gambling can also cut into revenues of established games. For example, in New Jersey, a report of the Governor's Advisory Commission on Gambling called horse racing a casualty of competition from other gaming. Similarly, a July 1992 report by the Illinois Economic and Fiscal Commission concludes that the introduction of riverboat gambling had a negative impact on revenues of horse and dog tracks located near the riverboats. The instant and lotto games of the South Dakota lottery suffered when the agency installed video lottery terminals across the state, although not enough to offset the huge gain generated by video lottery. West Virginia and Rhode Island have authorized placing video lottery machines at race tracks in the state in an effort to counter the decline in the racing industry.

Another disadvantage associated with gambling revenues is manifest in states where lottery revenues are dedicated for specific purposes, such as education. Says Borg, "Earmarking in most cases is detrimental to the cause you're trying to benefit. It initially enhances the cause, but over the years, funding is eroded." In Florida, where lottery proceeds go to education, funding for schools eventually decreased, partly because local voters turned down levy increases. "They don't realize just how small lottery revenue is as a total percentage of education funding. It's just a tiny portion," says Borg.

Even in states where revenues are

A problem gambler is likely to be female, low income or minority and a loner addicted to playing the lottery.

earmarked to create new programs, the volatility of gambling revenues can create problems. In Pennsylvania, lottery funds were allocated for property tax or rent relief, home care services, free or reduced transportation services, and reduced rates on prescription medicines for senior citizens. But because of lagging ticket sales, the Pennsylvania lottery fund has not been able to keep up with the ever-increasing costs of the programs. The legislature in recent years has had to shift programs that were initiated and funded by the lottery into the general fund.

States and communities have recently looked to casinos, not just for their revenue advantages, but also for the economic development and tourism benefits they bring. Voters in New Jersey approved casinos for Atlantic City in 1976, hoping to reverse urban decay and bring the city back to its 1920s glory as a premier resort and tourist attraction and to restore its reputation as a desirable place to live. Statistically, the economic and tourism benefits of Atlantic City are substantial. In 1991, casinos employed about 42,000 full-time workers. In addition to the $236 million the state collected in casino taxes, the casino industry paid more than $100 million in Atlantic City, Atlantic County and school property taxes in 1991. The city continues to hold the record as the No. 1 tourist destination in the country, attracting more than 30 million visitors in 1991.

Yet the economic picture painted by Atlantic City casinos is not entirely rosy. Even though many of the economic statistics present an overwhelmingly positive view, no other community has sought to model itself after Atlantic City. The "boardwalk of broken dreams," as *Time* labeled Atlantic City, still struggles to meet its initial goals. Gambling has failed to attract new residents; in fact, the city's population has declined: 10.9 percent from 1970 to 1977, 5.8 percent from 1977 to 1980, and 5.5 percent from 1980 to 1990. Economic benefits also fled the city. Many casino jobs went to

those outside city limits, leaving many poor inner-city residents still unemployed. Higher property values meant higher rents. Investments were limited to casinos, and didn't spill over to housing, municipal services or businesses other than gaming.

For 13 years after New Jersey voters approved casino gambling in Atlantic City, new casino proposals across the country were repeatedly defeated. In 1989, South Dakota voters set off a new trend when they authorized casinos for the small town of Deadwood. By 1992, casinos were legal in three mountain towns in Colorado, on riverboats in Iowa, Illinois, Mississippi and Louisiana, and in a complex to be constructed in New Orleans. In the four jurisdictions where casinos have been operating for more than a year (South Dakota, Colorado, Iowa and Illinois), the economic benefits are easily measured.

Casinos bring jobs and investment to communities. A University of South Dakota study noted that gaming establishments accounted for the addition of 800 to 900 jobs in Deadwood. City officials note that more than $30 million in private and public money has been invested in Deadwood. The Colorado Gaming Commission reports that casinos hired close to 5,000 employees in the first nine months of operation. The first three months of gaming brought more than a million people to Central City and Black Hawk, Colo., more than the two towns normally saw in a full year. In the town of Cripple Creek, Colo., more than $5.5 million went for infrastructure improvements in the first nine months of gambling, according to Mayor Henry Hack. In Iowa, more than $66 million has been invested in vessels and well over $100 million in land development since riverboat gambling began in April 1991. The Illinois Economic & Fiscal Commission attributes more than 6,000 jobs to riverboat gambling directly, and about 5,000 more to indirectly related jobs.

But experts warn that states and communities can't rely solely on gambling for sound economic development. Fort Madison, Iowa, borrowed $2.6 million to build a ticket center, pedestrian bridge and dock for the Emerald Lady riverboat. After only a year, the Emerald Lady and three other Iowa riverboats pulled up anchor and left the state for Mississippi, where the gaming laws are more liberal and the potential for profit greater.

Speaker Bob Arnould of the Iowa House of Representatives, one of the initial supporters of riverboat gambling legislation, notes that "by nature, gambling is a high-risk industry. Right now, the industry is going through a shakeout process. We advised our communities to invest in public improvements that were needed for the community, regardless of the success or failure of the riverboats." Casinos in the Quad cities have done very well, and riverboat gaming in Iowa will continue to be successful for those who make the right kind of investments, explains Arnould.

In Colorado, according to Patricia Stokowski, a University of Colorado researcher who has studied tourism development for 10 years, the economic boom gambling created in the three towns has been uneven. "Many shopkeepers who thought their stores would benefit from gambling had their leases canceled or bought out," says Stokowski. Many residents worry about increased property taxes. Bob Elliott, owner of a gift shop in Cripple Creek, saw his property assessment jump from $89,000 to $521,000 this year, even though he hasn't changed the building's use to gambling. Even those who opened small casinos found the competitive pressures too demanding. Many of the "mom-and-pop" casinos have folded as more and more of the larger casinos open, despite the state gaming commission's graduated tax rate that favors smaller casinos. According to Stokowski, "Seventy-five percent of the casino owners are from outside the area, about half of them from Denver and half from California and Nevada."

I. Nelson Rose, a gaming attorney and professor of law at Whittier Law School in Los Angeles, says, "Right now, we're coming out of a period of complete prohibition, so there's a lot of pent-up demand. Those who are in on the market first make a great deal of money, and get a high return on investment." Others who follow aren't as successful. Rose notes that in Atlantic City, the first casino to open made back its investment

in nine months. The 13th casino went bankrupt, and four others went down with it, he says. According to Rose, the market is nearly saturated in many areas. "There is an unrealistic idea that the gambling dollar is infinitely elastic and that the market will keep expanding." In many states, casino gambling is legalized in the hope of attracting tourists, but as gambling opportunities proliferate across the country, the majority of customers are locals.

In addition to competition from neighboring states, gambling communities face competition within their own borders. Indian tribes in 12 states have negotiated agreements with state officials to conduct gambling activities on tribal lands, and many more are currently in negotiation. South Dakota and Colorado found that legalizing casinos in limited areas led to pressure from other communities wanting gambling. In Colorado, four proposals seeking to expand legalized casino gambling to 27 communities appeared on the November ballot. Competition comes from across the country's border as well. Lotteries, video gambling machines and casinos are legal in Canadian provinces, and officials in Ontario recently authorized new casinos to be built in areas bordering several U.S. cities.

While gambling brings economic transformations, it also brings social changes. In Deadwood and the Colorado communities, a portion of gambling revenues goes for historic preservation. Since November 1989, Deadwood has received about $16 million for preservation efforts. Mark Wolfe, Deadwood historic preservation officer and city planner, notes that funds have gone to restore a library, museums, a train depot and a recreation center, among other historic preservation projects. The city also set up a revolving loan fund for private restoration efforts and a grants program for nonprofits. Wolfe believes gambling has been a plus for Deadwood historic preservation. He attributes Deadwood's success to the strict rules and review processes set up in the initial legislation authorizing Deadwood casinos. With more and more communities opting for gaming, "every community is going to have to fight to be something different. We're holding our own," Wolfe says. But he cautions that gambling has the potential to cause more damage than good for local communities. He notes that the National Park Service has placed the three

Colorado gambling towns on its list of most endangered historic landmarks because of the demolition of historic buildings and new construction associated with gambling.

Rapid development also created traffic and crime problems in Deadwood and the Colorado towns. In Black Hawk and Central City, traffic increased three-fold on canyon roads since gambling began, according to Stokowski. At the current pace, she says, the county will have more than 300 drunken driving arrests or citations in 1992, compared to 99 in 1991. And about 75 percent of all local police reports now are related to disturbances by casino patrons, Stokowski says. Air pollution, noise and litter also have increased. The Colorado Department of Health has ordered the three gambling towns to improve their overloaded sewer treatment plants, which are spilling pollutants into nearby mountain streams and the smell of raw sewage into the mountain air.

The riverboat gambling communities in Iowa and Illinois seem to have had fewer problems. Law enforcement officers in Alton, Ill., and Dubuque, Iowa, say they've had virtually no problems since riverboat gambling began. While traffic has increased in Alton, a spokesman from the city's police force says, "We've had no more calls from the riverboats than we would get from a K-Mart store." Speaker Arnould explains that the riverboat towns had experienced economic downturns, so there was plenty of empty space available to accommodate the visitors. Nor did riverboat gambling touch off a rapid inflation of real estate values, as it did in the Colorado towns and Deadwood, although it did boost the economy overall, notes Arnould.

Gambling's impact on communities differs, depending on geographic and demographic factors and on the type of gambling. According to Representative Joyce Hodges of South Dakota, the state lottery agency's introduction of video gambling machines statewide has had a pervasive negative influence in her small county. Even though the machines were originally intended to be only in bars, Hodges says, they ended up in any place holding a beer license, including family restaurants and convenience stores. Local business owners have told her they can detect video gambling cutting into their business. In addition, Hodges

> *Despite the risks, most gaming industry analysts forecast that gambling will continue to expand.*

claims that video gambling is "very, very addictive," particularly for young people, who have grown up with video games and computers. Individuals addicted to the machines, Hodges notes, cannot go to stores or restaurants without encountering their addiction. South Dakota voters did not envision this type of gambling when they amended the constitution to permit a lottery, she says. A citizen initiative gained enough signatures to earn a place on the November ballot, and if passed, will rid the state of the machines.

Valerie Lorenz, executive director of the National Center for Pathological Gambling, says, "There is no amount of money generated by gambling that would offset the costs to society." The costs are generated by problem gamblers and are measured in lost productivity at work, stolen money and taxes not paid, says Lorenz.

Lorenz says that while there are no long-term studies that definitively link increases in legal gambling to increases in the prevalence of compulsive gambling, there is evidence to suggest such a link. According to a study from the 1970s, she says, 1 percent of the U.S. population are compulsive gamblers, while the rate in Nevada is 2.5 percent. And today, Lorenz says, there's a new profile for the compulsive gambler. Since lotteries have come on the scene, a problem gambler is likely to be female, low income or minority and a loner addicted to playing the lottery. The typical problem gambler used to be a white male professional, 40 to 50 years old, hooked on racetracks or casinos, who at least initially had money to spend.

Lorenz doesn't necessarily advocate banning gambling, but she does believe every state should have a gaming commission and a gaming regulatory agency to research and mitigate the social problems associated with gambling. In addition, she says, every state should allocate funds for treating problem gambling. Currently, few states provide funding for such treatment. Iowa, an exception, designates 0.5 percent of lottery and riverboat gambling revenues for gambling education and treatment.

Speaker Arnould says that there is no strong indication that riverboat gambling has given rise to an increase in addictive gambling in Iowa. "Every state, whether they legalize gambling or not, has compulsive gamblers, but because of revenues from riverboat gambling we now have sufficient money for treatment."

A recent study in South Dakota emphasizes the difficulty of establishing social impacts of gambling. The study examined the sociological impact of all types of legal gambling in the state. The researchers looked at aid to dependent children and food stamp payments, child abuse and neglect and child support caseloads, divorce filings, property tax collections, bankruptcy and small claims filings, and real estate foreclosures. The study found significant increases in only two areas: chapter seven bankruptcy and small claims filings. But the researchers note that social changes take place more gradually than economic changes and require long-term study to establish firm causal relationships.

Despite the risks, most gaming industry analysts forecast that gambling will continue to expand. But it won't be profitable for everyone. Mary Ann Garfield, business director for Harvey's Resort Hotel and Casino, suggests policymakers consider several questions when considering gambling. "What strategic alternatives exist for you? If you chose gambling as a strategy, why did you? Are there options?" And, "If you choose casino gambling as a strategy and it fails for you, how do you get out of it and what are the exit costs? If concrete answers are not forthcoming, then your futures will be crafted haphazardly by circumstance—by people like me, and enterprises like mine, naturally taking advantage of opportunities to create our own futures."

The Tax the Public Loves to Hate

Although sometimes called unfair, the property tax stabilizes local finances and allows local governments to control their own affairs.

Ronald K. Snell

Ronald K. Snell is director of NCSL's fiscal affairs program.

When the president of the United States said he doesn't like broccoli, broccoli-haters everywhere took heart. Most Americans' attitude toward property taxes is about like President Bush's toward broccoli—best considered as compost. But the hard fact is that property taxes, like broccoli, are good for us. And while we can find substitutes for broccoli—the ever delightful brussels sprouts, cauliflower and spinach—there doesn't seem to be a substitute that will do the job of the property tax.

The property tax has two irreplaceable roles in America public affairs. First, it offsets the instability of the two other major state and local taxes—personal income and sales taxes. Income and sales tax collections wax and wane with the economy; the property tax's sluggish response to changing economic conditions helps maintain an even revenue flow. And second, in much of the United States, local governments' revenue from property taxes allows local citizens and local governments a degree of control over their own affairs that cannot exist otherwise.

Despite those roles, the public generally has considered the local property tax the "Worst Tax Except for the Federal Income Tax." When the Advisory Commission on Intergovernmental Relations began its annual survey of

public attitudes about taxes in 1972, a whopping 45 percent of participants declared that the local property tax was the worst tax of the possible choices—federal income, state income, state sales and local property. Reconsideration in 1973 brought the public around to the opinion it has held ever since: Except for the federal income tax, the local property tax is the least fair tax in the United States.

People who value fairness in taxation criticize property taxes because they bear no relation to people's ability to pay (ability to pay is usually considered a criterion of a good tax). The value of people's property, especially residential property, is not a key to their income, and elderly people especially can find that property taxes take a growing proportion of their income over time. Some people think it's just plain wrong to tax the unproductive bricks and boards that make up their houses.

Assessment practices and the length of time between assessments can make the tax unfair. Assessment is difficult, especially for properties that in any way are unusual. Market value is something that can only be guessed at until a property is sold. In addition, everyone has heard of assessors who manipulate values for reasons of their own. Elected assessors are said to be especially prone to do so, in order to stay in office.

Even with the fairest and least ambitious of assessors, problems can occur when years go by between assessments. Property values can grow slowly over the years, but the assessment reflects that growth only occasionally, so that

property owners are hit periodically by large and apparently arbitrary jumps in the taxable value of their property.

Differences between property taxes in different communities can undermine equity, fairness and hopes for economic development. When communities are forced to rely heavily on property taxes, communities with little taxable property suffer either from worse roads and schools than their neighbors or higher taxes or both. Such fiscal disparities are one of the major problems with the property tax, according to former St. Paul mayor George Latimer, now dean of the Hamline University School of Law: "Location ought not to control the level of social services." Reduction of such disparities is one reason for state aid to local governments or state assumption of former local services.

Every elected official is familiar with the disadvantages of the property tax, and all homeowners have felt the disadvantages at one time or another. But what can be said on the other side? Are there any reasons to preserve the traditional role of property taxes in state and local finance despite their bad press?

There are reasons to value the property tax. Some of them are fiscal, but the important ones are political—that is, they have to do with public policy. It is the political reasons that make the property tax truly irreplaceable in state and local government.

First, the fiscal reasons. Property taxes make up such a large part of state and local tax collections—over 30 percent—that any substantial reduction in property taxes takes either large reductions in government operations or large increases in other taxes. Where do those other taxes come from? The other taxes generally come from state government, which means that the blame for tax increases moves from local officials to state legislators and governors.

Nebraska, for example, has had two rounds of state tax increases in 1990 and 1991 in order to reduce residential and utility property taxes and to improve equity across the state. In 1990 the state increased state income taxes 17.5 percent and sales taxes 25 percent in order to provide 10 percent relief for property taxes. In 1991 the Legislature had to raise about $100 million in new state taxes to replace revenue lost because of a court decision requiring lower assessments of pipeline property. The state invented one new business tax—a surcharge of 2 percent on depreciation claimed on federal income tax returns—and raised other business taxes to make up the loss. So far the impact on business is unknown. Nebraska is a stark example of the magnitude of state tax increases it takes to cover significant property tax relief.

Nebraska faced the issue head on and raised state taxes to cover the lost local revenue that property tax reductions would mean. By contrast, California and Massachusetts over the years have discovered what happens if you reduce reliance on local property taxes without replacing the revenue.

In 1978 Californians amended their state constitution with Proposition 13, which capped property taxes at 1 percent of market value and limited increases to 2 percent a year until the property changed owners. The *California Journal* says that Prop 13 saves California homeowners and commercial property owners $15 billion a year—big money even in California.

But at what cost? Before Proposition 13 passed, counties spent about 30 percent of their budgets on "discretionary" items like libraries, parks and roads. The county supervisors' association reported that the percentage fell below 5 percent by 1988, because the counties' revenue had to meet obligations for law enforcement and public welfare. And over 10 years, property taxes fell from covering 52 percent of school district expenses to 19 percent. The state's share of school district funding rose from less than half to nearly three-quarters. The need for the state to replace property

taxes with general funds helped force the Legislature to increase various taxes by $7.3 billion in 1991. County governments and schools will get 75 percent of the increase ($3.5 billion more for schools than the year before, and over $2 billion more for county governments).

Massachusetts is another state where a local property tax limit has shifted the job of raising money from local governments to the legislature. In 1980 the voters used the initiative to pass a law capping the property tax, usually referred to as Prop 2-1/2. It has worked as intended to reduce the burden of property taxes. Local property taxes fell from $5.80 for every $100 of personal income in 1979 to $3.34 in 1989. Taxpayers were saving $2.8 billion a year by 1989, assuming that without Prop 2-1/2, property taxes would have claimed the same share of personal income in 1989 as in 1979.

Like California, Massachusetts achieved this miracle in part by shifting revenue raising from local governments to the state. State aid to local governments nearly tripled from 1979 to 1989, costing taxpayers $2.6 billion a year more in 1989 than in 1979. The tax burden shifted, almost dollar for dollar, from local property taxes to state sales and income taxes.

Some people might welcome that change, reasoning that state sales and income taxes show more growth than property taxes do and that many people consider sales and income taxes to be fairer than property taxes. But there's a downside too: The state governments that turn on the spigot of state aid can turn it right off again as well.

That's one of the ways state budgets got balanced in Massachusetts and New York in 1991—by cuts in aid to local government. Cities, counties, towns and school districts in those and other states see their fortunes rise and fall along with the vicissitudes of the state budget.

It's the same in California, where the governor and Legislature increased state sales and income taxes sharply to provide more aid to local governments. County officials in California think not enough was done, and they may be right. But in making that argument they are repeating a hard fact of life for California counties: They are at the mercy of state government finances. If California's fiscal crisis continues, state officials

might have to reconsider the decisions made in 1991.

And that's the real point about the irreplaceability of the property tax. Property taxes traditionally have protected the continuity of the basic services local governments provide—law enforcement and fire fighting, health and building codes, libraries, streets, parks and schools—the basic protections and structures of American community life. Senator Bob Jauch of Wisconsin says, "Locals can't depend on state and federal governments—they'll protect their own purses. Communities need their own sources of money." Representative Kitty Gurnsey of Idaho emphasizes how dependent local services are on property taxes. If a new property tax limit passes in Idaho, she predicts "there'll be a hue and cry for the state to take over senior citizens centers and youth programs and support to libraries."

Property taxes are ideal for funding basic services because property taxes are a stable revenue source—one that's there in bad years and good, not subject to rapid fluctuations because of a year's economic change. Richard Mattoon, an economist at the Federal Reserve Bank in Chicago, says that for Midwestern states the "relative stability of the property tax has proven to be an advantage during the recent recession."

A lot of the fiscal problems states have had in 1990 and 1991 have been due to the way personal income taxes, sales taxes and corporation income taxes respond to a recession. Collections fall fast. As soon as corporate profits decline, corporation income taxes go into freefall. Income tax collections drop as people are laid off or incomes are cut. Thrifty buying reduces sales tax collections.

Property taxes hold up better, providing, as Mattoon says, a "steady, sluggish revenue source for local governments." Even if property prices drop, there's a delay before property taxes reflect decreased market values. The property tax is unrivaled as the source of a steady revenue stream that can float local government services through good and lean times.

As a tax that belongs almost entirely to local government, it can provide independence for local governments as well as security. State and federal governments are suspect to many Americans. Mayor James Howaniec of Lewiston, Maine, says, "It seems that the further one gets from local government, the less accountable are the elected officials." Boston Mayor Raymond Flynn told Congress in February, "It's a lot different in the neighborhoods listening to the people than it is sitting in the statehouse listening to elected officials." Last winter when the White House floated a proposal to replace $15 billion in local government grants with new state block grants, New Orleans Mayor Sidney Barthelmy, president of the National League of Cities, responded that the proposal was unacceptable: "States' distribution of revenue does not meet the needs of municipalities and is often delayed before being allocated to us."

The frustration behind such mayoral remarks is at least partly due to the mayors' dependence on state and federal funding. That in turn is partly due to local governments' lack of taxing power, and that in turn to reduced reliance on property taxes. Maybe it's time to return responsibility for services and taxes to local governments through greater use of locally levied property taxes. That may be the best single way to make government responsive and answerable to the voters, and to make voters understand that services cost someone money.

This is not a suggestion that we go back to the days of 1902, when 86 cents out of every dollar state and local governments collected came from property taxes. That's plainly inappropriate in a post-industrial society where much wealth is intangible, where knowledge is as important a source of income as a broccoli farm or a two-family house.

Senator Jauch suggests an appropriate role for property taxes in today's system of state and local finance: It ought to be the foundation of the local revenue system, augmented by other kinds of taxes and state aid, but still the underpinning for necessary local services. George Latimer agrees; he points out the key is not to rely on the property tax so much that it creates serious fiscal disparities among communities.

Senator Jauch and former Mayor Latimer speak from experience in Wisconsin and Minnesota, where state governments have elaborate programs to limit the regressivity of property taxes. Minnesota refunds property tax payments to individual taxpayers based on their incomes, up to a maximum of $1,100. Wisconsin has an effective program for low-income taxpayers, although, Jauch notes, the property tax burden consequently is shifted to middle- and upper-income taxpayers. And, according to Jauch, the property tax credits have no political effect: "All people look at is their bill, not their credits."

It's pointless to hope that the property tax will ever be a popular tax, no matter how much is done to relieve burdens on low-income and elderly people; all that matters is that taxpayers tolerate it. It's important that they continue to do that.

The practice of decreasing local reliance on property taxes has meant more than relief to homeowners. It has imposed giant costs on state fiscal and political systems.

Reduced reliance on local property taxes increases the relative importance of state taxes that are just not as reliable a source of revenue when times get rough. That can mean tremendous threats for local governments if state budgets have to be cut.

Lawmakers at least should remember that every dollar they agree to send as a subsidy to local governments increases the likelihood of another tax vote in the legislature.

People who are concerned about the balance of authority among federal, state and local governments should remember that the power to tax is not just the power to destroy, as Justice John Marshall commented. The power to tax is also the power to create. Shifting the tax stream from local governments to state and federal governments shifts authority as well. Without a steady, reliable, strong flow of revenue, local governments cannot govern. And the best possible source of that power to govern is the property tax.

CRACKS IN THE CRYSTAL BALL

EILEEN SHANAHAN

Estimating revenue is as hard a job as there is in government. Come within 2 percent, and you can still be in trouble. But there are ways to improve the process.

Colorado's Curt Wiedeman sums up the realities of his professional life with a fatalism his peers will understand. "You're always going to be wrong," he says. "That's the one sure thing." Wiedeman is Colorado's chief revenue estimator.

His are hardly cheering thoughts, especially right now, as deadlines loom almost everywhere for making final decisions on next year's budget proposals and, with a little luck, the last major revisions of this year's, too. Perhaps Wiedeman is taking too much of the blame on himself, however, and on others like himself, because predicting what the economy will do is very hard, especially when it is moving from growth to recession, or vice versa. And that is only the first step. The more difficult task, nowadays, is converting the economic forecast into actual revenue estimates. Many old rules and formulas no longer apply.

In fact, revenue figures often miss by fairly small margins, frequently 2 percent or less in relatively stable times. That is not making such a bad job of it, given that the estimates must cover a fiscal year that will not end until a year and a half after the forecasts are made—two and a half years in the case of places with biennial budgets. Yet a mistake of that size often seems huge, to officials and the public alike, because it can force major cutbacks in spending. It hurts most when there is little or nothing in the bank to cushion the revenue shortfall, which is generally the case now.

When the criticisms come, estimators such as Wiedeman can plead that the problems are sometimes the fault of political interference with their revenue forecasts rather than bad estimates. That is true. They can plead that the huge annual spending increases that are now built into many state budgets far outweigh revenue-estimating errors as the cause of this year's widespread deficits and the pain of dealing with them. That is also true.

Nonetheless, budget professionals pretty much agree that the estimating process could be better than it is, and there is a major push to improve it right now in a variety of places. Many of the hoped-for improvements focus on gaining access to more detailed and more timely data. Others involve more sophisticated use of computers. Some are aimed at making it harder for elected officials to politicize the numbers.

That politics can intrude on the estimating process is a contention few deny. The past few budget seasons have produced some angry controversies over just that point. Maine was perhaps this year's prime example.

Steven Gold of the non-partisan Center for the Study of the States goes so far as to say that Maine "was the worst of the conspicuous cases where recent revenue estimates were warped by political considerations." He says Republican Governor John R. McKernan Jr. who faced a serious challenge in his campaign for a second term last year, "would have lessened his chances of re-election if he had been honest." Instead, Gold says, McKernan made "gargantuan revenue estimates, told the voters, 'We're all right, Jack,'" and right after the election, "Maine had to enact draconian budget cuts."

Charles Colgan, professor of public policy at the University of Southern Maine, defends McKernan, up to a point, at least. "If you look at the expert data in front of him at the time those estimates were made"—for example, the forecast of the New England Economic Project—"it did not show a rapid downturn in the Maine economy. Whether he exaggerated revenues deliberately or wanted to believe what the [computer] models were showing and deceived himself as much as anyone else, I don't know."

Richard L. Kaluzny, who is chief of New Jersey's Office of Tax Analysis, is not as generous in evaluating the performance of his state's former governor, Thomas H. Kean. "There weren't a whole lot of people who agreed" with the forecast of a big budget surplus that

Kean put out at the end of calendar 1990, Kaluzny says. "By that time, it was very clear we were in a recession. The legislature had predicted a deficit 10 months earlier." Kean wasn't even running for re-election, having already served the two terms that New Jersey permits. But Kean, perhaps in an effort to paint a flawless picture of his own accomplishments as governor, left a huge budget deficit for his Democratic successor, James J. Florio.

Gerald Miller, a respected budget specialist who formerly headed the National Association of State Budget Officers, complains that his state's former governor, Democrat James J. Blanchard, "dug an immense hole" for the man who defeated him, Republican John Engler, for whom Miller now works. In the past year, Michigan has had to revise Blanchard's final revenue estimate downward by more than $800 million—more than 10 percent. "If you could get people to tell you honestly what they knew in October of 1990," Miller says, "they probably knew three-quarters of that."

It is widely believed that mistakes in forecasting revenue always go in the same direction: they are too optimistic. The presumed motive is the desire of elected officials to increase spending, or at least to maintain it, at levels that a more realistic revenue forecast would not permit. But underestimates of revenue can be politically motivated, too. That is what is being said about Massachusetts now.

"Our economy really experienced a meltdown between the fall of 1990 and this spring," says James Wooster, chief economist in the Massachusetts Department of Revenue. "We just watched the revenues melt away. So the administration and the legislative leaders, for the first time in my memory, worked together to find a conservative estimate for '92, a safe estimate that wouldn't have to be revised down still another time." It is also true, others say, that the new Republican governor, William F. Weld, wanted a low revenue estimate as justification for some substantial spending cuts he wanted to make.

Ultimately, however, politics is only one of many reasons why revenue estimates go wrong. It is probably not the most pervasive reason. Overestimates consistently occur when the economy is sliding into a recession and underestimates when it is pulling out of one. It is simply hard to predict exactly when the economy will reach such turning points or how sharp the turn will be. Fiscal 1983 provides a famous instance of excessive pessimism by state estimators (which lasted into fiscal 1984 in many places), because the pace of the recovery from a major recession was underestimated.

Many states also underestimated their revenues for fiscal 1989, but for a different reason. That year, as any number of state budget officials insist on explaining, the commercial fore-

casting services that depend on giant computerized models of the national economy were warning that the long period of economic growth that had started in late 1982 must soon come to an end. But it didn't, not just then. The services, and the estimators who relied on them, were two years ahead of themselves.

When the proprietors of the econometric models recognized their error, they reversed course and overestimated economic growth—with near-disastrous results for many states' fiscal 1991 budgets. The problem was complicated further by the war in the Middle East, which so drastically affected consumer confidence and spending. But the fact is that the models missed the turning point, whereas many others—including economists at nine of the 12 regional Federal Reserve Banks, for example—saw a softening in the economy before Iraq ever invaded Kuwait.

State budget offices "all buy the same [econometric] forecasts," says Marcia Howard, research director of the National Association of State Budget Officers. "So when they're wrong, everybody's wrong."

Some old hands at state budgeting question the near-universal adherence to the forecasts of the econometric models—those of DRI/McGraw-Hill or the WEFA Group, or both—as the foundation for state (and some local) revenue estimates. In fact, many state officials say they continue to buy the

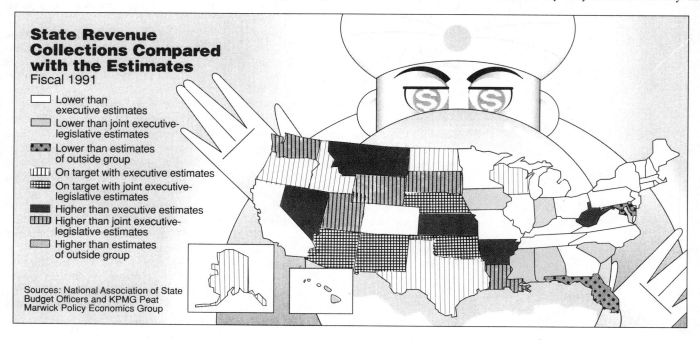

State Revenue Collections Compared with the Estimates
Fiscal 1991

☐ Lower than executive estimates
☐ Lower than joint executive-legislative estimates
▨ Lower than estimates of outside group
▥ On target with executive estimates
▦ On target with joint executive-legislative estimates
■ Higher than executive estimates
▦ Higher than joint executive-legislative estimates
▨ Higher than estimates of outside group

Sources: National Association of State Budget Officers and KPMG Peat Marwick Policy Economics Group

econometric services not so much for the forecasts as for the masses of data they provide and the software they get access to, which they then use in revising the models' forecasts.

"The major reason for bad estimates is the herd instinct," says Gerald Miller. "They have DRI and WEFA, and everybody buys in because it makes them feel more comfortable. They figure it won't be so hard to defend themselves when they're wrong if they can show they based their forecast on what the models were saying."

Miller thinks budget officials shouldn't be as timid as they are about deviating from the predictions the models come up with. "After all," he says, "the person that gets hurt when it's wrong is the governor."

The merits of econometric modeling aside, there's no doubt that arriving at sound revenue forecasts is harder than it used to be, whether or not a turning point in the economy is at hand.

"Economies are becoming so much more inter-dependent," says Kaluzny, the New Jersey tax analysis office chief. "It used to be, you just had to think about what was going on in your state and its neighbors. Now, it's your coast, or Ireland or Indonesia, or any place where there's cheap labor and good communications. And the taxes are getting more complicated. There are more opportunities for leakage—mail order sales, for one. And technological change. You can look at income and employment in your state and miss sales tax revenue by $100 million out of a total of $3 billion.

"Figuring corporate taxes was always hard," Kaluzny adds. "Profits fluctuate so. But now there are more and more problems of what gets allocated to your state. That depends, in part, on what's happening in other states. And the debt that's been piled up as a result of leveraged buyouts; that creates a big deduction against corporate income, far different in magnitude than it used to be."

There are still other reasons why a change in the economy of a state or locality doesn't translate into revenue the same way it once did. The increasing importance of both business and consumer services, which are not fully taxed in most places, is one. The growth in nontaxable deferred income and other employee benefits is another. Both of these developments alter the

linkage between economic improvement and tax receipts available for a government to spend.

And then there is always the oddball surprise. New Jersey got one when it changed its lottery rules, making it tougher to win so the games could offer larger prizes. State officials thought that would attract more betting and give the treasury a bigger take. It did the opposite.

Local governments, despite a general belief to the contrary, do not have it easy either when it comes to revenue estimating. Their main source of revenue, the property tax, is certainly more predictable than any of the other major taxes, those on personal income, corporate income or sales. Furthermore, property reassessments are generally done far enough in advance of budget time for up-to-date numbers to be used in working out the budget estimates.

But fluctuations in taxpayer delinquencies create a real problem. Allan Proctor, who heads the special New York state agency that keeps watch over the finances of New York City, says that "in bad times, people get what amounts to a loan from the government by not paying their property tax," even though the interest rate is a high 18 percent. So it is becoming a challenge, in bad times, to predict the amount of revenue that will be flowing in even from this most stable of tax sources.

Proctor wishes the state would give him more detail about the sales taxes it collects for local governments. "We need to know why sales tax collections have slipped—what kinds of things aren't selling as well? In what areas?— so we can make a better estimate next year," he says. Some of the 24 states that collect all sales taxes for their localities do provide this information, but many simply distribute the tax back to the localities on the basis of population, and don't know themselves, in any detail, what was sold where.

New York state's commissioner of taxation and finance, James W. Wetzler, says his agency may have the

ability to give Proctor what he wants in a couple of years, when it completes its long-term computer modernization program. But the main goal of upgrading the computers is to improve the state's ability to audit returns and collect unpaid taxes, he says. "Just improving data in a way that has no impact on audit or collections will come last."

Almost everywhere, the report card on revenue estimating says: Needs Improvement. Efforts to raise the grade are under way in many places.

One major trend is toward getting more input into the estimating process, particularly from business executives and others outside of government. "It used to be that the entire economic forecast was done by one person or a small group," says Harley Duncan, executive director of the Federation of

It's harder for politicians to disguise problems when the public knows what they've been told by outside groups.

Tax Administrators. "That worked pretty well when times were more stable." But not, he implies, anymore.

Calling in business leaders, and the economists who work for them, isn't just a matter of getting their opinions. It is the information they have, often long before the government gets it, that can be valuable. Colorado's Wiedeman notes that telephone companies "are counting their new hookups day by day; they tend to see things early. And power companies are forecasting their future loads all the time." He also talks formally with officials from the larger cities around the state. "They tell us about their building permits and employment trends." And local governments, which in Colorado collect sales taxes for themselves, can supply that information.

Business executives of all kinds "see their sales reports every single day," says Michigan's Miller. "And they're making decisions about capital expansion. You really need to talk to them at least a couple of times a year. They know what the people with the econometric models aren't picking up yet." Miller thinks it's best to talk to the business executives behind closed doors "because, especially if things are bad, they don't want to tell the truth in public."

James A. Zingale of Florida's Department of Revenue believes, on the other hand, that the public must be able to hear the discussions between state officials and their outside information sources—which is, in fact, required under Florida law. "What we're fighting against is the purely political forecast," he says. "Politicians are inclined to disguise problems in the hope that they'll go away." It's harder for them to do that if the public knows what they've been told by outside advisory groups.

Behind closed doors or out in the open, the use of outside advisers has one widely recognized defect: the more people involved in the process, the greater the tendency to compromise different views and arrive at a centrist position, whether or not that makes the most economic sense. "A consensus forecast is going to be less accurate, on the average, than a good single forecast," says Harley Duncan.

State and local governments are also doing more data collection on their own, and trying to improve their ability to analyze it. Linda Savitsky, director of finance for Groton, Connecticut, is trying to improve her analyses by "taking a hard look at longer-term historical patterns—not just back one or two years." Among the things she's trying to figure out is exactly how underlying economic conditions affect consumer use of "the softer services, like recreation and counseling," and thus affect the fees those services bring in.

Virginia, whose budget was clobbered this year by one of the country's worst real estate collapses, has launched a major effort to improve its forecasting. "We don't need more econometric models," says Secretary of Finance Paul W. Timmreck. "We need to disaggregate the Virginia forecast, to spot the regional trends earlier. And we need to disaggregate by business group. For example, sales of construction materials fell 16.9 percent in fiscal '91 compared with '90. We're going to gather that data more frequently, because we need to do a better job of monitoring and spotting the early warnings."

As part of its early warning system, Virginia is arranging to collect information from its larger cities on meal and lodging tax receipts. And the state has signed a contract with a professor at the College of William and Mary for an analysis of the impact of defense spending on Virginia's economy.

What will all this data collection and analysis cost, including a staff increase of two professionals? Timmreck says he's going to be spending some $400,000 this year for revenue estimating, which is $180,000 more than last year. It can be hard to convince legislators that it's worth spending that kind of money. "It's seen as a frill," says New Jersey's Kaluzny. "But not spending it is like flying a 747 without fixing the altimeter."

Many states formally include the legislature in the revenue-estimating process, though the details of how they do it and just who is involved differ substantially. Unfortunately, there's little evidence that either involving the legislature or using outside experts in a formal way yields more accurate results with any consistency.

The latest fiscal survey by the National Association of State Budget Officers shows that the fiscal 1991 revenue estimates of only nine of the 50 states were close enough to actual collections to be called "on target." Of the 14 states with a formal process for involving the legislature in reaching a consensus estimate, three were on target—a proportion that is barely better than the national average. Of the four states using a formal outside estimating group, none came in on target. (See graphic.)

There are reasons beyond simple arithmetic for adopting better means of estimating revenue.

"Nine times in ten," says New Jersey's Kaluzny, "when presented with a choice among a high forecast, a low and a most-likely forecast, a governor will pick the high or the middle one, though the greatest risk is in ignoring the possibility of the low estimate coming true. Excellent data has to be one key to convincing the governor to take the 30 percent risk of disaster seriously."

Michael O'Keefe, who used to work for a Republican governor of Kansas and now works for the Democratic governor of Rhode Island, thinks it is important to establish a system that requires the legislature and the governor to use the same estimates. "You must do all you can to give the widest body of people confidence in the numbers—and that very much includes the public as well as the legislature. People need to have assurance that even if the number is wrong, no one is getting a tactical advantage. It allows the legislature and the governor to work on the budget.

"Besides," he adds, "I'm troubled by the fact that because the numbers have been so bad for so long in Washington, people think that's the way it is in the states, too. That's not so."

Means Testing: Two Dirty Words We Need to Learn

PENELOPE LEMOV

The senior citizens of Philadelphia depend heavily on mass transit, and for most of the day they can ride it free. But when rush hour starts, the rules change. Those senior citizens who are poor still get a free pass. Those who aren't needy pay full fare, just like everybody else.

Philadelphia has been using a means test for its mass transit subsidy since 1989. It was not easy to enact, given the size and clout of the elderly population, but the threat of fiscal disaster got it through. It is now saving the city $4 million a year.

Milwaukee is means-testing its new school choice program. The state provides a subsidy for students from poor neighborhoods who choose to enroll at an approved private school. The "vouchers" are the equivalent of cash. But more affluent children can't use them. If they want to switch from public to private education, they have to do it with their own money.

Montana and Louisiana are two states that offer residents a homestead exemption from property tax liability. Montana exempts the first $80,000 in assessed value; Louisiana exempts the first $75,000. The means-tested Montana program, limited to those whose annual income is less than $15,000, costs the state $1.75 a person. The Louisiana program, available to rich and poor alike, costs $18.65 a person—$78 million a year out of a financially squeezed state budget.

It's good politics to make government help available to rich and poor alike. But we may not be able to afford it much longer.

Given the political danger of withdrawing benefits from the elderly or any other group of citizens already possessing them, it would be foolish to declare that the hour of means testing has arrived. This year's presidential candidates have been reluctant even to utter the words. But that the time is coming seems more and more clear. State and local governments, like the federal government, are currently spending billions of dollars every year giving benefits to people with no demonstrated need for them. Giving affluent people tax credits to buy home insulation is similar to giving them a government check—to do something they can likely afford to do on their own. It deserves the same sort of scrutiny that the check would receive. No matter how sensitive the issue of means testing might be, there is too much money involved for governments not to begin to take it more seriously.

One who takes the idea very seriously is Elizabeth Reveal, who was finance director in Philadelphia when that city means-tested its transit sub-

sidy, and is now finance director in Seattle. "One of the emerging issues of state and local government finance," she says, "is that the wealthy are a lot better off in the state and local tax system and enjoy a higher level of consumption of services for their relatively low investment. I don't think we can afford to keep giving breaks to those already getting a break."

Others argue that, politically risky as it may be to impose a means test on a popular program, the alternatives may be riskier. "When states want measures that are not so controversial," says Steven Gold, director of the Center for the Study of the States, "means testing might be less painful than an overt tax rate increase. Incidentally, it also may be good tax policy."

Unlike the federal government, state and local governments do not offer on their own that many direct subsidies or services that lend themselves to means testing. But there is one area in which the failure to impose a means test is costing these governments a fortune: taxes.

A few states have begun to apply some scrutiny to the exemptions they carve out of their income tax collection. Minnesota and Iowa phase out child care credits at high income levels. California phases out all its personal tax credits for high-income taxpayers. New York State is phasing out itemized deductions for higher-income taxpayers, and Wisconsin does the same with its standard deduction.

But it is retirement income—specifically Social Security payments and pension income—that could be the most important means-testing battleground in the states in the 1990s. Senior citizens are not the only beneficiaries of non-means-tested tax benefits, but they are, along with veterans and the disabled, among the biggest ones.

When the federal government pioneered its landmark entitlement programs during the 1930s, the idea was to be inclusive: Social Security was designed to offer a floor of protection against destitution in old age. So it provides benefits to all comers who pay into the system, even if they are millionaires in their retirement years. In this way, political support for the program flows from a wide base. Everyone owns a piece of the program; everyone is willing to invest in it. Support for Social Security has, accordingly, held steady over the years.

As late as the 1960s, there did not seem to be any real fairness problem. A disproportionate number of elderly people were still living in poverty, despite the existence of Social Security. In 1969, 25 percent of American elderly met the official definition of poor, where only 14 percent of children under the age of 18 did.

Since then, however, helped not only by Social Security but by Medicare and a variety of other programs at the federal and state level, elderly people have improved their economic position dramatically. In 1990, the percentage of elderly living in poverty was roughly half that of 1969—only 12 percent. Today, though many elderly continue to struggle, more than 20 percent of the annual benefits paid out through Social Security go to households with incomes in excess of $50,000 a year. As the population ages, these across-the-board benefits will become a much more significant drain on revenue.

And as elderly voters increase their clout at the voting booth—the number of Americans aged 55 or older will increase 11 percent during the 1990s, compared with 7 percent for the general population—the political possibility of imposing a means test on any popular but unaffordable benefit program may evaporate. "It may be now or never," says Steve Gold, "if we want to reform this area."

What happens to Social Security payments is mostly the federal government's business. But there is real money in retirement income for governments at every level. In the 1980s, when Minnesota tightened up its means test for income tax exclusions available to senior citizens, the state came out around $50 million a year to the good.

Since 1983, all states have had the right to tax Social Security benefits, as the federal government does to a very limited extent. Most states have ignored this opportunity to recapture revenue from affluent pensioners. Of the 41 states with broad-based income taxes, 19 piggyback on federal policies and tax a portion of Social Security income. The rest do not.

As to pensions and other retirement income beyond Social Security, a survey by Keith Carlson, a fiscal analyst for Minnesota's Senate tax committee, found 17 states offer tax exemptions of one sort or another. They range from North Carolina's $2,000 pension exclusion to unlimited exclusions in four states—Alabama, Hawaii, Illinois and Pennsylvania.

States were given an opportunity to revisit this issue three years ago, when the U.S. Supreme Court ruled that it was discriminatory for them to offer pension exclusions to their state and local employees while taxing federal government retirees at the regular rate. The 16 states that were doing this could have seized on the chance to rewrite their tax laws and offer the exclusion to government retirees—or all retirees—on a much stricter means-tested basis.

What they did instead was generally the opposite. They broadened the exclusion. There are now unlimited exclusions for all government retirement income in such states as Kansas, Kentucky, Louisiana, Massachusetts, Michigan and New York. Maryland and Colorado are also exceedingly generous in the amount of pension income that can be earned tax-free. Missouri, on the other hand, does limit its exclusion to those with income under $25,000.

The American Association of Retired Persons, the leading interest group of the organized elderly, remains adamantly opposed to means-testing either Social Security itself or the other pension benefits that older people receive. "Support for programs that are means-tested, such as Medicaid, tends to disintegrate more rapidly," says David Certner, a lobbyist for the AARP. "Social Security is a program that's so important to so many people that we really can't afford to have people lose faith in that system."

And Certner argues that no matter how much money a retired person may have, a pension is nearly always a fixed income—it loses its purchasing power with inflation. Over a period of 10 years or so—and most retirees live a good deal longer than that after retiring—a pension can lose half of its purchasing power, Certner says. "The exemption from taxation is," he concludes, "an understanding that those on wages can increase their incomes but those on fixed [incomes] see their incomes go the other way."

Many legislators, however, make a different argument: that if the elderly live on fixed incomes, they also have the highest discretionary income of any group in the society. Dean Conley, Ways and Means chairman of the Ohio House, would apply means testing to the property tax. "It makes no sense," argues Conley, "to give blanket property tax breaks across the board to all senior citizens when some are wealthy."

Forty-five states currently offer property tax relief in the form of homestead exemptions, which are a flat amount off a tax bill—usually a portion of the assessed value of the property. These exemptions often target the elderly, the disabled and veterans, although nearly one-half of the states make some sort of exemption available to all homeowners.

Most homestead exemptions were adopted in the 1930s when the Depression threatened property owners with loss of their homes. They were expanded after World War II to provide more generous benefits for veterans, and particularly disabled veterans. The exemptions were expanded again in the 1960s and 1970s to include a broader range of homeowners. At that time several states began imposing income tests to target the tax relief to low-income homeowners. According to a survey by the National Conference of State Legislatures, 19 states now means-test their homestead exemptions. Twenty-six do not (see map).

It isn't easy to change these programs. When Buddy Roemer became governor of Louisiana in 1988, he tried to lower his state's $75,000 homestead exemption to $50,000. Since any taxpayer living in a house valued at

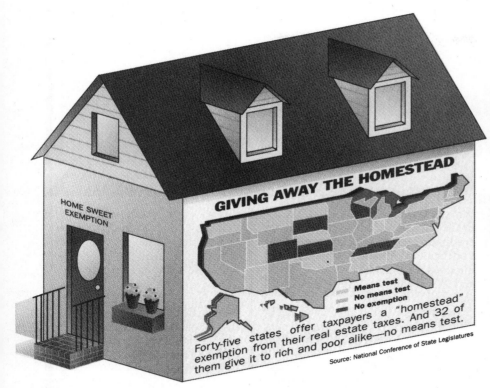

GIVING AWAY THE HOMESTEAD

HOME SWEET EXEMPTION

Means test
No means test
No exemption

Forty-five states offer taxpayers a "homestead" exemption from their real estate taxes. And 32 of them give it to rich and poor alike—no means test.

Source: National Conference of State Legislatures

$75,000 or less was absolved from paying property taxes, 85 percent of Louisiana's homeowners were not contributing to the tax base at all. But lowering the exemption would have taken a constitutional amendment, and Roemer was not able to get a majority of his constituents—many of whom benefited from the exemption—to go for it.

Many states have another property-tax break that *is* means-tested: the circuit breaker. Typically, it factors property tax against homeowner income and, like the electrical circuit wiring for which it is named, offers relief when there's an overload. The higher the tax and the lower the income, the more the relief. Most circuit breakers came into being in the 1970s; they tend to target the elderly and the disabled because they are the ones most often stuck using fixed incomes to pay rising property taxes.

Opting for circuit breakers rather than homestead programs does move the subsidy closer to the need, and there were minor expansions of circuit-breaker relief during the 1980s. But in the current fiscal climate, NCSL reports, further action along these lines is doubtful, and some cutbacks are possible. States that contemplate new circuit-breaker programs may be forced to raise other taxes in order to pay for them.

More likely are efforts to use means testing as a way of recovering more sales tax revenue. When states choose

not to impose a sales tax on food, as two-thirds of them do not, they make that decision in an effort to relieve low-income families of a regressive tax burden. But everyone benefits from the break—including those who can afford lobster and caviar. States could deal with this problem in a more rational way by taxing everyone for all the food they buy and then offering an income tax credit for low income residents. Hawaii and New Mexico already do this.

"Twenty to 30 percent of our food is purchased by visitors," says Richard F. Kahle Jr., the tax director for Hawaii. "We couldn't let that get away." Everybody who buys groceries in Hawaii forks over 4 percent of their bills to the state. Those below a certain income level get a rebate at the end of the year.

In New Mexico, where there is a food and medical-services rebate on sales taxes for low-income residents, the means-tested programs are part of what Laird Graeser, the state's director of tax research, calls "fighting to keep what tax base we have." The rebate is administered through personal income tax credits. "We don't ask retailers to make distinctions on what foods are taxable," Grraeser says. "Everything is." Even after the rebate is factored in, the sales tax on food provides New Mexico with about $78 million a year, or nearly 8 percent of the total sales tax collected in the state. That is money

that many other states are allowing to slip away.

So far, Hawaii and New Mexico are not generating too many imitators. But that could change. "I think we'll see more of this going on as states try to raise revenue by broadening their sales taxes," predicts Robert Cline, director of tax research for Minnesota's Department of Revenue. "They're going to have to be more creative about alternative ways of lowering taxes on low-income people."

For local governments, the same arguments ring true on the spending side. Many basic services that are provided free of charge could be means tested.

Several localities impose user fees for parks and recreation, and then provide means-tested relief from those fees. Some, such as Bloomington, Indiana, provide free swimming and tennis lessons for those who meet income-eligibility requirements. Others have found less cumbersome ways of offering free services to those who can't afford to pay. Some cities, for instance, apply a means test to recreation without actually forcing residents to provide details about their income. They simply charge less for recreational activities at parks in low-income neighborhoods than they do in the more affluent parts of town.

Is all this nickel and diming worth it? Probably not, if it's truly just nickels and dimes. The cost of administering a means test can be higher than the money saved. And the application of an income test has to make sense. "You can't ask people sitting in a city park for last year's income statement," says Seattle's Reveal. "The transaction cost-benefit is not there."

But it is not really nickels and dimes. No one knows for sure how much revenue could be raised by state and local government through the application of means testing, but on retirement income alone it is billions of dollars — and that does not even take in property tax relief and sales tax exemptions, let alone the means testing of services and direct subsidies such as those offered for mass transit.

"There just is not enough money," Reveal argues, "for governments to subsidize folks who don't need it. My father, who's an affluent resident of Philadelphia, rides the bus for free. That's ridiculous. And he thinks so, too."

The Third Wave of Economic Development

State policymakers are beginning to ask what really matters in economic development.

Dan Pilcher

Dan Pilcher is NCSL's economic development specialist.

In Wichita, Kan., a shortage of skilled machinists leads 33 aerospace subcontractors, helped by a state grant, to begin an apprenticeship program with area community colleges.

The Iowa Economic Development Department encourages the "clustering" of rural communities to work on economic development. The department helps small towns analyze their needs and solve mutual problems together.

Oregon measures its movement toward its stated economic, social and community goals through a "Benchmark" of more than 150 indicators.

These three examples illustrate principles that some experts say underlie the emerging "Third Wave" in economic development, which, since late 1990, has come to frame a lively debate about the future of state programs for economic growth.

The major strategies of the Third Wave are all long-term investments. Investments in people through education and workforce skills. Investments in distressed communities through help for the people and businesses in those communities. Investments in programs that encourage business and local government to work together.

The dilemma of the states' painful fiscal crunch and their deep worries about global economic competition is leading to the closest examination in more than a decade of what constitutes effective state economic development.

The Third Wave is a label coined by Bob Friedman of the Corporation for Enterprise Development (CFED), a Washington, D.C.-based research and consulting firm. Third Wave principles are also being applied to education,

> If "government is the answer to all problems" is the thesis, and if "government is the source of all problems" is the antithesis, then the Third Wave is the synthesis. It is a rethinking of what government can do and cannot do, and how it can do it more effectively. We've got to get smart.
> —R. Scott Fosler, Committee for Economic Development

school-to-work transition (including apprenticeship programs) and workforce training.

For the last decade and a half, when a state went into recession its legislature and governor invariably increased spending for economic development and adopted new programs. This changed in 1991. Legislatures in Illinois, Iowa, Kansas and North Carolina, for example, cut the budgets of economic development agencies and programs. Iowa cut its department by 30 percent. The Illinois legislature reduced the budget of the Department of Commerce and Community Affairs 40 percent, from $90 million to $51 million, resulting in the layoff of 108 staff. And Michigan is considering cutting its Commerce Depart-

ment—and thus its innovative programs—by 75 percent.

In other states, economic development fared better. For example, the Pennsylvania legislature increased program spending 32 percent, from $136 million to $180 million. Oregon is drawing national attention for its steps to reform education and the workforce and for being the first state to embrace explicitly the notion that its economic development effort should assist critical industries to help themselves become more competitive in the global economy.

This new way of looking at economic development concentrates on substance and how programs and services are delivered. It calls for a radical restructuring of state programs that includes the following principles to increase scale, quality and accountability:
• Relying on competition to ensure quality services from different public and private providers instead of relying on government as the sole supplier of services.
• Providing automatic feedback from businesses and communities.

• Providing comprehensive services at the local level.

• Using incentives to encourage clusters of firms to build their competitiveness and capacity to do business.

• Encouraging relationships between service providers and the communities and businesses who need them.

At this point, the Third Wave seems less a solidified theory of economic development and human investment than an emerging set of principles to guide lawmakers and others as they examine how to restructure state government and programs.

Some critics of the Third Wave say it doesn't help distressed rural and urban areas and poor people. The Third Wave focuses on how to deliver economic development programs, says consultant Brandon Roberts, "but—unstated and unquestioned—is the issue of 'to what end?'"

Brian Bosworth, a consultant and former president of the Indiana Economic Development Council, defines the traditional goals of economic development as increasing the standard of living, promoting equity and broadening the distribution of wealth, creating different paths of economic opportunity and choice for different people, and enhancing people's hope of improving their economic future.

In general, the new efforts under way involve a markedly different role for state government than in the past. For example, in Oregon the legislature created a special committee on the wood products industry that met with firms and developed legislation to help the industry help itself become more competitive.

Some states work through intermediary organizations. In Pennsylvania, the state's Manufacturing Innovation Networks program and nine Industrial Resource Centers have nurtured the growth of flexible manufacturing networks in critical industries. Florida and Massachusetts give money to community organizations that provide neighborhood residents with housing, job training and business assistance. The Texas international trade office helped establish more than 20 community offices that promote the export of Texas products.

To keep the state focused on a long-term vision and goals, at least four

This is Third Wave

Examples of economic development programs in both Europe and the United States that appear to deserve the Third Wave label include the following:

• The northern Italian region of Emilia Romagna, once among the poorest of that country, has relied on service centers for specific industries and business networks (machining and textiles, for example) to improve the competitiveness of small firms.

The nine service centers provide small firms and their networks with information and help in product design, marketing and technology transfer. Each non-profit center was created by a consortia of firms with help from ERVET, a quasi-public agency established by the regional government. The result has been that in 30 years Emilia Romagna has jumped from 17th to second in per capita income of Italian regions.

For example, in Modena about a half-dozen small firms work together to produce robots used in the manufacture of automobile engines. One business coordinates production while the individual firms contribute steel fabrication, knowledge of the market and customers' needs, electronic con-

trols and systems design.

• In the United States, at least 50 flexible manufacturing networks now exist in 14 states. A flexible manufacturing network is simply a group of small- or medium-sized firms that decide to cooperate in order to increase their competitiveness by attaining a goal that they cannot reach individually. Collaboration can mean many things, from sharing market information or working jointly on a project to training workers or sharing in the purchase of a new production machine. The industries range from heat treating in Ohio and machine tools in Pennsylvania to defense contracting in Montana and metal working in Arkansas.

• In North Carolina, the Rural Economic Development Center is a private non-profit organization established by the legislature. The center, funded by the legislature with $2 million per year, has raised $2.5 million from the private sector. Its programs include improving the quality of education, venture capital, rural leadership, capital financing for women and minorities, community development corporations, a micro-enterprise loan fund and flexible manufacturing networks.

states—Indiana, Kansas, Oklahoma and Oregon—have placed strategic economic development plans in permanent, quasi-public commissions.

To encourage grassroots action, Iowa, Kansas, North Carolina and Oregon give local communities money and assistance to develop and implement their own plans.

American state policymakers and economic development experts have been studying the success of the regional economies of Baden-Wurttemberg in Germany, Jutland in Denmark, Smaaland in Sweden and Emilia Romagna in Italy for several years.

The secret to the prosperity of these

regions "has been the broad recognition by business that cooperation is essential to competitiveness in an international economy," says C. Richard Hatch of the New Jersey Institute of Technology.

"The key unit of production is no longer the individual company but a decentralized network of companies," Robert Howard, associate editor of the *Harvard Business Review*, wrote recently. "These networks make possible continual innovation through a delicate balance of competition and cooperation, demands and supports." These networks can be found in Japan, Europe and California's Silicon Valley.

To help businessmen create and benefit from such networks, a new institutional context, a new kind of infrastruc-

The First and Second Waves

Bob Friedman and Doug Ross of the Washington, D.C.-based Corporation for Enterprise Development have characterized state economic development efforts as having three waves or phases.

Mississippi started modern state economic development (the First Wave) in 1936 with industrial recruitment, known as smokestack chasing, to lure branch plants down from the industrialized North.

Since then, recruitment has relied on such programs as national advertising, tax incentives, customized job training and subsidized infrastructure. As the economic woes of the United States worsened in the late 1970s, recruitment spread to states outside the South.

In the last decade, for a variety of reasons, recruitment has become perhaps the most widely debated part of state economic development. Critics have long questioned the effectiveness of recruitment programs and incentive packages because, according to several studies, state incentives are far down the list of what is most important to a business when deciding on a site.

Recruitment, though, is still alive and well, especially in the case of facilities that employ large numbers of people. State and local governments in 11 states, including Colorado, Indiana, Kentucky and Oklahoma, assembled incentive packages that run into the hundreds of millions of dollars to try to land a new $1 billion United Airlines maintenance facility.

Beginning in the late '70s and early '80s, a growing number of legislators and governors realized that most new jobs—80 percent to 90 percent—come from existing and new businesses.

Meanwhile, by 1980, 70 percent of U.S. products faced foreign competition within the nation's borders. Technology, workforce quality, capital, global market knowledge and customer service were the new factors in competitive advantage, as Japan and West Germany vividly demonstrated.

This led states to the "Second Wave": concentrating efforts on business activity within their borders. This label is applied to state programs in such areas as exporting, capital finance, managerial and technical assistance, workforce training, entrepreneurial development, technology innovation and deployment, product development and so forth across most major areas of business activity.

By fiscal 1988, the states were spending more than $1 billion on a bewildering array of programs, according to the National Association of State Development Agencies. About two-thirds of state economic development agencies were spending more on bolstering indigenous firms than on recruiting outside ones. Ross, a former Michigan Commerce Department director, likens the array of state programs offered to businesses to the offerings on a restaurant menu: "Please take one."

States found themselves under almost irresistible political pressure to adopt new programs if other states—especially those nearby—had adopted them.

Moreover, in the early and mid-1980s, most states undertook major investment and reforms in education, infrastructure, environment, taxes, workers' compensation and regulations. Motivated by worries over changes in the structure of the American economy and the effects of international competition, governors and legislators aimed these systemic efforts not at individual firms but at the state's economic foundation.

Second Wave initiatives sought to fill perceived market gaps and imperfections through government programs that directly provided economic development services to individual businesses. These services, however, were scattered across state departments and among divisions within departments, and they often operated independently from each other. In addition, they were usually based in the state capital, thus not easily accessible to firms across the state.

By the late 1980s, a number of states, legislators, program evaluation staff and others were increasingly troubled not only by sticky problems of how to measure the results of economic development programs but the inability of these efforts to make a real difference in the state's economy.

The most important criticism of Second Wave programs is that even if they work well, they may have only a marginal impact on a state's economic base because they lack sufficient scale to transform a state's economy substantially.

"On average, a state's economic development effort will affect only about 1 percent of the firms within the state," said Brian Bosworth, former president of the Indiana Economic Development Council.

"The states have a wealth of economic development models," said Bill Nothdurft, a public policy consultant, "but none of them is funded sufficiently to really make a difference."

---

ture is needed, according to Howard. State government, trade associations, labor unions, and other groups can play a role in creating this new infrastructure.

Helping communities and firms organize to help themselves by helping each other will not be easy for state policymakers. Competition, not cooperation, has long been the hallmark of relations among localities and businesses.

"The biggest [U.S.] institutional limitation—compared to our international competitors—is the weakness of trade associations, which view themselves as lobbyists rather than service providers to their member firms," said Anne Heald, program officer for the German Marshall Fund of the United States. The National Tooling and Machining Association, for instance, which has helped 20 of its 50 local chapters develop flexible manufacturing networks, is one of the few national trade groups that promote networking. Trade associations in Japan and Europe are more apt to provide services such as market information, sharing of technology and workforce training, to their members to improve their global competitiveness.

Beyond the issue of helping those

who will help themselves lies the question for state policymakers of political and financial accountability of Third Wave programs.

In the past, lawmakers exerted control over public spending by placing programs within state agencies. For legislators and governors, political accountability—in the sense of claiming credit for creating programs, appropriating funds and controlling the money and the programs—was inherent in most early economic development.

How to evaluate the tax money spent on Third Wave programs and private or quasi-public organizations is a thorny issue. Political control over the new round of efforts will likely be tenuous for governors and legislators.

Some legislators will be concerned that surrendering control of the purse strings for even a quasi-public organization may invite misuse of the funds. In many states, however, legislators serve on the boards of these agencies and can thus exert their influence on behalf of public policy and accountability. The legislature still holds the power of the purse if the agency depends on a regular appropriation.

In short, legislators and governors will have to confront the choice of relinquishing direct administrative and financial control if they want to reap the possible benefits of Third Wave programs. In theory at least, the new way of looking at economic development holds the potential for a greater political constituency to support it if groups of communities and key industries can be mobilized to help themselves.

In state after state, there is a growing consensus that improving the quality of the state's workforce will improve its competitiveness in the long run. "The challenge of economic competitiveness is the challenge of competence," says Bill Nothdurft, a public policy consultant who has studied European education and workforce training systems. "To the extent that there is a secret weapon in Europe's rise in international competitiveness, it is that they are continuing to produce a steady stream of highly skilled, motivated, educated and competent workers."

Friedman of CFED says that one goal of the Third Wave should be to offer people incentives and resources to

Oregon Looks to Europe for a Model

Oregon is gaining national attention for undertaking a new approach to economic development that encourages small businesses in the same industry to work together to become competitive in the global market.

Oregon's economy, based heavily on timber and agriculture, faces significant declines because of concern for the environment, which includes protecting endangered species such as the spotted owl and the native salmon. The future of Oregon's economy, therefore, depends on its ability to add value to a limited or even declining resource base.

With help from the German Marshall Fund of the United States and the Northwest Policy Center at the University of Washington, a group of Oregon and Washington legislators, economic development officials and business leaders in September 1989 examined Western European programs. The Oregon team paid particular attention to Italy, where flexible manufacturing networks—groups of small firms cooperating to compete effectively in global markets—have driven the economic resurgence of several regions.

Denmark also provided a model for Oregon's plan. The Danes have made small business networks the centerpiece of their national strategy to compete in the 1992 single market of the European Community.

"In Denmark, we saw an impressive program to make small businesses internationally competitive by encouraging cooperation in international

marketing," said Senator Wayne Fawbush, co-chair of the legislature's Joint Trade and Economic Development Committee. Denmark established a program of network brokers, who bring together firms to define and solve common problems and offer feasibility grants of up to $10,000 to groups of three firms.

The American delegation noted that the best European programs:
• Emphasize individual industries, not individual businesses.
• Focus on services such as market information and new technologies that improve the competitiveness of firms, instead of government subsidies.
• Encourage businesses to manage and finance these services.

During the 1991 session, the Oregon legislature, using some of these ideas, created a wood products competitiveness corporation to encourage businesses in the timber industry to work together. The corporation, composed of industry representatives, will receive $2.25 million from the state to encourage small groups of firms (networks) to solve mutual problems. Firms in the network might share the cost of acquiring a new production process or training their workforce, the cost of common services such as marketing and accounting, and work together to produce a product.

"The legislature," says Fawbush, "expects this independent quasi-public corporation to fashion a strategy for competitiveness that addresses the industry's needs and gets wide participation from firms throughout the state."

support themselves and their families through jobs or their own businesses.

"Think of the policies in American history that have generated significant, widespread, long-term economic growth," says Friedman. "They are policies like the GI Bill and the Homestead Act—democratic investments in the common genius of the American people." The Third Wave must have modern versions of such policies, he says.

Is the Third Wave a breakthrough in economic thinking, or just a new way of looking at old economic development techniques?

Whatever the answer, one thing is clear: The field is in lively ferment and accepted approaches are being challenged. The model that emerges will probably define in large measure state economic development for the 1990s and into the 21st century.

TAXES AND THE WEALTH OF STATES

Richard Vedder

Richard Vedder is professor of economics at Ohio University. He is coauthor with Lowell Gallaway of Out of Work: Unemployment and Government in 20th Century America *(Holmes and Meier, 1993).*

In the lifetimes of readers of this article, state and local governments in America have grown enormously in size and scope. In the 1980s alone, state and local governmental expenditures more than doubled. While various means have been used to finance this activity, the dominant one is taxation. State and local taxes have grown with government. Before the 1930s, the typical state had neither an income nor a sales tax, whereas today most states have both. Do these increasingly important taxes affect our rate of economic progress? In short, do taxes matter? The answer clearly is "yes," confirmed by a large and growing body of research conducted over the past two decades.

The tax-growth relationship is usually demonstrated by economists through the use of elaborate statistical models, but the same results are obtained through the use of some simple comparisons. Recently, in a study for the American Legislative Council, I looked at a period of roughly one generation, from 1967 to 1990. I compared the ten states in the union with the greatest economic growth (as measured by income per capita) with the ten states possessing the smallest growth rates. As figure 1 shows, the ten states with the greatest growth rates raised their taxes, on average, about 35 percent less than the ten slowest growing states. Alternatively, looking at the ten states with the biggest increase in tax burdens over the same pe-

riod, the growth rate was fully 20 percent less, on average, than in the ten states with the smallest increase in tax burdens.

The same sort of relationship holds when economic vitality is measured in terms of job growth, population change, or capital movements. It also holds over shorter time horizons. For example, I compared the net migration of population in the ten states with the highest state and local tax burden in fiscal year 1979 over the 1980 to 1988 period with the net migration in the same period with the ten states possessing the lowest tax burden. The ten high-tax states had a net *outflow* of thirty-six thousand persons. More persons left those states than entered.

This may not seem particularly startling, until one realizes that nearly 5.6 million persons migrated *into* the United States from other countries in the same period, so the average state gained perhaps one hundred thousand population through new migrants. Not the high-tax states, however.

What about the low-tax states? They gained some 2,970,000 migrants over eight years—over half the national total. Every day (Saturdays, Sundays, and holidays included), over one thousand persons on average moved into the low-tax states. People entered these "lands of opportunity" where the government taxed the populace lightly, while they avoided the high-tax areas where a relatively larger proportion of the fruits of economic endeavors were taken by the state or local governments in the form of taxes.

To illustrate the point, let us look at one of our largest and wealthiest states, New York. Two generations ago, in 1929, New York was easily the richest state in the

United States. Its per capita personal income was 12 percent higher than its nearest competitor, Delaware. More than 16 percent of the nation's income was generated in the Empire State. With the passage of time, however, New York's economic preeminence has diminished. Several states—including neighboring New Jersey and Connecticut—have surpassed New York in terms of income per capita. New York's share of American personal income has been nearly cut in half and is now well behind California's.

What happened? In part, New York's relative economic decline was the natural consequence of forces of the market system at work. The market has great equalizing properties, working to reduce income and wealth disparities over time. Economists speak of a "factor price equalization theorem." Over the past several decades, workers in low-income states, mainly in the American South, moved north to earn higher wages, increasing the labor supply in the high-income states of the North and thus depressing wages there somewhat. The departure of workers in the lower-wage areas sometimes created labor shortages in those areas, leading to higher wages there. In seeking better lives for themselves and their families, American workers moved in such a manner to reduce interstate inequalities in income and wealth.

Similarly, capitalists seeking to maximize profits moved plants and equipment to the lower-wage areas, often in the South. Capital moved south, while labor moved north. The huge capital advantage that northern workers had, enhancing their productivity, was largely erased by the mobility of capital and labor resources. This movement explains much of the reason why the typical New Yorker earned nearly *five times* as much as the average South Carolinian in 1929, but only about 25 percent more today.

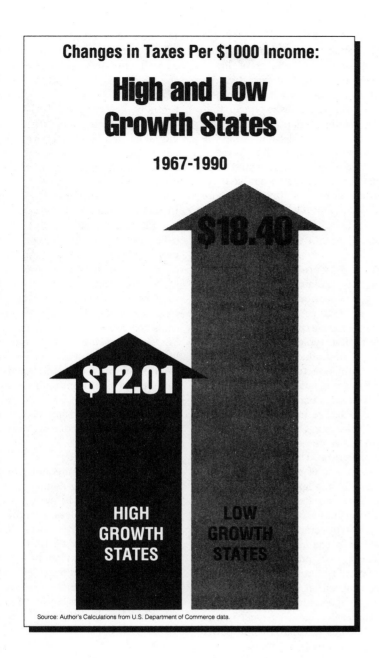

Source: Author's Calculations from U.S. Department of Commerce data.

ing differences in population growth between the states is migration. There is a voluminous literature demonstrating that people move into states where economic opportunities are good and growing, and they leave states where the chances for financial well-being are poor and not expanding.

As late as 1950, there were more people living in Montana than in Idaho. Today, the population of Idaho far exceeds that of Montana. It is not a coincidence that tax burdens have risen more in Montana than Idaho. Similarly, it is not an accident that the two fastest growing states over the past six decades, Nevada and Alaska, have no personal income tax, a distinction also held by such other rapidly growing states as Florida and Texas.

To put it succinctly, taxes matter. That is not to say that "taxes *alone* matter." Texas, Florida, and Nevada have benefited from low taxes—but also from air-conditioning. The discovery of North Slope oil has made a difference to Alaska. The growth in defense installations during two world wars and the Cold War helped several states, while paying for those installations has hurt other ones. The growth in the federal government generally has been a boon to the economies of Virginia and Maryland but probably, on balance, has drained resources from the industrial Midwest and Northeast.

The aggregate statistics disguise some of the debilitating effect that taxes have on economic activity. Let us return to our first example, New York State, and compare it with two of its neighbors, New Jersey and Connecticut. The Empire State's income superiority over its neighbors eroded in the 1930s and 1940s as the market's natural equalizing tendencies were at work. By 1950, income per capita in the three states was nearly identical. The relative economic status of the three states stabilized over the next two decades, with income differentials being very small as late as 1970.

Beginning in the 1960s, however, New York began to vigorously raise the tax burden on its people, far more than was the case in neighboring New Jersey or Connecticut. The tax differentials between the three states grew considerably again in the 1970s, in large part because New York had a highly progressive state income tax that absorbed ever-larger proportions of the income of New Yorkers because of inflation-induced bracket creep.

Yet the natural convergence of incomes over time does not explain why New Jersey, with a per capita income fully 20 percent lower than New York in 1929, has *higher* income levels today. It does not explain why New Hampshire's income superiority over neighboring Vermont has *grown* over time, rather than diminish as economic theory would predict. It does not explain why Kansas has surpassed Iowa, or why Virginia has surpassed West Virginia, in terms of the most comprehensive measure of economic well-being.

A key factor in explaining these trends in economic growth has been the level and types of taxes imposed by state and local governments. New York became one of the nation's highest-tax states, and suffered economically relative to its lower tax neighbors Connecticut and New Jersey (not to mention Pennsylvania, Massachusetts, or Vermont). Iowa, in general, imposed higher taxes than Kansas and grew less. While the situation with respect to Virginia and West Virginia is more complex, again West Virginia imposed higher taxes on income than its neighbor to the east, and suffered for it.

The same conclusions hold if one measures economic vitality in terms of population growth rather than per capita income growth. The major factor explain-

By contrast, Connecticut had no income tax in this period and New Jersey enacted a modest rate tax only in the mid-1970s. As a consequence of New York's aggressive tax increases, a new income differential between the three states began to develop—with New York now having the lowest income.

In the 1980s, New York very modestly reduced its aggregate tax burden on the citizenry, in that the proportion of income absorbed by taxes declined by about 6 percent. The top income tax rate, for example, was significantly reduced. Yet New Jersey engaged in even more aggressive tax reduction (about 12 percent), and Connecticut also reduced its aggregate tax burden, already the lowest of the three states. As a consequence, New York grew—but less than its neighbors. By 1990, income per capita was almost 14 percent higher in New Jersey than in New York (whereas it had been *lower* as late as 1970). In Connecticut, the differential was even greater by 1990, over 15 percent.

Other examples abound. Compare the two big Sunbelt states that have for decades attracted hordes of retirees and tourists from the North—California and Florida. Florida has maintained a relatively low tax climate, refusing to enact an income or inheritance tax. California, by contrast, has had fairly high levels of taxation, with heavy reliance on individual income taxes. Partly as a consequence of this, Florida has outperformed California economically by almost any measure. Whereas in 1967 income per capita was over 30 percent higher in California than in Florida, by 1990 the differential had fallen to 12 percent. In percentage terms, population growth has been about one-third larger in Florida, despite the higher population densities in that state.

The tax-growth relationship applies if one looks at smaller (cities) or larger (nations) geographic areas. Looking at data on over twenty leading industrialized nations in the 1980s, I took the five that raised their taxes the most as a percent of gross domestic product and compared them with the ones that raised taxes the least. The average growth rate of the top five tax-increasing nations (Spain, Ireland, Italy, Denmark, and Greece) was 1.72 percent a year. By contrast, the average growth rate of the five nations that decreased taxes the most or increased them the least (Norway, West Germany, the United States, Austria, and Turkey) was 29 percent higher—2.22 percent a year.

The compounded effects of lower growth are staggering. Suppose two nations both had incomes of $15,000 per person in 1980. Suppose, as was typical, that the tax-increasing nation grew 1.72 percent over the ensuing decade, while the tax-decreasing nation grew 2.22 percent. By 1990, per capita income would have been $894 higher in the nation that restrained the growth of taxes, or more than $3,500 for a family of four.

WHY DO TAXES MATTER?

Why are taxes important in explaining the changing economic fortunes of states? Taxes "crowd out" private economic activity, and the "bottom line" is that, typically, private sector activity is more productive, dollar for dollar, than public sector programs. How does the "crowding out" take place?

Consider sales taxes, the most important revenue source in many states. The burden of sales taxes is shifted from the retailer to the customer, leading to higher consumer prices. This reduces the real purchasing power of consumers, leading them to buy a smaller physical quantity of goods. Less private output is sold to the taxpaying public.

Also, the true compensation of a worker is lowered by the imposition of a sales tax, since the real purchasing power of each dollar is reduced. It is a well-established proposition in economics that the amount of labor supplied is directly related to the real wage. Since sales taxes lower real wages (the purchasing power associated with any given money wage), they lower the number of hours individuals are willing to work.

This is even more vividly seen with income taxes. Indeed, income taxes might influence where a given worker will locate. Suppose a computer scientist is considering jobs in Florida and California. Suppose that both jobs are equally challenging, that the climate is the same in both communities, and so forth. Where will he locate? If both firms offer him $60,000, he probably will choose to move to Florida, since in California, state and local income taxes might take close to $5,000 of his pay. Thus, California's income taxes can (and do) drive productive "human capital" to locate elsewhere.

To be sure, the California firm might be able to lure our mythical scientist by offering more money, say $65,000, to overcome the tax differential. But in doing so, the California firm finds its labor costs higher than its competitor's in Florida, potentially lowering firm profits and the rate of return on capital. Thus, high individual income taxes can adversely impact on companies. That is why studies have shown that high-technology firms relying on high-priced brainpower tend to be very sensitive to personal income taxes in making business location decisions.

Similarly, profit-maximizing businesses will find their profits reduced by high property taxes or high corporate profit taxes. It may seem to the reader that these items are small compared with labor costs and other considerations. Property taxes are equal to 2 percent or less of sales for most businesses, for example. Yet since corporate profits typically are less than 10 percent of sales before taxes, even comparatively small expense items can make a significant difference with respect to profits. Also, as indicated above, taxes can impact significantly on the most important cost to most firms, namely labor expenses.

All taxes crowd out private sector activity. This does not mean, however, that all taxes are equally damaging to economies. For example, the evidence suggests that sales taxes are less harmful than income taxes or property taxes. In part, the reason for this may be that sales taxes can be avoided by saving, and saving has positive economic effects, as economists since Adam Smith have observed. By favoring savings over consumption, sales taxes are less harmful than income taxes.

Flat-rate income taxes seem to be better than steeply progressive ones from the standpoint of maximizing economic growth. High marginal tax rates tend to have stronger disincentive effects on work effort than moderate tax rates. Therefore, a flat-rate tax with a 4 percent rate probably would be less detrimental to economic growth than an income tax with a range of 1 to 8 percent that raises about the same amount of money as the flat-rate one does. This realization was behind the move to lower federal marginal tax rates in the 1980s, and also led several states (including New York) to lower their top marginal tax rate.

In recent years, it has become particularly appealing for states to raise excise taxes on alcohol, cigarettes, and gasoline.

It is argued that these types of taxes are "good" because they discourage the consumption of things that pollute or cause health hazards. Generally speaking, economists are wary of taxes on specific commodities that distort the allocation of resources. The fact that the products taxed are consumed heavily by lower-income individuals adds equity concerns. Still another major problem is administrative in nature: High excise taxes lead to extensive cross-border activity that actually can harm the state imposing the tax. Some of my colleagues and I recently ascertained that 43 percent of the cigarettes consumed in Cincinnati and some of the surrounding areas in Ohio were purchased in Kentucky, simply because Ohio's cigarette tax is six times that of Kentucky.

WHY DO POLITICIANS RAISE TAXES?

Taxes are unpopular with voters, and the evidence suggests that they are bad for economic development. Why, then, do the politicians keep imposing new ones? Nearly all states have constitutions with balanced budget provisions that require taxes to be used to finance governmental services. Taxes are imposed because of demands placed on lawmakers for governmental services. Those demands have risen over time, in part because rising population and incomes increase voter demands for services, and in part because of agitation by special interests—the education establishment, welfare lobby, contractors, and automobile clubs (wanting highways), and so forth.

Some of the new tax-financed projects approved at the instigation of special interest groups may not be desirable—the costs to society exceed the benefits. However, most voters are "rationally ignorant" and go along with the legislative decisions. Specifically, the benefits to projects typically accrue largely to a relatively small number of members of special interest groups. With the benefits concentrated on a small number of persons, these persons will wage a lengthy battle to get the benefits approved.

By contrast, the costs of most projects are spread over millions of taxpayers, and the typical taxpayer loses only a little welfare or income on any given boondoggle that is approved. It simply is not worth the time and effort to fight every government project that is going to cost the individual voter a dollar or two. Thus the voters remain "rationally ignorant" of many undeserved projects that get approved, necessitating more tax revenues.

The problem is aggravated by evidence that the economically debilitating effects of taxes are not fully felt until two or three years after adoption. Thus a tax increase approved in 1992 might start hurting a state's economy in 1994 or even 1995. By then, voters will not associate the economic stagnation with the tax increase passed years earlier, and politicians can blame the poor economy on other factors.

USES OF TAX REVENUES AND ECONOMIC GROWTH

As this discussion hints, not only does the economic impact of taxes vary with the type of tax levied, it also differs with the use made of the tax revenues. Some governmental expenditures promote economic growth, offsetting part or even all of the adverse effects of the taxes (the crowding out of private activity). Other spending, however, is detrimental to growth, so the adverse impact of the activity is even greater than the negative effect of the tax itself.

On the positive side, spending on public investment seems to be growth enhancing. New highways often lower transportation costs to private sector businesses, for example. The correlation between highway spending and economic growth is not very strong, however, suggesting that the negative effect of the taxes is roughly offset by the positive effect of the investment financed by the taxes.

The evidence is mixed regarding educational expenditures. Some economists have purported to observe a positive relationship between educational spending and economic growth, but this author consistently observes a negative statistical relationship. The more states spend on education in relation to the state's economic resources, the lower the rate of economic growth.

This seems counterintuitive. Education, after all, creates "human capital," giving people skills that ultimately should make them more productive in the workplace. At the highest levels of higher education, persons not only obtain valuable skills needed to operate complicated capital equipment, but they also discover new ways of doing things that enhance output. Technological progress is intimately associated with education and human capital formation.

At the same time, there are literally scores of studies that show virtually no association between expenditures per pupil (or some other measure of resource use) and learning in public schools. Eric Hanushek of the University of Rochester has written two survey articles reviewing the entire literature and has concluded that, on balance, the studies find no relationship between spending and learning. To be sure, there are high-spending school districts with high levels of student achievement, but there also are school districts spending huge amounts per pupil with very low levels of student performance.

Indeed, the major studies show that the factors that influence student learning are parental involvement, family environment (traditional two-parent families are superior to other living arrangements), the school's level of independence (schools that are relatively autonomous do better), the level of expectations, and so forth. Spending itself makes little difference. More money for schools often means higher salaries for members of the education establishment, but little else.

One form of expenditure that many scholars have observed has clearly adverse effects on economic growth is public assistance. Jurisdictions with relatively high levels of tax-financed public assistance expenditures tend to suffer economically as a consequence. The reason is that welfare spending tends to have significant work disincentive effects, and additional adverse effects in traditional family structures that promote a work ethic consistent with economic growth.

The larger the welfare benefits are, the smaller are the rewards for working. Consider an unwed mother with two children living in the nation's largest state, California. She very well might receive over $600 a month in AFDC payments, Medicaid benefits worth $250 a month, and $250 in other benefits—food stamps, WIC payments, SSI, housing subsidies, and so forth. If the mother took a full-time job paying $7 an hour ($14,000 a year), she might lose all benefits. Yet her benefit package is worth nearly $14,000—so why work? There is no incentive in taking a low-paying job, and the "tax" in the form of welfare benefits forgone is high even for persons having the option of a moderately well paying ($9–10 per hour) entry-level job.

PRIVATE VS. PUBLIC PRODUCTIVITY AND EFFICIENCY

Tax-financed expenditures lead to lower private sector spending and higher public sector activity. There is no inherent reason this should lower the rate of economic growth, particularly if a significant proportion of the public activity promotes infrastructure development that might enhance economic growth in the long run. Yet the evidence rather consistently suggests that economic growth is impaired by tax-financed public spending. Why? Private sector entrepreneurs can improve their economic welfare by cutting costs—increasing economic efficiency. If costs are reduced in relation to revenues, profits grow. Owners get larger dividends. Managers can make money on stock options, profit sharing, and other incentive programs. Even rank-and-file employees often share at least indirectly in the profits arising from increased efficiency. The market system provides financial rewards for raising productivity. On the demand side, the system rewards those who devise new products that people want. Incentives lead business leaders to want to please their buying public.

Public sector executives, like their private sector counterparts, want to improve their economic welfare. But, with some small exceptions, they are not selling their products in a market. Their "consumers" are forced to buy their goods and services via taxation. The bureaucrats providing services are typically monopolists, not having to worry too much about pleasing customers to maintain market share.

On the supply side, the typical private sector manager tries to reduce costs by cutting staff and other expenses. The average government bureaucrat tries to increase his budget, add staff, and otherwise use resources. Why? Managers are not rewarded on their efficiency, which in any case is hard to measure given the absence of a financial "bottom line." Indeed, managers usually have more power, more perks, and possibly even a bigger salary the *larger* the number of persons they have performing their assigned tasks. Moreover, the staff is happier if they have more persons to help them do the work.

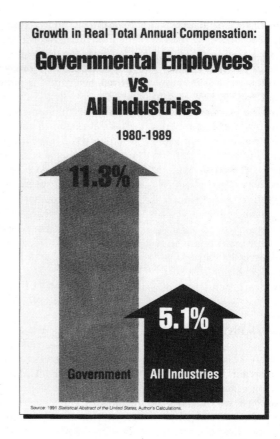

Growth in Real Total Annual Compensation:

Governmental Employees vs. All Industries

1980-1989

11.3%

Government

5.1%

All Industries

Source: 1991 *Statistical Abstract of the United States*, Author's Calculations.

I briefly was one of these public sector managers myself, serving as the chair of my department at a public university. I maneuvered to hire more staff, increase my supply budget, and get money for staff travel. My colleagues applauded my efforts, and no one condemned me for increasing departmental costs in relation to my unit's "output." If, on the other hand, I had been running a unit for a profit-maximizing corporation, more staff would have been allocated only if I were able to demonstrate that I could increase my output and the firm's income sufficiently enough to cover the added resources commanded. That thinking simply does not exist in most public sector activities.

The average citizen is aware that United Parcel Service outshines the publicly owned U.S. Postal Service. Telephone service is invariably better in countries where there is private ownership and control. Municipal garbage service tends to be more costly and less pleasing to customers than privately provided services. The late Soviet Union was a monument to the inefficiencies of publicly provided goods and services, as nearly every resident of that former nation will tell you.

It is no wonder, then, that the crowding out of private sector activity by public sector programs through the tax mechanism lowers the growth of output. A growing economy is one where output is growing faster than input—where productivity is rising and scarce resources are serving more human needs.

Another reason why public sector expenditures seem to have a limited payoff in terms of economic development is that individuals attempt to use government in order to redistribute income to themselves in a manner that is detrimental to economic progress. Economists call these individuals "rent seekers," and they often band together in what Mancur Olson calls "distributional coalitions." Special interest groups try to extract tax revenues to serve their own needs.

One of the biggest groups of "rent seekers" is public employees themselves. As tax revenues soared in the 1980s with the Reagan era prosperity, teachers and other public employees successfully fought to get their own compensation and benefits increased relative to the private sector. Money that taxpayers thought was going to improve the quality of education, for example, often merely increased the incomes of existing employees without increasing accountability or performance.

As figure 2 shows, real total compensation (including fringes) of all governmental employees (including federal government workers) rose far more in the 1980s than for all workers (a group that is predominantly nongovernment workers). Looking just at state government employees, in 1988 the average wage or salary was 24 percent above the average for all employees. In California, the average public sector employee earned an astonishing 60 percent more than the average for all employees, private and public.

DISGUISED TAXATION AND ECONOMIC GROWTH

Official government statistics on taxation ignore some "disguised taxes" or burdens that citizens of states and localities face. For example, workers' compensation is a program with a worthy objective, namely a no-fault form of insurance protection for those injured on the job. Yet the payments under this program have soared in recent years, a significant financial obligation to employers that is not officially considered a tax but that has the same debilitating impact on the rate of return of productive endeavors. Similarly, unemployment compensation insurance payments are another "disguised tax" that almost certainly impact negatively on growth.

Regulatory behavior of governments is not considered a form of taxation, but from the standpoint of economic factors regulations have much the same effect as taxes. Extremely stringent environmental rules can raise business costs in much the same manner as corporate income taxes, for example. Finally, mandated benefits (e.g., health insurance provisions) can similarly increase labor and other costs in much the same fashion as an explicit tax.

AN OPTIMAL TAX POLICY FOR THE STATES

Taxes matter. Areas with high levels of taxation tend to have lower levels of economic well-being. Therefore, what should states do? From the standpoint of economic growth, an optimal fiscal policy would be centered around low levels of taxation. The optimal state would have a moderate sales tax, low property taxes, and no state income tax. On the expenditure side, the state would spend moderately generously on highways and perhaps some other forms of public investment, would not spend highly on education, and would have minimal provisions for public assistance.

Actual policies increasingly deviate from optimal policy. In large part, this reflects the institutional imperfections of the American political system. Key to moving toward the optimal fiscal policy is institutional reform that reduces the inordinate power of the "distributional coalitions" whose political clout is responsible for much of the modern increase in spending and taxation. Put bluntly, it is too easy to buy the support of legislators. Spending and tax limitation, term limits for legislators, and tying public employee compensation to economic performance are but three ways of dealing with this problem. We need to experiment with new rules of politics, for the old adage is largely correct: The power to tax is the power to destroy.

The Pros and Cons of Investment Incentives:

How Do You Know You Get What You Pay For?

Andrew P. Grose

Economic development incentives are a little examined sector of state public policy which would benefit from research and debate. This article, while far from definitive, points out some of the advantages and disadvantages of state incentive packages for economic development. The author notes that good incentive programs are directly correlated with overall economic development strategy, that states must do a better job of correlating the cost of benefit packages with long-term benefits, and that good incentive programs ultimately serve overall social goals. The article intends to stimulate a critical look at incentives by both the academic and practitioner communities.

INTRODUCTION

For almost six years, through the end of 1989, I directed Nevada's economic development program. By most traditional measures, it was a very successful endeavor. Nevada led the nation in new jobs during the last three of those years, led in per capita creation of new businesses in the last two, and ranked as the best state for manufacturing in the West by Grant Thornton. Also, during those six years, the department grew from a staff of eight and a budget of $800,000 to 32 people and a budget of $5.2 million. That's bureaucratic success, if nothing else.

I also oversaw the preparation of a comprehensive state economic diversification plan, the first in Nevada history. But I must confess that except for a half dozen businesses, representing maybe 100 jobs, I could not conclusively say which jobs were attributable to our efforts and which would have come anyway. I believe we contributed to many more, but I can't prove it, although I always had a strong case to present to the Legislature. That's the nature of economic development work. You don't always know what influences business location decisions.

The question of the efficacy of investment incentives is a perfect subset of the greater uncertainties in economic development. Do incentives work and are they worth it?

There is no clear answer. You cannot say with certainty if it was an incentive package that closed a deal in comparison to many other variables, and you can't really say if an incentive package is cost-effective because no one has developed a generally accepted methodology to determine what a job is worth to a community.

The issue of incentives is one of several conundrums of economic development. Others are:

Are low taxes or stable taxes more important?
How high do wages have to be before it's a "good job?"
Or is the only good job a union job?
What is a primary job—an exogenous job is the new term—and what is not? Does the distinction mean anything anymore?
What jobs are wealth creators versus wealth circulators?
Is the goal jobs creation or wealth creation?
Is it more important to attract new business or expand existing ones?

I would submit that far more state economic development programs are based on what other states are doing rather than any objective criteria of programmatic success. A very few states, such as Minnesota, are trying to bring measurement and accountability to the field, and are to be applauded. But short-sighted interstate competitive bidding continues.

WHAT THE RESEARCH SAYS ABOUT INCENTIVES

First, we need to be clear about definitions. Any number of things, including a good education system, dry climate, location, a right to work law, transportation system, political leadership, presence of a skilled work force and a low degree of unionization can be incentives for particular businesses.

Our purpose is to talk about a narrower set of incentives that we will define as *direct payments to a business or on behalf of a business, tax reductions or infrastructure improvements that are for the sole or at least primary benefit of a particular business or other job-creating project.* With this definition, we are talking about conscious decisions about public resources going to benefit a business or other project in order to get a business or project to locate in a particular place or to keep one from going elsewhere.

Another way of looking at incentives of this sort is that they are not available to all businesses or even to classes of businesses. Rather, they are available on a case-by-case basis.

I would submit that far more state economic development programs are based on what other states are doing rather than any objective criteria of programmatic success.

Are there guidelines or other benchmarks to determine what incentives are to be offered to which kinds of jobs producers? Basically, no. Are incentive deals logically consistent within a state? Not that anyone has ever been able to show. Does anyone measure the cost of incentives against jobs created and the salaries? Not really. And why not?

It is not clear why there is so little introspection about what sort of deals make sense and which do not in the economic development field. I found my state economic development colleagues notably uninterested in the topic. My own theory is that those in key positions in economic development are beneficiaries of the new development right away while the costs fall elsewhere and over a period of time. The benefits accrue to two groups of people: 1) political leaders, especially governors and legislators, for whom job creation is a widely supported goal, and 2) the private sector supporters of new jobs including developers, banks, real estate people, the building trades, the utilities and other businesses who see their well-being in terms of growth. People in the second category tend to be politically influential as well.

For both these groups, public outlays to create jobs make excellent political and economic sense. For the general taxpaying citizen, it may not make much sense at all, but he or she is not at the policy table. At the policy level, any push for incentives is opposed by existing businesses who see it as unfair competition, but this is usually limited to inconsequential grumbling since most businesses want growth.

Every state offers some kind of incentives to new and expanding businesses. But there is a tremendous range in the extent and cost of incentives, from industrial development bonds, which really cost a state nothing although they cost the federal government lost taxes, to huge infrastructure and training costs and tax breaks that can go into the hundreds of millions of dollars. Add in that local governments also can provide incentives and so can utilities. Just as the general taxpayer foots the bill for taxes reduced for someone else, the general ratepayer will make up for any utility cost breaks.

We are not talking small numbers. By the early 1980s, according to the National Governors' Association, states were spending, in direct outlays or in terms of taxes foregone, up to $20 billion a year to attract business. Even the federal government openly encourages bidding wars for things like the Supercollider and the Bureau of Engraving and Printing's western facility. To compete for the Supercollider, states as a minimum had to provide the several thousand acres of land required, and the bidding went up from there. Kentucky's 1988 deal with Toyota was estimated at $150 million, or $50,000 per job. Indiana's attraction of United Airlines will cost $172 million, or $28,000 per job.

What makes sense and how can you say how much a job is worth? It would seem that the job should, at the very least, return the equal amount in tax revenue over the life of the business. As simple as it sounds, there is no agreed-upon methodology to measure this. It would seem that a lot of smoke and mirrors are being used when the governor of Indiana says United will return $500 million in revenues. The multiplier effect would have to be carried out quite far to reach these kinds of numbers. And I would wager that figure does not consider the added costs to state and local governments year to year in public services, education and so on.

The literature is clear on one point. Many incentives are wasted. Numerous studies over the past 15 years show cases where a site decision already was made and then incentives were negotiated. The state officials involved usually didn't know this, but sometimes they did. Two of the oldest bureaucratic rules come into play. One, if you don't spend money one year, you'll lose it the next; and two, if you convinced legislators that a program was needed, and then it's not used you look bad. These combine to mean that some incentive money is wasted.

In 1989, General Electric initiated the process of closing its Cicero, Illinois plant and consolidating in Decatur, Alabama. Company officials told Illinois they had made the decision, but Illinois still offered to put together an incentive package. That was enough for Alabama to do the same, which, of course, General Electric accepted.

The literature is clear on one point. Many incentives are wasted. . . . [S]tate officials involved usually didn't know this, but sometimes they did.

The question is how many companies in General Electric's position are equally candid and how many go to two or more states saying they are candidates when a decision already has been made based on other factors. Judging from my own experience, the number is large. Certainly, this applies to a majority of cases. We frequently sat around a table at National Association of State Development Agencies meetings and compared notes, after the fact, on how a company had played us off against each other. The trouble is, you can't really do that while the negotiating is going on. You are not going to share your offer with a competitor in hopes that you ultimately can hold costs down.

[A]ny company that is more interested in tax breaks or subsidized financing than trained workers is very likely to move on again. It is not a good prospect upon which to build a stable economy.

On the whole, the research is not very supportive of incentives. From a macroeconomic point of view, they produce nothing of value and do not increase national wealth. They merely transfer resources from the public to the private sector. Otherwise, they are a zero-sum game. Other economic development efforts, such as introducing new firms to the export market, actually increase U.S. wealth. Nonetheless, there will continue to be competition among states for new investment, and foreign firms are every bit as adept at the game as American ones. For them, this aspect of the federal system is a delight!

Given that incentives are not going away, what can you say about them that is good? First, they provide an opportunity for government to influence private development to support public goals. In the wake of the Los Angeles riots, talk of urban enterprise zones has surfaced again, with passage of legislation in Congress probable. This is a good example of using incentives to achieve a social goal. Giving tax breaks or other incentives to get businesses into a rural area is a similar exercise. The French have a massive program in place to get businesses to move out of Paris. The Japanese have disincentives to keep regional businesses out of Tokyo. Highway programs serve as a major incentive to firms to locate in some places as opposed to others.

Not all incentives have the same impact. A state that spends money to train workers for a new business makes a human resources investment. Similarly, building infrastructure is an investment in yourself. Tax breaks are simply money lost for which there is nothing to show when the business leaves.

It should be kept in mind that virtually every survey on the subject shows that taxes rank very low in location decision. Site locators will tell you that taxes are important, "all things being equal." But the fact is that all things are almost never equal. This means any company that is more interested in tax breaks or subsidized financing than trained workers is very likely to move on again. It is not a good prospect upon which to build a stable economy.

What about other forms of incentives such as financing? In a market economy where capital moves freely, it is a tough question whether there is a legitimate need for state financing programs. Some of the same arguments apply to industrial development bonds. How many of those businesses are built only because of lower interest rates? Are there legitimate business proposals for which conventional financing is not available? Absolutely.

Low-interest financing costs the taxpayer. The question is why should a sound business have to pay market rates while an unsound, or at least weaker competitor gets subsidized rates? The answer is that this is legitimate to further some other goal such as minority business development. But the case is harder to make in terms of general job creation.

Finally, what about incentives in the form of government-funded research. Again, the question is why government should fund it for some businesses and not for others. This does not mean that governments should not support first-rate research institutions that any business can access. This is an investment a state makes in itself, not in a company that may be gone tomorrow.

CONCLUSION

Isn't there some quantifiable way to look at incentives? We know which states have which programs. Why should comparisons be so hard? Because there are considerable differences in the importance of different incentives and because importance can differ for different companies. However, in the interest of creating some comparable numbers, I have taken data from a 1989 study of state business incentives done by The Council of State Governments and compared them to two recent measures of economic development success. The results, while not scientifically conclusive, are nonetheless interesting. Keep in mind, however, the old warning about confusing correlation with causality. Though fire engines are commonly seen at fires, they don't cause them.

[I]ncentives . . . should be investments that accrue to the state and its citizens as well as the business and that will remain if the business leaves.

From *State Policy Reports,* we have 1991 data on new and expanded corporate facilities by state adjusted for population. We also have 1989 CSG data on state incentive programs. CSG identified 14 tax incentives and 14 financing incentives. A top score for incentives then would be 28. Table 1 shows the top and bottom 10 states for new and expanded facilities and the total number of tax and financing incentives, and the total of those scores. Interestingly, the most successful states had lower total scores than the least successful.

Table 2 uses a different measure of success, something called economic momentum, and again how the top and bottom 10 states. The first thing to point out is that seven states are in the bottom 10 on both rankings, while only one state, Nevada, is in the top 10 on both. Again, however, the top 10 states had lower incentive scores than did the bottom 10.

These tables show correlation only. We cannot conclude that incentives cause comparative economic failure. In fact, the more likely case is that states with liabilities over which government has limited or no control (such as climate, location, skill levels, etc.) try to compensate for those problems by creating incentives. They could make the plausible argument that without incentives, their problems would be worse

So, what does this say about incentives? Are they a bad thing that we'd all be better off without? Not at all. But there are some key considerations.

First, incentive programs should be based on an overall economic development strategy that recognizes the changes in the world and the implications of those changes for certain kinds of business. Are incentives going to businesses with a national and international future, or are they feeding dinosaurs? The Connecticut pension fund bailed out Colt Firearms for $25 million and a 47 percent interest rate two years age. Now Colt is in Chapter 11 and the state is guaranteeing another $2 million loan. Chances are the state will be out $27 million. While it can be tempting politically, there is great danger in trying to save those the market would destroy.

Second, there has to be some agreed-upon calculus for relating the value of incentives to long-term costs and benefits of a new or expanded business. That calculus should be part of the strategy. A credible national organization should develop a set of guidelines that states and the private sector can use as a recognized standard of measurement. There would be no right or wrong ratio, but at least there would be comparability from one project to another and from one state to another.

Third, the incentives, to the maximum extent possible, should be investments that accrue to the state and its citizens as well as the business and that will remain if the business leaves. This means education, training and infrastructure as opposed to tax breaks and financing subsidies.

Fourth and finally, incentives should be used to pursue a strategy that has overall social goals. It is not enough to have jobs as the object of a development strategy. It should be particular kinds of jobs in particular places in order to effect certain desired changes. When a business or other project fits a strategy of this sort, and when other site selection criteria are met, then incentives make sense.

Unfortunately, I know of no state that administers an incentive program based on these four criteria or even some of them. And the only thing that will change the

Table 1
New and Expanded Corporate Facilities by State
(per million population — 1991)

Top 10 states	Incentives Tax	Business	Total
Mississippi	12	12	24
North Carolina	5	4	9
Kentucky	8	19	18
Alabama	11	9	19
South Carolina	10	11	21
Oklahoma	10	7	17
Indiana	11	13	24
Florida	13	11	24
Nevada	6	7	13
Wyoming	5	9	14
		Total	183
Bottom 10 states			
Rhode Island	10	10	20
New York	12	14	26
New Hampshire	6	6	12
Pennsylvania	11	12	23
Massachusetts	13	7	20
New Mexico	7	8	15
Vermont	7	10	17
Connecticut	12	14	26
Maine	11	10	21
Montana	12	9	21
		Total	201

Table 2
State Economic Momentum — March 1992
and State Business Incentives

Top 10 states	Incentives Tax	Business	Total
Nevada	6	7	13
Utah	8	6	14
Nebraska	10	6	16
Idaho	10	2	12
Arkansas	9	11	20
Oregon	9	14	23
Hawaii	4	10	14
Texas	5	6	11
Arizona	9	4	13
South Dakota	8	9	17
		Total	153
Bottom 10 states			
Georgia	4	4	8
Maryland	11	12	23
Vermont	7	10	17
New York	12	14	26
New Jersey	7	10	17
Connecticut	12	14	26
Maine	11	10	21
Rhode Island	10	10	20
New Hampshire	6	6	12
Massachusetts	13	7	20
		Total	190

current process is for us to see several more examples like Colt in Connecticut or Volkswagen in Pennsylvania. Or examples of major polluters who received big incentives from the same government that is dealing with their pollution. Things like this will give incentives a black eye and generate a lot more caution. I think we are already seeing that. The huge deals are drawing at least as much criticism as applause, and that is not a balance any politician finds attractive.

In summary, then, are incentives good or bad? Neither. The problem is they have been used to such an extent to win a competition rather than to accomplish clearly defined goals. Of course it is perfectly American to concentrate on winning. But that doesn't hold up too well with regard to business incentives. The misplaced and haphazard use of incentives can end up being like winning the javelin catching competition. The thrill of victory is soon replaced by economic agony.

Searching for New Jobs, Many States Steal Them

Joel Brinkley

Special to The New York Times

SALT LAKE CITY—In state capitals across the nation, just as in Washington, government leaders are casting about for approaches, new and old, to reinvigorate their economies. And the key to that, where ever it is tried, is creating jobs.

For decades most states have taken the easy, politically expedient approach. They have offered lucrative tax incentives, a proven technique that lures businesses away from neighboring states, enabling politicians to put hundreds or thousands of their constituents to work before the next elections.

Among the states relying on this approach even today are Arkansas, the home state of President-elect Bill Clinton, and Kentucky, which has perhaps the most generous such program.

But here in Utah, as in a handful of other states, officials are trying new methods. Utah is looking to its own people for creative ideas that can be turned into marketable inventions. When one emerges, the state helps to turn it into a business venture, creating home-grown enterprises that sell new high-tech products.

To Meet Competition

Economic development experts say that if the nation is to remain competitive internationally, Washington cannot rely only on large-scale Federal public works projects and tax incentives to create jobs. They say the Government should also encourage the creation of innovative businesses, as Utah does. Even though most of these start quite small, such new companies, with patented, cutting-edge products, hold the greatest potential to keep the nation competitive.

One such enterprise may have been born at a meeting of scientists, engineers, venture capitalists and marketing specialists who had been brought together here this month by Utah economic development officials.

Dr. Paul Savello, a professor at Utah State University, told the group that in five years, "there will be no more whole milk for sale in grocery stores."

He explained: "People are concerned about the fat, and in 15 or 20 years people are going to want to move away from 2 percent milk, too. But the problem is, they just don't like the taste and the appearance of skim milk. It's watery."

"It looks blue," an investor, Lee Smith, interjected with a dismissive laugh.

"Well," Dr. Savello went on, "we have firmly developed a way to make skim milk indistinguishable from 2 percent milk in blind taste tests. We don't add anything; it's still regular skim milk. All we're doing is manipulating the protein structure."

That caught everyone's attention, and the investors immediately peppered Dr. Savello with questions about marketing, distribution, costs. He didn't have many answers. "I'm just a scientist," he said, almost as an apology. But he did say, "the cost of the process is probably under one-tenth of a penny per gallon."

With that, a businessman, Jim Dreyfous exclaimed, "This could be the Nutrasweet of milk!" And within a week Dr. Savello had heard from several eager suitors, venture capitalists and others eager to join forces with him—start a company, build the equipment, hire employees and begin licensing the technology to local dairies nationwide.

"We're really excited about this," Rick Sherle, a Utah entrepreneur who was a breakfast guest, said later. "We're putting together a business plan."

Down the street, at Utah's economic development department a few days later, Michael Alder, head of the state's job creation office, was smiling. He is the one who organized the breakfast. And now, Mr. Alder said, "it looks like the skim milk is taking off."

Mr. Alder's office had helped finance Dr. Savello's research; over the last two years the state had given him almost $200,000. Dr. Savello and Dr. Ault are just two of several dozen scientists and engineers at Utah's universities who have been given $16.5 million for research in the last six years, grants that have been matched 10 to 1 by the Federal Government, foundations and private companies.

The state money is awarded with the clear instruction that it must be used to produce cutting-edge commercial products. Economic development experts say this program is among the nation's most innovative projects for creating jobs. About two-dozen other states offer aid to inventors in universities, said Walter Plosila, an economic development official in Maryland who was hired to evaluate Utah's program last year. "But very few of them are oriented to moving the inventions into industry," he said.

Now with Dr. Savello's work, once again Utah appeared ready to create jobs in an innovative field, jobs that might never have been created without the state government's help.

A Mistake
'I Did Overdo It,' Clinton Admits

Among economists, social scientists and others, state economic development programs are generally held in low regard. Most do not create jobs. Usually they simply shift them from one place to another, often at great cost.

To many states, economic development means tax rebates and other costly incentives to lure businesses away from their neighbors—"smokestack chasing," it is called.

But those tax breaks, while often successful at attracting low-tech businesses in search of bargains, can at the same time deprive state governments of revenue they need. Without that money, states often cannot improve their schools and universities, enhance their roads, bridges and other elements of the infrastructure—or in general prepare themselves for the high-technology industries the nation needs to remain competitive in the world.

Tax incentives were the key to Mr. Clinton's economic development program in Arkansas. In the last decade, it produced impressive growth in basic manufacturing jobs, as Mr. Clinton often noted in his campaign speeches.

But most of the new jobs were in new, expanded or relocated plants that generally hired low-wage workers. And even with all those new taxpaying employees in Arkansas, the business-tax rebates insured that Mr.

Clinton still had to cut state spending to balance the budget and then raise other taxes to pay for school improvements and other social programs.

In his book "Laboratories of Democracy" (Harvard Business School Press, 1990), David Osborne profiled Mr. Clinton's administration. This study, otherwise generous with praise for Mr. Clinton, criticized the Governor for the size of the tax credits he gave businesses, noting that they cost Arkansas at least $10 million in 1986 alone.

"I asked Clinton about this once," Mr. Osborne said in an interview. "And he said: 'Yup, I plead guilty. It was a mistake.' " In Mr. Osborne's book, Mr. Clinton is quoted as telling the author several years ago: "In 1983, unemployment was 13 percent, and for three years I was desperate to do anything to keep manufacturing jobs. But I think I did overdo it."

Largesse
Most Aggressive In Tax Incentives

Kentucky is similar to Arkansas in many ways. Half Southern, half Midwestern, it is largely rural and poor. By many national measures of wealth and education, Kentucky, like Arkansas, ranks not far from the bottom when compared with other states.

Last summer Kentucky began what may be the nation's most generous tax-incentive program to recruit new businesses, and it has already attracted several hundred jobs. But it also touched off a regional war.

The most visible part of Kentucky's program is the television advertisements. Since late summer, the state has been running 30-second commercials on CNN showing Gov. Brereton C. Jones leaning toward the camera from behind a polished, dark-wood desk.

"As Governor, I'm asking you to consider Kentucky for your business location," he says. "Locate your white collar jobs in Kentucky, and the state will pay half your rent for 10 years and up to half your start-up costs."

In another ad, the Governor promises: "Locate your manufacturing

plant in Kentucky, and the state will reimburse your entire investment. In Kentucky, we're serious about jobs!"

The lucrative tax rebates were Lieut. Gov. Paul E. Patton's idea. His elected position has no duties, so early this year Mr. Jones appointed him head of the state's economic development cabinet as well. Very quickly he drafted the tax incentive plan, the legislature passed the bill and the new law took effect in July. Officials in Ohio and Tennessee promptly cried foul.

"It's the most vicious piece of legislation I have ever seen," Mayor Dwight Tillery of Cincinnati complained.

Almost immediately, Ohio's General Assembly prepared its own generous economic incentive bill, and at the hearings in August, one state senator summed up the general sentiments when he said: "Ohio can't stand by and be a patsy."

After Gov. George Voinovich told the state Senate this was a "must pass" bill, it was enacted. So now Ohio, too, has a generous tax-rebate program—along with all the economic burdens it brings along.

In Jackson, Tenn., meanwhile, officials were preparing to announce late last summer that the International Paper Company was going to build a plant there. It would employ 400 people manufacturing paper labels for cans.

But just before the announcement, International Paper heard about Kentucky's new program and reconsidered. The company's project manager, Kris Schmaling, told the Nashville Business Journal that Kentucky's tax incentives were worth $39 million to International Paper, so "we literally took the Jackson construction plans and modified them for Bowling Green," in southwestern Kentucky.

That was not the only new plant Tennessee lost to Kentucky, and economic development officials were furious. They, too, began lobbying that state's legislature to enact similar incentives.

But at Middle Tennessee State University, Tony Eff, a professor of regional economics, warned Tennessee not to join the regional smokestack chase.

"That was a good strategy 20 years ago, when what made us competitive was low-cost, hard-working workers," he said. "But if employers want that now, they can go to Mexico." And in fact, several states that have used temporary tax-rebate programs to lure businesses are finding that as soon as their rebates expire, some of the companies move away to take advantage of incentives elsewhere.

Now, Dr. Eff says, Tennessee must begin manufacturing new, high-technology products that other countries cannot easily produce. Businesses of that sort usually are not after tax rebates. They look for states with attributes like strong universities, educated and well-trained citizens and advanced communications.

As for tax incentives, Dr. Eff says, "I don't think we can afford it."

Lieutenant Governor Patton says he has heard the argument that Kentucky cannot really afford the incentives, either. But he argues that even though large tax benefits are given to the companies, the state still gains revenue. The new employees "pay sales taxes, property taxes, gasoline taxes," he said.

At the same time, however, these people and their children fill more classrooms, add traffic to the highways, make additional demands on the state Medicaid program. The list goes on. So determining whether the state wins or loses in the end is difficult if not impossible.

"Some people say it's the wrong way to go, that we are eroding our tax base," Mr. Patton acknowledged. "But in Kentucky's situation, we still have high employment and as long as we bring in jobs for local people, it's helping us."

A Big Score
Kentucky Lands Toyota's Plant

Kentucky generally prospered in the latter half of the 1980's, largely a result of several lucky strikes. The most notable was Toyota's decision to build an assembly plant in Georgetown, after the state offered $140 million in incentives.

But the economic consulting firm DRI-McGraw Hill projects that Kentucky will rank 34th in the nation in job creation next year. The Corporation for Economic Development, another national consulting firm, ranks Kentucky 39th, and its annual report card on the states gives Kentucky D's for both economic performance and development capacity.

The same two firms rank Utah 10th and 8th respectively in job creation. And in the same two categories the report card gives Utah two A's. This is largely because Utah puts most of its energy into a different approach.

Mr. Alder's office, the Centers of Excellence program, is a central part of that. It seeks out promising research in university laboratories in the state—professors with projects that ordinarily might produce interesting articles in academic journals but seldom much more.

The state encourages these professors to refocus their work toward commercial applications. And then twice a year, professors across the state can enter a competition of sorts for state financing up to $300,000 a year that must be used to move their work from university labs to new commercial ventures.

Start-up businesses of this sort generally take several years to get going. But since the program was begun in 1986, it has led to the creation of 65 high-tech companies employing almost 1,500 people, plus about 1,000 more people hired to carry out additional work in the associated university labs. Not all of these companies will survive. But those that do provide jobs that were not simply shifted here from other states. They did not exist before, and most of them pay higher than average wages.

A Success
Utah Seeks Out Cutting Edge

In northeast Salt Lake City, right beside the university campus, the entrance sign to a modern industrial park reads: "University of Utah Research Park: Technology, Creating Industry, Creating Jobs."

Inside are rows of squat, red-brick industrial buildings housing more than 50 start-up concerns, all of them born of research in the university's labs, many of them financed in part with money from Mr. Alder's program.

Not many universities encourage their professors to start businesses; in fact the whole idea seems contrary to the philosophy of academia. But "this institution has a view that we are an important part of the regional and local economy, and one thing we can do for the state is commercialize our research," said Richard Koehn, the University of Utah's Vice President for Research.

That's not just an altruistic view; by a variety of arrangements the university shares in the profits from commercial ventures born in the school's labs. "Last year we took in $1.3 million," Dr. Koehn said.

And it is also true that his university is known for unorthodox experiments. It was here in 1989 that two researchers announced that they had achieved cold nuclear fusion, a claim that was later largely discredited. And it was here, seven years earlier, that Dr. William DeVries implanted the first permanent artificial heart in a patient, Barney Clark. He died three months later.

On a trial production line in one of the industrial-park buildings, a wide strip of special, porous plastic material rolls past, and steel nozzles just above spit small globs of clear gel at designated intervals, 70 of them a minute. A few inches father along, another layer of plastic is laid on top, a punching device cuts the sheets into individual two-inch squares. And then these little patches of medication are dumped into a basket ready for packaging—the first products market with an estimated potential value of $1 billion.

The squares are transdermal patches of testosterone, the male sex hormone. They are like the nicotine patches many people use to help them quit smoking, though far more sophisticated. Pasted most anywhere on the body of a patient suffering from malfunctioning gonads, they dispense testosterone through the skin to replace the testosterone the body should be producing on its own, under a new, patented process unknown before it was pioneered in a University of Utah laboratory.

Creation of the process was financed in part by more than $1 million from the state, Dr. Sun Wan Kim, one of the inventors, said. With encouragement from both the university and Mr. Alder's office, he founded a company, Theratec Inc., which produces the patches and several other novel drug delivery technologies.

Theratec made a public offering of its shares early this year, and the over-the-counter stock has grown to be a darling of some financial analysts. "The unappreciated gem of the drug delivery area," an analysis by Vector Securities said early this year. Last month, Kidder, Peabody & Company said "the uniqueness and proven benefits of these products gives us confidence in the company's profitability."

Now Theratec employs 80 people in a field that did not exist just a few years ago. And the company is almost certain to grow after it gains Food and Drug Administration approval for its initial products. Already, the average salary of Theratec's employees exceeds $40,000 a year. But like most speculative new companies, Theratec's early days were not easy.

"It would have been tough getting going without that money from the state," says Dinesh C. Patel, the company's president. "The state stepped in where most new companies fail."

Dr. Kim said, "Because of the state funding, we were able to initiate many new areas of research," adding that the Clinton Administration should look to Utah for ideas.

"The new Government in Washington has to stimulate small technologies like ours," he said.

Stephen C. Jacobsen has a similar view. He is a professor of engineering at the same university, and with help from the state, among others, he created a successful robotics company now employing 120 people. He put it this way: "People like us create the headwaters of innovation that can enable this country to stay ahead of Japan. But in the beginning, it's a minefield, and that's where the state helps."

If the Federal Government "doesn't do something to help entrepreneurs, something like the state does here, then we'll be in trouble."

Service Delivery and Policy Issues

- **Service Delivery (Articles 53–55)**
- **Policy Issues (Articles 56–63)**

One only has to look through a daily newspaper to realize the multiple and diverse activities in which state and local governments engage. Indeed, it would be an unusual American who, in a typical day, does not have numerous encounters with state and local government programs, services, and regulations.

State and local governments are involved in providing roads, sidewalks, streetlights, fire and police protection, schools, colleges, day-care centers, health clinics, job training programs, public transportation, consumer protection agencies, museums, libraries, parks, sewerage systems, and water. They regulate telephone services, gambling, sanitation in restaurants and supermarkets, land use, building standards, automobile emissions, noise levels, air pollution, hunting and fishing, and consumption of alcohol. They are involved in licensing or certifying undertakers, teachers, electricians, social workers, child-care agencies, nurses, doctors, lawyers, pharmacists, and others. As these incomplete listings should make clear, state and local governments affect many, many aspects of everyday life.

Among the most prominent state and local government functions is schooling. For the most part, public elementary and secondary schools operate under the immediate authority of local school districts. Typically headed by elected school boards, these districts are collectively responsible for spending more than 100 billion dollars a year and have no direct counterparts in any other country in the world. State governments regulate and supervise numerous aspects of elementary and secondary schooling, and school districts must operate within the constraints imposed by their state government. In addition, most states have fairly extensive systems of higher education. Tuition charges are higher at private colleges than at state institutions, and taxpayers make up the difference between what students pay and actual costs of operating state colleges. While the national government provides some aid to elementary, secondary, and higher education and involves itself in some areas of education policies, state and local governments remain the dominant policy-makers in the field of public education.

Crime control and order maintenance make up another primary state and local government function. Criminal statutes, police forces, prisons, traffic laws (including drunk driving laws and penalties), juvenile detention centers, and courts are all part and parcel of state and local government activities in the area of public safety. Presidential candidates sometimes talk about crime in the streets and what to do about it, but the reality is that state and local governments have far more direct involvement with this policy area than the national government does.

Singling out education and public safety in the preceding two paragraphs is not meant to slight the many other important policy areas in which state and local governments are involved: planning and zoning, roads and public transport, fire protection, provision of health care facilities, licensing and job training programs, and environmental protection, to mention just a few. Selections in this unit should provide greater familiarity with various activities of state and local governments.

The first section of this unit focuses on the issue of service delivery. It is important to distinguish between *provision* and *production* of goods and services by state and local governments. For example, a local government may be responsible for *providing* garbage collection for residents and might meet that responsibility by paying a private firm or a neighboring unit of local government to *produce* the service. Similarly, a state government may be responsible for providing penal institutions to house certain kinds of criminal offenders, but might meet that responsibility by paying a private concern or another state government to *produce* (plan, build, organize, and operate) a prison where offenders will be suitably confined. In recent years, the concept of privatization has figured prominently in discussions and decisions about the best ways for state and local governments to deliver services.

The second section of this unit treats issues facing state and local governments in various policy areas. Interactions among national, state, and local governments frequently play important roles in shaping such policy issues.

Topics in this unit of the book can be viewed as the consequences of topics treated in earlier units. Intergovernmental relations and finances, elections, parties, interest groups, and governmental institutions all shape the responses of state and local governments to policy issues. In turn, policies that are adopted interact with other components of state and local politics and modify them accordingly. Thus, the subject matter of unit 8 is an appropriate way to conclude the book.

Looking Ahead: Challenge Questions

List all the occasions in a typical day in which you come into contact with state and local government services, programs, regulations, and the like. Compare your list with a similar list of daily encounters with the national government.

Identify some policies pursued by your state govern-

ment or one of your local governments that you consider undesirable. Identify some desirable policies, too.

What do you think about the pros and cons of state and local governments contracting with others to produce goods and render services such as garbage collection, fire protection, school maintenance, prisons, and so forth? What does *privatization* mean to you and how do you feel about it? Do you think that the private sector can generally do a better job in producing goods and services than the public sector can? Why or why not?

Do you think it is fair that parents who send their children to private or parochial schools still have to pay property taxes to support public schools in their school district? What about people without any children? Should they have to pay taxes to support public education? Why or why not?

Do you think that your state's system of higher education is satisfactory? Why or why not? Do you think that students attending state colleges should have to pay tuition? Or should state colleges be free in the way that public elementary and secondary schools are?

Is it right for state and local land-use regulations to restrict how private citizens can use property that they own? Do you approve of the power of state and local governments to take property away from citizens through *eminent domain*?

What do you think is the single most important service that state governments are primarily responsible for providing? Local governments? The national government?

If you were an elected state government official, on what policy areas would you concentrate your efforts? If you were an elected local government official?

Privatization Is a Means to "More With Less"

JOHN R. MILLER and CHRISTOPHER R. TUFTS

John R. Miller is a partner with Peat Marwick Main & Co. in New York City, and National Director of the firm's Government Services Practice. He is a member of the board of directors of the National Civic League. Christopher R. Tufts is a senior manager in the Washington, D.C. office of Peat Marwick.

America's industrial leaders have come to realize that to be competitive in the global economy they must demonstrate to the buying public that their products represent the best value. Such mode of economics-based decision making is now being applied by taxpayers to the goods and services produced by government. Taxpayers and consumers alike are demanding the best quality and value for their hard-earned dollars.

Companies realize that in order to win in the marketplace and make a profit, they must "accomplish more with less"—fewer people, less money, less time, less space and fewer resources in general. To be competitive and profitable, many companies are adopting "downsizing" business strategies. Key components of downsizing include: productivity and quality improvement programs; mergers, streamlining operations; and divestiture of businesses in which they are not competitive. These strategies must be balanced by more creative management.

Government has a comparable challenge. Faced with public demand for increased or improved services in a period of diminishing resources and a changing pattern of accountability, government officials must also develop innovative solutions to win public confidence. This article discusses the concept of downsizing government and specifically focuses on privatization of service delivery as one alternative.

Downsizing

Government downsizing is the selective application of a broad range of management and cost reduction techniques to streamline operations and eliminate unnecessary costs. These same techniques can be applied to the development or expansion of government service, as well as to maintaining service levels, improving quality, and reducing existing government service cost. In all cases the objective is the same: Identify practical solutions and implementation plans that best serve the public through more effective management and delivery of government services, while saving or avoiding unnecessary costs.

Downsizing alternatives can be grouped into five major categories:

- Productivity and quality improvement programs;
- Consolidation (intra-and inter-government cooperation);
- Privatization;
- Program reduction;
- Program abandonment.

The objective of "accomplishing more for less" is most frequently achieved by exercising a combination of downsizing alternatives. For example, a government may initiate a productivity and quality improvement program in its health services; consolidate, through a multijurisdictional agreement, to provide shock trauma medical treatment; contract with the private sector to provide drug prevention programs; attempt to reduce the demand for service through the imposition of user fees for ambulance service; and eliminate minor injury treatment services at government hospitals. Each potential opportunity for downsizing must be approached creatively to ensure the public still receives the best service at the lowest possible cost.

Privatization As a Downsizing Choice

As many corporate leaders are retrenching to do better what they do best, so too must government be willing to do the same. Peter Drucker, in his book *The Age of Discontinuity,* called for "reprivatization" of many government functions, saying "The purpose of government is to make fundamental decisions and to make them effectively. The purpose of government is to focus the political energies of society. It is to dramatize issues. It is to present fundamental choices. The purpose of government, in other words, is to govern. This, as we have learned in other institutions is incompatible with 'doing.' Any attempt to combine governing with 'doing' on a large scale paralyzes government's decision-making capacity."

One downsizing alternative for government to consider is to competitively engage the private sector to produce goods and services that are readily available from many commercial sources. Although the current impetus for privatization is largely pragmatic, the guiding political philosophy behind it is as old as the nation itself. Americans have long alternated between the Jeffersonian and Hamiltonian philosophies of government. However, the new momentum for privatization transcends political and ideological boundaries, and is rooted in the determination of creative government managers to develop innovative solutions to serve the public interest.

Today a broad and growing consensus recognizes that privatization, properly implemented, is a viable and legitimate response to a wide range of philosophical and practical concerns. Experience is showing that the private sector can indeed provide many services rendered by

Reprinted by permission from the March/April 1988 issue of *National Civic Review*, pp. 100-111. National Civic Review, 1601 Grant Street, Suite 250, Denver, CO 80203.

government with equal or greater effectiveness, and at lower cost. Consequently, privatization is likely to exert a powerful influence over the shape of political and economic institutions in coming years.

What is Privatization?

George W. Wilson, Distinguished Professor of Business and Economics at the Indiana University School of Business, defines privatization on a philosophical plane. He writes, "The broader and more relevant meaning of privatization must refer to nothing more or less than greater reliance upon market forces to generate production of particular goods and services."

In practical terms, privatization is a process by which government engages the private sector to provide capital or otherwise finance government programs, purchase government assets, and/or operate government programs through various types of contractual arrangements.

As privatization usually occurs in combination with other downsizing initiatives, so too do many privatization transaction involve a combination of methods. For example, private sector capital financing, using such vehicles as leveraged leasing, lease purchases, and turnkey contracts, is frequently accompanied by operation of government programs through one of four types of arrangements: franchises, grants, vouchers, or contracts.

Privatization is nothing new. It can be traced to the first Bank of the United States which served as the Federal government's fiscal agency and principal depository of the Treasury and was owned by private shareholders. When the Federal government wanted to deliver mail to its citizens west of the Mississippi, it contracted with 80 horseback riders and spawned the Pony Express. The Homestead Act gave settlers government-owned land for a small fee if they would cultivate soil for a fixed period.

In the last decade, privatization has expanded from capital construction and professional service contracts to traditionally in-house administrative and public service programs. The majority of governments now contract for at least some legal, medical, engineering, technical and other professional services. Indeed, state and local government spending for public services performed by the private sector rose from $27.4 billion in 1975 to well over $100 billion in 1985. The trend toward privatization will continue to grow even though the growth rate for state and local governments appears to be slowing.

State governments, though less active than local governments with privatization, are experimenting in many areas. The state of California alone in 1985 wrote 7,000 contracts, worth over $2 billion, to carry out administrative or public service functions, including mental health, corrections, and a full range of administrative services.

Objectives of Privatization

What are the primary objectives of privatization? They are:

• To improve the use of scarce resources by reducing the costs of providing public services, particularly where private enterprise is strong and government is assured of more effective services at lower costs;

• To modify the role of government from that of a primary producer of goods and services to that of governing;

• To enable government to meet responsibilities that might otherwise be abandoned because they are too costly;

• To reduce the debt burden;

• To limit tax rates.

Privatization of government services should be considered:

• When government's operations are unrelated to the central function of governance. Examples of governance are legislative, judicial, and certain financial activities (e.g., rate setting, debt issuance, revenue policy);

• When current government service is in direct competition with services operated by the private sector;

• When the cost of an existing government-provided service exceeds the available or projected resources;

• When current government operations are inefficient and/or service is of poor quality and all remedial actions have resulted in insufficient improvement.

Privatization Successes

As already noted, privatization transactions cover a wide range of services. The following are examples of applications of various types of privatization.

Fire Protection. Rural/Metro Fire Department Corporation, a privately-owned company, serves half a million people in Arizona (one-fifth of the state's population), and 100,000 more in Tennessee. Rural/Metro Corp.'s $4.3 million contract with Scottsdale, Arizona for 1987-88 averages out to $36 per capita per year, compared with an average of $50 for public fire departments in similar cities. Scottsdale's fire insurance rates are average.

Ambulance Service. Newton, Massachusetts, estimates saving nearly $500,000 by privatizing its ambulance service while at the same time increasing ambulance availability and coverage.

Street Light Maintenance. The City of New York is divided into eight service areas for the provision of street light maintenance. All eight are competitively bid. No single company can "win" more than two service areas.

Legal. In Los Angeles County, Rolling Hills Estates broke off a contract it had with the County Prosecutor to handle all its cases, mostly involving violations of building and other town codes. Rolling Hills Estates now pays a private law firm to act as Town Prosecutor.

Grounds Maintenance. The school district of Rye, New York, recently contracted for grounds maintenance with a private company at an estimated savings of $34,000.

Prisons. The Dade County Jail is run by the Corrections Corp. of America, which runs several correction facilities throughout the United States, including two for the United States Immigration and Naturalization Service in Texas. Some interesting questions arise in privatizing corrections. Who chases escapees? Who is liable for the prisoners and their actions? Is prisoner rehabilitation compatible with profit? (Court decisions so far indicate that both the government and private contractor are liable for the actions of private guards.)

Fleet Maintenance. The city of Philadelphia contracts for the repair, maintenance and replacement of its motor vehicle fleet at an estimated savings of more than $4 million over the past four years.

Health Care. In Corsicana, Texas, the Navarro County Hospital was old, losing money, and about to lose its accreditation. To put it in shape, $12 million was needed. The county turned it over to the Hospital Corporation of America, which built a new hospital right next to the old one. The former hospital cost taxpayers $50,000 a year to operate. The new one is paying taxes of over $300,000 a year. In a similar vein, in 1983 the city of Louisville, Kentucky turned over the operation of a teaching hospital at the University of Louisville to the Humana Corporation. This hospital now benefits from the advantages of mass purchasing, gained by being part of Humana's 85-hospital chain.

Public Defender Services. Shasta County, California, reported a $100,000 per year savings in indigent-defense court costs by contracting its entire public defender program to a private firm run by a former member of the district attorney's staff in a association with six full-time lawyers, three secretaries and a part-time investigator. The switchover was prompted by a study that showed Shasta's in-house Public Defender's Office was about one-third more costly than contract services would be.

Data Processing. Orange County, California, whose population has doubled to over two million since 1973, estimates that it has saved more than $3 million over the past 12 years by hiring a private firm to run its computer center. "Without automation and the professional know-how to use the computers efficiently," said Howard Dix, manager of the center's operations, "the county would have faced an explosive growth in costs for personnel and facilities."

Privatization Failures

Let us now look at some failures in privatization, and the pitfalls they illustrate.

Two towns in Ohio hired a private security firm to provide police protection. The equipment provided was totally unacceptable. Both towns fired the private company and hired the guards to be public police officers.

In another case, a city contracted for trash pickup at one cent per household per month less than the city could provide the service. The company could not work that cheaply. Within months, the company was raising cash by selling equipment given it by the city. At Thanksgiving and Christmas, garbage piled up faster than the company could collect it. A new company took over the contract. Said the mayor of the city, this "case makes me a lot more cautious. It was false economy to take a bid that was low by one cent per household per month."

New York City's Parking Violations Bureau scandal is a sore reminder of what can happen in contracting for services. Several public officials and business people pled guilty to, or were convicted of, serious crimes involving contract corruption. Two contracting corporations, without admitting any guilt concerning the alleged bribes, reached an out-of-court settlement with the city wherein the companies paid $600,000 in damages.

In a New Jersey city, private trash haulers bill residents directly. As local landfills close, the haulers' costs rise dramatically, and they in turn raise the rates they charge. Complaints to the haulers have been unavailing, and the reaction of some residents is to cancel service and dump their own garbage illegally in any open space. This has precipitated a limited health emergency. City officials are now considering eliminating use of the franchised haulers and instituting municipal trash collection, even though it will require raising property taxes.

How To Accomplish Privatization Transactions

To avoid the pitfalls of the failure examples, a careful process should be followed. The process should begin with analysis of privatization alternatives (franchises, grants, vouchers, and contracts) relative to the current delivery methods practiced. This analysis should examine implementation feasibility, technical performance, and costs. Its objectives are to determine which services may be privatized, select the most appropriate privatization method, and develop a scheduled work plan for implementation of the privatization transaction.

In order to meet these objectives, a multi-disciplined team approach should be followed. At minimum, this team should consist of personnel with technical experience in the function under review; legal, personnel, fiscal, and contracts staff; and political advisory and independent review support. The team approach provides the appropriate balance of expertise to ensure that all issues are identified and practical solutions are formulated. In addition, the use of political and independent review advisory support will assist in building the necessary consensus and commitment to change among all constituent groups. Most important, the team approach provides appropriate balance between program, fiscal, and political considerations.

Implementation Feasibility Analysis

Implementation feasibility analysis is the study of the political, legal, market, government operations, and other factors of each privatization option relative to the status quo, to anticipate the difficulties in accomplishing each option. The team approach provides the appropriate expertise to identify issues and barriers and develop solutions to minimize the impact of the issues and eliminate the barriers. The objective of the implementation feasibility study is to develop action plans identifying the specific objectives, scope, process, responsibilities, and timing for implementation of each service delivery option. The implementation feasibility study must address:

Political Barriers. Are the current coalitions of beneficiaries, near beneficiaries, service providers, government administrators, officials, political activists, unions and general populace amenable to change? How do you build the coalitions necessary to support the change process?

Legal Issues. What are the statutory, regulatory and tax law barriers, incentives, and/or requirements for privatization? What modifications to union agreements or ongoing contracts are required? What is the impact on liability?

Market. Is the private sector market mature or developing? Has the private sector shown interest through unsolicited proposals, industry studies, or research by industry experts? How capable is the private sector of providing quality goods or services? Is there a sufficient number of qualified bidders to ensure competition and provide the government a favorable risk/reward ratio? Does the private sector perceive a favorable risk/reward ratio? What is the private sector track record in government contract performance?

Government Operations. Will privatizing selected functions disrupt continuity of operations? How will the affected employee be treated? What effect will privatization have on accountability? Who will monitor the private sector? How, and with what frequency will the private sector be monitored? What performance measures will be used to determine whether performance standards have been met? How will the government control the quality, timing and cost of delivery of services to be privatized? What are appropriate penalties (or incentives) to ensure compliance with performance standards and service requirements?

Other Factors. Who will have control over the staff, equipment, and facilities? Are the resources available to do the necessary analysis, conduct the planning, preparation, and execution of privatization transactions?

Technical Performance Analysis

Once a government has examined the implementation feasibility of the privatization options, it needs to compare the overall implementation difficulties anticipated against the total benefits to be derived. Each option must be evaluated in terms of technical performance criteria including, but not necessarily limited to: availability, quality and effectiveness, risks, and program impacts. Through review of historic experience within and outside the jurisdiction, demographic and geographic studies, and/or the performance of pilot programs, analysis can be performed to evaluate each option. Criteria should be weighted and each alternative scored to determine the optimal anticipated technical performance option. At a minimum the criteria should include:

Availability and Costs to Citizens. Will individual consumers obtain improved choices of supply and service levels? Will all consumers including disadvantaged groups or geographically remote regions be served? If user fees are charged, will disadvantaged users be able to afford the level of service they need? Will the service cost to all consumers be fairly distributed? Will the overall cost to citizens increase?

Quality and Effectiveness. Will government objectives be achieved more effectively? Will the quality of service improve?

Risks. Will service disruptions be more likely? What contingencies will be required? A risk analysis that quantifies the technical, implementation, and cost risks associated with each of the alternative delivery options provides a comprehensive and disciplined approach towards reducing uncertainty and focuses the attention of the team on the most critical issues.

Program Impacts. What synergies or benefits will be derived? Will the government benefit from new technology? What impact will there be on the operations of other departments, especially if the program or service is for internal government use?

Cost Analysis

Since privatization is heavily influenced by cost, a thorough costing, economic, and pricing analysis must be performed for each option. The purpose of this analysis is to estimate potential savings, assess the economic impact, determine specific costs, and establish pricing requirements. The three types of studies most frequently performed are:

Financial Feasibility Studies. A determination of the current and future gross and net costs or savings of the planned privatization transaction in relation to the costs of the current method of operation.

Cost Benefit Analyses. A determination of the costs of new methods of providing services or doing business, compared against the benefits of the alternatives, to identify the methods that are the most cost-responsive.

Cost and Pricing Studies. An identification and examination of the direct, indirect, fixed, variable, opportunity, and oversight costs associated with a privatization transaction for different levels of service; a definition of what will happen to total costs as the service levels change;

and the recommendation of pricing strategies and/or prices to achieve desired utilizations, cash throw-offs, and/or rates of return.

For each study the first step should be to determine what constitutes cost, where the data should be obtained, how costs should be calculated, and how costs should be projected for future years. For a cost comparison between government service performance and a service contract between government and a private vendor, the major cost elements to examine include:

Government Performance Costs

• Personnel costs: basic pay (salaries or wages), other entitlements (e.g., night differential, hazardous duty differential), fringe benefits (e.g., FICA, pension, workers' compensation), other (e.g., overtime, uniform and meal allowances);

• Materials and supplies costs: costs of raw materials, replacement parts, repairs, office supplies, and equipment, necessary to provide a product or perform a service;

• Overhead costs: operations overhead (e.g., supervision) and general administrative overhead (e.g., personnel, data processing, legal);

• Other specifically attributable costs, such as rent, utilities, maintenance and repairs, insurance, depreciation or use charges, travel;

• Additional costs, unusual or specific circumstances that occur only under government operation or don't fit other categories.

Contractor Performance Cost

• *Realistic* contract price: the contractor must be able to deliver the service at the quantity and quality desired at the bid price, and still make a reasonable profit, for a contract price to be realistic;

• Start-up costs (e.g., learning curve);

• Contract administration costs, including execution of quality assurance monitoring, payment processing, negotiation of change orders, and contract close-up;

• Conversion costs (e.g., disposing of expendable items, retraining, severance pay, lease termination penalties, conducting the privatization transaction);

• Additional costs (e.g., lost volume discounts).

Cost Advantage Based on the Above Costs

The cost advantage is defined as the difference between the total government performance cost and the total contractor performance cost, adjusted for additional or lost tax revenues. Because of the risks involved in implementing such a change, public managers should generally look for a major cost advantage before shifting to new modes of service delivery, to avoid being caught short like the city that changed to contracted trash pickup for only a one cent per household cost differential.

Selection and Implementation

Having completed implementation feasibility, technical performance, and cost analyses, a government manager can select the preferred method of service delivery. Privatization can be one of several downsizing alternatives available to government managers. It is not a panacea for challenges facing government managers. If analysis shows that government provides a service more efficiently and effectively than the private sector, it should continue to do so. Privatization offers an opportunity to introduce the cost-saving, creative, service-generating aspect of competition into the public arena. It is important that public managers retain both decision-making and ultimate responsibility for public services. It is they who must decide what services will be privatized and who will provide them.

Not all methods of privatizing will benefit all parties or work in all situations. The concept works best when public managers carefully examine public assets and services to determine which could be replaced by private functions, thoroughly evaluate private sector competition, assemble representatives from all affected parties to agree on alternatives and solutions, and analyze the combination of tactics to satisfy a broad range of constituents. The key is to develop a workable mix of program and fiscal alternatives.

Privatization is an appealing concept because it offers governments flexibility in meeting their public responsibilities and, at the same time, presents entrepreneurs with a new set of challenges. Entrepreneurs, as George Gilder notes in his book *The Spirit of Enterprise,* are "engineers of change." The challenge to public managers today is to identify and manage change.

Privatization
Presents Problems

HARRY P. HATRY
Harry P. Hatry is Director of the State Policy Center, the Urban Institute, in Washington, D.C. This article is adapted from a presentation at the American Political Science Association Annual Meeting September 4, 1987 in Chicago, Illinois, as part of the session on "The Politics of Privatization."

Admittedly, public officials should periodically consider options for greater use of the private sector for delivering their services. This is good public policy and good public management.

But public officials should also examine existing instances of private sector delivery and consider the option of switching *back to public employee delivery.* This is also good public policy. For a number of reasons, private delivery can become inefficient or have quality problems.

The Best of Times, the Worst of Times—to Contract

Our work at The Urban Institute indicates that the appropriateness and success of using a particular privatization option is *highly situational.* Success depends on many factors that are individual to the particular public agency, in the particular location and at the particular time. Success of a privatization approach depends on:

• The current level of performance of the current delivery system. A government agency may indeed be delivering the service quite efficiently and with good quality—leaving little room for improvement. (As hard as some people find it to believe, often public employee delivery *does* work very well.) In other situations, the service may be inefficient or of poor quality. This is the situation that provides the mayor opportunity for successful change.

• The way the option is implemented. Without good implementation even the best ideas will go away. For example, in a switch to contracting, the quality of the request-for-proposal process is key to assuring that a capable contractor is selected. And a sound, sustained contract administration and monitoring process is essential to assuring that contractor performance remains up to par.

Threat of Privatization is Often Enough

I believe that the major advantage of the privatization movement is not that the private sector can reduce costs or improve service to a great extent, but that consideration of privatization encourages public officials and public employees to innovate and to break down obstacles to improving public employee efficiency.

Increasingly, examples occur where employees and their unions agree to changes, such as reductions in the size of garbage collection crews, when faced with a city council threat to contract the service.

Other governments have introduced procedures that involve direct competition between public and private agencies. In the "Phoenix Model," public agencies such as the City of Phoenix Public Works Department submit proposals that compete directly with bids received from private firms for services such as garbage collection and street sweeping. (The City Administrative Services codified this in January 1985 as "Management Procedure: Procedure for Preparing Cost Estimate City Services Under Consideration to be Performed by Private Industry on a Contractual Basis.")

In a third approach, Kansas City, Phoenix and other cities have split their work, such as garbage collection, into districts, some of which are served by private contractors (if they win) and some by public employees. The city reports on comparative costs, encouraging competition between public and private service providers.

Private Isn't Necessarily Cheaper

Lower cost with improved efficiency is the most frequently given reason for contracting. I am not convinced, as some others are, based on the evidence thus far available, that privatization lowers costs in most instances. Hospital care is one of the few areas that has been extensively studied in recent years. A University of California study of contracting the management of public hospitals in a number of counties in California did not find evidence that the contractors had achieved cost savings. The study did find evidence that the private firms were better at securing revenue. [1] Last year's National Academy of Sciences study of private versus public hospital care found that "studies of hospital costs that control for size (and in some cases for case mix and other factors) show for-profit hospitals to have slightly *higher* expenses than not-for-profit public and private institutions." [2]

The Urban Institute recently worked with two states (Delaware and Maryland). In three of the four programs that the states considered for a change to contracting, we found that state employees were likely to achieve costs similar to or lower than the private sector. In one, food service for inmates of Delaware's prisons, we surveyed ten other states that had contracted for inmate food service. Six reported higher costs with contracting, three lower, and one reported about the same costs. Delaware's own current costs appeared to be similar to those expected if the service were contracted. The department is still considering contracting, its motivation being the difficulty in hiring prison kitchen supervisors and, secondarily, the desire of some prison administrators to reduce the administrative headaches in arranging for meals.

Columbia University's classic 1970's analysis of solid waste collection costs found higher *average* unit costs for public employee delivery than for contractor-delivered service. [3] But it also found that the most expensive delivery method was delivery by franchised firms— firms that dealt directly with households and not through a government. The more recent Ecodata study of Los Angeles County also private vendors were, on average, cheaper. In all these comparisons, however, averages hide the fact that in some cities the unit costs were lower for public employee delivery than in some contracted cities.

Vouchers, while often an excellent way to give consumers more choice, do not necessarily involve lower costs. It depends on how the government sets the value of the vouchers. Hennepin County (Minnesota) in

Reprinted by permission from the March/April 1988 issue of *National Civic Review,* pp. 112-117. National Civic Review, 1601 Grant Street, Suite 250, Denver, CO 80203.

its trial of day care vouchers found that total costs increased when it switched to vouchers.

It is dangerous to generalize as to the success of privatization options. There will be situations where a switch will be worthwhile and cases where it won't be.

Three Important Potential Problems With Privatization

Three major potential problems in privatization, are almost always raised by public employee unions. While these problems are acknowledged by advocates of privatization, they are often treated too casually, as if they were easy to overcome, only minor inconveniences. These three problems are: 1. potential for corruption; 2. possibility of reduced quality of service; and, 3. possibility of reduced access of disadvantaged citizens to services.

Corruption. High financial stakes introduce great temptations to individuals to engage in illegal action. We have frequent examples—New York City's Parking Violations Bureau; recently, in the District of Columbia, in all sorts of contract awards; and, over the years, the City of Chicago has had its share of problems. The American Federation of State, County and Municipal Employees (AFSCME) has taken great pains to document numerous instances of hanky-panky in public sector contracting.[4] The possibility of corruption can be reduced by establishing sound procurement procedures, and in the case of divestiture, by installing appropriate regulations. Nevertheless, the threat remains.

Possible Reductions in Service Quality. Again, when substantial payments are involved, a natural temptation is to do whatever is necessary to maximize profitability and skimp on quality to save dollars, particularly in for-profit organizations. This temptation becomes even greater when a firm gets into financial difficulties. This sometimes happens even with private nonprofit organizations. The principal protections against poor quality are performance contracting and adequate performance monitoring. The need for these protections has been noted by both proponents and opponents of privatization. A classic example of this problem is recent shoddy aircraft maintenance in deregulated airlines facing major financial problems. Some airlines have been assessed large fines for inadequate maintenance.

However, it is much easier to say that monitoring is needed than to provide it. Most government contracts I have seen in recent years have very weak or non-existent performance requirements. To make matters worse, performance monitoring of contracts is very sparse.

Possible Reduced Access to Services for Disadvantaged. The incentives to private firms—particularly for-profit firms—are to avoid clients for whom securing payment for services is likely to be difficult, and to avoid clients who may be particularly difficult and expensive to help, such as disadvantaged clients.

This problem has become particularly acute in the delivery of medical services. Persons without medical insurance or other funds have reportedly been turned away from private hospitals and even from emergency room care. The National Academy of Sciences study cited earlier concluded that access is a major national concern. The study found that for-profit hospitals served fewer uninsured patients and had a smaller proportion of uncompensated care than non-profit hospitals. The researchers felt that although the percentage differences were small among the types of providers, they could nonetheless "translate into large numbers of patients: Data from four of five states demonstrate that not-for-profit hospitals provide two or three times as much uncompensated care, on average, than for-profit hospitals. (Both types provided less uncompensated care than public hospitals.)"[5] Debate continues about what laws and regulations should be introduced to encourage or require private hospitals to admit patients regardless of their ability to pay, particularly emergency-care patients.

This problem can be alleviated through contractual and statutory requirements and the provision of subsidies. Alleviating the problem, however, will often reduce the benefits of privatization.

Conclusion

Privatization should be viewed as neither panacea nor poison. It is simply one tool available to public officials. Before they attempt to apply it universally, there are points they should remember:

• The success of privatization is highly situational, dependent on local circumstances and how well the new approach is implemented.

• Periodically consider options that involve greater use of the private sector.

• Periodically consider switching *back* from *private* delivery to *public* delivery.

• Give serious attention to the three potential problems of privatization-corruption, reduced service quality, and reduced access of the disadvantaged to services.

Perhaps the main virtue of the privatization movement is that it encourages public employees to improve their own productivity in order to help ensure their own competitiveness in the face of privatization. Increasingly, the message to the public sector is that if a service has problems in efficiency or quality, the agency needs to "shape up or be shipped out." The net result should be less costly and higher quality services for all the public.

Notes

[1] William Shonick and Ruth Roemer, *Public Hospitals Under Private Management: The California, Experience,* Institute of Governmental Studies, University of California, Berkeley, 1983, Chapter 5.

[2] Bradford H. Gray, Editor, *For-Profit Enterprise in Health Care,* National Academy Press, Washington, D.C., 1986, p. 93.

[3] Barbara J. Stevens and E.S. Savas, "The Cost of Residential Refuse Collection and the Effect of Service Arrangement," Graduate School of Business, Columbia University, September 1976.

[4] See, for example, John D. Hanrahan, *Government For Sale,* American Federation of State, County and Municipal Employees, Washington D.C., 1977.

[5] *Ibid.,* p. 116.

Getting in Touch with Government

California's new automated government information system lets people get a lot of what they need from government on their own time at their nearby store. It may save money, too.

Jo Martinez

Jo Martinez is director of NCSL's Legislative Information Systems/Services Program.

How do I get license plates for my car? Who can help me settle a dispute with my landlord? How do I obtain a license to operate a day care center? Is there a carpool that would work for me? What jobs are available in my neighborhood?

For residents of Sacramento and San Diego, the answers to these and other questions no longer require calls or visits to government agencies but a single trip to the local grocery store. Grocery store? Yes, California is trying out its new automated information system, Info/California, with information kiosks installed where the people are—in shopping malls, grocery stores and libraries.

The state embarked last fall on a nine-month trial of multimedia computer system to answer some of the questions most commonly asked of state agencies. If it works out, the system will go statewide and be expanded to allow all citizens to conveniently transact their business with state and local government. They will be able, for example, to obtain copies of birth certificates, renew their driver's licenses and reserve campsites in state parks all in the same place—a sort of "one-stop shopping" for government services.

Info/California comes through a video screen in a specially designed station, or kiosk, that looks like an automated teller machine. For phase I of the project, 15 kiosks have been set up in shopping malls, grocery and discount stores, a senior citizens' center, public libraries and on college campuses.

For information on any of 90 subjects, citizens merely follow the instructions of the on-screen narrator and the graphic display to select their topics from a number of options. Touching a picture on the screen activates a videotape that gives the requested information in Spanish or English.

The categories currently available are employment, the legal system and business, education, health, environment and natural resources, transportation, family and children, and general assistance. (For example, is any of the unclaimed state property mine, or how can I prepare for an earthquake?)

Under Transportation, for example, citizens can get information about California's boating laws and driver's licenses, registering vehicles, joining Rideshare programs, and applying for license plates and placards for the disabled.

A special interactive program on the system allows citizens to use the state's "Job Match" program. By touching a series of screens, individuals define the type of work they're interested in. The computer presents the number of jobs currently available in the selected category and location and the salary range. The job information is updated daily.

The individual can use the "keys" on an on-screen keyboard to complete an application form, which the system prints out along with the name and address of the nearest employment office. The applicant can take the completed form to the employment office, thus saving time for both the applicant and the interviewer. This process formerly required a long, face-to-face interview.

"Info/California is a fresh approach to providing citizens with the attention and service they demand," says Governor Pete Wilson, "while containing the escalating cost of government services."

Info/California was made possible by a 1988 law sponsored by Senator Rebecca Morgan, whose district includes California's Silicon Valley. Senator Morgan's legislation authorized the state to work with private industry to explore ways to increase public productivity with information technology.

"We are always looking for ways that we can increase government service without increasing government employment," Senator Morgan explained. "By using the technological advancements of the private sector, we can provide more government service for less."

The law established requirements for state government participation with business in advanced technology projects, and it authorized two major data centers, the Teale and the Health and Welfare Agency data centers, to allocate funds from certain unencumbered surpluses for projects that demonstrate or develop advanced information technologies.

Info/California is a product developed by the state in partnership with the IBM Corporation and North Communications. To date, the state has spent approximately $300,000 on the project, while IBM's out-of-pocket expenses, not including personnel costs, have been $750,000. In addition, for the pilot project IBM and North Communications lent the state software and equipment valued at $3 million to $4 million, according to IBM project leader John Allen.

Information Kiosks Are Coming Up All Over

All around the country, people are using automated information systems to find out about the services of cities, counties and states. In Kansas City, Mo., they can go to "City Hall in the Mall"; in Orlando, Fla., they can learn "Orlando A thru Z"; and they can find out that "You Count" in Orange County, N.C.

Besides the usual rundown of how to get permits or financial aid for students, the systems offer some special services.

• A feature bound to appeal to politicians is offered by "The County Connec-

tion" in Anne Arundel County, Md. There, a visitor can touch the "Your Voice in Government" option on the screen and point out his residence on a map, and a picture of his council representative appears on the screen, delivering a taped message.

• Better than a list of rules is the most popular video of Plano, Texas' Municipal Center in the Mall, "Fireworks," which explains fireworks regulations through a colorful, dynamic display.

• "AutoClerk," a kiosk operated by Long Beach (Calif.) Municipal Court, al-

lows people to pay a traffic ticket using a credit or debit card or a personal check, plead not guilty, sign up for traffic school or choose a court date. The kiosk is open 24 hours a day and gives instructions in English or Spanish.

• Mobile kiosks give cities, counties and states flexibility in getting information where it's needed. Hillsborough County, Fla., located its mobile unit of The 24-Hour Courthouse in a library in an area of the county where the people felt they had not received their fair share of county services.

The network uses state-of-the-art multimedia technology incorporating video, computer graphics, high-quality stereo and computer touchscreen operations. The technology was first developed for IBM's "24-Hour City Hall/County Courthouse" project in the late 1980s. The goal of this project was to make government more accessible to the public by providing access in convenient locations, not just local government offices, and by expanding delivery of government services beyond the 9-to-5 work day.

Working with Public Technology Inc. (PTI), a non-profit technical arm of the National League of Cities, the International City/County Management Association and the National Association of Counties, IBM developed multimedia touchscreen access systems for a number of local governments.

The California system is based on "Hawaii Access," a dramatically successful experimental touchscreen network started in 1990. Hawaii's multimedia network provides health, human services and employment information in English, Samoan and Ilocano (spoken in the Philippines). During its six-month pilot project, the Hawaiian system was used by 30,260 people, 216 percent ahead of projections for use.

Californians seem to like Info/California, too. In its first four months, 54,357 people used the 15 kiosks—that's an average of 33 contacts a day per kiosk and 10 percent more than projected. Although use of the system dropped from

an average of 52 contacts a day the first month, officials attribute most of the decrease to the especially low use of the kiosk in the senior center. At the busiest sites, more than 50 people a day used the kiosk after four months.

Half of the users said Info/California saved them a phone call, letter or trip to a government office; 79 percent found the system easy to use.

Most of the people (57 percent) used the system outside regular weekday work hours. Eighteen percent of the usage overall was in Spanish; at one Sacramento grocery store 30 percent of the "customers" chose Spanish. (Usage statistics are compiled automatically.)

The most popular topics were Job Match, student aid, beaches, driver's licenses, the California State University system, in-demand jobs, community colleges, state parks, the University of California system and AIDS/HIV.

In the second phase of the project, which began this spring, citizens pay for services, such as copies of birth certificates or driver's license renewals, with credit cards. Currently, the certificates or licenses are delivered by mail, although the Health and Welfare Data Center is exploring ways to produce and dispense birth certificates from kiosks, according to center Director Russ Bohart. Each kiosk can "read" the magnetic strip on new California driver's licenses, allowing the system to verify the user's identity and record the name and address automatically.

Over the long term, Info/California may be integrated with other informa-

tion systems to offer a broader range of services. Automated systems already in operation in California include the Tulare County kiosk used to prequalify residents for AFDC; the Long Beach municipal court kiosk, "Auto Clerk," which accepts major credit cards, personal checks or debit cards in payment for traffic fines; and the San Diego kiosk, which provides information about local services.

Bohart says the wave of the future may be kiosks that provide access to all levels of government service—city, county, state and federal. Integrated systems would allow citizens to resolve problems, obtain quick answers to their questions, and order, pay for and obtain government documents without the hassle of locating the correct government office and then getting to it during working hours.

"We're talking to [agencies and departments that handle] student aid, fish and game, licensing for health professionals, hairdressers—we're talking literally to every program in state and local government," Bohart says.

Making all these services available through an "information backbone," he says, would greatly simplify and expedite government service by providing a "single face to government" for all citizens.

A network of kiosks throughout the state could be paid for, Bohart suggests, by re-directing funds currently used for public education and outreach. The state could recoup the cost of operating the kiosks, estimated at $2,000 a month per kiosk, by charging agencies a fee for the video information provided.

Another potential revenue source is the money saved from existing budgets. Bohart explains that the California Department of Motor Vehicles currently processes about 250,000 address changes each month, at $5 each. If individuals made changes using the kiosks, the data center could provide address changes to the DMV in electronic form for $1 or $2 each, which would go toward operating the kiosks and would improve DMV's cost–effectiveness. Customers also could share the costs through user fees on special services received from kiosks, such as instant copies of birth certificates, Bohart says.

Shirley Marshall, IBM's project manager for "24-Hour City Hall," says that in a time of shrinking resources, multimedia technology can help governments provide quality services to an increasingly diverse and growing population.

Michael North, president of North Communications, explains that pro-

grams like Info/California also provide the opportunity to improve government efficiency. By turning over to the kiosks the repetitive tasks of answering the same questions, such as which office to contact, which documents to bring and how to fill out forms, government workers are free to spend time meeting people's special needs. Agencies with "intersecting missions," such as providing day care and child nutrition information to single mothers, can coordinate and consolidate their functions. North says that advanced technology can reduce the costs of administering government services and make dealing with government easier for citizens.

Other states are starting to use kiosks for some services. In February, New Jersey began offering "TAG, the Motor Vehicle Self-Service Helper" to process automobile registration renewals automatically. The machines placed around the state allow users, for a small fee, to connect with the state motor vehicle database and receive

copies of vehicle registration cards on the spot. The TAG system was developed by the NCR Corporation.

Delaware, Maryland, New York, Pennsylvania, Virginia, West Virginia and the District of Columbia offer job information through Automated Labor Exchange (ALEX) kiosks, financed by the U.S. Department of Labor. Job seekers can find lists and descriptions of positions open around the country. More than 1,000 people a week were using the machines in Virginia.

California's Health and Welfare Secretary Gould says that Info/California is an example of government working "smarter."

"People want government to be responsive to their needs, regardless of which level—federal, state or local—is responsible," Gould says. This technology is a tool to improve government efficiency and productivity while at the same time "bringing government directly to people's fingertips."

The Challenge Ahead:

The State Agenda for the Coming Years

The mid-1990s promise to be extremely challenging years as state leaders and institutions struggle to bring accountability and predictability back into their political systems. Faced with continuing budgets troubles, increasing demands for services and a shift of responsibility from the federal to the state level, the American states will be hard pressed to satisfy constituent needs or improve state services. However, the tough times may result in long-term improvement in state government, as administrators streamline agencies, legislators trim inefficient or redundant programs and state leaders generally seek new and cost effective solutions to social and economic problems.

Dag Ryen

Dag Ryen is executive editor for The Council of State Governments.

A great deal of fermentation is going on in state cauldrons. Having achieved a level of influence and activity unprecedented since the 18th century, state governments face extremely challenging problems and decisions in the coming years. Across the country chief executives and legislators are evaluating which problems to tackle, which issues to confront and which activities to regulate. In one way, states are coming into a new understanding of their full potential. But with that understanding comes an additional appreciation for the responsibilities and difficulties of governance in the modern age.

On the one hand, state leaders feel they can step into the logjam created by an overly politicized national leadership to meet the real needs of constituencies. On the other, there is a real sense that state governments cannot be all things to all people, that priorities must be set and hard choices made. Given a complex and often adversarial environment, it is difficult to predict with any accuracy how state governments will evolve in the near future in response to such conflicting forces. But change is in the offing, change that may be more profound than is immediately apparent.

Clearly, states have moved into almost every area of government activity, including many regulatory and program areas once considered the exclusive preserve of the federal government. Indeed, some expansion of state activity has come as a result of federal mandates. Whether states can continue to refine and improve their services and products over such a broad range remains to be seen.

The number one priority in most state capitals over the coming biennium will be fiscal rehabilitation. Despite massive budget cuts and tax increases in the first three fiscal years of the decade, most states continue to experience difficulties in bringing their budgets into balance. In fiscal 1991, 29 states were forced to reduce their enacted budgets. In 1992, that number rose to 35. Projections for fiscal 1993 and 1994 indicate modest growth at best, with most states forced to hold expansion of general fund expenditures at 3-5 percent. (NGA/NASBO 1992)

While the national recession has had an impact on the states, it is not the only cause of the fiscal crunch. Phenomenal growth in state revenues during the 1980s has tapered off due to major structural changes in the national economy. Services now constitute a larger share of retail activity and since most states do not tax services, state revenues have slowed accordingly. Also, the wide diversity in state tax environments has created a climate where corporations and partnerships easily can limit their tax liability.

A second major cause of fiscal turmoil is the rising cost of services over which the states have little control. Most important among these is health care. The national bill for health care is rapidly approaching $1 trillion a year. Through required contributions to Medicaid, state employee benefits and other programs, states pick up a significant portion — about 8 percent — of these costs. Every year states spend more than $200 per resident on health care.

The cost of health care continues to increase, as does the proclivity of the federal government to pass costs on to the states. From 1989 to 1990, health care costs rose by 9.2 percent. Over the past five years, the costs have gone up almost 50 percent. Health care costs consume nearly a fourth of all state revenues. (CSG 1992)

Another area of rapid growth in state expenditures is corrections. Between 1960 and 1985, state spending for corrections grew by 218 percent largely as a result of demands for better public safety and crime prevention. The national crackdown on criminal behavior has proven costly, with average annual expenses of keeping an inmate in a correctional facility running at $12,000-$15,000. A recent study by WESTRENDS, a research group established by the Western Legislative Conference to monitor changes in the Western states, indicates that 180 new 500-bed prisons will have to be built in the West in the coming five years to accommodate the expanding prison population. Last fall, Texas voters approved a $1.1 billion bond issue for prison construction in that state alone. All of the most populous states face similar problems.

States have adopted many strategies to keep budgets in balance while still meeting constituent needs. The solution often entails tax increases, including sales tax hikes, new or expanded excise taxes, restructuring of corporate and individual income tax rates and taxes on services. In 1992, states raised an additional $15 billion in revenues through tax increases, and governors' budget requests include an additional $5.1 billion for fiscal 1993. (NGA/NASBO 1992)

Other budget reduction strategies include across-the-board cuts, layoffs, bond issues, hiring and travel freezes and raiding surplus or rainy day funds. Most, however, are short-term solutions at a time when comprehensive reforms are needed to achieve fiscal stability.

Looking Ahead: Education

Even in the face of tough fiscal times, states continue to provide a wide variety of services and to improve the delivery of those services. But tight budgets have forced the elimination of most public service frills and have led state decision-makers to concentrate on the basics. Education, health care and economic development have been singled out as high priority areas for reform and refinement.

Education reform continues to receive a great deal of attention. Arguing that a well-educated population is the most important factor in ensuring economic health and competitiveness in a global economy, state leaders are championing major education reform packages. Many of these programs are tied to national education goals adopted by President George Bush and governors from the 50 states at a national "education summit" in 1990.

School reform got a jump start in Kentucky, Texas, Montana and New Jersey when courts in those states ruled that the existing education system was inequitable. All have since made major changes in education funding. Kentucky's comprehensive education reform act, which mandates school-based decisionmaking and a new state watchdog agency, is being used as a model by other states. Texas legislators met in special session four times before finalizing a $528 million reform package that is still subject to controversy and New Jersey's $600 million school aid reform was financed by increased sales, income and excise taxes.

Similar suits have been brought in at least 20 other states, several of which have initiated reform efforts to pre-empt further judicial action.

Among recent reform packages is Oregon's "Educational Act for the 21st Century." The Oregon program includes expanded Head Start and other early childhood programs, performance assessments, learning centers to help dropouts, a tracking system to monitor the performance of individual schools and an expanded school year.

A sweeping reform package adopted in Minnesota allows educators to start their own so-called charter schools. The new Minnesota law calls for streamlining the management bureaucracy in elementary education, lengthening the school year by 20 days over the next 10 years and bolstering parental involvement in the schools.

School reform also is a high priority in Arkansas, where a $287 million fund has been established to bolster teacher salaries and fund pilot programs in school restructuring; in Iowa, where recent legislation allows home education when children continue to pass annual tests; and in North Dakota, which now requires newly elected school board members to undergo in-service training.

Health Care

Another area of significant state activity is health care. Legislators and administrators who advocate health care reform are motivated in part by fiscal reality and a desire to bring down rising costs. But they also share a desire to help the more than 30 million Americans who have inadequate health insurance coverage. Ironically, the rolls of uninsured have grown as a result of the national recession, at a time when state wherewithal to help them is decreasing.

The most significant, and controversial, innovation in health care reform remains Oregon's Medicaid care priority system that restricts expensive medical procedures while extending basic and preventive care to all medically needy citizens. State officials submitted a formal waiver application to the Health Care Financing Administration in Washington almost two years ago and are still awaiting a decision from the Bush administration.

Variations on the Oregon rationing scheme have been discussed in other states, including Colorado and New York, but copycat programs are unlikely to be adopted before the federal government takes a stand on the issues involved.

Complicating the debate are proposals for national health care reform. Several Democratic members of Congress are advocating national health insurance, while the Bush administration has floated a proposal called "pay-or-play," which would mandate expanded employer coverage while relying on the current multi-provider system. Shifting responsibility for financing health care from the private to the public sector, as envisioned in the Democratic proposal would entail an initial tax increase, but ultimately would result in savings to businesses and the economy. A recent study indicates a one-payer system could result in savings of $1.3 trillion. (Robert Wood Johnson Foundation 1992) On the other hand, the president's proposal would allow both employers and the states greater flexibility in designing their own health benefits programs.

Many states are encouraging insurance companies to expand the policies available to small businesses and low-income workers either by providing tax credits or direct subsidies to the insurance provider. Maine Washington, New York, Ohio and Connecticut provide direct subsidies to individual policyholders. (Riley 1992) Florida and Minnesota in 1992 passed laws to subsidize health insurance for the working poor.

Meanwhile, states are looking for ways to improve access to health care while reducing costs. Among the most popular solutions is managed care, systems that use networks of health care providers much like HMOs while discouraging unnecessary or ineffective treatment. Statewide managed care plans for Medicaid patients long ... offered by Arizona and Kentucky are now being picked up by other states.

Economic Development

The governors of Texas and Kentucky have established task forces to develop legislation on comprehensive health care reform. In Delaware, legislation building on a public/private partnership with the Nemours Foundations, has been presented to ensure health care coverage to all children under the age of 18.

The trend in economic development is toward greater interstate cooperation.

A third area of intense state activity is economic development. With the economy faltering, unemployment rates running high and corporate investment dropping, states have expended considerable energy and resources to attract business, create jobs and improve the economic climate. Economic development programs have become more innovative and tailored to the specific assets and needs of the individual state.

For the most part, states have stepped back from the bidding wars for new industrial plants that characterized economic development during the 1980s, swayed in part by studies that showed such factors as educational facilities and skilled labor pools to be more important to industrial siting decisions than the size of state incentive packages. But an occasional business opportunity still generates interstate competition, as in the tug-of-war over the siting of United Air Lines' maintenance facility. And, in 1992, Nebraska and South Carolina were actively competing for a BMW assembly plant.

The trend in economic development is toward greater interstate cooperation. Responding to the challenges of international competition, five American states have joined with two Canadian provinces to form the Pacific Northwest Economic Region. The goal of this organization is to enhance the economic competitiveness of the region through cooperative policies, uniform legislation and common import-export initiatives.

The grandfather of interstate economic development organizations, the Southern Growth Policies Board, continues through seminars, leadership programs and research efforts to identify growth and trade opportunities for the Southern states. Further evidence of the trend toward multistate cooperation is provided by the establishment of shared foreign trade offices. And, in the Northeast, an effort is underway through the Eastern Regional Conference of The Council of State Governments to set up a shared electronic data base linking state foreign trade offices in that region.

In Alaska, Gov. Walter Hickel has promised to continue to push for Congress to open the Arctic National Wildlife Refuge to oil exploration and development, which according to the governor would create more than 700,000 jobs nationwide. In Iowa, officials are banking on a $93 million fiber optics network to attract business to the state's rural communities as well as improve their educational options.

Other states are looking to infrastructure and public works projects to help stimulate the economy and create jobs. Many hope to reap significant benefits from the $151 billion six-year transportation package passed by Congress in 1991. Among the projects that will be financed in part by federal transportation funds are a high-speed rail line through Florida and a major reconstruction of public transportation facilities in New Jersey.

Other Issues

While scarce revenues will limit the programs states can fund, state decisionmakers will continue to confront a wide range of regulatory and policy issues in addition to the major areas of education, health care and economic development. Efforts will be made to reduce state expenses by cutting back on questionable programs or by turning programs over to private vendors. Also, many issues relating to the political process will be addressed.

Among the topics likely to be considered in the coming biennium is the value and structure of general assistance programs. Major changes in general assistance have been implemented in Ohio, Michigan, New Jersey, Massachusetts, Minnesota, Maryland and Oregon and are pending in several others. In many instances the reforms entail reductions in cash and medical benefits as well as limitations on who qualifies. In Michigan and Oregon, the programs were changed to exclude hospitalization benefits.

In New Jersey, all welfare recipients whose children are 2 or older will be required to participate in educational programs or job training. The new act also denies additional benefits to mothers who have more children while on welfare.

Welfare reforms stem in part from state reaction to changes in the federal Aid to Families with Dependent Children (AFDC) program. States found themselves creating administrative structures to collect child support, administering work and training programs and ensuring health care to more and more lower income families. Supporting such efforts alongside their own general assistance programs have become a significant financial burden. Moreover, the changes reflect a growing sentiment among state leaders that entitlement programs should be remedial, not open-ended. Whether reforms will result in long-term savings without increased human suffering remains a serious question.

Another topic that will be hotly debated in some states is workers' compensation reform. The cost of workers' compensation doubled from 1985 to 1990 and many state insurance pools were brought to the brink of bankruptcy due to high medical costs, benefits abuses and frequent litigation. Reforms are likely to be proposed in Massachusetts, Tennessee, Pennsylvania, Texas,

---

> ### The most significant ideas being debated in state government include:
> - Site-based school management as core of education reform
> - Public and/or private school choice
> - Health care rationing waivers to Medicare/Medicaid
> - Multi-state foreign trade initiatives
> - Workfare and other restrictions on welfare entitlements
> - Expansion of sales tax to services and mail order purchases
> - Creating markets for recycled materials
> - Alternatives to incarceration
> - Restrictions on abortion
> - Redefining standards for lobbyist-legislator relations

Alabama and Minnesota, among others. (*Governing* 1992)

One tool that helps cut state costs is privatization and public/private partnerships. In the short-term, states are expected to review the possibility of turning such programs as state-owned liquor stores and public hospitals over to the private sector. Proposals for private toll roads have been presented in Colorado, Illinois, Minnesota and Virginia.

Significant initiatives also can be expected in the area of the environment. While state and local recycling efforts have been stymied by the scarcity of markets for recycled products, concern over the problem of solid waste disposal remains high. Many states are considering action to increase state purchases of recycled goods.

Considerable activity also is likely in the area of clean air standards. While California remains the only state with a regulatory agency to set standards and monitor emissions on all vehicles, Massachusetts and New Jersey already have adopted California's standards and others are giving the program serious consideration.

Adjusting the political process

A final area of intense activity in the coming years is likely to be the political process itself. Armed with polling results showing increasing public disenchantment with politics and politicians, legislators and executive branch officials will seek to bring greater accountability into the system. Indiana recently enacted a bill adding more stringent provisions to state ethics laws for members of the executive branch. Major legislation on campaign financing and ethics reform are pending in several states, including Rhode Island and Kentucky.

The furor over term limitations has lost some of its steam. But initiatives to limit the terms of state legislators will appear on the ballot in a handful of states and proposed legislation is likely to be presented in several others. Heated debate is expected in Texas, Wisconsin and Florida. Even without term limitation, turnover in state legislatures will likely rise as a result of retirement, the growing demands of holding public office and voter dissatisfaction. A recent study by the Midwestern Legislative Conference of The Council of State Governments showed that only 42 percent of the legislators who were in office in that region in 1983 remained in office 10 years later.

Conclusion

The American states in the near future face a time of refinement and of major challenges to their role in the federal system. Following a period of expanding state activity in the 1980s, states now find themselves struggling with declining revenues and, in many cases, faltering efficiency. A period of retrenchment, particularly with regard to major social programs, can be expected as states seek to bring maximum efficiency to the delivery of basic services.

At the same time, a major national debate is brewing on the relationship between the states and the federal government. Smarting from the imposition of unfunded federal mandates, states are seeking to bypass federal guidelines with innovative programs in such areas as health care, international trade and the environment. Whether Congress and the White House will allow states the flexibility to experiment with major programs remains to be seen.

A period of retrenchment, particularly with regard to major social programs, can be expected as states seek to bring maximum efficiency to the delivery of basic services.

In asserting their role as "laboratories of democracy," the leaders of the American states must also be conscious of the dangers of fragmentation. In other parts of the world, in Europe and in Asia, nations are moving toward aggregate trading blocs with uniform policies and standards. As states seek to blaze their own path in the absence of strong bipartisan national leadership, they must be careful not to lose the cohesion that through 200 years has kept them vital and responsive to the needs of their citizens.

Schoolhouse Equality

JULIE KOSTERLITZ

The renewed push to equalize spending on schools is giving states increasing power over localities, shifting tax burdens and raising politically touchy questions of economic class.

"Today, the disadvantaged are doubly mistreated: First, by the accident of their environment, and second, by the disadvantage added by an inadequate education. The state has compounded the wrong and must right it."

This is not the rhetoric of a 1960s anti-poverty activist. It is part of a sweeping and unanimous ruling by an ideologically mixed New Jersey Supreme Court early last month that found the state's public school financing system to be unconstitutional.

Topping off a nearly decade-long lawsuit, the ruling placed the blame on a system that relies heavily on local property taxes. The result, the court said, was vast disparities between the funds available to students in wealthy districts and those in poor districts in which the system failed to provide all students with the "thorough and efficient" education required by the state constitution.

As a remedy, the state would have to equalize school spending so that students in poor areas receive as much as those in wealthy ones. What's more, the court said, to ensure disadvantaged children an equal chance in life, the state might have to spend more money on them than on affluent children.

In New Jersey, quite suddenly, equality of educational opportunity has become more than an abstract concept. Thanks to the court and the state's activist Democratic Gov. James J. Florio, who has embraced the call for change, school finance reform has emerged as a legal imperative that is revolutionizing the state's tax system.

Florio has turned New Jersey's political traditions upside down by pumping millions in school aid and tax relief to the poor and middle class while handing the bill to the rich. "Any system that says 'You'll get a quality of education based on where you live' is not only unfair, but stupid—it's designed to fail," Florio said in an interview. "The people of this state know they have to invest in students if all are to be adequately prepared for the future."

The New Jersey court isn't alone in challenging school financing arrangements. In a flurry of activity not seen since the early 1970s, courts in Kentucky, Montana and Texas have also mandated overhauls in state education financing, and the possibility of other court challenges lingers, by some counts, in another half-dozen states.

In Congress, meanwhile, retiring House Education and Labor Committee chairman Augustus F. Hawkins, D-Calif., has introduced legislation that would require states receiving federal education aid to maintain equitable school financing systems and that would push for equity in education spending among states. The legislation currently has little momentum—equity among states would cost the federal government a bundle—but hearings have given the issue some recent visibility in Washington.

Opinions vary on whether the renewed interest in school equity is the natural swing of history's pendulum or the fruits of work by its persistent advocates. But what's clear is that school equity has become an important current in the national debate over how to shore up the quality of American education, at a time when business leaders and politicians have come to see education as the key to the country's ability to thrive in the global marketplace.

The movement is also helping accelerate a long-term trend toward giving states more responsibility for—and localities less control over—their schools. In part, the decline in local control is a result of the fact that the mechanism used to finance schools at the local level, chiefly the property tax, no longer works and is being superseded.

But the decline also coincides with society's current view of education as a matter of sufficient national concern that it can no longer be left to the whims or preferences of localities. "We have to question now the way we've traditionally implemented local control," said Allan Odden, professor of education at the University of Southern California. "There's a growing realization among all sectors and educators that education is key to increased [economic] strength and survival. We still want local school implementation [of education policies], but there's a growing consensus that we need nationwide goals."

The movement, though, has its critics. Conservatives see it as an attempt to throw more money into an education system that has been short on results. The affluent, many of whom habitually resist tax hikes and the redistribution of income, are particularly incensed in states such as New Jersey and California, where school equity means setting not only a spending floor, but also a ceiling on the amount wealthy districts can spend for their own children. That, critics say, undermines the cherished tradition of local control and forces a downward leveling of spending that invites mediocrity for all.

Public acceptance of efforts to equalize school spending, it seems, hinges on two features: how much of a new tax bite citizens face and what kinds of results they can expect from the new investment in schools.

That poses tough challenges for state governments, which must not only craft tax packages carefully, but also wander through the ambiguous terrain of education reform, where opinions are as abundant as hard evidence is scarce.

Reform will require patience, its advocates say, because results won't be tangible overnight, and may require waiting until one generation of schoolchildren passes through the new system.

RICH SCHOOL, POOR SCHOOL

Local control and financing of public schools is a tradition that sets the United States apart from most other Western democracies, which have national curricula and national student examinations. Americans, imbued with mistrust of big government, have long delegated responsibility for education to the states, which in turn, by tacit agreement, have farmed out the responsibility to local school districts, which now number roughly 16,000.

With limited taxing authority, localities traditionally turned to the one tax that hadn't already been usurped by federal or state authorities: the property tax.

As early as the 1930s, however, it became clear that relying on local property taxes creates disparities in the monies available for schools in different localities. High-value residences and active economic development in affluent areas meant that only the wealthy neighborhoods could afford more-sophisticated buildings and equipment, higher teacher salaries and enriched class offerings and extracurricular programs.

State legislatures have periodically tried to enact plans to equalize expenditures, "but the politics are very difficult at

the state level," said Arthur E. Wise, a longtime school finance equity advocate recently hired to head the National Council for Accreditation of Teacher Education in Washington. "You can only go so far in this area [because] legislators need to bring home the bacon" to their own districts.

By the late 1960s, education activists, inspired in part by the civil rights movement's talk of equal opportunity, homed in on the idea that the big gaps in spending between rich and poor districts might violate the Constitution's guarantee of equal protection under the law. In other words, their cause might best be advanced through the courts. "If one school district spends five times what the other spends, is that equal protection?" asked Wise, whose book *Rich Schools, Poor Schools* (University of Chicago Press, 1968) helped launch the idea of a legal basis for school finance reform.

Finance equity advocates initially hoped their suits would elicit a Supreme Court ruling on the order of the famous *Brown v. Board of Education* decision, which voided segregation in public schools. But when a 1973 ruling by the Court found that equal access to education was not a fundamental right guaranteed by the Constitution, the activists began peppering the states with lawsuits.

These suits brought considerable success. As many as 25 states either were ordered by courts to overhaul their school finance systems or voluntarily took action to ward off such court orders. From 1970-80, Wise said, spending gaps narrowed and states picked up a larger share of the education tab.

After activists let up on the pressure, however, the gains from these early legal efforts began to erode. Legislative compromises gave concessions to affluent areas and failed to update equalization for-

mulas to reflect current costs of schooling. Educators' mounting concerns about declining quality shifted attention away from the equity issue. Moreover, the public climate didn't favor equalization, because of what Wise called a "wave of conservatism in the 1980s."

A Congressional Research Service analysis of the most recent Census Bureau education spending data (from 1987) shows evidence of inequalities in all states, with stark contrasts in a few: In Illinois, the 10 highest-spending elementary school districts spent $6,260 per child—more than three times the amount spent by the 10 lowest-spending districts; in Texas and Ohio, the ratio of spending between the 10 top districts and the 10 lowest was about 2.8-1; in New York, it was 2.6-1; in New Jersey, 2.4-1.

Other analyses show that disparities in some areas have not only persisted but have also mushroomed over time. In New Jersey, where a 1973 state Supreme Court order had theoretically required equalization, plaintiffs in a 1981 suit showed what had happened as the Legislature's vigilance on the issue waned during the 1980s: The gap between per-pupil spending in wealthy Cherry Hill and blighted Camden went from $336 in the 1975-76 school year to $1,531 in 1984-85 to $2,443 by 1988-89, a pattern found consistently in pairings of New Jersey's poor urban areas and nearby suburbs.

Such inequalities translate into tangible differences in the classroom. "It's easy to be misled and think that the numbers aren't serious, but a $2,000 difference per kid in a classroom of 25 kids means the difference of $50,000," Wise said, a sum roughly equal to the annual salaries of two teachers. "Over the course of a school career, that differ-

Revenue Sources for U.S. Public Elementary and Secondary Schools, 1920-87 (percentages of total)			
School year ending	Local	State	Federal
1920	83.2%	16.5%	0.3%
1930	82.7	16.9	0.4
1940	68.0	30.0	1.8
1950	57.3	39.8	2.9
1960	56.5	39.1	4.4
1970	52.1	39.9	8.0
1975	48.8	42.2	9.0
1977	47.8	43.4	8.8
1979	44.6	45.6	9.8
1981	43.4	47.4	9.2
1982	45.0	47.6	7.4
1983	45.0	47.9	7.1
1984	45.4	47.8	6.8
1985	44.4	48.9	6.6
1987	43.9	49.8	6.4

ence for one kid can add up to $26,000."

Indeed, critics of the New Jersey system documented in detail just what the disparities meant for students in different school districts in that state: Princeton schools are able to offer one computer for every 8 students, but in Camden, there is just one computer for every 58 children; Princeton requires its fifth-graders to take a half-year each of French and Spanish and offers a variety of other languages for its high schoolers; in Paterson, foreign language instruction isn't offered until 10th grade. Such comparisons run parallel in the realm of art and music offerings, athletics and shop, with the poorest districts lagging far behind the richest.

20-YEAR CYCLES?

Why the renewed interest in school equity? The spate of new rulings and threatened suits on school finance equity are seen by some as a sign of society's renewed interest in equality, after a decade of policies that belittled the value of public programs for low-income people and stressed individual motivation as the cure for societal ills.

"This goes in cycles 20 years apart, because the country emphasizes individualism so much, then they come to the extreme and ask whether they're being fair," said John F. Jennings, counsel for the House Education and Labor Subcommittee on Elementary, Secondary and Vocational Education.

But the activists who brought the suits say that they've been there all along, and that the recent successes don't reflect society's change of heart as much as the persistence of a small core of activists. "To say it's cyclical is in error. We've been at this a while," said Marilyn J. Moreheuser, executive director of the Education Law Center, a nonprofit group with offices in Newark, N.J., and Philadelphia that is concerned with issues of education for disadvantaged kids. Moreheuser, the lead lawyer in the *Abbott v. Burke* case that brought the recent New Jersey Supreme Court ruling, noted that she filed the case nine years ago.

What is new, all concede, is the receptiveness of courts. "Those who press these claims have done so in the 1960s, but this time they're getting a sympathetic hearing from the state Supreme Courts," said Mark G. Yudof, dean of the University of Texas Law School, who served on a panel appointed by Republican Gov. William P. Clements Jr. to advise the state government on school finance reform in the wake of the Texas Supreme Court ruling. Twenty years ago, Yudof said, activists in Texas preferred to take their case to the federal courts, writing off the state courts as unsympathetic. But this year, the Texas

Supreme Court, which, Yudof said, often splits 5-4 along ideological lines, voted unanimously to find the school system unconstitutional.

It's hard to know what has spurred the new attitude of the state courts, but it's worth noting that these decisions come at a time when business and political leaders have changed their views of education. From about the mid-1980s on, a growing awareness of global economic competition, declining domestic productivity and a work force that increasingly will have to rely on employees with disadvantaged upbringings has fostered a new interest in education and child welfare previously associated only with social do-gooders. As these attitudes changed, education was viewed as more than just the preserve of local authorities.

Actually, a shift away from local control was already under way: Localities' shares of school revenues had been dropping steadily since 1920. (See table.)

Part of the shift has to do with problems with the property tax. Aside from inequalities between districts with expensive homes and those with poor homes, there are problems created by the location of special high-value developments. A large shopping center or factory may draw shoppers and workers from all surrounding areas but fall within the taxing jurisdiction of a school district that serves only some of the area's children. Property value is not always a good measure of wealth. Family farmers, for example, may own valuable property but have scanty incomes. Similarly, elderly home owners who live on small, fixed incomes may own homes that appreciate in value.

In some cases, rapid inflation of housing values has meant tax bills that outpace home owners' gains in incomes. Finally, not all property owners support higher school spending—elderly home owners whose children are grown, for example, might not. Over time, perpetual upward pressure on property taxes, combined with other state and federal taxes, have provoked the kind of ire seen in 1978 in California, where voters imposed a cap on the rate of increase in property taxes.

As states stepped into the breach with more money, they also exerted more authority over the schools. During the 1970s, states took a harder line: If they were going to give money to the schools, schools were going to have to show it was being used well. "With the accountability movement of the 1970s came more state control," Moreheuser said. Indeed, she noted, school districts that failed to meet minimum state requirements, such as those in Jersey City, N.J., and Oakland, have been placed in "receivership" and come directly under the control of the state.

So, when opponents of school finance equalization in New Jersey argued that finance reform would undermine local control, the court noted that the such a transfer of power had already taken place.

The trend toward state control has been accelerated by the mounting interest of business and political leaders in education as an economic tool. Recognizing that about a fourth of students in the public schools are poor and probably disadvantaged, and that this share is slated to rise to a third within 10 years, they are concerned about the quality of education in many poor school districts, the high dropout rates and the level of graduates' skills.

As concern has mounted, it has even spurred calls for help and guidance beyond the state level, as was demonstrated by the unprecedented meeting of the nation's governors and President Bush in Charlottesville, Va., late last year to set national goals for public education. The meeting may not have presaged a boost in federal aid—it was held mainly to appease the governors. Nevertheless, local authorities were notably unrepresented.

"If the country depends on the [kindergarten through 12th grade] education systems," the University of Southern California's Odden said, "if that's where it's all won or lost, as the evidence shows, the question becomes, can we leave these matters to 50 states and 16,000 districts? The answer is increasingly no."

THROWING MONEY

Still, it's one thing to contemplate the quality of tomorrow's work force from the lofty perspective of political leaders and heads of large corporations, and another to engineer a tangible transfer of wealth from rich to poor and to tell localities that states plan to take greater control of their finances and operations.

Plans to equalize schools' finances encounter a traditional set of arguments from opponents. Chief among them is the notion that more money won't solve the problems of ineffectual schools, wherever they are. In March, Education Secretary Lauro Cavazos told a special session of the Texas Legislature convened to consider school finance reform that "money is clearly not the answer to the education deficit" and that research had disproven the "notion that dollars equal educational excellence."

A paper published in May by Lewis J. Perelman, a senior research fellow at the conservative Hudson Institute in Indianapolis, expands on this theme and argues that increased spending wouldn't help even disadvantaged kids: Witness, he writes, the poor results obtained with disadvantaged kids in the District of

Columbia, which spends well over the national average per student. "No studies have shown any sustained benefit from the billions of dollars spent on the major national program for compensatory education . . . ," and the program may indeed have "the effect of inhibiting at-risk children's ability to learn," Perelman writes. Instead of focusing on money, he and others argue, educators should concentrate on improving the delivery of services, a less expensive type of reform.

Residents of affluent districts often express a variant on this theme, saying that money transferred to poor districts will merely be wasted. A common reaction of her affluent neighbors, a New Jerseyite reported, has been "Why give the money to Newark? They're just going to waste it. Those kids can't learn."

Advocates of school finance reform have ready responses. To the charge that money is irrelevant to school quality, they ask the affluent to apply that line of reasoning to themselves. If there's no correlation between education spending and academic achievement, "Why not take all the money and divide it equally" between districts? Hill aide Jennings asked. The affluent reject that idea, he notes, when they say, "Wait, we'll have to stop French classes and close the gym."

Granted, what it takes to improve academic achievement is more complicated than money, public education reform advocates acknowledge—most of the state equalization plans come with a host of requirements for school reforms—but it's wrong to assume there's no correlation merely because studies on this topic are ambiguous.

It's tough to disentangle the impact spending has on an individual student because of a host of other complicated, interwoven factors, such as family background, school administration and teaching techniques. Even when the factors can be disentangled, the lessons are ambiguous. "The main determinant of success is the educational attainment of the mother—we know that from studies," Jennings said. "But what does that mean [for poor kids]? Tell them to have different mothers?"

Indeed, the huge disparities themselves create misunderstanding. New Jersey, Moreheuser points out, has the second-highest per capita income of any state, but is also home to 4 of the 11 most distressed U.S. cities. "What bothers me about the kind of reaction we've gotten," she said, "is that, although the state is geographically small, there are two divided segments that . . . have no notion about [conditions] on the other side."

Even though advocates believe more money can bring improvements in the quality of education in poor areas, they also say that the absence of a definable link between money and quality is beside the point. The wording of most state constitutions, they argue, makes it clear that the state owes children equal opportunities, and equal spending is still the best measure of that guarantee.

CAPPING THE AFFLUENT

But advocates are divided over whether equal opportunity requires absolute equality in per-pupil spending. At issue is what the goal of equalization should be: to help poor districts achieve a level of adequacy, or to ensure that no district spends more per pupil than any other.

States have answered the question differently. Texas, for example, has decided its obligation is merely to even out the inequalities created by different property values. Thus, while some districts with property tax rates above the state average at present can still wind up with fewer dollars because the property available to them is worth substantially less than property in other areas, the state plans to level the playing field, to compensate for disparities in property values, thereby ensuring that districts that tax their property at equal rates will get equal sums. But the state will not compensate for differences incurred by a district's decision to tax itself at a lower rate than other districts.

New Jersey has gone a different route. The state Supreme Court held that districts must be able to spend equal amounts per student, regardless of differences in property value, or in the rate at which they tax themselves. Rich districts were free to spend as they chose, the court said, but it was up to the state to make sure poor districts could spend just as much. Faced with the prospect of incurring major costs trying to help poor districts keep up, the state has imposed caps on the amounts affluent districts can spend.

That move has come in for criticism, even from some supporters of school finance reform. "It's a mistake to restrict districts who want to spend more," said Michael J. Kirst, a Stanford University professor of education who has been active in the finance reform movement. Capping expenditures by affluent districts will "cut back on the emulation of the Joneses. Everybody tries to catch up to the wealthy districts. If you cut them off at the knees and say you can't spend more even if you want to, you have more of a leveling [downward.]"

Kirst and others cite the example of California, which moved to a capped approach in the wake of Proposition 13. "It's been a tragic mistake," Kirst said,

"and one of the reasons [the state] is 31st in spending on education."

Yudof of the University of Texas said strict equalization patronizes local communities. "The question is, who will decide what's adequate? . . . I trust poor communities [to make that decision]. I don't accept the view that there is something magical about a state board or legislative body that is more knowledgeable than leaders in a predominantly black community."

Worse yet, said former San Antonio Mayor Henry G. Cisneros, who now heads his own assets management company and who sat on the state task force on school finance reform, capping expenditures is a tough political sell. "It becomes very difficult to tell people they can't spend their own money to improve their own schools," he said. "In the realm of what's politically achievable, it's crossing the line to say what's locally gained can't be locally spent."

Another group of reform advocates disagrees. Allowing some districts to spend more than others merely because they can afford it and want to "is a very elitist attitude," Jennings said. "If you can afford more for your kid, as a member of society, you have to help the poor kid have a chance. The obligation of a citizen is not to be greedy but to be concerned with the good of society."

A child's education shouldn't be held hostage to the levels of taxation local school districts vote for themselves, others argue. It isn't fair to penalize a child who lives in an area dominated by elderly people not interested in paying taxes for education, Wise said. And there's some evidence to suggest that people's willingness to spend on education is tied to their own levels of education and income, the Congressional Research Service reports. Thus, it seems, the highly educated and affluent are not only more able, but also more willing to pay higher taxes for public education, at least in their own areas.

The provincialism of affluent areas on the matter of school spending, their critics say, reflects their slowness to grasp, as business and political leaders have, how dependent the nation's future is on the well-being of all children. "To destine a child to a lower quality of life based on where they happen to be in school is not only unfair, but shortsighted," Wise said.

Caps on local education spending make sense, Wise added, because they will force those concerned about the quality of their own schools to channel their activism to the state level and push for more spending on all schools. Such caps are important for another basic reason: Without a requirement for equal spending on each student, Moreheuser said, disparities inevitably grow between rich and poor. Thus, New Jersey, which set about repairing inequities after the state Supreme Court's 1973 ruling without imposing caps, gradually let political pressures undermine the principle, allowing the huge inequities that prompted the 1981 suit.

MAKE THE RICH PAY?

Until the affluent are persuaded that they stand to benefit from school equalization plans, state politicians trying to implement these plans face delicate problems in handling vocal and powerful segments of their electorate. Texas tackled the problem by striking compromises over how much equalization it would insist on, how much it would spend to get there and how quickly it would move to get there. If Texas has appeased the affluent, it has also drawn criticism from advocates for the poor and from some Hispanics for not going far enough.

In New Jersey, Florio has decided not to placate the well-to-do, but instead, to isolate them politically. He is raising much of the revenue from taxes on the rich and using some of the proceeds to offset higher tax burdens in middle-class districts.

In June, he narrowly pushed a package of tax increases through the Legislature, including a hike in income taxes that will double the rate for those earning upwards of $75,000 a year ($150,000 for couples), an increase in the state sales tax and some excise taxes. Adding insult to injury, the state simultaneously plans to slash aid to affluent school districts and make them pick up the hefty costs of teachers' pensions—on the theory that the state shouldn't subsidize wealthy school districts that offer high salaries and generous retirement plans.

"The combination of losing that aid, picking up the pension costs, capping expenditures and making the wealthy in these [well-to-do] districts bear the brunt of the new taxes is making people very scared about being able to keep the level of education they have now," said Susan Fuhrman of the Center for Policy Research in Education at Rutgers University. "There's been plenty of politicking,

and the plan got through [the Legislature] very narrowly" because of resistance by representatives of affluent Bergen County and teachers' unions that were unhappy about the new pension arrangements, she said.

Ironically, she noted, a result of the reductions in state aid and the shifting of pension costs will be to lessen the impact of the controversial caps on the amounts affluent districts can spend. That's because these new expenses are likely to absorb any new monies that would have previously gone to raise over-all spending levels.

Asked about the recriminations from the rich, Florio sounded a defensive note and emphasized the gains to the vast majority. "There's no backlash," he said, adding that people have yet to realize that three-fourths of the state's school districts will end up net winners as a result of the plan, and that the package includes substantial tax relief for many. But the state isn't entirely unmindful of the affluent's distress signals. It has already relented a bit on the proposed total cutoff in state education aid to their districts.

Despite some grumbling about higher taxes, however, observers in various states see signs that the reform plans are winning public acceptance. In Texas, even though the Legislature had to hold three special sessions before the governor accepted a plan to raise $528 million in taxes to pump funds into poor schools, Cisneros said he was "very pleased. . . . Despite the bloodbath that [school finance] equity could have been in Texas, most of the recriminations were limited to the Legislature and did not extend to the public like I thought it would.

"I thought the day when courts mandated leaders to be funders of equity, with Hispanics at the front of the pack [of those who stood to gain], there would be major social disruption," Cisneros said. "But people understand the disparities. They're sophisticated enough to know what it means to their future, despite pockets of resistance." The proof he said, was the lack of support for the governor's opposition to new taxes. "He

thought he had a mandate . . . , but he didn't, and he ended up signing a major tax bill."

Likewise in New Jersey, where the political outcome of Florio's gambit has yet to be seen, Fuhrman detects some acceptance. "I think most people see [school finance equalization] as a good cause and a necessity and are accepting that the current system is not constitutional. They're mostly arguing about the wrinkles" in the plan to correct it now, she said.

Echoing sentiments heard elsewhere, however, Fuhrman added that people will be waiting to see whether the increased spending on poor schools produces visible rewards. "It's hard to sell people on [income redistribution] when they can't see results," she said. Other welfare programs can show they've raised income levels, or fed more people, she said, but even if school finance reform produces new buildings or science labs, that won't be enough. "People want to see increased achievements."

Many observers say that Kentucky may show the best results, because its Supreme Court, in finding the public school system unconstitutional in June 1989, insisted not only on overhauling the state's education finance system, but also the structure and function of the school system.

State legislatures eager to produce results, however, will have to tread carefully through the minefield of conflicting theories of what kinds of reforms, aside from new funds, will improve academic achievement, and which are the best measures of such improvements.

School equity advocates say a few improvements are almost immediately measurable: dropout rates and college attendance rates, for example. But major improvements may take time. "One of the reasons it's hard to see [results from higher spending] is that for many years, we will be reaping the results of past neglect," Moreheuser said. "There will not be results overnight."

"By the time a child goes through 13 years in adequately funded circumstances, you can expect to see changes," Wise said. "But don't ask to see results until you have fully schooled a whole generation."

Reform School Confidential

What we can learn from the failure of three of America's boldest school reforms

Katherine Boo

Katherine Boo is an editor of The Washington Monthly.

When *A Nation at Risk* toppled American educational complacency back in 1983, I was just out of high school, working as a typist for the federal government. Beside me was another just-graduated clerk named Peggy, who had gone to D.C.'s Coolidge High School. Peggy was pleasant and industrious, with a reverence for horror movies. Before long, I realized that she was also functionally illiterate. She had learned to type, slowly but cannily, by matching letters on the page to letters on the keyboard. When she needed to know what something actually *said,* she asked her coworkers to read for her.

One heard a lot of stories like Peggy's back then, as it began to dawn on America how broke the public education system was, especially in the cities and among the poor. There were illiterate honor students, kids who graduated after missing months of school, teachers who couldn't spell competence, let alone demonstrate it. Here in D.C., those stories begat blue-ribbon commission, tens of millions of dollars in new funding, and perhaps as many new programs as there are schools—from Afrocentric education to early-learning centers to magnet schools. And with each came the expectation that there'd eventually be fewer Peggy stories to tell.

A few weeks back, weary of school officials' talk about how nicely reform efforts were progressing, I started wondering how those reforms had played out at Peggy's alma mater, Coolidge. In 1982, when she graduated, the school's average reading levels were more than two grade levels below the national norm—scores among the worst in a pretty sorry school system. Today, after all the reports and research, refinancing and retooling, Coolidge students' reading

scores are *exactly* the same as they were. And those are the scores of the slim majority of kids who stayed in school—another statistic frozen in place.

Figures like these, I think, help explain why half of Americans now claim to support educational vouchers. It's not really a profound faith that this country's St. Anthonies and Oxford Preps will cure what ails education. The recent results of the Bush administration's own National Assessment of Educational Progress show that kids about to graduate from private school don't do any better than public school kids when you control for family background. Rather, the polls lay bare our lack of faith in the public schools' willingness and ability to transform—a faith strained to breaking by some of America's most celebrated and ambitious reform efforts.

Rochester, New York. Chelsea, Massachusetts. Chicago, Illinois. In those places in the mid-eighties, some of education's most committed reformers seized upon a few bold ideas, drummed up some cash, and embarked on a seeming revolution from within, generating hype and hope in the process. Rochester's goal was to beef up the quality and status of teachers. Chicago sought to give parents control over the way the schools were run. Chelsea focused on leveling the playing field for poor kids. Theirs are still the experiments educators point to when they ask for more time to fix the system. But today, each of them is foundering, leaving communities, students, even the leaders who propelled them disillusioned.

On one level, the stories of these efforts reinforce what many Americans apparently believe: We've tried public school reform. It didn't work. Let's ditch the whole idea. Yet before we start dismantling public education, perhaps we should

Reprinted with permission from *The Washington Monthly,* October 1992, pp. 17-24. *Tne Washington Monthly,* 1611 Connecticut Ave., NW, Washington, DC 20009. (202) 462-0128.

215

check out why even these tremendous efforts have failed—explanations rooted, not in money or theory or intention, but in an educational establishment that has managed to thwart the most righteous of reforms.

The greenback attack

In the world according to liberals like Jonathan Kozol, the key to school reform is in the bank: money to hire good teachers, money for innovative programs, money for books, money to relieve students' socioeconomic disadvantages. But it was probably no accident that Kozol, when researching *Savage Inequalities*, didn't spend much time in Rochester. Five years ago, in a school district of 33,000 students—most of them poor and almost half from single-parent households—Rochester launched one of America's most expansive and expensive efforts to rebuild a system whose test scores and dropout rates consistently ranked it as one of the worst in New York State. Goaded by a "Call to Action" by the Rochester Urban League and funded by hundreds of millions of dollars from taxpayers and local corporations like Eastman-Kodak and Bausch and Lomb, chilly Rochester in 1987 became, as *U.S. News* put it, the hottest place on America's education map.

Rochester's throw-money-at-it approach was not without a guiding, and good, idea: freeing the hands of teachers to do what they're supposed to do—butt into the lives of kids and make them learn in whatever way works. What Chris Whittle, in his obsession with uniformity, fails to realize is that good schools leave room for passion, giving people freedom to experiment, adjust, and respond. But in the unreconstructed Rochester schools, as in most others, administrative dicta spewed forth on everything from what days to read *Silas Marner* to assignments on the

WHITTLE, DOWN TO SIZE

Everything you really need to know about Chris Whittle sits in downtown Knoxville, Tennessee. There, the media mogul has erected a $55 million headquarters that relentlessly replicates Thomas Jefferson's spread at Charlottesville. With its red-brick arches, wrought-iron gates, and 120-foot clock tower, it's a massive, unexpected building—rich, as Whittle has said, in "energy and youthful spirit."

Big, spirited, and unconventional are precisely what Whittle aims to be, whether the subject is magazines in doctors' offices or, lately, how Americans educate their kids. With his $3.1 billion Edison Project, Whittle plans to build and operate a huge, perhaps revolutionary, network of for-profit schools by 1996.

That's got public-school defenders worried. This, after all, is the man who saved *Esquire* in the early eighties by exploiting untapped advertising possibilities, the guy who invented Channel One for schoolchildren and built himself a media empire before he reached middle age. That glitzy résumé explains why what would be viewed as a doomed venture if proposed by a lesser mortal is being treated as a potential death blow to American public education. Yet what's overlooked in breathless accounts of the Edison Project is that the great innovator often has trouble following through. It is as an inventor—a maker of images and markets—that Whittle has earned his reputation. But behind much-chronicled "successes" like Channel One, there are folded magazines, discarded "poster media," and struggling current publications. Whittle has gone from 42 media properties in 1989 to 26 in 1992, and he just laid off 100 of his 1,100 employees.

What is it with Whittle? Perhaps his self-proclaimed "youthful spirit" is a phrase more telling than he realizes. When it comes to conjuring up moneymaking schemes, he's got as much spunk as a caffeine-wired sophomore. What he doesn't have is the dedication to the details that turns high concept into real change.

Con Edison

It's not surprising that Whittle has only a vague sense of what the classrooms of the Edison Project will look like, what will be taught and how, who the students will be, or—perhaps most important from a businessman's standpoint—how in the world he's going to pay for it. The numbers don't add up: He says he can do it for the current per-pupil cost of $5,500 a year, but that's the barebones cost in schools—public and private—where they already have buildings and desks and books. Hence the widespread speculation that he's expecting the federal government's embrace of vouchers to fuel the project.

But the Edison Project isn't the first time Whittle has ignored the all-important details. Once, years ago, he produced a sports information poster to hang in bars, but in doing so neglected to consider an important fact: Bars are dark. As catchy as the posters may have been, no one could read them and the project, funded by ads, collapsed.

Whittle's real interest is the big gesture, which explains not just his office building but his joy in luring Yale President Benno Schmidt to Edison. In weekly cafeteria detail. Correspondingly, teachers worked to the rule, got raises like clockwork, and earned the minimal respect they deserved. Students learned, if they were lucky.

Fortunately, renegade Rochester Teachers Union leader Adam Urbanski and Superintendent Peter McWalters, a former Peace Corps Volunteer and veteran teacher, didn't think that was the wisest way to reach at-risk kids. So they battered out a historic agreement. Teachers would receive a 40 percent pay increase over four years—vets could receive as much as $70,000—but they'd damn well have to earn it. They would go to students' homes, stay late, and tutor individually. They'd mentor weaker teachers, develop curricula, plan special programs and events. So empowered were teachers by the changes that administrators actually sued for being cut out of the supervisory process. There was a tradeoff, of course. Rochester taxpayers now demanded teacher account-

ability. And Urbanski's union, to collective amazement, agreed to waive some seniority rights, tie pay in part to performance, and give officials a little help in weeding out incompetent teachers.

Today, mention of the district's modest improvements in elementary reading and math scores still pops up from time to time in the education press. But statistics tell a more complicated story. There are still almost as many dropouts as graduates. Only half of Rochester high schoolers passed the state's Regents math and English test, down from more than 60 percent two years ago. The number of black students who averaged a B or better through four years of high school is the lowest in five years. Last year, the Urban League summed it up: These are the same "crisis conditions" as in the bleak days preceding reform.

But why? Rochester respected its teachers. Rochester empowered its teachers. Rochester paid its

The unmiraculous past of education's latest savior

one blow, Whittle got clout, prestige, and publicity. "[Schmidt] shares our belief that our mission could make a vital difference to our country's future," Whittle exulted. "His joining is confirmation of our goals."

With Whittle, talk of a pending project is always sweeping. Ever since the 44-year-old entrepreneur founded his first company shortly after graduating from the University of Tennessee, he has inaugurated his business ventures with more metaphors than a *New Yorker* short story: Walls are kicked down, new lands conquered, scouts sent ahead. You'd almost forget, listening to his grand promotional lines, that his fortune has been built on producing arcane media for advertisers to reach captive audiences: *Pet Care Report*, for instance, or *La Familia de Hoy*, "a multimedia system in Spanish." And you'd also have to struggle to remember that the talk doesn't always match the result. In a 1989 interview with *The New York Times*, Whittle predicted his revenues would hit $315 million by 1991. He came in at $207 million.

Consider his controversial Channel One, developed to be shown in schools. Introduced in 1989, the daily, 12-minute television program offers a superficial look at current events buttressed by two minutes of ads, usually by corporations like Burger King or Nike, to its captive student audience. Early on, Whittle promised advertisers an audience of 6.6 million teenagers. According to Whittle himself, only 3.8 million actually watch Channel One; the National Education Association says only 2.6 million do. What are the kids getting? A University of Michigan study of Channel One's first year

found that watching the MTV-like show increased students' knowledge of current events by a not-so-revolutionary 3.3 percent.

Still, Channel One has survived longer than Whittle's home-state magazine, *Tennessee Illustrated*, founded in 1988. Whittle was executive editor and chairman; the magazine also included a column under his byline and photo, a Whittle Communications first. And its prepublication publicity offered a sense of the kind of hype Whittle would use on endeavors to come: This was going to be big—*really big*. It would reach two million Tennesseans by subscription and distribution—in other words, virtually the state's entire adult population (and, coincidentally, the number of students Whittle says Edison will be serving "shortly after the turn of the century").

Whittle wasn't just market-wise; he was politically savvy. His friend and consultant, Lamar Alexander, had just left the governor's office, so Whittle scooped him up. Alexander—now Bush's secretary of education and a potential source of school vouchers for the Whittle schools—would be a stockholder and adviser not only on the magazine but later on Channel One. (Whittle needed political leverage to lobby Channel One through skeptical legislatures and school boards; he'll need it even more if Edison gets off the ground.) In the case of *Tennessee Illustrated*, Alexander helped Whittle run a minicampaign for the magazine, barnstorming the state and lunching with mayors and power-structure types to sell the venture.

Tennessee Illustrated, Whittle said, was to be a
(Continued on next page)

teachers like accountants. So how good are those teachers? In Rochester, that question is irrelevant, since it's virtually impossible to fire the bad ones.

Thanks to the same state and union requirements that make getting rid of poor instructors arduous and expensive across the country, the head of Rochester school personnel estimates that only about 2 of more than 2,000 tenured teachers have been removed—or "counseled out"—every year since reform began. Meanwhile, the Rochester teacher's union has rejected all pay-for-performance criteria in its contract, essentially reneging on its original agreement. The upshot? Even Urbanski admits that the epic reform hasn't changed the way teachers teach.

"We have teachers who fraternize—I mean, *have sex with*—teenagers, and they're still teachers," says Marvin Jackson, head of Rochester's District Parent Council and a parent of five. "We had a middle-school teacher hit a kid. Parents freaked, but absolutely nothing happened to that teacher. But mostly, we just have some plain old bad teachers, and nothing ever happens to them."

In fact, at current levels of pay, in five years three quarters of those teachers will make $60,000 just for showing up—a fact that gives Whittle and other acolytes of educational competition real claim to the moral highground, and not just in Rochester.

Of course, with a million bucks of his own money countering the education lobby, Ross Perot did manage to secure merit pay in Texas; Bill Clinton obtained a one-time-only basic literacy test for Arkansas teachers back in 1983. But there, in that corner of the map, you have all the significant state-level reform in teacher training and evaluation since *A Nation at Risk*. Almost everywhere else, a diploma—earned with a host of questionable pedagogical courses, a few weeks of practice teaching, and virtually no testing of subject knowledge—still equals a license to teach. Once teachers get those licenses, you can only hope that the semi-literate ones also have a predilection for pedophilia; little else will get them dismissed.

Teacher quality is an educational necessity that liberals are particularly shoddy at confronting. Teachers obviously deserve protection from unfair job actions, just as they deserve decent pay and working conditions. But as Rochester parents understand viscerally, there is another issue here—one of expectations. While pay can't be tied inextricably to performance until the wonks create the perfect test or

Whittle, Down to Size

(Continued from previous page)

"new restaurant of words. Expect the unexpected from *Tennessee Illustrated*. We are going to celebrate the past, clarify the present, and contemplate the future, be intelligent without being overly sophisticated, objective without being cynical, fun without being ribald, and provocative without being antagonistic." It was hyped as the next *Texas Monthly*, a dynamic voice for the state.

But *Tennessee Illustrated* didn't have time to find that voice. For the 12 issues that comprised its short life, a colorful format featured pieces on the myth of Davy Crockett, a visit with Alex Haley, and a selection of 20 Tennesseans as "Good Folks." There was little controversy and less hard-hitting politics. Whittle's most forceful editorial suggested that the state ban billboards in favor of tourist-information radio channels.

Tennessee Illustrated may have made dull reading, but it made decent political sense for the impresario. At the time, it was clear that Whittle had political ambitions, but he had not said which party he favored. Add that to a dependence on ad revenue from utilities and banks—important political players in the state—and there was a clear reason for Whittle to stick to campaigning, as he did in his column, for apple-pie issues: in favor of small towns, against "unsightly" billboards, and for innovative education. Political magazines, he said later, are "a bad business." Opinions, since they divide, often are.

Helping kill *Tennessee Illustrated* was not only that uncertain editorial approach but money. Whittle had used his famous "category-specific" advertising approach—selling ads to a single producer of a given product—and four giants in the state bought in: South Central Bell, Baptist Health Care System, First Tennessee Bank, and the Tennessee Valley Authority. TVA invested $750,000, but pulled its ads after a year to cut costs. The loss of the sponsor, coupled with vanishing revenues, drove the magazine from a bimonthly to a quarterly, then out of business altogether.

Yet as *Tennessee Illustrated* was dying, an undaunted Whittle was making what he called "the most successful magazine launch in history" with six *Special Report* publications—one on sports, one on health, and the like—blanketing doctors' offices across the country each quarter. The advertisement-gorged magazines entered the market (Whittle thinks in market terms, not audience) with the understanding that doctors, who'd get the magazines free, would not be allowed to have more than two non-Whittle magazines in their waiting rooms. It was a new idea, and the advertisers loved it. But again, it didn't necessarily have staying power.

As the years passed, the six quarterly publications dropped to three; now, there is one bimonthly the administrators fill classrooms with uniform percentages of good kids and bad, allowing teachers to teach with no real-world standards has predictable consequences. In Rochester, for example, state-level reform recently changed the way students would learn math; the new thing, sensibly, was mastering concepts and critical thinking instead of memorizing formulae. Yet what was good for students was a pain in the neck for their teachers, who would have to revise their ancient lesson plans. With no incentive to change their ways, they balked, clinging to the old memorize-the-Pythagorean methods. Droves of students failed their state math exams.

Even sadder was the fizzling of one of Rochester's most promising ideas. Every high school and middle school teacher had agreed to counsel 20 pupils and get involved with their parents—a plan to ensure that in reformed Rochester no child would slip quietly between the cracks. But some teachers refused to visit their poorer students' homes. They were petrified. Parents across the city quickly organized "diplomatic corps"—local parents who'd escort teachers into the projects. But the teachers wouldn't use them. Now the corps don't exist any-

more, the teachers aren't making their visits, and you can almost hear the cracks widening.

Office politics

If Rochester's plan was to shower money and power on teachers, Chicago's plan was to wrest it from administrators and give it to parents. And when you ask Chicago school officials about the success of their dramatic decentralizing plan—one the *Tribune* called the most radical assault on the administrative power structure in American educational history— you invariably hear the story of Spry Elementary. There is a good lesson there, but not perhaps the one the central office wants to convey.

A few years back, the overcrowded, underfunded Spry was the fief of a Bad Old Principal whom parents routinely complained about to an indifferent central office. Then came reform, which usurped the central office's power and gave local councils composed of parents, who know what's best for their kids, the power to fire principals and set policy for individual schools. Heady with this new control, the first thing the Spry council did was dump that Bad Old Principal for someone more responsive and ag-

Special Report, and that's part of what Whittle calls an "interactive multimedia system" of TV shows, magazines, and take-home booklets. That means that while waiting in the doctor's office, you get to watch Joan Lunden host a 60-minute television show—described by the corporation as "a mix of expert advice, hard-hitting investigations, consumer and health updates, quick quizzes, commentary, comedy, slice-of-life features, and celebrity profiles and interviews." And here's the Whittle touch, the innovative, break-the-mold feature: "The system is made unique by its interactivity: Segments on the show frequently refer viewers to complementary or follow-up information in the booklets or magazine."

A *Special Report* vice president says the move from print to video in his division of Whittle reflects the companywide trend toward electronics, the more profitable venture of the two. And, lately, profits matter more than ever. This year, Whittle Communications' have plummeted.

What could be the problem? Whittle has made his fortune by eliminating divisions between public and private, bringing commercialism into contexts that were previously free of such forces. He did it with Channel One in public schools; in his Whittle Books division, he sticks ads from corporations like Federal Express into books by John Kenneth Galbraith and George Plimpton. But Whittle has

never demonstrated sustained devotion to any idea except one: that amorphous new "media" are out there waiting for him to exploit.

Schools are about ideas. They're about books that should be read whether they pay for themselves or not; they're about rising above market forces, however briefly, and instilling a larger sense of the world. If a magazine fails, you can close it. If a school fails, you have failed students, not customers. Whittle likes the big gesture, and he seems to crave respect. But he is a salesman, and the bottom line always comes first. It came first with *Tennessee Illustrated*, and it came first with *Special Report*.

And so, as the romance with Whittle and Schmidt trips along, remember that Whittle has failed in the past for many of the reasons Edison is at risk: raising long-term capital; informing a product with discernible, intelligent content; and sustaining the promise of the pitch. That should be some comfort to those who fear the Whittle plan's effect on public schools. But only *some* comfort, since one thing makes the Edison Project more dangerous than the rest. If we keep exaggerating Whittle's invincibility, people may begin to believe that it's safe to ignore the public schools—which will leave those schools even worse off if Whittle's latest brainchild gets abandoned, half-grown, by its impatient father.

—Jon Meacham

gressive. Today, Spry's classes are smaller and its test scores are inching up. Parents are happy, teachers are happy, students are happy. In fact, everybody seems happy except the students at Clay School across town. That's where the Bad Old Principal now collects his salary.

From Chicago and Cincinnati to Washington and San Diego, decentralization of school administration is the latest banner of the reform crusaders, and its premise is a sound one. By cutting bureaucracy and loosening central office control, principals and teachers can be more responsive to the needs of their particular kids. And without the central office gobbling up funds, they'll have more money to respond with. Yet a peek behind the press releases suggests that this new trick is nothing against one of the oldest: bureaucratic inertia.

When William Bennett called Chicago the "worst school system in the country" back in 1988, he was stepping onto a pretty sturdy limb. Half the students dropped out before graduation, and high school achievement scores ranked in the lowest 1 percent of American schools. The administration, on the other hand, was doing fine. Central office workers were spending twice as much every month to trim and water the plants in their offices as they handed out for school supplies in the city's poorest elementaries. Meanwhile, layers of administrators couldn't even accomplish their most fundamental task: getting teachers into classrooms. Every day, thousands of students arrived at school to find neither a teacher nor a substitute in front of the class. "It's just a fact of life," one administrator reassured the *Chicago Tribune* at the time. "It's always been like this."

Finally, Chicagoans' frustration erupted. Unprecedented public, business, and press support led to the 1988 reform legislation that set a cap on the size of the administration and reallocated money to the schools. An astounding 17,000 people—mostly parents—ran for 4,300 seats on the newly empowered school councils in 1989, and more than 300,000 people turned out to vote. But by last year, a third of the council members had quit, frustrated; only 3,000 ran for the empty seats. What went wrong? Well, if you think you can't fight City Hall, try the school administration, whose "Club Med mentality," as parent Ron Sistrunk dubs it, has proved as durable as the roaches in the lunchroom.

Consider the number-one decentralization "strategy" issued by the administration: "Disassemble the Central Service Center" at the central office. A perusal of the restructuring plan shows what it really means isn't dismantling, but *renaming*—as the "Central Resource and Training Center." Another job-preserving technique comes under the heading "eliminat[ing] administrative impediments": not cutting staff or streamlining procedures, but researching and writing a series of procedure manuals that include development of "a master matrix . . . of the stakeholder groups."

How do administrators get away with this rearguard action? Easily. School boards come and go; parents get frustrated with inertia and arcana. Thus

administrators have been able to wait out "reform" until public interest wanes. And that's apparently what Chicago Superintendent Ted Kimbrough intends to do. In fact, all this harping over administration sort of bores him. Instead, he says, "We need to focus on the classroom."

So let's. When the Consortium on Chicago School Research recently polled thousands of Chicago teachers, 57 percent of them reported that the restructuring has had no effect on what they do in their classrooms. Now come closer and see how reform has changed Farren Elementary, where geography—it's nestled into the world's largest housing project, Robert Taylor Homes—has traditionally been destiny.

Here, the city reports that *100 percent* of the student body is low-income, and test scores are among the city's lowest. Has reform come to the rescue? This year, Farren's supply budget was cut 95 percent. To purchase the necessary paper and paper clips, Principal William Auksi had to shift the money from programs for kids with remedial learning problems.

"They had enough money," Auksi shrugs. Not surprisingly, tiny Farren does have enough funds to support two handsomely paid assistant principals.

No comprendo, teach

So even a "reformed" education establishment manages to keep bad teachers on the payroll, strangle creativity, and lavish on itself funds meant for kids. But perhaps the most damaging thing isn't what that establishment inflicts, but what it fails to share—power with the parents who have the most to gain and lose from the quality of their children's schools. In Chicago, that's a side effect. In Chelsea, Massachusetts, it's a disease unto itself. There, the disenfranchising of parents has sabotaged one of the most promising and well-intended reform movements in the country.

When John Silber's Boston University (BU) finally obtained a 10-year contract to run the Chelsea schools over the fierce objections of the teachers union and school administration, it was a little like winning a vacation home in Love Canal. The small district was the poorest and arguably the worst in the state. A third of the mostly hispanic student body couldn't do coursework in English, and its dropout rate, the highest in the state, was just barely higher than the rate at which its teenaged girls had kids. But BU was anything but daunted. "I don't want to be arrogant or grandiose," John Silber said at the time, "but I don't think it's utterly fanciful to say we're testing the future viability of American primary and secondary education."

As expected, the conservative Silber took on the patronage-laced administration with ferocity, and by 1990, with a salary boost as sweetener, he cajoled the teachers union into merit pay. But when it came to the classroom, he had a plan that would warm Hillary Clinton's heart. In Chelsea, teaching kids would begin outside the classroom, with health care, parent literacy programs, early training in English. In short, the Chelsea plan would hand over to teachers kids who were, in the education catchphrase, ready to learn. It was a swell idea—indeed, probably the most important in educating underprivileged, at-risk kids, who currently make up about a third of America's public school population. But Silber's perestroika overlooked one thing. More than half of Chelsea parents couldn't even understand BU's various projects, let alone participate in them.

As the schools' new leaders went on cross-country speaking tours to discuss their plans, parents fumed that none of the all-important hearings BU held to air its plans were in Spanish, nor were any of their reports translated. And the university was fairly clumsy with its symbolism. It abolished a longstanding position of bilingual program director, deputizing a non-hispanic teacher to take over the vestigial work.

Silber and company, justly proud of their programmatic accomplishments—elementary school reading and math scores had increased, while Chelsea High SAT scores shot up 14 points in a year—treated the unhappy parents as kevetchers: "the ain't-it-awful crowd," one BU administrator dubbed them. Weren't they giving them good health care, a rich assortment of afterschool programs, and, for once, accountable teachers? Still, the first state study of the takeover, in 1990, sided with the moms and dads, calling the BU contingent "arrogant and devaluing to parents and others who are members of minority groups." A federally funded study a year later echoed the charge. As the state panel observed in fluent educationese, "The university seems to have underestimated the need for continuous socialization of important issues with various constituencies." The community was more direct. When Silber attempted to speak to parents about the schools' financial problems, he was drowned out by jeers.

Failing to translate reports or hire hispanics seems rather forgivable in the context of a huge reform plan. Yet four years after the historic contract was signed, oversights like those have proven pivotal, because Chelsea parents didn't just express their hostility with noise. City leaders, keying into residents' feelings, cut the schools' budget dramatically, crowding classrooms and stymieing many of BU's planned reforms. The results of that underfunding are now being felt acutely: The reading and math scores that leapt up in the first years of reform recently sank beneath pre-takeover levels. "It's just a big monster," charges Juan Vega, member of the Chelsea Commission on Hispanic Affairs, of the reform effort—not seeming to realize that it was all supposed to be done for his kids, not *to* them.

Chelsea's current crisis is an extreme manifestation of a standard problem in education reform. From Rochester to Chicago to D.C., even well-intentioned reformers tend to act like summer-stock Coriolanuses when it comes to parent involvement. They pay lip service to the notion but work doggedly to keep the masses from messing with their plans. Unfortunately, longitudinal studies suggest that the treacly concept of getting moms and dads engaged is almost certainly the linchpin of students' educational success. That task isn't very difficult when your student body is middle class and raised in families that value learning. The challenge is students who are poor, usually urban, possibly hungry, and brought up a world in which education isn't necessarily a priority. Administrators have to *work* on and with these parents. And while the payoff for doing so can be astounding, administrators tangled up in the details of running a school tend to find apathetic moms and dads more convenient.

Convenient, that is, in the short run. It may not be tomorrow, or even next year, but, as Chelsea's parents indicate, citizens excised from the reform process can prove far more toxic to change through their votes in elections and on bond issues than by their "meddling" in a third grade class. This fall, hispanic parents actually threatened to keep their kids out of school, while BU muttered about taking a hard look at the practicality of its long-term investment in Chelsea.

"At this point, it would be a blessing if BU just left," says Juan Vega. The university's hand-picked superintendent, Peter Greer, has already taken the hint. Earlier this year, he resigned to run a private school in New Jersey.

"F"ing school reform

To be sure, from each of these hope-freighted reforms have sprung some triumphs: Spry Elementary's makeover, the rising elementary scores in Rochester and Chelsea. And in the context of so much bad news about public schools, it's tempting to be grateful about good news, however small. Perhaps the goal is, as Churchill said about democracy, to be, not the best, but the least bad.

But the trouble with toasting Rochester, Chicago, and Chelsea for slender gains is that they had the leadership and the motivation to be a lot more than least bad. They aimed to empower good teachers and get rid of bad ones; to wrest money and control from bureaucracies; and to include families, whatever the class differences and difficulties, in a learning process that precedes and transcends the classroom. In their early days, these three cities held the keys to real reform. And then they lost them.

The dampened hope in Rochester, Chelsea, and Chicago should make liberals not just furious, but determined. If we really believe that funneling public money into private schools is wrong, we have a moral obligation to address the politically hazardous sources of public school reform's continued failure—tenured incompetence, administrative protectionism, parental detachment and alienation. Until we do, there's little guarantee that the next Brilliant Ideas for reforming our schools from within won't be more wasted efforts. Only this time around, the casualty list may include, besides all those Peggys unleashed into the economy, the notion of public education itself.

The New Welfare Debate: What the States Are Hoping to Accomplish

An Editor's Report

ON FEBRUARY 3, the Senate Finance Committee's Social Security and Family Policy Subcommittee held a hearing on proposed restructuring of state welfare policies. The subject matter sounds routine, but some of the changes being proposed—and the national debate they are inspiring—are anything but.

Driven by anorexic budgets and a growing conviction that the welfare policies of three decades are doing more harm than good, state governments from California to New Jersey are moving ahead with sweeping policy revisions that welfare expert Lawrence Mead, who was among the witnesses on February 3, says have taken on some aspects of "a national movement." The discussion was broad, but specific attention was given to newly enacted New Jersey reforms. Testimony ranged from the actuarial to the philosophical. It also included the practical when Democratic State Assemblyman Wayne Bryant of Camden, New Jersey, one of the nation's poorest cities (80 percent there get public assistance), took the witness chair to describe the bills he authored and Governor James Florio recently signed. Excerpts from his remarks follow on the next page.

The Nation

In his testimony, Douglas Besharov, director of the Social and Individual Responsibility Project at the American Enterprise Institute, outlined some of the changes that are being discussed throughout the country today. Some are already in effect. They include:

■ The Wisconsin Learnfare program, started in 1988, that reduces welfare payments to teen mothers or to families with teen dependents who fail to meet school attendance requirements.

■ The Ohio Learning, Earning, and Parenting Program, started in 1989, that gives teenage parents on Aid to Families With Dependent Children (AFDC) who have dropped out of high school and returned a bonus of $62 for each month they have less than five absences (no more than two of which can be inexcused).

■ California Governor Pete Wilson's proposed initiative for the November 1992 ballot that stipulates that AFDC payments no longer be increased when a mother has additional children and that grants to teenage mothers be given only if they live with their parents or guardians, with the grant going directly to the older generation. Welfare grant levels would be reduced 10 percent for all recipients, with an additional 15 percent reduction after six months for any family headed by an able-bodied unemployed adult.

■ "Bridefare" or "Wedfare" provisions in some states that seek to encourage couples to marry and work by allowing married recipients to retain more of their earnings than single recipients.

■ Bonuses to mothers in Women, Infants and Children programs who have their children immunized.

In the debate among Democratic presidential candidates on January 19, the contenders focused specifically on New Jersey reforms. They were asked whether they thought Governor Jim Florio of New Jersey should sign the legislative package Bryant authored. Nearly all the candidates favored reforming welfare, but only one, Senator Bob Kerrey, said that he might sign the legislation. Florio signed it on January 21.

In his testimony, Mead speculates that the new state policies "are probably a spin-off from workfare," those programs in which granting welfare is conditioned on education and training, and following that, on a job. These programs, he says, "are widely viewed as effective."

A second rationale, he says, is that states are trying to "extend controls from public forms of behavior to more private ones." Rather than simply requiring recipients to work or stay in school, the new policies "attempt to shape their personal lives. Society has an interest in whether children are well prepared for adulthood, and it must do something forceful to protect that interest." Third, Mead says, "The states are reacting to the fact that voluntary social programs have failed to halt the violence, child abuse, and school and unemployment problems in low-income areas. Merely to offer people new benefits or services does not cause them to live more constructive lives, or does so only marginally. That failure is the underlying reason why local leaders now want to get tough. The traditional idea that caregivers ought to be unjudging toward their clients is giving way to a more directive posture."

Economic conditions also explain why welfare restructuring is occurring now. Rapidly expanding welfare rolls predated the economic downturn, but the recession has contributed to their expansion. A. Sidney Johnson, executive director of the American Public Welfare Association, estimates that between July 1989 and November 1991, 2,000 children per day were added to the AFDC rolls nationwide. "Welfare costs of the states have soared by nearly $1.7 billion since July 1989," he said, "and total Medicaid for the poor in the last year was nearly $31 billion, an increase of 20 percent." Besharov notes that federal rules make it impossible for states to cut Medicaid spending, so they cut AFDC payments instead, knowing that federal Food Stamp payments will rise automatically to cushion the impact of the cuts on the poor. Johnson added that the implementation of the last major welfare reform, which required able-bodied recipients to get education and training or lose benefits, is being slowed by the recession. The downturn has caused, in Johnson's words, "unprecedented increases in caseloads, unprecedented costs to states, and a dramatic reduction in state revenue needed to fund state services."

But the "economic motive is not uppermost," Mead says. Only in California are there calls for across-the-board cuts in AFDC benefits. He believes that "the new proposals are designed to change the character of government much more than its scale. The aim is to get recipients to do something more to help themselves in return for welfare." And that, he says, has long been the desired approach of the American people, who "want to be generous to the poor, but also demanding." Those goals have long been seen in Washington, he argues, as opposites.

A New Jersey Report

This is the context in which reforms are now being proposed and implemented. Scholars and policymakers will long debate the merits of what some are suggesting is a less-than-benign form of social engineering. But for now, states are acting, and many of these actions appear to have public support.

Much of the media attention to New Jersey's approach has focused on the provision to eliminate the $64 increase in welfare payments for each child born after parents enroll in AFDC. But the legislation is much broader. Actually a collection of six reforms, it contains education and training requirements and allows women to retain welfare benefits after they marry. Additionally, when it takes effect in July, it would allow a woman with a new child to work and keep wages equal to half of her monthly grant without losing welfare benefits. Richard Nathan, director of the Nelson A. Rockefeller Institute of Government in New York, described the $64 cutback as "shooting at a popular and safe target; children on welfare can't return the

fire." Wayne Bryant, author of the reform, disputes the contention. Excerpted here are portions of his testimony.

Bryant's Testimony

For decades, well-meaning policymakers at every level of government have crafted and implemented a host of programs designed to help the poor.

As governmental programs go, welfare is the one most associated with dealing with the problems of poverty. However, the traditional welfare system itself can also be blamed for sustaining the existence of an underclass society. It is also

> "Anyone who believes that the welfare system offers genuine hope for the poor to escape from the clutches of poverty should simply ask the opinion of any recipient."
>
> —Wayne Bryant
> Democratic Assemblyman
> Camden, N.J.

the only governmental program that aggravates poverty conditions by having rules which destroy family unity.

Anyone who believes that the welfare system offers genuine hope for the poor to escape from the clutches of poverty should simply ask the opinion of any recipient. In case after case, they will hear stories of despair.

The individuals they talk to will, more than likely, have limited reading and writing skills and lack marketable job skills. Statistics show that more than 50 percent of AFDC recipients in New Jersey never complete high school.

And more than likely, the individuals they talk to will have already tried to find or keep a good-paying job, only to become demoralized by educational and vocational limitations.

The welfare system does nothing to abolish those limitations. It is not a system of transition. It is a system of entrapment that condones complacency

and passiveness and robs individuals of dignity and self-respect.

In crafting changes in New Jersey's system, I was guided by my experiences with recipients who felt enslaved by welfare. However, my primary inspiration came from those recipients who struggled furiously for a way out.

I found them in places like the Work Group in Pennsauken, New Jersey. There, welfare mothers work toward their high school equivalency diploma, learn computer skills, and make themselves marketable for good-paying, full-time jobs in the private sector. My reform laws embrace this spirit of self-sufficiency.

The other major focus of my program is to reunite the fragmented welfare family. We will begin fortifying the family by eliminating financial disincentives to family unity built into current welfare laws. The eligibility rules in our welfare system have helped to create a sub-society of "invisible men"—men who fear that if they make their presence known, they would put the welfare mother at risk of losing benefits to her and her children.

The system has also penalized family unity by reducing welfare grants by 30 percent when both natural parents are married and in the home. Two of my laws will instead create financial incentives for fathers and father figures to stay with the family.

Under New Jersey's new program, the Commissioner of Human Services is directed to allow full benefits to the AFDC program to those families in which both parents are married and reside in the same home, without placing restrictions on the employment of either parent whose income does not exceed the state's AFDC eligibility standard.

The second measure is commonly referred to as the "step-parent law." An eligible parent who is married to a person who is not the parent of one or more of the eligible parent's children will not be eligible for benefits if the household income exceeds the state eligibility standard for benefits. The eligible parent's natural children *will* be eligible for benefits according to a sliding income scale which excludes the income of the eligible parent's spouse if the total annual household income does not exceed 150 percent of the official poverty level. The eligible parent's spouse and the spouse's natural child who is not the eligible parent's natural child, who is living with the family, shall not be eligible for AFDC benefits.

The cornerstone of my package is the Family Development Initiative Act. In addition to establishing educational and vocational achievement as a condition for welfare benefits, this provision directs the state to craft and monitor an assistance program tailored to an individual family's needs. So if a welfare mother needs child care services while she works toward her high school equivalency diploma, the state will provide them. If a child in the family needs tutoring, the state will provide it. And if a member of the family requires substance abuse counseling or treatment, that, too, will become part of the plan.

The law stipulates that a recipient whose youngest child is two or older shall participate in education and employment activities. A recipient whose youngest child is less than two shall participate in counseling and vocational assessment activities and the development of a family plan and may voluntarily participate in education, vocational training, or employment activities.

The services to be provided under the program shall include, but not be limited to: job development and placement in full-time permanent jobs, preferably in the private sector; counseling and vocational assessment; intensive remedial education, including instruction in English-as-a-second-language; financial and other assistance for higher education, including four-year and community colleges, and for post-secondary vocational training programs; job search assistance; community work experience; employment skills training focused on a specific job; and on-the-job training.

The program shall be designed to ensure that each participant and member of the participant's family, as age appropriate, has attained the equivalent of a high school degree, before assigning that person to a vocational-related activity.

The program will also provide supportive services to a program participant as a last resort when no other source is available and when these services are included in the family plan. The supportive services will include, but not be limited to, one or more of the following: day care services for the participant's child; transportation services; health insurance coverage, to be provided by a participant's employer, or through a continuation of Medicaid benefits.

The protection afforded AFDC recipients is a major disincentive to public assistance recipients who are considering employment. While the federal government has recognized the relationship between medical coverage and successful employment initiatives through its policy of allowing limited extensions of Medicaid to former AFDC recipients who lose eligibility for both programs as a result of employment, only 12 percent of those entering employment receive Medicaid extensions for more than four months because of strict income eligibility.

A person who becomes ineligible for financial assistance under the AFDC program due to earnings from, or increased hours of, employment, or receipt of benefits under the "employment compensation law," is eligible to continue receiving Medicaid benefits for 24 consecutive months, commencing with the month in which eligibility for AFDC ceases.

Another component of my package, disallowing increased AFDC benefits to adult recipients who have additional children, is also about responsibility. It suggests that individuals on welfare can make responsible decisions. Life is about decisions, and decisions often revolve around the family.

A middle-class wage earner does not go to his boss and say, "I'm having another child, so I'm entitled to a raise." The wage earner works extra hours, gets a part-time job, or adjusts the family budget to compensate for the new arrival. There is nothing wrong with instilling this responsible work ethic in poor people as they become better educated, better skilled, and self-sufficient.

This component of my plan has generated a spirited debate. But let me emphasize here that the debate has focused principally on the first part of a two-part law. This law also changes welfare rules to allow adult recipients to collect their full benefits while earning an income equal to 50 percent of their grant in order to support the new arrival. The alternative is for government to hand out an additional $64 per month for the additional child. To earn that paltry income, a recipient would have to work a half hour per day for a month at minimum wage. The welfare recipients, who will be educated and trained for placement into skilled private sector jobs, can do much better than $64 a month.

New Jersey's new welfare law is founded upon four fundamental principals: family, responsibility, education, and opportunity. It represents a holistic approach in dealing with the welfare family and empowers people with real tools—dignity, self-sufficiency, and confidence—to reverse the vicious cycle of poverty and welfare dependency.

Do we need more prisons?

Point ▶ ▶ ▶ ▶ ▶ ▶ ▶ ▶ ▶ ▶ ▶

Ann W. Richards

Ann W. Richards is governor of Texas.

I f government's most sacred and fundamental obligation is to protect its citizens, government is failing to meet its obligation. Throughout this nation, crime and the fear of crime have fundamentally altered the way we live. People all over America, Texans included, lack the assurance that the criminal justice system is making their cities safer, their homes more secure, their streets free from violent crime. We read too many newspaper stories, see too many horror stories on the evening news, talk with too many friends and acquaintances who have been crime's victims, to believe that we have made our communities safe places for our families.

Making America a safer, more secure place to live is not an easy task. It requires a comprehensive approach, a battle on numerous fronts. Building more prisons is an absolutely crucial component of this multifront strategy.

If our criminal justice system is to be effective, the perpetrator of a crime must know that punishment will be swift and sure. Violent criminals must know that many years will pass before they walk free again. They must serve the bulk of the sentence assessed. And we must be assured that the criminal comes out of prison a changed human being.

To meet those objectives, we have to build enough prison cells to end the revolving-door system that turns criminals loose after they have served only a fraction of their sentences. Last year in Texas, our prisons admitted more than 46,000 new prisoners, enough to fill almost all the space we have. Obviously, something has to give. Either you let some out, or you don't let new ones in — or you build more space. Other states confront the same dilemma.

We need more prison space. Here in Texas, we have no choice. Our prisons are so crowded that we have had to resort to releasing violent prisoners after they have served a mere fraction of their sentences. Some 17,000 felons are clogging up our county jails, because our prison cells are occupied. Thousands of warrants go unserved because of a lack of space.

Even though we have added thousands of prison beds in the past two years and have nine prisons under construction, the backlog is so great that jail overcrowding will continue. With a backlog larger than the total prison population of 36 states, Texas has to build more prisons.

Building more prisons is not a panacea; we understand that fact. If prisons are mere holding spaces,

◀ ◀ ◀ ◀ ◀ ◀ ◀ Counterpoint

Anne M. Larrivee

Maine Rep. Anne M. Larrivee serves on the Joint Select Committee on Corrections, the Maine Criminal Justice Commission and is a member of the Campaign for an Effective Crime Policy.

W e only need more prisons if they're working. So, let's take a critical look at what has happened in the last 10 years. As statistics from the American Correctional Association clearly show, per 100,000 of population we have doubled the number of people behind bars from 1980 to 1990. And in 1992 according to *Americans Behind Bars: One Year Later*, the U.S. rate of incarceration rose 6.8 percent to 455 per 100,000 population, number one in the world. In second place was South Africa, with 311 per 100,000 incarcerated. Their rate declined in 1991 by 6.6 percent. Our incarceration rate has risen more than 100 percent in the last decade and is still going up. If incarceration works to deter crime, ask yourself if you feel 100 percent safer from crime than you did in 1980. Our streets do not feel safer to me. There has been little impact on crime rates in relationship to the tremendous increase in numbers incarcerated. A recent FBI report shows that 1991 was the bloodiest on record with murders up 5.4 percent from the previous year.

There is no disagreement that perpetrators of violent crimes (rape, robbery, assault) must be incapacitated by prison sentences. However, a study by the National Council on Crime and Delinquency found that 80 percent of those going to prison are not serious or violent criminals but are guilty of low-level offenses; minor parole violations; and property, drug and public disorder crimes. Alternatives such as intensive probation, electronic monitoring, restitution and fines for appropriate offenders have shown to be more effective and less costly than incarceration. Warehousing these prisoners at a cost of about $50,000 per bed for construction and $20,000 per year must be rationally analyzed. We must be sure we are not reacting to cries for a popular "get tough" philosophy by simply increasing the number of prisons and the length of the sentences when we can show no better than a negligible effect on crime. If the goals of incarceration are incapacitation, deterrence, punishment and rehabilitation we must scrutinize the effectiveness of our current sentencing structures and building plans. And we must avoid being lured into decisions to satisfy the need for a politically correct voting record.

Most people understand the need to fund prisons, but want to know their investment is working. They want to be assured that they will be safer, criminals will be punished, and that imprisonment will work.

Point	Counterpoint

nothing but criminal warehouses, we will never be able to build all that we need.

We must make sure that the right people are occupying prison cells. We must use the prisons to keep violent criminals off the street. We must lock away the people who have no regard for the life or safety of other human beings.

Of course, we cannot look the other way when nonviolent crime occurs. But too often, the hot-check writer or the young first-time burglar ends up occupying prison space that ought to be reserved for murderers and rapists. That's not smart. We need what the professionals call "alternative sentencing" — electronic monitoring, restitution centers, boot camp, intensive supervision probation. We have to make sure that tax money does not become a scholarship to crime school, otherwise known as prison.

Finally, we need to make sure that the prison experience cuts into the cycle of crime, especially into the escalating cycle created by drugs in our society. We know that eight out of 10 people serving time in our state prisons committed crimes that were directly related to their abuse of alcohol and drugs. Six out of 10 prison inmates are rearrested within three years of their release, and drug offenders have a recidivism rate 25 percent higher than other offenders.

Here in Texas, we have set aside 12,000 prison cells for inmates who were put in prison because drugs or alcohol took insidious control of their lives. We are telling them in no uncertain terms that if they want to get out and stay out, they must undergo rigorous treatment and stop alcohol and drug use.

When inmates are forced to confront their addiction and the harm it has done to their lives and the lives of others, three out of four serve their time and never come back. We know we are cutting costs and crime when an inmate leaves prison clean and sober and determined to stay that way. That is what prisons are supposed to do; they are supposed to change people's lives for the better.

We know that building more prisons will not, in and of itself, eliminate crime. But refusing to build them does not work either. Prisons have their place in a carefully designed, comprehensive system of criminal justice. Our job is not only to build them, but to make sure they function effectively.

Prisons are a crucial component of a multifront strategy against crime.

Building more prisons has not made us safer.

I doubt that you could find a handful of voters who think we have crises licked because we now put 100 percent more people behind bars. When informed that from 1982 to 1989 the cost for corrections for the nation per $100 of personal income rose 54 percent while education costs increased only 6 percent, they would wonder how much more good money should be thrown after bad to the detriment of education, health care, early intervention and other methods of building a healthier society.

When we rely on putting people behind bars to decrease crime rates what we fail to recognize is that 98 percent of inmates *will* be out on our streets again. With the trend moving toward incarcerating more and more, funding that could be used for treatment within the prison walls is going to bricks and mortar. The effect is that many inmates are walking out the door with their proverbial new suit and $3 in their pocket with the same problems they brought in, with the same behaviors intact and most likely, new ones learned behind bars. If certain of those inmates had escaped two weeks prior to release, we would have put out APB's, started the manhunts and advised citizens to lock their doors. Ask your corrections officials who's due to be released in the next year from your prisons and if they would feel safe having those inmates in their neighborhoods. Simply building more capacity has not worked.

The answer to the question "Do we need more prisons?" must be no. No, because prison terms are not working; and no, because we are not safer. When the only tool you have is a hammer, every problem looks like a nail. Justice does not mean prisons and only prisons. In an era of scarce resources, we must use more tools, cheaper tools and more effective tools than simply "locking them up," which is costing taxpayers dearly while doing precious little to insure their safety.

Let's look deeper.

Of LULUs, NIMBYs, and NIMTOOs

Herbert Inhaber

Herbert Inhaber is principal scientist for the Westinghouse Savannah River Company in Aiken, South Carolina.

In high school, we were told by our mathematics teachers that a proof in geometry had to be both necessary *and* sufficient. The present way we choose sites for hazardous and radioactive wastes in this country, replete with elaborate environmental impact statements and risk analyses, is in some ways necessary. But it isn't sufficient. If it were, we wouldn't have so much trouble finding sites for these locally unwanted land uses—LULUs, in the jargon.

Siting protests have become frequent, and some have even turned violent. In April 1990 an anti-LULU riot broke out in Caneadea, New York (in Allegany County). Protesters charged police lines set up to protect officials who were trying to inspect a proposed low-level radioactive waste (LLRW) site. Hundreds took part in the melee, many wearing masks reading, "Allegany, No Dump." Six men riding horses charged the police. A group of elderly citizens chained themselves across a bridge to prevent the state inspectors from getting through. Thirty-nine people were arrested.

A poll taken around that time showed that about 91 percent of local residents were opposed to the site. Feelings ran so high against the proposed facility that the local prosecutor had no luck getting a grand jury to indict the rioters, despite the fact that the violence was captured on videotape and witnessed by many bystanders.

THE PRESENT APPROACH

How can a LULU site be built without setting off riots or endless litigation? The "scientific" approach to finding sites for these LULUs has clearly failed. Everyone is in favor of finding a place for a LULU, as long as it is at least a hundred miles away from them. Is there another way, perhaps market-based, of finding a site? Will those responsible for finding a site for these LULUs always be confronted with counter-acronyms: NIMBY (not in my backyard) or NIMTOO (not in my term of office)?

There *is* a way out of this predicament. It involves simple and proven market principles. Environmental standards, cumbersome as they sometimes are, do not have to be diluted or reduced.

Before I discuss how the market can again solve a seemingly intractable problem, consider the approach leading to the New York riots and many other less violent confrontations. On its face, who could quarrel with it? It is strictly scientific and objective, complete with risk assessments and elaborate ecological studies. As a risk analyst, I cannot quarrel with these studies. Yet, as I noted above, while necessary, these detailed examinations are not sufficient.

The solution envisioned by most siting agencies is education. Who could be against that? To carry this out, public meetings are held in which the potential host communities are lectured by scientists and administrators. The experts usually explain that the risks are very small (which they are) and that the chances of environmental damages from a well-engineered facility are almost negligible (also true). Then they sit back and wait for nods of agreement from the locals.

The nods never come. As University of Southern California professor Elihu Katz has noted, "In spite of the blind belief of advertisers, politicians, some academics and the public that media campaigns are capable of inducing massive changes in opinions, attitudes and actions—always somebody else's, not one's own—the research evidence continues to say otherwise."

In Allegany County, according to one newspaper report, one public information meeting attracted about 5,000 people, "many of them chanting 'no dump,' [who] hooted and hollered their opposition." While this was undoubtedly one of the major examples of public participation in that sparsely populated county's history, it could hardly be described as a meeting in which the people were educated by the scientists.

I was formerly coordinator of the Office of Risk Analysis at Oak Ridge National Laboratory in Tennessee. As part of my job, I attended public meetings dealing with the proposed (and semi-abandoned) Monitored Retrievable Storage system, whereby nuclear fuel rods would be "temporarily" stored until a final repository was built. In

Reprinted from *The Public Interest*, No. 107 (Spring 1992), pp. 52-64. Copyright © 1992 by National Affairs, Inc.

these meetings, I was nervous about standing up and saying something that could be construed as possibly supporting the viewpoint of the scientists who were being shouted down. So much for public interaction and dialogue, the ostensible purpose of these gatherings.

The system is not supposed to work like this. It is supposed to begin with a neutral evaluation of the need for a facility. Then a map of the state or region under consideration is examined to eliminate unsuitable places, such as swamps and big cities. The narrowing-down process, performed only by experts, continues until a specific, presumably the "best," site is chosen. The inhabitants of that community are told that their increase in risk, as calculated by yet other experts, will be small. After some consideration, they agree, and construction begins.

That is the way it looks on the blueprint. But the preceding examples suggest that the elaborate plan, with its series of milestones and deadlines, rarely is implemented.

EDUCATION AND RISK

While educating the public on any technical subject is a good idea, in the case of LULUs it has worked fitfully at best. Locals often perceive contempt in the attitude of technicians who lecture them along these lines: "Here are the facts. There's no appeal, because we know what the truth is. If you had any sense, you'd accept what we say."

Much of the debate ultimately centers on risk. Risk analysts contend that the hazards are small, but the people in affected areas meet this with disbelief. Part of the disparity in viewpoints is normal, deriving from who is performing the risk analyses, and who is expected to understand them. Chauncey Starr, the former head of the Electric Power Research Institute in Palo Alto, would illustrate this disparity with a story about bread-cutting:

Go to the grocery store and buy a loaf of unsliced bread. When you get it home, start slicing. Note how far your thumb is from the knife. Now call in a neighbor, your spouse, or even a stranger walking down the street. You again hold the loaf, but this time let the other person hold the knife. Now see how far your thumb is from the knife. Chances are it's much farther away.

In other words, when you are in charge of your own risk, you may be nonchalant. If somebody else is controlling the hazards, you are much more cautious.

This proposition was self-evident at the Tennessee meetings I attended. I made a brief observation of the other vehicles pulling into the parking lot. Very few of the drivers and passengers were wearing seatbelts. And the air in the meeting halls was filled with cigarette smoke. Most risk analysts would say that smoking or driving without seatbelts would produce much greater risk than any conceivable LULU.

Such instances may give the impression that the public is somehow irrational about LULUs. It is not. Consider the following imaginary analogy: Suppose it had been

shown by batteries of scientists that green cars cause less eye strain, and in addition reduce global warming due to their absorption of certain solar rays. But suppose that consumers preferred red cars. Any manufacturer who decided that customers were unreasonable in ignoring the scientific evidence, and produced only green autos, would soon find himself with shuttered factories. No LULU site will ever be built by debating just who is or is not being logical. If the facilities are to be constructed, fruitless arguments of this type must be put aside.

In truth, those who live around a potential LULU site are exhibiting intelligence, although it may not be readily apparent to the beleaguered scientists and engineers dodging verbal bullets on the platform. As Gail Bingham of the Conservation Foundation writes,

Although it may sound heretical or obvious, local *residents are acting rationally in opposing hazardous waste facilities* [emphasis in original]. Those wishing to site new hazardous waste facilities must begin by acknowledging (at least to themselves) that even good proposals are likely to impose more costs than benefits on local residents. The reason local residents oppose new facilities is that they have every incentive to do so—the new facility makes them worse off. Thus, the most direct way to respond to such opposition is to change the incentives that motivate people's behavior.

THE ROLE OF INCENTIVES

Incentives are key here. Incentives of varying types propel much, though not all, of human behavior. Is it inconceivable that they can be used to find sites for LULUs?

The rush to the barricades begins. "You can't mix the environment with money," the cry arises. "People's health and environmental quality are too important to be rung up on a cash register."

Perhaps the best response to this was offered by a fellow risk analyst at the University of Tennessee. He had long been active in studying the nuclear waste management process, and observed:

In a perfect world, environment and dollars might be in separate compartments, kept apart by an impermeable barrier. But in the real world, they're already intermingled, whether or not the neighbors of a waste site get a penny themselves. The funds to 'educate' the people that the risks are smaller than they imagine have to come from somewhere. They're taken from the pockets of the rest of us, of course. And the various siting commissions spend freely. I should know—some of my research is paid for by them. The states have spent tens of millions of dollars, if not hundreds of millions, without an ounce of radioactive waste being put into the ground. The federal program for high-level radioactive wastes has spent hundreds of millions, with about the same results.

So let's not pretend that there are no incentives in the hazardous-waste siting process. There are plenty of them—but they go to government bureaucrats, university professors like myself, and consulting firms. The people whose lives would be most affected by the waste site see precious few of these incentives.

But does the use of incentives for accepting LULUs constitute a bribe to the local population? In a word, no. Bribery has three elements that a properly designed incentive system does not. First, bribery is only used in pursuit of an illegal act. Finding a LULU site is not only legal, almost every citizen is in favor of it, as long as it's not in his backyard. Second, bribery is almost always done under the table. A viable incentive system would avoid closed doors. It would make the level of payments publicly and widely known. Third, bribes are always targeted. An appropriate incentive system will not zero in on any specific county, town, or other political jurisdiction, as is often done under the "objective" procedure now in place. Rather, it will let the potential site neighbors decide for themselves if the level of incentives matches any level of harm they perceive coming from the site.

Incentives to take socially approved action would not be a new phenomenon if applied to hazardous-waste sites. For example, walk into a post office and chances are you will see photos of real or alleged felons. Above their fuzzy snapshots will be the word "Reward." In a perfect world, we would all be so civic-minded that we would be on continuous outlook for these fugitives, without any thought of recompense. In the real world, the state has found that it can achieve its goals—bringing these individuals to justice—by offering an incentive to do so.

WHY NEGOTIATION FAILS

If incentives should be supplied to the people who would be affected by a LULU near them, what system should be used to set the level? The obvious and intuitive first choice would be negotiation between the siting authority and the affected community.

But that process holds a defect that, as I noted above, will engender charges of bribery, if not worse: the element of secrecy. Most negotiations are carried out behind closed doors. I cannot envision the entire population of a town or county bargaining simultaneously. While negotiation over compensation works in most other contexts, it faces severe difficulty in the LULU context.

The implicit model used for negotiation in trying to site a LULU is that of labor-management bargaining. Admittedly, most labor-management talks end in success, in that a contract of some sort is signed. But these discussions have one element that arguments over LULU siting do not: a deadline. That is, both labor and management know that at some point a strike or lockout can occur. Even when that date is postponed, it still looms in all negotiators' minds.

Nothing of the sort happens in LULU-siting talks. All participants know that any deadlines specified are easily ignored. When Congress passed the Low-Level Radioactive Waste Policy Act of 1980, for example, it required states to form "compacts" that were to build waste-storage facilities. By 1985, all the elaborate deadlines set

down in the legislation had passed, so Congress passed amendments to the original law. Seven years after the new legislation got the President's signature, most of the new deadlines have been forgotten. States and localities are still arguing over where the radioactive wastes should go.

About the same thing happened with respect to high-level nuclear waste (mostly spent fuel rods from nuclear reactors). After years of the Department of Energy setting its own deadlines, Congress got involved in 1982, establishing a whole new set. Few if any were met. Five years later, a new law was passed, producing still more deadlines. Even those have been missed by years, due in part to legal wrangling. So when a siting system for a LULU is proposed, with an elaborate schedule of milestones, the targeted community generally knows it can avoid them.

AUCTIONS: DIRECT AND INDIRECT

One way out of the negotiation-deadline trap is a public auction. The reasons for holding auctions of any type were summarized by Ralph Cassady in his authoritative book on the subject, *Auctions and Auctioneering:*

> One answer is, perhaps, that some products have no standard value. For example, the price of any catch of fish (or at least of fish destined for the fresh fish market) depends on demand and supply conditions at a specific moment of time, influenced possibly by prospective market developments. For manuscripts and antiques, too, prices must be remade for each transaction. For example, how can one discover the worth of an original copy of Lincoln's Gettysburg Address except by auction method?

To follow Cassady's reasoning, there would be no point in using an auction system in conjunction with the millions of catalytic converters attached annually to our cars to reduce air pollution. The converters are generally similar. But each hazardous- or radioactive-waste site, or other LULU, is a unique combination of calculated risks, geology, nearby population, engineering design, and, most importantly, the attitudes of potential surrounding neighbors. For this reason, an auction is the best way to decide the appropriate level of compensation.

Although almost everyone has participated in an auction at one time or another, we may be unfamiliar with their use in public policy. One recent example was the siting process for the superconducting supercollider (SSC), the physically largest and most expensive scientific project in history, which took place via an indirect auction among the competing states.

AN AUCTION IN DISGUISE

The gigantic particle accelerator, estimated recently to cost about $8 billion, will dwarf all past scientific endeavors. When finished, it will employ about 3,000 scientists, engineers, and technicians, with an annual payroll of about $270 million.

The SSC was, and is, clearly a desirable installation. It is thus vastly different from a LULU. Yet both share one characteristic: they both can be built in a variety of locations. Because there are then many potential "bidders," an auction could, in principle, have taken place for the SSC.

Almost every state expressed at least some interest in having the lucrative installation within its borders. About two dozen submitted formal applications. Congress wanted the selection to be done in an "objective" way, and so forbade direct financial bids by the states. That is, Pennsylvania could not say, "We hereby offer $500 million for the SSC."

In that sense, there was never any auction held for the accelerator. But as Congress often does, it left a loophole in the law big enough to drive the entire SSC installation through. States were not precluded from bidding *indirectly* on the project. As far as the theory of auctions is concerned, an indirect bid, with goods and services offered instead of currency, is equivalent to a direct bid.

Since all states were aware of the size of competing indirect bids, for all practical purposes an auction was held for the SSC. The auction took place at the same time as the "objective" search by a committee of the National Research Council (NRC), an arm of the National Academy of Sciences.

Of the indirect bids, Texas's was the largest, at approximately $1 billion. Some of it was in the form of an electricity subsidy over the lifetime of the installation, providing electricity at the rate of one cent per kilowatt-hour. About one-eighth of the current average national rate, this is an enormous indirect subsidy, since the SSC will be a prodigious user of electricity. Illinois offered $570 million in roads, housing, and fellowships. Colorado offered a package of $300 million in road and railroad improvements; many other states offered comparable packages.

The NRC awarded the SSC to Texas, which, as it happens, made the highest indirect bid. So if the "objective" method had been dropped in favor of an auction, Texas would have also won. The results were the same as if an auction *had* been held.

THE REVERSE DUTCH AUCTION

The economic literature is filled with descriptions of many types of auctions. Which one is best to site LULUs?

Consider the English auction, the one with which we are most familiar: this variety is held in Sotheby's, churches, synagogues, and farm yards. In an English auction, the auctioneer's cry might be as follows: "I have ten dollars, ten dollars. . . . Do I hear fifteen? Fifteen—I have fifteen. Now, is there someone at twenty? The gentleman in the back row offers twenty. Anyone for twenty-five?"

The English auction almost always has multiple bids. But this is probably too much to expect when finding a site for a LULU. One adequate volunteer would be sufficient. That would be one more than the number that usually volunteer.

What then is left? The Dutch auction (sometimes called Chinese) starts with a high price that falls. This form is used to speed up the auction process, since the English auction can be time-consuming. The Dutch auction begins with a silent appraisal by the auctioneer of a reasonable price for the goods on the block. For example, he might decide that a consignment of cut flowers is worth about $50. He does not announce this. On that basis, he might start the bidding at $100, hoping that a bid of more than $50 will be made. The cry in a Dutch auction might then be:

I will start the bidding at $100. Any takers? I will reduce the price to $95. No hands at that price, so I will lower it to $90. Going once, going twice to $85. The lady in the front row raises her hand, so she gets the lot for $85.

The Dutch auction differs considerably from the English version. From the viewpoint of finding LULU sites, the prime dissimilarity is that there is only one bid. In the above example, when the hand was raised at $85, the auction ended immediately. There was no chance for reconsideration or second chances.

This feature then corresponds to what society needs in finding a LULU site: a community that is certain of what it wants and the price it deserves.

HOW IT WORKS

The Dutch auction deals in desirable objects, like flowers or cheese. But a LULU is clearly a different matter. In a Dutch auction, the bidders pay *for* the object on the block. In dealing with LULUs, we have to pay money *to* the community making a bid. This then suggests a *reverse* Dutch auction, in which a community bids to be paid.

In the reverse Dutch auction, another feature of the ordinary Dutch auction is retained. The price level is set by the auctioneer, not the participants. In the example noted above, the auctioneer, if he had been so inclined, could have changed the price in increments of $100 or $1. The participants in a reverse Dutch auction therefore cannot arbitrarily raise the price they will be paid for accepting the LULU. The auctioneer—in this case a siting authority—is in control.

Thus, in a reverse Dutch auction, the price would rise until a town or county came forward with an environmentally acceptable location. After that sole bid the auction would end.

The reverse Dutch auction would of course be proposed via the usual official documents. But if an oral announcement to a meeting of officials from potential siting communities were made, it might sound approximately as follows:

We have this radioactive waste (or prisoners, or municipal trash, or incinerator) we wish to site. We have abandoned the previous technique of pretending to listen to you and then forcing the facility on a community regardless of its wishes.

What have we substituted in place of this discredited method? We propose to let the market determine the site, subject to existing environmental regulations. Any community that does not want the facility under any circumstances does not have to participate in the auction. This will ensure that the facility will never be within its boundaries.

The increase in the size of the bonus should draw the attention of those communities that are not absolutely and irrevocably opposed to the facility. Of course, if a community waits too long to decide, it runs the risk of seeing the bonus go to another community.

We are not going to choose the site. You are. Admittedly, most communities don't have the scientists and engineers needed to do any required studies. Feel free to hire as many as necessary, and send the bill to us. But don't employ them to prove you shouldn't have the site in your area. If you don't want the site at any price, just don't bid.

For the first month of the auction, we're offering a $10 million bonus [or any arbitrary amount] to a community that volunteers. After that, the bonus will rise $10 million monthly, until a community comes forward. And we know that one will volunteer, when the price is right. That should end, once and for all, the waste controversy in our state. All unproductive activity—lawsuits, threats, and riots—can now come to an end. We have found the key to making the volunteer community happy that it has stepped forward.

SOURCE OF THE BONUS

Where would the money for the reverse Dutch auction come from? For LULUs built to accommodate wastes the initial source would be the waste generators. Ultimately, of course, the costs will be passed on, in one form or another, to the rest of us. As a nation, we have been crying "NIMBY" without having to pay any price. But the privilege of living ten, one hundred, or one thousand miles from a LULU surely has an economic value. Whatever the level of the bonus in the reverse Dutch auction, it is the true social cost of the facility. Put another way, it's the price the rest of us have to pay so the wastes aren't in *our* backyard.

Waste generators won't like new taxes. But at least they would be getting something for their money. No bonus would be paid until a real site was found and approved. Contrast this to the search for a low-level radioactive waste site in New York State. Roberta Lovenheim, a consultant to the New York State Low-Level Waste Group (an organization of radioactive-waste producers), says that $37 million has been spent to date in the so-far fruitless quest. The federal government has spent hundreds of millions of dollars on a site for high-level waste, battling Nevada and the governors of other states. The nuclear fuel rods still wait patiently in their pools at the reactors. The moral? It's better to pay for a Mercedes, if you're definitely going to get it, than for a Yugo that never appears.

Is this just a technique for foisting LULUs on the poorest communities? Not really. Under the reverse Dutch auction, if a poor community volunteered, it could anticipate a substantial bonus heading its way. The bonus might be on the order of hundreds of millions, depending on the particular facility, the size of the state, the competition in the auction, and other factors. Modern Landfill Incorporated has offered every citizen of Lewiston, New York, $960 annually for the next twenty years for the right to expand a landfill, from which hazardous wastes would be excluded. The price per citizen could very well be higher for hazardous and radioactive wastes, although the bonus would only be decided as the reverse Dutch auction proceeded.

Contrast this with the battle over the low-level radioactive waste site in Allegany County. The state offered to pay the county $1 million annually in lieu of taxes. This works out to about $20 per person each year. Although Allegany County residents have been derided as irrational, in reality they were behaving in accord with economic logic, if a little violently. They were each asked to accept $20 a year for wastes that most people, rightly or wrongly, regard as more dangerous than regular garbage. Yet people three counties away are offered $960 annually to enlarge an ordinary landfill.

A WAY OUT OF THE MAZE

Of course, LULUs do get built, sometimes without significant opposition. Penitentiaries arise and homeless shelters are located, occasionally without the slightest protest. An economist would say that in these instances the perceived social benefits to the nearby community outweigh the costs. For example, in some areas, a prison might be regarded as a valuable source of employment. In those cases, no reverse Dutch auction would be necessary. In others, the odium of the facility may outweigh the promise of hundreds of jobs.

In general, though, LULUs—especially waste sites—will tend to be regarded negatively by most communities. And those who cry "NIMBY" are in an important sense rational. They are telling us that the cost, real or perceived, of a LULU in their vicinity is high *to* them.

One critic has labeled the present system of finding waste sites "DAD," perhaps in honor of its paternalistic nature: "Decide, Announce, and Defend." Under the present system, a siting commission decides on a specific site behind closed doors, announces its decision, and spends the rest of its time defending the decision from the slings and arrows of outraged citizens.

The objections of these citizens have been a useful signal, like a toothache telling us of decay. Now is the time to respond to that sometimes noisy message in a fair and equitable way, using the reverse Dutch auction to settle LULU disputes.

State universities are scrapping programs and jobs as they feel the pinch of tough economic times.

Dismantling the ivory tower

Ben Zion Hershberg

Ben Zion Hershberg is a staff reporter with The Courier-Journal *in Louisville, Ky.*

hen the University of Nebraska planned last fall to drop two respected programs and lay off more than 20 tenured professors, its faculty rebelled.

One of the programs — classics — had been around since the school's beginning in 1865 and was one of the busiest departments, teaching mythology and ancient literature in translation to hundreds of students. The other intended victim — speech communications — also had a large enrollment and was especially profitable for the university because it used a large number of inexpensive teaching assistants.

"That's what bothered people," said Linda Pratt, an English professor. "There was no good reason for cutting those cost-efficient departments."

Eventually, after weeks of faculty and student protest, the administration backed off and accepted faculty proposals for making the 3 percent budget cuts required by a reduction in state funding, Pratt said.

The Nebraska cuts are being made without eliminating departments or laying off tenured faculty. But class sizes have been increased to make up for a reduction in part-time, non-tenured instructors. And other costs have been cut to the bone, including cleaning and maintenance, photocopying of faculty research materials and even the availability of office telephones.

The future could be even worse, said Larry Scherer, associate academic officer for the Nebraska Coordinating Commission for Post-Secondary Education. The state is trying to redesign its tax system after decisions by state courts saying the current system's methods of taxing personal property are unfair.

State revenue projections indicate there will be deficits next year, requiring larger cuts in funding for higher education and many other state programs, if a new system isn't developed soon.

The failure of legislative efforts to redesign the state tax system and boost revenue could mean a repetition of the budget battle next year for the Lincoln-based university, Pratt said.

Nebraska's problems are tiny compared with Connecticut's. The state has cut its higher education budget 13 percent for the next fiscal year starting July 1, said Rep. Nancy Wyman. That follows a cut of more than 10 percent for this fiscal year.

The state has been struggling with a recession for at least three years, while primary and secondary education, Medicaid and social services have soaked up larger shares of a declining budget. Colleges and universities have laid off faculty and staff, cutting the number of classes.

That's meant much larger classes and slower graduation rates, since most students can't get into all the classes they need to graduate in four years, Wyman said.

The Legislature is redesigning the state system of higher education and is considering consolidating administrative layers to save money, Wyman said.

The fund shortage is nationwide. Fourteen states have lower budgets for higher education this year, and 17 others increased their higher education budgets less than the rate of inflation.

State-supported universities in 28 states expect cuts in the next fiscal year, said the *Report of the States*, an annual budget survey by the American Association of State Colleges and Universities.

The association estimated state funding for higher education nationwide fell $1.3 billion — about 3 percent — in the past two years.

"This is the first time states have slipped behind in higher education spending in 30 years," said Robert M. Sweeney, policy analyst for the American Association of State Colleges and Universities.

Most often, the decline in state spending on higher education is caused by some combination of four factors: shortfalls in state revenue because of the national recession, increased spending on primary and secondary education, increased spending on prison systems and rising Medicaid costs.

The increased state spending on large government programs, such as health care and the penal system, results from a shift in the burden of many government costs from the federal to the state level during the 1980s.

In Nebraska, like many states, the public's reluctance to accept new state taxes to fill the gap created by the

federal retreat left the governor and Legislature with nothing to do but cut where they could. That meant sizable hits for higher education.

Many other states are experiencing similar problems. For example:

• Maryland cut its $900 million higher education budget by 9 percent this year because of a shortfall in state revenue. That meant a 6.2 percent reduction in funding for four-year colleges and a 25 percent cut for community colleges.

State government left most budget-cutting decisions to university administrations. But it ordered a halt to out-of-state travel by university employees and prohibited vehicle purchases.

On their own, Maryland universities eliminated equipment and construction expenditures where possible and cut payrolls. Some universities have reduced faculty research time and required professors to teach more. They have increased the average class size so fewer faculty members teach more students, lowering costs per student.

Maryland plans to rebuild its budget for higher education and some other state programs next year by cutting more than $600 million from state operating budgets and boosting taxes by at least $500 million. More dollars for education will come from imposing sales taxes on business and professional services, higher taxes on cigarettes and alcoholic beverages and boosting corporate income taxes if legislative proposals are successful.

• North Carolina cut more than 3 percent from its $1.4 billion higher education budget for this year after averaging increases of more than 5 percent annually since 1986.

To make part of the cut, the state ordered a hiring freeze early last year and began closely reviewing all large equipment purchases.

**Higher education budget cuts made in FY92
and comparison with overall state cuts
(as of fall 1991)**

State	% cut	Comparison with overall cuts	More or new cuts expected
Alabama	6.0	Higher	Unsure
Colorado	3.0	Same	Unsure
Connecticut	NR*	Higher	Yes
Florida	5.3	Same	Yes
Georgia	7.5	Higher	Yes
Idaho	3.0	Same	No
Kansas	1.0	Same	No
Kentucky	5.0	Higher	No
Maine	7.66	Higher	Unsure
Maryland	4.0	Higher	Yes
Mississippi	2.0	Higher	No
Missouri	8.0	Lower	Yes
Montana	5.2	Lower	No
Nevada	1.0	Same	Unsure
New Hampshire	3.5	Same	No
New York	3.0	Same	No
South Carolina	3.0	Same	No
Virginia	3.0	Lower	No
Wisconsin	5.0	NR*	No

* NR = No rating available.

Source: American Association of State Colleges and Universities

---

For the University of North Carolina system based in Chapel Hill, the cuts will mean eliminating 210 of the system's 8,000 faculty positions, more than 300 jobs among maintenance, clerical and other support staff, and emergency budget reserves.

The North Carolina state auditor's office also studied faculty work loads at several state campuses and found professors on average taught two to three courses a semester. That is expected to increase to ease the budget crunch. And tuition also is expected to increase sharply, despite a tradition of low-cost access to higher education in the state, said the report by the American Association of State Colleges and Universities.

• Despite a healthy economy, Oregon cut funding for higher education by 11.5 percent, or $86 million, this year. The reason was a successful referendum that limits property tax rates and the portion of those taxes that can be spent on education, requiring the state's already strained general fund to make up the difference.

To make the cuts required by the tax changes, the system's

eight campus presidents developed plans to lay off up to 700 faculty and staff and cut enrollments by about 3,000 students this year—about 5 percent of the system total. The state also imposed a $600 surcharge on each student's tuition to help cover this year's budget cuts.

To deal with its budget problem, Southern Oregon State College decided to "take out entire, vertical slices" of programs, eliminating some academic departments, said president Joseph Cox. That approach was designed to let the university at Ashland maintain the quality of its remaining programs, Cox said.

He and his provost met with groups of faculty and staff to review each of the university's academic programs by four criteria: quality, cost, productivity and centrality to the university's mission as a regional university.

Some of the evaluation was subjective, while some was based on objective standards, such as accreditation, success in licensing or professional examinations and so forth.

That review last summer led to eliminating a degree program in business education that was available from other state schools, dropping a program in library science and cutting out three of the five tracks in the university's physical education program.

Cox also reorganized the university's 10 schools into five, simplifying the administrative structure at the 5,000 student university.

The cuts eliminated 24 of the schools' 240 faculty positions, including some tenured faculty members, Cox said. And they eliminated half of the university's 10 deans and their staffs.

Cox didn't cut the budgets for the university library or its computing services center, because he felt those areas needed to develop rapidly to improve Southern Oregon State's quality.

"I took some heat for that," Cox said.

His school has come through the 1991 budget cuts pretty well, Cox said. But he's worried about the future, because the property tax limits enacted last year will mean additional cuts for each of the next three years unless the public accepts a tax increase.

"I think we're involved in a total redefinition of this country's standard of living and its priorities," Cox said. And he's not sure where that will leave state-supported higher education.

Jan Bargen, administrator for Oregon's joint interim education committee, said Gov. Barbara Roberts hopes to call a special legislative session this spring to overhaul the tax system. The plans for additional tax changes haven't been completed, and it's uncertain how any new plan would affect higher education, she said.

It's also not clear whether voters would accept a new tax system that might raise their costs. Without such changes, higher education will face even larger budget cuts in the future, Bargen said.

The picture is just as grim in Nebraska.

"There are no easy solutions," Pratt said, explaining that state government is debating tax changes but hasn't found any answers to its budget needs.

"I think the nation will find that changing its tax structure is one of the most painful ordeals it's ever faced."

OTHER PEOPLE'S GARBAGE

The new politics of trash: A case study

Elizabeth Royte

Elizabeth Royte is a journalist living in New York City. She has written for Esquire, The Atlantic, *and* The New York Times Magazine.

At the end of Lower Shannon Branch, a dirt road that winds for six miles through West Virginia's hill country, there sits a vast, bowl-shaped hollow, its sides carpeted with 6,000 acres of second-growth hardwood trees. This particular piece of land holds little attraction for most people in rural McDowell County. It's not especially scenic—it looks like a thousand other wooded hollows in southern Appalachia that were first timbered and then mined. But the valley's ordinariness and resolute quiet belie a brewing national storm. Like many out-of-the-way sites in poor, rural communities across America, this hollow is considered by some an ideal place to dump the disposable diapers, orange rinds, Coca-Cola bottles, and chicken bones of several million people who live very far away.

The scarred hillsides of this valley provide a good vantage point from which to view the nation's garbage wars. For here, two shaky vectors have converged—a community in acute financial distress and a corporation looking to build a landfill that no one really wants. It is a scenario that promises to become increasingly common as the nation's trash piles mount, municipal landfills are ordered shut, and waste-management companies propose megadumps in those pockets of the country most desperate for cash and the promise of a financially stable future.

I went to McDowell last fall because, in agreeing to become home to one of the largest dumps in the country, it represented the future of garbage in America.

This was no abstract notion for me: as a New Yorker, I'm part of a community that's gobbling up landfill space faster than any viable alternatives for disposing of our trash can be found. New York City's last local dump will close within the decade, and the city already ships trash, by truck and by train, to places well beyond the Hudson River. If my garbage was going to be traveling far away, I was curious to trace its complex route—a route that promised to land it in McDowell County.

Welch, the county seat of McDowell, is a coal camp set smack in the middle of what was once the most productive coalfield in the country. During its heyday, in the Forties and Fifties, McDowell County produced 21 million tons of coal a year. Welch boasted three movie houses, three hospitals, and no fewer than forty-two beer joints. Its frontier spirit even inspired such cosmopolitan accoutrements as houses of prostitution and gambling. The reins of power in McDowell County were firmly held by the coal conglomerates; King Coal rented houses to its workers, and furnished them with heat, water, and electricity. It provided a company store, doctors, and schools. But in the early Eighties, the bottom fell out of the coal market, and increased mechanization within the industry sharply reduced the number of workers needed to mine those few veins that still produced. Like a colony that exists only to feed a remote power, McDowell suffered when the coal empire collapsed: the big companies pulled out, taking with them most of the county's mineral wealth, natural gas, and timber. They left behind an epidemic of disease, decrepit shacks, barren hillsides, and a legacy of resentment toward those who own what is left of the region's wealth.

Welch is no longer a sophisticated place. It's the sort of town where people go on the radio to swap guns, where the arrival of a Long John Silver's restaurant is much anticipated. Nearly a third of the stores on McDowell Street stand dusty and closed; the Greyhound no longer pulls into the depot across from City Hall. There are no movie theaters or bookstores left to enliven the hours after work. In fact, there's precious little work to be had. Figures vary, but Tony Johnson, publisher of the ten-page *Welch Daily News,* puts the county's unemployment rate at about 60 percent.

Though McDowell County has always referred to itself, somewhat defensively, as the Free State of McDowell, the region in many ways has come to resemble a dependent Third World nation. More than a quarter of McDowell's 35,000 people live in poverty; thanks to poor diet and heavy smoking, it's not uncommon for men of forty to die of heart attacks. In 1989 the county's infant mortality rate was a third above the national average. And one in ten residents receives disability payments for black lung disease. As one unemployed McDowell man told me, "If it weren't for black lung and Social Security, there'd be nothing here." The people's despair can be measured most starkly in suicide attempts, of which the hospital reports no fewer than two a week.

McDowell's future is bleak: the county lacks the basic infrastructure that might convince a company to choose it as the site for a new factory or branch plant. Thanks in part to its terrain, which is fractured by countless streams and mountain ridges, McDowell doesn't have a single four-lane highway; within its borders, it takes an hour and a half to drive fifty miles. Welch's mayor, Martha Moore, has been forced to lay off the town's meter maids and the entire fire department, and to cancel city workers' pension plans. The county, which owes a quarter of a million dollars to vendors and can barely meet its bare-bones payroll, recently laid off several sheriff's deputies.

The rare projects that are offered to McDowell are the ones that have already been turned away by people who can afford to say no. Within the last five years the county's economic salvation has loomed first in the form of a federal prison, to be built atop a strip mine; then it was going to be a facility for holding spent nuclear fuel rods. Neither scheme panned out, to the relief of many, but still McDowell kept looking for a way to stop, or at least stall, its precipitous decline. In 1987 that search ended; a new means of salvation had appeared. This time it was garbage.

Garbage is a simple matter: people make it, then they want it to go away. They pay to have it picked up from their curbs; their communities pay to tip it into dumps or to truck it somewhere else, preferably somewhere far away, beyond their borders— out of state, out of mind. And the amount we discard keeps growing: by the year 2000, according to the Environmental Protection Agency's estimates, we'll be producing five pounds of garbage per person per day, more than double the output of thirty years ago.

Most of this garbage—about 80 percent of it—ends up in the ground, buried in landfills, But by the mid-1990s, one half of the 6,500 municipal landfills still operating in the United States are expected to reach capacity (since 1978, 14,000 landfills have closed). Already the Fresh Kills landfill on Staten Island, the nation's largest city dump, turns away 10,000 of the 27,000 tons New York City generates each day. When it peaks at 505 feet, within the decade, Fresh Kills will be almost as tall as the Washington Monument.

EPA requirements introduced last September will force still more landfills to close: the new rules mandate that over the next six years landfill operators will have to shut down every dump that lacks the high-tech monitoring systems and liners that are supposed to stop toxic seepage. But these features carry a big price tag, and so, for most small communities, up-to-snuff dumps have become prohibitively expensive. Nationally, the solution would appear to be fewer but larger landfills; in relative terms, giant dumps are cheaper to build than small ones. To these strategically placed, privately run sites will be trucked, or hauled by rail, garbage from surrounding regions, even from out of state. Ironically, the EPA's ruling, which ought to have offered some environmental safety, instead introduced the prospect of a Faustian bargain, in which huge waste-hauling companies offer to alleviate the economic woes of desperate communities—in exchange for a place to put a megadump.

It was just such a deal that was presented to McDowell County in 1987 by a Pennsylvania businessman named Jack Fugett. Fugett, a personable urbanite who affects a folksy manner as soon as he turns off I-77 into McDowell County, is the president of Capels Resources, a subsidiary of the Berwind Corporation. The Philadelphia-based industrial conglomerate is well known to the people of McDowell: Berwind owns the mineral rights under almost a third of the surface land in the county. Fugett wanted to build a huge landfill in Welch, one that would accept 300,000 tons of out-of-state waste a month. The garbage would arrive by rail, filling an estimated 182 cars a day.

When Martha Moore became mayor in 1986, she stepped into a quagmire. In addition to its crushing fiscal troubles, Welch was under court order to clean up its water: the city has no sewage-treatment system, and the fecal coliform levels in its rivers were as much as 50,000 times higher than the EPA's recommended limits. The cost of feasibility studies for a treatment system had already eaten up what little funding the town had for installing it. And though it seemed the least of her woes, Moore also had garbage troubles: in 1987, under pressure from the state, McDowell agreed to close its only landfill, a low-tech dump down the road in Marytown.

In this respect, McDowell is like many communities across the nation, suddenly faced with the news that they can no longer use their landfill. But unlike most of these towns, Welch has plenty of places to put its trash: residents have no qualms about using one of the county's many undeveloped hollows to bury the 1,100 tons of garbage they produce each month. As a rule, Welch does not recycle. Its roadsides are littered with paper bags from the town's half-dozen fastfood outlets. One survey found 180 illegal dump sites around the county.

Although McDowell Countians didn't mind keeping their trash nearby, they certainly didn't want to pay higher sanitation fees to do so. But after the county began poking around, looking for a suitable site for a new landfill, they discovered they couldn't afford one. Thanks to the new EPA rules, landfills now cost upward of $10 million to construct.

The search for a replacement landfill for McDowell was led by Charlie Thomas, a retired auto-body mechanic who, at the time, sat on the county's solid-waste board. When Thomas learned that the parcel of land he wanted for the landfill—on Lower Shannon Branch—was owned by Berwind, he contacted Jack Fugett. But Fugett turned the tables on Thomas, suggesting a much larger project. Thomas was skeptical at first, but Fugett kept talking. The landfill would have a "state of the art" liner—a complicated layering scheme of dirt, clay, plastic liners, and gravel—and sixty wells for testing water quality. The electronic monitoring and transfer stations would be fully enclosed. In addition to local inspections, the EPA, the Occupational Safety and Health Administration, and the state Department of Natural Resources would have their pokes at it, too. The seven families that lived on Lower Shannon Branch, who rented their houses from Capels, would be compensated and relocated. When the dump was full, in fifty years, it would be a flat, grassy field, the kind of place a factory might want to locate, Fugett said. Thomas began to come around. "Nothing like this had ever been done before," he later explained. "This landfill would have been a tourist attraction."

Charlie Thomas introduced Fugett to Mayor Moore just as the county's woes were coming to a head. They had nowhere to dump their trash and no money to pay their bills, and if the mayor didn't clean up the sewage mess soon, she would be going to jail for defying the court order. "Something clicked in my mind when I heard about [Fugett's] plan," she remembers. "I thought, let's take two negatives—sewage and garbage—and turn them into a positive. It was a natural." Moore knew that fifteen similar super-landfills had been proposed and shot down in other West Virginia counties, but those counties, she reasoned, didn't have

McDowell's problems. The mayor knew a good deal when it came along. Jack Fugett, she decided, would treat Welch's sewage, deal with its garbage, and pay for the privilege.

The idea was not outlandish. Nationwide, Moore knew, money swirls around garbage piles—about $30 billion a year, with industry analysts predicting a doubling of revenues within the next five years. County officials did some research. They learned that for agreeing to accept a landfill, operators pay towns "host fees" based on tonnage received. The fees range widely, reflecting each town's negotiation skills. Although the waste companies are prepared to pay as much as ten dollars a ton, they often get away with per-ton fees as low as twenty-five cents. As part of the deal, a host community pays nothing to dump; operators make their money charging the neighboring towns and distant cities whose garbage ends up in the landfill. Waste haulers may also sweeten deals with such tokens of appreciation as community centers and scholarships.

Fugett's sales pitch to McDowell County got a boost from the fact that a similar landfill had just gone up in nearby Charles City County, Virginia. Before the landfill was built, that county had had no supermarket, no drugstore, not even a bank. But since the facility began accepting its allotted 105,000 tons of garbage each month, the county has cut property taxes and begun building new schools. Dee Milom, a broad-shouldered Welch resident with graying hair and piercing blue eyes, happened to visit the Charles City landfill last year and found it a model enterprise. "It didn't smell," he told me later. "It didn't look like anything. Nobody paid it any mind." An out-of-work carpenter, Milom was hoping to get a job at the Capels landfill; on one of his regular sweeps through town last summer, Fugett had promised to hire him. Fugett had shown him intricate drawings of the landfill's liner, and Milom believed Fugett when he said that it wouldn't leak. And even if it wasn't fail-safe, that was a risk Milom was willing to take. "You gotta get pollution to get jobs," he said, his voice hard. "We're gonna die anyhow. We'll starve to death."

Chip Lawson, a jeweler on Welch's main street who's seen business plummet these past couple of years, agreed. When I visited his store one morning, the only customers he had were asking him to appraise pieces they wanted to sell. "I'd rather be the garbage capital of the world than the welfare capital of the world," he said. "I'm for anything that will bring jobs. This is one of the last businesses we can have here." When asked if he worried about environmental degradation, he answered, "Will the landfill be any worse than our open sewer?" Obviously, he thought not. And if it contained toxics, would he still be for it? "Yes. They have monitors." What about nuclear waste? "Sure," he answered, smiling. "Then we'd get highways."

Throughout 1988 Fugett met once a month with Thomas and other county officials. They talked about trash, about liners and sewage, tipping fees and revenue. The McDowell representatives liked what they heard, but they pushed for more. They knew that landfill owners can afford to be generous: garbage dumps are hugely profitable. Gross profits run upward of 50 percent of revenue at large dumps (one Texas company had profits of $24 million on revenue of $39 million last year). And because landfills are built in small sections, with revenue coming in as each section fills, the costs of construction are spread out as the money rolls in. In Mobile, Arizona, for example, Waste Management Inc. is spending a total of $240 million on a dump that it projects will bring in $2.26 billion over its fifty-year lifespan.

In the windowless meeting room of McDowell's county commission building, a deal began to take shape. There would be money—between $6 and $8 million for the county. There would be 367 jobs, with a payroll of $10 million. Capels would clean up the illegal dump sites around the county; Welch would dump its garbage for free. And Capels would treat the town's sewage. In November 1988 the first contract was signed, and the landfill proposal began its journey through the state bureaucracy.

Given what was at stake, it is surprising how little the people of McDowell discussed the proposed landfill during the three years it was under consideration. The city council had been talking about the landfill at public meetings, which were advertised in the local paper. There were TV programs and radio shows on the project. But very few people took any notice. Only five citizens directed questions to the county office set up to facilitate the landfill. Moore herself spent little time worrying about selling the project to constituents: she didn't think she had to. "We didn't have a strategy to win the landfill," she told me later. "The sewage treatment was so important that the garbage was minor." Moore spoke about the landfill to any group that invited her; Charlie Thomas handled the Rotary, the Lions, and the Kiwanis. "I wasn't hiding anything," Moore said. "I'd shout it from the rooftops. The people of Welch couldn't wait to get this thing. The bigger the better, they said. The more dollars, the more jobs."

But a political surprise awaited Mayor Moore. As if out of nowhere, opposition to the dump began to materialize in the spring of 1991. It is unclear whether there had always been anti-dump sentiment in the county, smoldering under the surface, or whether sophisticated political organizing by environmentalists in the state capital had fanned a small ember into a firestorm of discontent. But a town that had seemed desperate to embrace this giant landfill suddenly became the scene of bitter protests against it.

The first stirrings of dissent began with the Reverend Jeffrey Allen, a local Methodist minister. Allen first heard about the landfill in January 1990, but by then, he was told, Fugett had already signed agreements with the county. He didn't know Moore herself had yet to sign the deal—she was hoping to get more money out of Fugett—but he believed there was little he could do to stop it. His doubts were confirmed by the number of signatures he collected on a petition to put the landfill to a county-wide referendum: three.

Allen abandoned his campaign against the landfill until February 1991, when he received a phone call from Norm Steenstra, an organizer with an activist environmental group in Charleston. There are people all over McDowell who are upset about the landfill, Steenstra told Allen, and you should bring them together. But Steenstra's promised crowds were slow in coming. When Allen held his first meeting, only eight people showed up. The next time around, though, a few more people came, and by May, Allen was drawing audiences of forty or fifty, whom he organized into a group called TEARS/WV: Team Effort Against Ruining Southern West Virginia.

But why had it taken so long for opposition to the dump to coalesce? "People hadn't heard about the landfill," Allen explained to me, somewhat improbably. "You have to understand Appalachia. If the power elite decides something isn't going to be an issue, it isn't." He blames, in part, the extreme regionalization of the county. Rough terrain enforces isolation, and coal operators, who didn't want their workers to keep in contact with one another, institutionalized apathy: dialing a telephone number five miles away counts as a long-distance call. Few people in the county read the newspaper closely, and the publisher, who supported the Capels project, didn't run a single anti-landfill story.

Allen's group began to look more closely at Fugett's deal, and they didn't like what they saw. Although Fugett had promised more than three hundred jobs, the United Mine Workers local learned that similar landfills employ fewer than one hundred people, at low wages and with few benefits. They heard that one West Virginia landfill, run by out-of-staters, had fired several employees just before Christmas for trying to unionize.

TEARS wanted to know if Capels jobs would be safe jobs. Fugett had promised the public that the landfill would accept only municipal solid waste, sewage sludge, and incinerator ash. It would take no medical or nuclear waste—nothing, Fugett said, that was hazardous or toxic. But incinerator ash can contain high levels of dangerous metals, including arsenic, cadmium, lead, and mercury. The ash can contaminate soil, ground water, and surface water; in the form of fly ash, it can be ingested or inhaled. Nor is household refuse entirely benign: the average household generates fifteen pounds of hazardous waste per year—cleaning agents, fertilizers, paint, automotive products, and so on—most of which goes out with the eggshells and cereal boxes. In addition, virtually all landfills release methane, a toxic gas, and some emit vinyl chloride, a known carcinogen. Neither gas respects landfill boundaries: tests done in California have shown that illegal levels of gases accumulate not only over landfills but over nearby residential areas as well.

The more TEARS learned, the more outraged they became. According to the EPA, they discovered, 3 percent of all municipal-waste workers are injured each year through handling or exposure to hazardous substances. Of 1,235 Superfund sites—the environmental messes the EPA has assigned the highest priority for cleanup—about 240 are municipal landfills, most of them haunted by the slow and inexorable drip of leachate, the toxic gunk that seeps through trash and settles to the bottom of a landfill, where it has the potential to contaminate surface water or, even more insidiously, continue its journey all the way to the water table.

The community's growing suspicions that the dump might be more dangerous than they had been told were intensified by memories of the coal years, when companies, as a matter of course, misled their workers about environmental hazards and job security. To those who'd been burned by King Coal—the hundreds who didn't have clean drinking water or whose houses, shoved into narrow valleys, suffered yearly floods and endured mud slides that poured down from denuded mountains—the landfill began to look less like an exercise in cooperative capitalism than like a return to colonialism. "You've got the county dependent on the benevolence of a private corporation," Reverend Allen explained, "and suddenly it's not 1991 anymore but 1891."

The issue that stirred up the most powerful opposition to the dump wasn't neocolonialism, dubious liners, or tipping fees; it was the specter of out-of-state garbage. McDowell County didn't mind burying its own trash, but many residents had deep-rooted fears of outsiders' garbage. And they particularly didn't want trash from New York and New Jersey, which together export more than all other states combined. Throughout last summer, the national media conspired to heighten awareness of the perils, real or imagined, of imported waste: there were television programs about Mafia involvement in East Coast landfills and newspaper stories about cargo trucks spilling out-of-state garbage onto the highway. One TEARS broadsheet suggested the landfill would spread AIDS, be run by the Mafia, and accept hidden toxics and nuclear waste.

It's difficult to say exactly why Eastern trash is

maligned so, but the infamous *Mobro* barge, which roamed the Atlantic for four months in 1987 with garbage from Long Island, offers a clue. If no one wanted that trash, perhaps there was good reason. Were mobsters "cocktailing" household garbage with toxics? Maybe New Yorkers were hiding medical waste or New Jerseyites were disguising sewage sludge. A Welch artist preyed on these fears with his eight-foot-high billboard, erected on a lawn along Route 52. In vivid, angry colors, the sign depicted a skinny, bearded Fugett squatting atop a mammoth trash heap of crossbones, nuclear symbols, hypodermic needles, and other sinister detritus, surrounded by the letters NY, NJ, and PA. The sign read, "Home of the world's largest cancer-causing water-polluting rat-infested toxic waste dump. Best kept secret has finally leaked out in McDowell County. Say no to Capels Landfill."

It is precisely to counter this sort of "negative advertising" that the garbage industry has lately been working hard to change its image. Nobody even calls the stuff garbage anymore—it's "solid waste"—and dumps have been rechristened "landfills" or "transfer stations." To calm fears about transporting large quantities of solid waste, rail companies now use newfangled waste containers that don't smell, leak, or offend the eye. They're often kept cleaner and shinier than the rest of the cars in the train.

Yet no matter how thorough garbage's image makeover, the persistent distrust of out-of-state waste, particularly from the East, promises to become a powerful political issue across the country. Under the new EPA rules, landfills need vast quantities of trash to be lucrative; as McDowell County found out, the only way to make garbage pay is to import it from far away. Already, forty-two states both import and export municipal waste, and the trucks, barges, and trains that move the trash are becoming potent political symbols. In a state like West Virginia, out-of-state garbage is the sort of emotionally resonant issue that can decide an election—something that Governor Gaston Caperton was quick to grasp.

Throughout the summer of 1991 the battle raged in McDowell County. Pro-landfill county officials ran ads calling their opponents "environmental radicals" and "outside agitators." Employers received anonymous phone calls informing them which of their workers had attended TEARS meetings. There were taunts in the street. Mayor Moore and other local politicians began to press for a referendum on the landfill. Fugett was all for it: he wanted to prove once and for all that a majority favored the project. But TEARS, which was born out of a drive for such a vote, now opposed a referendum. It was a curious move. Didn't TEARS believe it could win? "We've got 90 percent of the county behind us," one member told me. "We'd win that election tomorrow."

Yet TEARS was apparently unwilling to risk losing on a popular vote; they realized they had a better chance of appealing directly to Governor Caperton, who was up for re-election in the fall and in no mood to enrage a well-organized citizen's group. TEARS turned on the heat. On September 31 carloads of landfill opponents began streaming into Charleston for a week's worth of rallying and lobbying lawmakers. They were followed closely by a band of Fugett's newest friends, most of them unemployed, who were bused in by Fugett to fight for what they saw as their best shot for a decent job.

By the afternoon of October 15, the battle was over. Caperton, acutely aware of garbage's new political power, agreed to a bill limiting the size of West Virginia's landfills to 30,000 tons a month. For McDowell, though, he made a slight exception: on a referendum vote, the people could increase the capacity of their landfill to 50,000 tons. Caperton probably would have preferred to simply ban garbage imports outright, but the U.S. Constitution protects interstate commerce, making such a move, however politically attractive to a governor, impossible. Nevertheless, Caperton's solution amounted to a de facto ban—even at 50,000 tons, a landfill that meets EPA standards can't make the kind of money that the waste-hauling industry has come to expect.

TEARS members rejoiced; to them, the decision marked the end of McDowell County's decades of exploitation. Jack Fugett and the county officials who had negotiated the landfill deal were predictably crushed. Mayor Moore took Caperton's decision especially hard. "We lost not because people thought the landfill was dangerous but because it's an election year," she said. "Caperton knew that fifty-four counties didn't want a big landfill and only one did. But nobody cared to listen to the facts." She blamed TEARS for ruining not only a hard-won scheme but any hope that Welch would soon be back on its feet. "For four years we worked on this," she said angrily, "and now what do we have? Nothing."

G arbage tends to concentrate in depressions: it rolls downhill until it hits those places most desperate to deal. McDowell had seemed to be such a place—far too needy and weak to withstand the temptations of a gigantic project like Capels's. So what happens to 300,000 tons of trash a month when a place like McDowell suddenly decides not to play the role the waste industry, and the American economy, had assigned to it? In all likelihood, this garbage—which is my garbage, indeed all of our garbage—will find an-

other, even poorer and less well-organized place to settle.

The EPA regulations have made the economics of gigantic regional landfills irresistible. Garbage will increasingly be shipped from the richer, more populous parts of this country to those places that, out of economic desperation or lack of political strength, cannot refuse to take it—places like Third World and Eastern European countries, where waste traders have since 1986 exported 5 million tons of toxics; places where minorities live (two recent studies show that 60 percent of blacks and Hispanics live in communities with one or more unregulated toxic-waste sites). And perhaps onto Indian reservations: because they aren't subject to state and local environmental laws, landfill operators have increasingly targeted reservations as potential dumping grounds. Waste-management companies have approached nearly every reservation in the country; federal officials over the last several years have invited around three hundred reservations to become repositories of high-level nuclear waste. So far, nine are considering accepting.

There are, of course, other, forgotten alternatives to these giant landfills: massive recycling, combined with composting, incineration, and salvaging, can reduce the waste stream by up to 90 percent. But in my own city, the sheer volume of our trash has stymied the best efforts to reduce our garbage output. Three years into a court-ordered citywide recycling program, most of New York still recycles only newspapers, which for lack of a market often end up riding a truck—along with cans, bottles, plastics, and compost—to a landfill in Taylorville, Illinois.

The garbage will find a place to go, but what about McDowell? Exactly what sort of "victory" can the county be said to have won? There are those in Welch today who speak of a renewed sense of pride and self-worth among McDowell Countians, who have proved to themselves that together they can resist the sort of powers that have historically had their way in this region. But still there is no sewage system, no up-to-snuff landfill, and Mayor Moore is as far from balancing her budget as ever. Soon after Caperton signed the landfill bill, ten months of negotiations to get a major retail chain to open a local store all but collapsed. Moore stands in contempt of court for refusing to sign a second consent decree to clean up the city's water, but the citizens can't afford the $63 a month per household that a new treatment system would cost. Still, the mayor plans to run for re-election this fall. The garbage issue dogs her, but she figures that once this election year is over, things might calm down a little. Then, she thinks, people are going to have to reconsider whether McDowell County can really survive without other people's garbage.

Credits/ Acknowledgments

Cover design by Charles Vitelli

1. Early Commentaries
Facing overview—Library of Congress.

2. Intergovernmental Relations
Facing overview—Houston Chamber of Commerce photo by James R. LaCombe.

3. Linkages Between Citizens and Governments
Facing overview—A. Tannenbaum/Sygma.

4. Government Institutions and Officeholders
Facing overview—Florida Department of Commerce/Division of Tourism.

5. Regionalism and Variations Among Regions and States
Facing overview—EPA Documerica.

6. Cities and Suburbs
Facing overview—USDA.

7. Finances and Development
Facing overview—Bay Area Rapid Transit Photo.

8. Service Delivery and Policy Issues
Facing overview—The Dushkin Publishing Group, Inc., photo.

ANNUAL EDITIONS ARTICLE REVIEW FORM

■ NAME: _____ DATE: _____

■ TITLE AND NUMBER OF ARTICLE: _____

■ BRIEFLY STATE THE MAIN IDEA OF THIS ARTICLE: _____

_____

_____

_____

_____

■ LIST THREE IMPORTANT FACTS THAT THE AUTHOR USES TO SUPPORT THE MAIN IDEA:

_____

_____

_____

_____

_____

_____

■ WHAT INFORMATION OR IDEAS DISCUSSED IN THIS ARTICLE ARE ALSO DISCUSSED IN YOUR
TEXTBOOK OR OTHER READING YOU HAVE DONE? LIST THE TEXTBOOK CHAPTERS AND PAGE
NUMBERS:

_____

_____

_____

_____

_____

_____

■ LIST ANY EXAMPLES OF BIAS OR FAULTY REASONING THAT YOU FOUND IN THE ARTICLE:

_____

_____

_____

_____

■ LIST ANY NEW TERMS/CONCEPTS THAT WERE DISCUSSED IN THE ARTICLE AND WRITE A
SHORT DEFINITION:

_____

_____

_____

_____

_____

ANNUAL EDITIONS:
STATE AND LOCAL GOVERNMENT, Sixth Edition
Article Rating Form

Here is an opportunity for you to have direct input into the next revision of this volume. We would like you to rate each of the 63 articles listed below, using the following scale:

1. **Excellent: should definitely be retained**
2. **Above average: should probably be retained**
3. **Below average: should probably be deleted**
4. **Poor: should definitely be deleted**

Your ratings will play a vital part in the next revision. So please mail this prepaid form to us just as soon as you complete it.
Thanks for your help!

Annual Editions revisions depend on two major opinion sources: one is our Advisory Board, listed in the front of this volume, which works with us in scanning the thousands of articles published in the public press each year; the other is you—the person actually using the book. Please help us and the users of the next edition by completing the prepaid article rating form on this page and returning it to us. Thank you.

Rating	Article	Rating	Article
	1. *The Federalist* No. 17		33. State Stats
	2. *The Federalist* No. 45		34. School Days' Primer
	3. Nature of the American State		35. Business Flees to the Urban Fringe
	4. American Federalism: Past, Present, and Future		36. Snow White and the 17 Dwarfs: From Metro Cooperation to Governance
	5. Rethinking Federalism		37. A Tale of Two Suburbias
	6. Federal Government Mandates: Why the States Are Complaining		38. Health Problems of Inner City Poor Reach Crisis Point
	7. Set Us Free		39. Cities Get Into the Game
	8. Maps That Will Stand Up in Court		40. How to Hold a Riot
	9. Dickering Over the Districts		41. After the Los Angeles Riots
	10. The Mirage of Campaign Reform		42. Rediscovering the Village
	11. Throwing Out the Rascals (and Those Who Aren't)		43. In Suburbs, a Stealthy War Against Infiltrating Students
	12. Local Redistricting: The Demographic Context of Boundary Drawing		44. Revenue-Raising Partners
	13. Should Judges Be Elected?		45. Not Quite the Pot of Gold
	14. News Judgments		46. The Tax the Public Loves to Hate
	15. Civic Strategies for Community Empowerment		47. Cracks in the Crystal Ball
	16. Is the Initiative Process a Good Idea?		48. Means Testing: Two Dirty Words We Need to Learn
	17. The Legislature 2010: Which Direction?		49. The Third Wave of Economic Development
	18. An Embattled Institution		50. Taxes and the Wealth of States
	19. Running a Town the 17th-Century Way		51. How Do You Know You Get What You Pay For?
	20. Practicing Political Science on a Local School Board		52. Searching for New Jobs, Many States Steal Them
	21. Gubernatorial Styles: Is There a Right One?		53. Privatization Is a Means to "More With Less"
	22. Wisconsin's 'Quirky' Veto Power		54. Privatization Presents Problems
	23. "City Managers Don't Make Policy": A Lie; Let's Face It		55. Getting in Touch With Government
	24. The States' Lead in Rights Protection		56. The State Agenda for the Coming Years
	25. View From the Bench: A Judge's Day		57. Schoolhouse Equality
	26. Justice by Numbers		58. Reform School Confidential
	27. The High-Tech Court of the Future		59. The New Welfare Debate: What the States Are Hoping to Accomplish
	28. Charter Reform in the 1990s		60. Do We Need More Prisons?
	29. Bringing Government Back to Life		61. Of LULUs, NIMBYs, and NIMTOOs
	30. Legacy of the '80s: Richer Rich and Poorer Poor		62. Dismantling the Ivory Tower
	31. Resurgence of Multistate Regionalism		63. Other People's Garbage
	32. The Delta Looks Up		

(Continued on next page)

ABOUT YOU

Name_____ Date_____

Are you a teacher? ☐ Or student? ☐

Your School Name _____

Department _____

Address _____

City _____ State _____ Zip _____

School Telephone # _____

YOUR COMMENTS ARE IMPORTANT TO US!

Please fill in the following information:

For which course did you use this book? _____

Did you use a text with this Annual Edition? ☐ yes ☐ no

The title of the text? _____

What are your general reactions to the Annual Editions concept?

Have you read any particular articles recently that you think should be included in the next edition?

Are there any articles you feel should be replaced in the next edition? Why?

Are there other areas that you feel would utilize an Annual Edition?

May we contact you for editorial input?

May we quote you from above?

ANNUAL EDITIONS: STATE AND LOCAL GOVERNMENT, Sixth Edition